Course Overview

Poets Prescribed for Higher Level

JUNE 2011 EXAMINATION

Wordsworth (pages 25–52)

Dickinson (pages 53–76)

Hopkins (pages 77–110)

Yeats (pages 111–155)

Frost (pages 156–182)

Kavanagh (pages 183–207)

Rich (pages 207–344)

Boland (pages 437–463)

JUNE 2012 EXAMINATION

Frost (pages 156–182)

Kavanagh (pages 183–207)

Larkin (pages 239–269)

Kinsella (pages 270–306)

Rich (pages 307–344)

Plath (pages 345–373)

Heaney (pages 374–404)

Boland (pages 437–463)

JUNE 2013 EXAMINATION

Shakespeare (pages 1–24)

Wordsworth (pages 25–52)

Hopkins (pages 77–110)

Bishop (pages 208–238)

Kinsella (pages 270–306)

Rich (pages 307–344)

Plath (pages 345–373)

Mahon (pages 405–436)

JUNE 2014 EXAMINATION

Dickinson (pages 53–76)

Yeats (pages 111–155)

Bishop (pages 208–238)

Larkin (pages 239–269)

Kinsella (pages 270–306)

Plath (pages 345–373)

Heaney (pages 374–404)

Mahon (pages 405–436)

[Ordinary level: see pages iv–vii]

Poems Prescribed for Ordinary Level

JUNE 2011 EXAMINATION

Wordsworth	She Dwelt among the Untrodden Ways (p. 26)	**Herbert**	The Collar (p. 467)
	It is a Beauteous Evening, Calm and Free (p. 28)	**Auden**	Funeral Blues (p. 486)
	From *The Prelude*: Skating [ll 425-463] (p. 30)	**Morgan**	Strawberries (p. 495)
Dickinson	I felt a Funeral, in my Brain (p. 60)	**Wilbur**	The Writer (p. 500)
	I Heard a Fly buzz – when I died (p. 67)	**Levertov**	What Were They Like? (p. 508)
Hopkins	Spring (p. 87)	**Murphy**	Moonshine (p. 514)
	Inversnaid (p. 100)	**Adcock**	For Heidi with Blue Hair (p. 519)
Yeats	The Wild Swans at Coole (p. 118)	**Kennelly**	A Glimpse of Starlings (p. 526)
	An Irish Airman Foresees his Death (p. 122)	**Durcan**	Going Home to Mayo . . . (p. 546)
Frost	The Tuft of Flowers (p. 158)	**Shuttle**	Jungian Cows (p. 551)
	Mending Wall (p. 162)	**Monahan**	All Day Long (p. 557)
	'Out, Out –' (p. 170)	**Hardie**	Daniel's Duck (p. 560)
Kavanagh	Shancoduff (p. 188)	**Muldoon**	Anseo (p. 563)
	A Christmas Childhood (p. 194)	**O'Callaghan**	The Net (p. 568)
Rich	Aunt Jennifer's Tigers (p. 308)	**Duffy**	Valentine (p. 571)
	The Uncle Speaks in the Drawing Room (p. 311)	**Armitage**	It Ain't What You Do . . . (p. 578)
	Trying to Talk with a Man (p. 328)		
Boland	Child of Our Time (p. 444)		
	This Moment (p. 456)		
	Love (p. 458)		

Note: In the Ordinary level exam in June 2011 there will be one question on the poems in the left-hand column and one question on the poems in the right-hand column. Candidates are required to answer only one question.

New Explorations

Complete Leaving Certificate Poetry
for examination in 2011 and onwards

UNIVERSITY *of* LIMERICK

TELEPHONE: 061 202158 / 202172 / 202163

Items can be renewed from BORROWER INFO on the Library Catalogue
www.ul.ie/~library

PLEASE NOTE: This item is subject to recall after two weeks if
required by another reader.

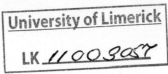
Gill & Macmillan Ltd
Hume Avenue
Park West
Dublin 12
with associated companies throughout the world
www.gillmacmillan.ie

978 07171 4548 5

Design and page make-up by Mike Connor Design & Illustration

The paper used in this book is made from the wood pulp of managed forests. For every tree felled, at least one tree is planted, thereby renewing natural resources.

For permission to reproduce photographs the author and publisher gratefully acknowledge the following:

AKG IMAGES: 292, 379; ALAMY: 90, 103TL, 103TR, 103BL, 103BR, 155, 204, 206, 244, 267, 382, 385, 388, 428, 451, 548; THE ART ARCHIVE: 27, 39, 42, 138; BARBARA SAVAGE CHERESH: 522; BORD FÁILTE: 154; BRIDGEMAN: 1, 25, 29, 45, 58, 77, 161, 174, 308, 312, 315, 321, 329, 473; CHICHESTER CATHEDRAL/ A F KERSTING: 253; COLLINS PHOTOS: 270, 525; CORBIS: 60, 339, 345, 497, 537, 541; DEPT OF THE ENVIRONMENT: 121B; DEREK SPEIRS: 545; ELIZABETH BISHOP/ ALICE HELEN METHFESSEL: 209, 218, 224; GED CLAPSON: 78; GERARD BURNS PHOTOGRAPHY SERVICES: 184; GETTY: 157, 273, 302, 479, 485, 507, 515, 551, 562, 578; HARVEY L STAHL/ THE GALLERY PRESS: 559; THE HUGH LANE GALLERY: 111, 131; IMAGEFILE: 80, 166, 357, 403, 454; IMPERIAL WAR MUSEUM LONDON: 259; IRA WOOD: 531; JOHN SKELTON/ THE PATRICK KAVANAGH RURAL AND LITERARY RESOURCE CENTRE: 186; JOHN WHEATLEY/THE GALLERY PRESS: 583; KEVIN CASEY: 437; KIM HAUGHTON: 565; LEBRECHT MUSIC & ARTS: 519; LLOYD FRANKENBERG/ VASSAR COLLEGE LIBRARIES: 210; MARK GERSON: 510; MARY EVANS PICTURE LIBRARY: 53, 97, 150, 343, 467, 470, 476; MICHAEL MARKEE/ WILLIAM STAFFORD ARCHIVES: 488; MUSEUM OF MODERN ART NEW YORK/SCALA: 234; NATIONAL LIBRARY OF IRELAND: 145; NEIL RYAN: 201; PA PHOTOS: 307; PHOTOCALL IRELAND: 375, 405, 513, 573, 580; PROFESSOR CONNOLLY/ ST JAMES HOSPITAL: 202; ROYAL GEOGRAPHICAL SOCIETY: 432, 433; SALMON POETRY: 557; TOPFOTO: 121T, 208, 240, 305, 482, 491, 494, 500, 534, 571; ULSTER MUSEUM: 392, 413.

The author and publisher have made every effort to trace all copyright holders, but if any has been inadvertently overlooked we would be pleased to make the necessary arrangement at the first opportunity.

JUNE 2012 EXAMINATION

Note: In the Ordinary level exam in June 2012 there will be one question on the poems in the left-hand column and one question on the poems in the right-hand column. Candidates are required to answer only one question.

JUNE 2013 EXAMINATION

Note: In the Ordinary level exam in June 2013 there will be one question on the poems in the left-hand column and one question on the poems in the right-hand column. Candidates are required to answer only one question.

JUNE 2014 EXAMINATION

Dickinson	I Felt a Funeral, in my Brain (p. 60)	**Herbert**	The Collar (p. 467)
	I Heard a Fly buzz – when I died (p. 67)	**Williams**	This is Just to Say (p. 479)
Yeats	The Wild Swans at Coole (p. 118)	**Thomas**	Do not go Gentle into that Good Night (p. 492)
	An Irish Airman Foresees his Death (p. 122)	**Nemerov**	Wolves in the Zoo (p. 497)
Bishop	The Fish (p. 210)	**Beer**	The Voice (p. 511)
	The Prodigal (p. 220)		
	Filling Station (p. 233)	**Kennelly**	Night Drive (p. 528)
Larkin	Ambulances (p. 262)	**Piercy**	Will we Work Together? (p. 531)
	The Explosion (p. 266)		
Kinsella	Thinking of Mr D. (p. 272)	**Gallagher**	The Hug (p. 542)
	Mirror in February (p. 278)	**Lochhead**	Kidspoem/Bairnsang (p. 548)
Plath	Poppies in July (p. 366)	**Shuttle**	Zoo Morning (p. 554)
	The Arrival of the Bee Box (p. 368)	**Hardie**	Daniel's Duck (p. 560)
	Child (p. 372)	**O'Callaghan**	The Net (p. 568)
Heaney	A Constable Calls (p. 386)	**Duffy**	Valentine (p. 571)
	The Underground (p. 394)	**Sirr**	Madly Singing in the City (p. 574)
	A Call (p. 398)	**Wyley**	Poems for Breakfast (p. 581)
Mahon	Grandfather (p. 407)	**Wheatley**	Chronicle (p. 584)
	After the Titanic (p. 412)		
	Antarctica (p. 431)		

Note: In the Ordinary level exam in June 2014 there will be one question on the poems in the left-hand column and one question on the poems in the right-hand column. Candidates are required to answer only one question.

New Explorations Critical Notes

CD 1 attached to the inside cover of this book contains detailed *Critical Notes* on all the prescribed poems (except those by Adrienne Rich, for copyright reasons) for Higher and Ordinary Level English for students sitting the Leaving Certificate examination in 2011–2014.

To access the content on the CD-ROM:

Windows XP/Vista

Once the CD is inserted a screen will open up automatically with three options:

1. Open Critical Notes
2. Install Adobe Reader 9.0 if it is not already installed
3. Download Latest Adobe Reader – clicking here will take you to the official Adobe Reader download web page

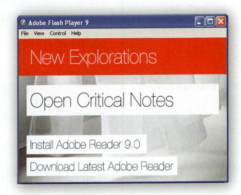

Mac OS X

Insert the CD and double click the **New Explorations** icon on the desktop. In the Finder window the same three options are available.

Contents

P = poem also prescribed for Ordinary Level

P = poem also prescribed for Ordinary Level

P = poem also prescribed for Ordinary Level

P = poem also prescribed for Ordinary Level

P = poem also prescribed for Ordinary Level

14 Derek Mahon (1941–)   Pages 405–436

15 Eavan Boland (1944–)   Pages 437–463

P = poem also prescribed for Ordinary Level

Ordinary Level

Contributors:
- Carole Scully
- John G. Fahy
- Bernard Connolly
- John McCarthy
- David Keogh

William Shakespeare
1564–1616

prescribed for Higher Level exams in 2013

William Shakespeare was born in April 1564 in Stratford-upon-Avon, Warwickshire, the son of John Shakespeare, a glover, and Mary Arden, the daughter of a gentleman farmer.

John Shakespeare was a man of some importance in the town of Stratford, eventually becoming the equivalent of mayor and achieving considerable wealth and property in the 1570s but losing it again in the 1580s, when for some unknown reason his fortunes took a turn for the worse.

William Shakespeare probably attended the local grammar school; he never went to university but was self-educated to a very high standard. He was an avid reader. There is a tradition, which cannot be substantiated, that he was for a time an assistant country schoolmaster. Certainly he was familiar with the Latin authors used in Elizabethan grammar schools: Plautus, Ovid, and Seneca.

> Lucius, what book is that she
>   tosseth so?
> —Grandsire, 'tis Ovid's
>   Metamorphoses.
>   [*Titus Andronicus*, IV, i]

There are also references to these writers in *The Merry Wives of Windsor* and *Love's Labour's Lost*.

However, Shakespeare was also an 'out-of-doors' man. From the evidence of his writing it seems that he was addicted to sports of all kinds: deer hunting, hare coursing, hawking, bowls, and archery.

> I do follow here in the chase,
>   not like a hound that hunts,
> but one that fills up the cry.
>   [*Othello*, II, iii]

> When the wind is southerly I know
>   a hawk from a handsaw [young
>   heron].
>   [*Hamlet*, II, ii]

So he was an all-round 'Renaissance man'.

In November 1582, at the age of eighteen, Shakespeare married Anne Hathaway, who was eight or nine years his senior, and six months later their first daughter, Susanna, was born. In 1585 a twin son and daughter, Hamnet and Judith, were born. Hamnet died, aged eleven, in August 1596. Shakespeare wrote his grief for his only son into the play he was composing at the time, *King John*:

> Grief fills the room up of my
>   absent child,
> Lies in his bed, walks up and
>   down with me,
> Puts on his pretty looks, repeats
>   his words,
> Remembers me of all his
>   gracious parts   [III, iv]

Shakespeare left Stratford to follow a career in acting and the theatre, though there is no hard information about which company he was with or exactly when he went to London. But we know that he was working with Lord Strange's Company in London in 1592. In 1595, when the company was renamed the Chamberlain's Men and organised on a shareholding basis, Shakespeare was wealthy enough to become one of the eight shareholders.

His early attempts at comedy, tragedy and history — *The Comedy of Errors*, *Titus Andronicus* and *Henry VI* — were popular successes. But, more important, he had acquired a patron in the young Earl of Southampton, to whom he dedicated his narrative poems 'Venus and Adonis' and 'The Rape of Lucrece' in 1593 and 1594. It was rumoured that Southampton's financial bequest of a thousand pounds for this gesture enabled Shakespeare to buy in to the Chamberlain's Men, thereby securing his financial future (as it was generally the acting company that held the copyright of a play). This meant that Shakespeare had continuous remuneration for both writing and performance. And write he did: at least thirty-seven plays in about twenty years, among them *Romeo and Juliet*, *The Merchant of Venice* and *Julius Caesar*, as well as the tragedies *Hamlet*, *Othello*, *King Lear* and *Macbeth*. He also wrote the long narrative poems and over 150 sonnets. So he was a prolific writer, as well as an actor and producer.

Shakespeare achieved fame as well as fortune in his lifetime, his players performing twice as frequently as any other company at court during the reigns of Queen Elizabeth I and her successor, James Stuart. With his wealth he bought property in his home town of Stratford, to which he retired in 1613. But his retirement was brief, and he died in April 1616.

The sonnet form

At its most basic, a sonnet can be described as a fourteen-line poem with a formal rhyming scheme and a fixed structure for its ideas. There are two principal forms of the sonnet, Petrarchan and Shakespearean. The Petrarchan sonnet (after Francesco Petrarca, 1304–1375) is structured in two parts. The first eight lines or octave make the chief statement, describe the situation, pose the question or problem. There follows a turn or volta, featuring a new statement, or a refinement of the first statement, or a solution to the problem, expressed in the final six lines or sestet.

Each section may embody a different thought process: often the octave is merely descriptive, plainly reporting an event, with the speculation on that event following in the sestet. There may also be a change of mood or tone in the sestet. There is a strict rhyming scheme to be followed — abba abba cdcdcd or cdecde. The Petrarchan sonnet has been an influential and popular poetic form.

The sonnet was introduced into English poetry in the sixteenth century, reaching its full flowering in the second half of the century. The first English sonneteers, such as Sir Thomas Wyatt and Sir Philip Sidney, followed the Petrarchan model. Shakespeare, a near contemporary of Sidney's, developed a form of his own, which consisted of three groups of four lines (quatrains), and a rhyming couplet to conclude. The couplet was meant to be epigrammatical — a pithy conclusion, rounding off the poem with a moral or a truth. Shakespeare used it in a variety of ways. The quatrains are distinct but linked in theme to the main idea of the sonnet. Shakespeare favoured the rhyming scheme abab cdcd efef gg.

Perhaps because of these numerous divisions in structure, the Shakespearean sonnet tends to read as a reasoned argument. The brevity of the sonnet form demands great discipline of thought from the writer as well as technical skill with rhyming. It is particularly suitable for the development of a single idea and has been popular as a vehicle for love poetry down through the ages.

Editions of the sonnets: a note on the text

During 1609 the volume entitled *Shakespeares Sonnets: Never before Imprinted* was published by Thomas Thorpe in a quarto format (a large page size). This edition is now referred to as the Q text. Shakespeare had engaged a well-known printer, George Eld, to print the volume. Thirteen copies of Q have survived, .and it is the authoritative text on which all subsequent editions are based.

There have been some adulterated editions of the sonnets down the years, most notably the second edition published by John Benson in 1640. Benson rearranged Thorpe's 1609 edition, omitting the dedication to 'Mr W. H.', running some sonnets together to form longer poems, and completely omitting eight of the originals. Among other changes, he substituted some feminine nouns and pronouns for the masculine, so giving the impression that the poems were addressed to a woman rather than to a man. He even invented some titles. Benson's edition became the source for many of the eighteenth-century editions of Shakespeare's sonnets, until Edmund Malone's celebrated scholarly edition of 1780. Malone restored the Q text, though with some emendations and modernisations, according to the style and literary taste of his own time.

There have since been many editions of the sonnets by editors holding different scholarly opinions on the spelling, punctuation, word usage and order of the poems (most modernise the spelling); but there is general agreement that the order of the poems in the 1609 edition is authoritative and likely to have been overseen by Shakespeare. The selection here follows in general the Cambridge University Press modern spelling edition of 1966 edited by G. Blakemore Evans.

Sonnet 12

When I do count the clock that tells the time,
And see the brave day sunk in hideous night,
When I behold the violet past prime,
And sable curls all silvered o'er with white,
When lofty trees I see barren of leaves,   5
Which erst from heat did canopy the herd,
And summer's green, all girded up in sheaves,
Borne on the bier with white and bristly beard:
Then of thy beauty do I question make
That thou among the wastes of time must go,   10
Since sweets and beauties do themselves forsake,
And die as fast as they see others grow,
        And nothing 'gainst Time's scythe can make defence,
        Save breed, to brave him when he takes thee hence.

Notes

[4]   **sable:** black
[6]   **erst:** erstwhile, formerly
[14]   **brave him:** defy him

Explorations

First reading

1. List the images used, particularly in the first eight lines. Consider what they have in common. Does this give you a clue to what the poem is about?

Second reading

2. Could we say that the poem falls into two separate categories, more like a Petrarchan than a Shakespearean sonnet? Identify the two sections and the different considerations of each.

3. List all the images dealing with change and ageing. Do they deal mainly with two different life forms? Comment on any patterns you notice.

4. Examine the connotations of some of these images.

Third reading

5. Can you now state briefly what the poet's main considerations (or themes) are here?

6. Do you find his argument convincing? Explain.

Fourth reading

7. Read the critical commentary. What points do you agree with? Which points do you disagree with? Substantiate your views with reference to the text.

8. Read the poem aloud. Can you hear the poet's voice? What is his mood?

9. Make your own notes on the poem, under headings such as:

   • theme

   • development of argument

   • force of the imagery

   • tone of the poem.

Sonnet 18

this poem is also prescribed for Ordinary Level exams in 2013

Shall I compare thee to a summer's day?
Thou art more lovely and more temperate:
Rough winds do shake the darling buds of May,
And summer's lease hath all too short a date;
Sometime too hot the eye of heaven shines,   5
And often is his gold complexion dimmed;
And every fair from fair sometime declines,
By chance or nature's changing course untrimmed:
But thy eternal summer shall not fade,
Nor lose possession of that fair thou ow'st,   10
Nor shall Death brag thou wand'rest in his shade,
When in eternal lines to time thou grow'st.
    So long as men can breathe or eyes can see,
    So long lives this, and this gives life to thee.

Notes

[4] **lease:** legal agreement allowing use of property, land, etc. for a specified time
[7] **fair from fair:** beautiful thing from beauty
[8] **untrimmed:** stripped
[10] **thou ow'st:** you own or possess

EXPLORATIONS

First reading

1. In describing the Friend, Shakespeare first suggests an analogy with a summer's day, but then dismisses it. Why does he find the analogy inadequate?

2. What qualities of the Friend are praised, both in direct statement and by implication?

3. What is the poet's underlying worry here, and what is his solution?

4. The notion of the transience of youth and the swift fading of summer energy is introduced in line 4. Trace its development through the second quatrain.

5. What view of human life is communicated by the octave of this sonnet?

6. 'But thy eternal summer shall not fade.' How does the poet go on to justify this paradoxical statement?

7. Can you now state the main themes in a few succinct phrases or sentences?

8. How would you describe the tone of the poem: worried, intimate, supremely confident, arrogant, or what? Justify your comments by reference to the text.

9. What does the poem reveal about the writer?

Fourth reading

10. Read the critical commentary and discuss it.

11. What unanswered questions have you about this poem?

Sonnet 23

As an unperfect actor on the stage,
Who with his fear is put besides his part,
Or some fierce thing replete with too much rage,
Whose strength's abundance weakens his own heart;
So I, for fear of trust, forget to say   5
The perfect ceremony of love's rite,
And in mine own love's strength seem to decay,
O'ercharged with burthen of mine own love's might:
O, let my books be then the eloquence
And dumb presagers of my speaking breast,   10
Who plead for love, and look for recompense,
More than that tongue that more hath more expressed.
    O, learn to read what silent love hath writ.
    To hear with eyes belongs to love's fine wit.

[1]   **unperfect:** imperfect, doesn't know his lines
[2]   **is put besides his part:** cannot play the character
        with conviction
[6]   **rite:** ceremony
[9]   **books:** of poems
[10]   **dumb presagers:** silent foretellers or spokespersons

EXPLORATIONS

First reading

As often with a Shakespeare sonnet, the first line gives us the clue. Take the first simile as the guiding clue: he is comparing himself to an inadequate actor.

1. What type or types of actor does he identify with? Are there more than one? What are their inadequacies? Examine the first quatrain.

2. What 'part' does the poet wish to play? What does he see as his inadequacies? Examine the second quatrain.

3. What is his solution? Examine the final six lines.

Second reading

4. Explore what exactly the poet wants to communicate. Examine, in particular, lines 6, 8, and 11.

5. What is his emotional state? Examine, in particular, lines 1, 5, 8, 11, and 13.

Second reading continued

6. Comment on the tone of the poem.

7. Did you notice that the poet can still be clever and witty — using paradoxes, and punning on words? Read the poem again. Do you need to re-evaluate your comment on tone?

Third reading

8. What exactly is the poet saying about the communication of feelings?

9. Evaluate the appropriateness of the similes and metaphors that he uses to communicate his dilemma.

10. Comment on the energy of the language.

Fourth reading

11. Write up your notes on this poem.

Sonnet 29

When, in disgrace with Fortune and men's eyes,
I all alone beweep my outcast state,
And trouble deaf heaven with my bootless cries,
And look upon myself and curse my fate,
Wishing me like to one more rich in hope,   5
Featured like him, like him with friends possessed,
Desiring this man's art, and that man's scope,
With what I most enjoy contented least;
Yet in these thoughts myself almost despising,
Haply I think on thee, and then my state,   10
Like to the lark at break of day arising
From sullen earth, sings hymns at heaven's gate;
    For thy sweet love rememb'red such wealth brings,
    That then I scorn to change my state with kings.

Notes

[1]   **disgrace:** out of favour
[3]   **bootless:** useless, in vain
[7]   **art:** skill, talent
[7]   **scope:** opportunities
[10] **haply:** by chance

EXPLORATIONS

First reading

1. This is very much a mood poem. Reread the octave and pick out the key words that indicate the writer's mood.

2. What picture of the speaker emerges?

3. Reread the sestet. Pick out the key words that indicate the mood here. Describe it.

Second reading

4. What is the link between the two moods?

5. Can you express the theme in a few sentences?

Sonnet 30

When to the sessions of sweet silent thought
I summon up remembrance of things past,
I sigh the lack of many a thing I sought,
And with old woes new wail my dear time's waste.
Then can I drown an eye, unused to flow,   5
For precious friends hid in death's dateless night,
And weep afresh love's long since cancelled woe,
And moan th' expense of many a vanished sight;
Then can I grieve at grievances foregone,
And heavily from woe to woe tell o'er   10
The sad account of fore-bemoanèd moan,
Which I new pay as if not paid before:
     But if the while I think on thee, dear friend,
     All losses are restored and sorrows end.

Notes

[1]	**sessions:** sittings of a court
[4]	**new wail:** newly bewail
[4]	**my dear time's waste:** the wasting or destruction by time of things dear to the poet
[6]	**dateless:** endless
[7]	**cancelled woe:** sorrow that has been forgotten or cancelled because it has been paid for
[8]	**sight:** probably 'sigh', reflecting the then current medical belief that sighing adversely affected the health; so he is lamenting the sighs of sorrow that wasted his health years before
[9]	**foregone:** former
[10]	**tell:** count
[11]	**fore-bemoanèd:** previously lamented

Explorations

First reading

Once again the opening metaphor gives us the clue. It is a legal image: the 'sessions' are the sittings of a court to which all his memories are summoned in evidence.

1. List the regrets he has.
2. Are they all selfish sorrows? Explain.

Second reading

3. List the key words that indicate his mood.
4. In the first three quatrains, do you think he manages to gain some measure of control over his depressed state, or does it deepen? Explain.
5. Do you find the couplet convincing?

Third reading

6. Trace the line of legal imagery through the poem: i.e. list the words that could have legal connotations.
7. How does this imagery fit in with the theme? Do you think it appropriate? Is it effective?
8. Comment on any other imagery you find effective.
9. How does the poet use the sounds of the words to create the atmosphere?

Fourth reading

10. Outline the theme, and comment on the development of it in this sonnet.
11. Would you agree that the sentiment is overdone but that the poem's main value is in the startling and graphic imagery?
12. Reread Sonnets 29 and 30 and compare them under the following headings:
    - theme and its depth of treatment
    - coherence and convincing nature of the argument
    - sincerity and depth of feeling
    - imaginative and colourful expression.

Sonnet 60

this poem is also prescribed for Ordinary Level exams in 2013

Like as the waves make towards the pebbled shore,
So do our minutes hasten to their end,
Each changing place with that which goes before,
In sequent toil all forwards do contend.
Nativity, once in the main of light,   5
Crawls to maturity, wherewith being crowned,
Crookèd eclipses 'gainst his glory fight,
And Time that gave doth now his gift confound.
Time doth transfix the flourish set on youth,
And delves the parallels in beauty's brow,   10
Feeds on the rarities of nature's truth,
And nothing stands but for his scythe to mow.
    And yet to times in hope my verse shall stand,
    Praising thy worth, despite his cruel hand.

Notes		
	[4]	**sequent:** successive
	[4]	**contend:** struggle, compete
	[5]	**nativity:** the newborn child
	[5]	**main of light:** ocean of light, i.e. the universe in sixteenth-century cosmography
	[7]	**crookèd:** malign
	[7]	**eclipses:** natural phenomena seen as a manifestation of evil in the universe
	[8]	**confound:** destroy
	[13]	**times in hope:** (imaginary) better future times

Explorations

First reading

1. What words and phrases stand out on a first reading?
2. Do you notice any repetition of words or ideas? Do these give you any clue to what the poem might be about?

Second reading

3. Read the first quatrain carefully. What picture comes into your mind? Describe it.
4. What words or phrases in particular create this picture of movement?
5. If this is taken as a metaphor for life, what does it suggest?
6. Read the second quatrain carefully. If you use the words 'nativity', 'crawls to maturity' and 'eclipses' as stepping-stones, can you make out what the poet is describing?
7. List the phrases you don't understand in this quatrain. Look at the notes and read it again.
8. What general impression of time comes across from the third quatrain? Concentrate on the verbs.

Second reading continued

9. List the phrases you don't understand, and investigate them in the notes and the commentary.
10. What is the new idea the poet introduces in the rhyming couplet?

Third reading

11. Briefly outline the poet's argument in this sonnet.
12. Examine the various characteristics of time as communicated through the imagery. Do you find these threatening?
13. Do you find the rhyming couplet convincing? Explain your views.
14. Do you think this poem communicates the deeply felt personal fears of the poet, or do you find it more of a clever, learned and well-crafted performance piece? Discuss.

Fourth reading

15. Briefly express the theme.
16. What is your personal reaction to this poem?

Sonnet 65

Since brass, nor stone, nor earth, nor boundless sea,
But sad mortality o'ersways their power,
How with this rage shall beauty hold a plea,
Whose action is no stronger than a flower?
O, how shall summer's honey breath hold out   5
Against the wrackful siege of batt'ring days,
When rocks impregnable are not so stout,
Nor gates of steel so strong but Time decays?
O fearful meditation! Where, alack,
Shall Time's best jewel from Time's chest lie hid?   10
Or what strong hand can hold his swift foot back,
Or who his spoil of beauty can forbid?
    O, none, unless this miracle have might,
    That in black ink my love may still shine bright.

Notes

[1]	**since:**	since there is neither
[3]	**rage:**	fury
[3]	**hold:**	maintain
[4]	**action:**	case, as in a legal action
[6]	**wrackful:**	destructive
[9]	**alack:**	an exclamation of pity or regret
[10]	**Time's best jewel:**	beauty — probably in reference to the Friend
[10]	**Time's chest:**	Time's coffer, with overtones of 'coffin'
[12]	**spoil:**	plunder
[14]	**my love:**	my beloved — a reference to the Friend

EXPLORATIONS

First reading

1. Read the sonnet aloud a number of times. Do you get the impression that some of it, at least, is dealing with power and strength? What creates that impression?

2. Is the entire sonnet in this vein, or are there contrasting images and phrases? Where, and what are they about?

Second reading

3. The first quatrain carries the essence of the argument. Can you work it out? Look at the notes if necessary.

4. Do you think the contrast in the first four lines is effective, or is it overdone?

5. Does the argument of the second quatrain resemble that of the first?

6. What metaphorical context for time do the images of the second quatrain suggest?

7. How does the poet view Time in the third quatrain?

8. Do you think the use of the term 'miracle' is appropriate in the couplet? Explain.

Third reading

9. What exactly is being threatened by Time in the sonnet?

10. Do you find the threat convincing? Discuss.

11. What would you say are the poet's feelings here? Justify your view by reference to the text.

Fourth reading

12. Read Sonnets 60 and 65 again. Which do you think has the greater depth of feeling? Explain.

Sonnet 66

Tired with all these, for restful death I cry,
As to behold desert a beggar born,
And needy nothing trimmed in jollity,
And purest faith unhappily forsworn,
And gilded honour shamefully misplaced,   5
And maiden virtue rudely strumpeted,
And right perfection wrongfully disgraced,
And strength by limping sway disablèd,
And art made tongue-tied by authority,
And folly (doctor-like) controlling skill,   10
And simple truth miscalled simplicity,
And captive good attending captain ill.
    Tired with all these, from these would I be gone,
    Save that to die, I leave my love alone.

Notes

[2]	**as:**	for instance
[2]	**desert:**	a deserving person
[3]	**needy nothing:**	a nobody, lacking in virtue
[3]	**trimmed in jollity:**	dressed up as for a celebration
[4]	**forsworn:**	perjured
[5]	**gilded:**	golden, covered in gold
[6]	**strumpeted:**	debauched, prostituted
[8]	**limping sway:**	incompetent power
[11]	**simple:**	pure
[11]	**simplicity:**	foolishness or ignorance
[12]	**attending:**	subservient to, waiting upon

EXPLORATIONS

First reading

1. 'Tired with all these . . .' What are all these sources of dissatisfaction for the poet? Consult the textual notes and make a list in your own words.

Second reading

2. In your own words, what are Shakespeare's criticisms of (a) class structure, (b) social and moral values, and (c) the use of power, as he sees them operating in his society?

3. In brief outline, trace the framework of Shakespeare's argument in the sonnet.

4. How would you describe the poet's mood? What leads you to this conclusion?

Third reading

5. Does this poem give us any greater insight into Shakespeare's mind than we get from the other sonnets read so far? Explain.

6. Contrast this with any two of the other sonnets, using as headings:

   • preoccupations of the poet

   • philosophy of life

   • attitude to death.

Sonnet 73

That time of year thou mayst in me behold
When yellow leaves, or none, or few, do hang
Upon those boughs which shake against the cold,
Bare ruined choirs where late the sweet birds sang.
In me thou seest the twilight of such day   5
As after sunset fadeth in the west,
Which by and by black night doth take away,
Death's second self, that seals up all in rest.
In me thou seest the glowing of such fire
That on the ashes of his youth doth lie,   10
As the death-bed whereon it must expire,
Consumed with that which it was nourished by.
  This thou perceiv'st, which makes thy love more strong,
  To love that well which thou must leave ere long.

[4]   **choir:** the part of the church where the choir sang; this may allude to the destruction of the monasteries at the time of King Henry VIII

[4]   **late:** of late, lately

EXPLORATIONS

First reading

1. 'That time of year . . .' What time of his life is he referring to here?

2. On a first reading, what do you see in this poem? What images make the biggest impression on you?

3. Each of the three quatrains uses a metaphor to express the theme. Examine each quatrain in detail, and explain what is suggested by the imagery and what exactly the poet is saying in each.

4. To whom do you think the poem is addressed?

Second reading

5. What is his theme here, death or love? Explain, with reference to the text.

Second reading continued

6. How would you describe the mood of the speaker: despondent, nostalgic, confident, hopeful, or what? Trace the variations in tone throughout the poem. Examine the tone of the final couplet.

7. What view of death informs the poem?

8. Do you find any truth or wisdom in the poem?

Third reading

9. 'The beauty of this sonnet has a lot to do with the simplicity of language and the honesty of feelings.' Would you agree?

10. Do you read this as a completely depressing poem?

Sonnet 94

They that have pow'r to hurt and will do none,
That do not do the thing they most do show,
Who, moving others, are themselves as stone,
Unmovèd, cold, and to temptation slow:
They rightly do inherit heaven's graces,   5
And husband nature's riches from expense;
They are the lords and owners of their faces,
Others but stewards of their excellence.
The summer's flower is to the summer sweet,
Though to itself it only live and die;   10
But if that flower with base infection meet,
The basest weed outbraves his dignity:
    For the sweetest things turn sourest by their deeds;
    Lilies that fester smell far worse than weeds.

Notes

[4] **Unmoved:** unaffected by emotion or excitement; calm; steadfast.

[5] **heaven's graces:** the grace or benevolence of heaven

[6] **husband:** to cultivate or manage carefully; to economise

[6] **expense:** money spent; consumption; loss

[8] **steward:** an official who controls the domestic affairs of a household for the master or lord

[11] **base:** here probably means inferior, mean, debased, worthless

[12] **outbraves:** surpasses

EXPLORATIONS

Before reading

1. Do you have any experience of people who appear well-meaning and friendly but are not what they appear to be? How do you think the friend of such a person might feel when he/she discovers this deception? Make a list of possible reactions.

2. In pairs or groups discuss this issue in general, without naming names or referring to actual people. Discuss the morality of it and the effect on others.

First reading

3. Read the first six lines. What do you think the poet is saying here? Share your ideas in groups.

4. Look at the commentary on these lines. Do you consider the first six lines a neutral statement, or might there be a hint of criticism? What words, images or statements influence your view? Explain your thinking.

5. How do lines 7 and 8 fit in with the argument made by the poet?

6. Read the sestet. What do you find different from the octet? Discuss this in groups.

First reading continued

7. Does the sestet influence your view of what the poet is saying in the entire poem? Explain.

Second reading

8. In your own words, and remaining faithful to the poem, trace the argument the poet is making.

9. Explore the images used. Do you think they are effective in conveying the argument?

10. Do you think the rhyming couplet at the end is an effective punch line to the argument? Explain your thoughts.

Third reading

11. What questions would you like to ask Shakespeare about the sonnet?

12. Do you view the speaker here as a highly moral person who has been hurt or just a 'whinger' who lost out?

13. Do you think the poem has anything to contribute to the lives of people today?

Sonnet 116

Let me not to the marriage of true minds
Admit impediments; love is not love
Which alters when it alteration finds,
Or bends with the remover to remove.
O, no, it is an ever-fixèd mark   5
That looks on tempests and is never shaken;
It is the star to every wand'ring bark,
Whose worth's unknown, although his height be taken.
Love's not Time's fool, though rosy lips and cheeks
Within his bending sickle's compass come;   10
Love alters not with his brief hours and weeks,
But bears it out even to the edge of doom.
    If this be error and upon me proved,
    I never writ, nor no man ever loved.

Notes

[2] **impediments:** legal obstacles — a reference to the marriage service in the Book of Common Prayer
[5] **mark:** sea marker
[7] **the star:** the North Star
[8] **whose worth's unknown:** whose astrological influence is uncertain
[8] **his height be taken:** its altitude has been calculated (for navigation purposes)
[9] **Time's fool:** Time's sport or plaything
[10] **compass:** range
[11] **his:** Time's
[12] **bears it out:** lasts, survives
[12] **edge of doom:** Judgement Day
[13] **upon:** against

681273 2
University of Limerick

EXPLORATIONS

Before reading

1. Read the first one-and-a-half lines. What do you think the poem is going to be about?

First reading

2. What do you notice about this sonnet? List your thoughts, in any order.

3. Shakespeare describes love by comparing it to some things and contrasting it with others. First examine the comparisons in the second quatrain. What do they suggest about the quality of love?

4. Examine the contrasts: lines 2–4 and 9–12. What is suggested about the quality of love here?

Second reading

5. How would you describe the type of love dealt with in this sonnet: erotic love, friendship, soul-mate love, or what? Substantiate your views with reference to the text.

6. Would you consider Shakespeare's idea of love to be unreal and too idealistic? Comment.

7. Examine the couplet. What does it mean? Do you think it makes a good conclusion or not? Explain your view.

Third reading

8. Briefly outline the theme of this poem.

9. Do you think the images used adequately convey the performance of true love and also the dreadful ravages of time? Examine the effectiveness of one usage of each type.

10. How would you describe the tone of this poem: serious, defeatist, confident, arrogant, or what? What words or phrases lead you to this conclusion?

11. 'In this sonnet we find an interesting treatment of love — tender, yet not sentimental.' Discuss this statement, supporting your views by reference to the text.

Fear no More the Heat o' the Sun

Guiderius:

> Fear no more the heat o' the sun,
> Nor the furious winter's rages;
> Thou thy worldly task hast done,
> Home art gone and ta'en thy wages:
> Golden lads and girls all must,   5
> As chimney-sweepers, come to dust.

Arviragus:

> Fear no more the frown o' the great;
> Thou art past the tyrant's stroke;
> Care no more to clothe and eat;
> To thee the reed is as the oak: 10
> The sceptre, learning, physic must
> All follow this and come to dust.

Guiderius:

> Fear no more the lightning-flash,

Arviragus:

> Nor the all-dreaded thunder-stone;

Guiderius:

> Fear no slander, censure rash;   15

Arviragus:

> Thou hast finish'd joy and moan:

Both:

> All lovers young, all lovers must
> Consign to thee and come to dust.

Guiderius:

> No exorciser harm thee!

Arviragus:

> Nor no witchcraft charm thee!   20

Guiderius:

> Ghost unlaid forbear thee!

Arviragus:

> Nothing ill come near thee!

Both:

> Quiet consummation have;
> And renownèd be thy grave!

[11] **sceptre:** royal staff, symbol of rule
[11] **physic:** medicine, i.e. doctors
[14] **thunder-stone:** meteorite

Context of the song

This elegy is taken from *Cymbeline* (IV, ii), one of Shakespeare's later comedies (c. 1609–1610). Set in Roman Britain, it is a play of uneven quality, full of sinister scheming, gratuitous horror, and a great deal of confusion. One of Shakespeare's biographers, Garry O'Connor, likens it to a forerunner of nineteenth-century music-hall entertainment, 'designed to appeal to bored middle-class sophisticates and philistine royal families with a short attention span.'

Imogen (daughter of Cymbeline, king of Britain), while travelling in disguise through the forest, has fainted and is presumed dead by her companions (really her disguised half-brothers, Guiderius and Arviragus), who are moved to sing this dirge.

EXPLORATIONS

First reading

1. Can you imagine the setting, the positions of the speakers, the position of the person addressed? Describe what you see.

2. In what tone of voice should this be spoken or sung? Why?

Second reading

3. What categories of things are no longer to be feared by the dead person?

4. What view of death is conveyed in this song?

5. Compare this view with references to death found in sonnets 18 and 30.

Third reading

6. What attitude to society comes across through this song? Compare it with the poet's view of society expressed in sonnet 66.

Fourth reading

7. Compare the metre of this poem with that of the sonnets. What effect does the metre have on the mood of this poem?

8. What characteristics of writing style and other Shakespearean qualities do you think this poem shares with the sonnets?

2 *William Wordsworth* (1770-1850)

prescribed for Higher Level exams in 2011 and 2013

William Wordsworth was born on 7 April 1770 in Cockermouth, Cumberland. The family was well-to-do and had a good social standing. Dorothy, his sister, was born in December 1771 and the two children developed a close relationship that was to continue into adulthood. Sadly, when he was eight years old his mother died, and five years later his father also died. Wordsworth attended Hawkshead Grammar School and at the age of 17 entered St John's College, Cambridge.

In 1790, during his summer holidays, he went on a walking tour through France and the Alps. After receiving his BA, Wordsworth returned to France and became interested in the revolutionary movement. He had an affair with Annette Vallon, who bore him a daughter. Under pressure from his friends, who were anxious about the political instability in France, Wordsworth returned to England and published some of his writing. The books received little attention, but they did lead to his friendship with Samuel Taylor Coleridge. Together they worked on a book of poems entitled *The Lyrical Ballads*, generally recognised as marking the beginning of the Romantic Movement in English poetry. For much of his life Wordsworth lived with Dorothy, his wife Mary, and his children in the beautiful Lake District. However, he enjoyed travelling on the Continent as well as around Britain and Ireland.

Although Wordsworth's work was not generally popular, among the literary set he was recognised as the initiator of a new form of poetic writing. Towards the end of his life he became more generally appreciated. In 1843, he was appointed Poet Laureate and received a state pension. He died in 1850 at the age of eighty and is buried in Grasmere churchyard.

She Dwelt among the Untrodden Ways

this poem is also prescribed for Ordinary Level exams in 2011 and 2013

She dwelt among the untrodden ways
Beside the springs of Dove,
A Maid whom there were none to praise
And very few to love:

A violet by a mossy stone   5
Half hidden from the eye!
— Fair as a star, when only one
Is shining in the sky.

She lived unknown, and few could know
When Lucy ceased to be;   10
But she is in her grave, and, oh,
The difference to me!

Notes

[1]   **dwelt:** lived
[1]   **untrodden:** not stepped on
[2]   **springs:** a place where water wells up from the earth
[3]   **Maid:** a girl

EXPLORATIONS

First reading

1. Describe in your own words the type of life that Lucy led. What sort of environment did she live in? Do you think she was happy with her life? Why? Would you be happy to live like this?

2. Wordsworth does not tell us directly what Lucy looked like. In the second stanza he uses two images to suggest some of her qualities. Discuss what you consider these qualities to be. How would you react if someone compared you to a 'violet' or a 'star'?

A contemporary painting of peaks in the French Alps,
which Wordsworth visited in 1790

3. What is Wordsworth's mood in this poem? Choose one phrase from the poem that you feel clearly signals this mood. What tone of voice should be used to read this poem?

Second reading

4. Do you think the first stanza is an effective way to open a piece of poetry? Why/why not?

5. What do you learn about Wordsworth himself from reading the poem? Can you suggest what sort of relationship he had with Lucy?

6. Examine Wordsworth's use of rhyme. Were you aware of it as you read the poem? How does the rhyme contribute to the overall effect of the piece?

Third reading

7. Wordsworth claims that Lucy's death made a 'difference' to him. Do you feel that the poem communicates death as distressing? Can you think of a reason why he might not be too upset?

8. Do you think that this poem conveys the flesh-and-blood Lucy, or was Wordsworth more interested in describing something else?

9. Wordsworth wanted to write poetry using 'the language really spoken by men'. Does he succeed in doing this here? How did his choice of words affect your reaction to the piece?

10. Is this poem too simple to be really interesting? Does simplicity in writing necessarily mean that it is easy to understand?

It is a Beauteous Evening, Calm and Free

this poem is also prescribed for Ordinary Level exams in 2011 and 2013

It is a beauteous evening, calm and free,
The holy time is quiet as a Nun
Breathless with adoration; the broad sun
Is sinking down in its tranquility;
The gentleness of heaven broods o'er the Sea: 5
Listen! the mighty Being is awake,

And doth with his eternal motion make
A sound like thunder — everlastingly.
Dear Child! dear Girl! that walkest with me here,
If thou appear untouched by solemn thought,   10
Thy nature is not therefore less divine:
Thou liest in Abraham's bosom all the year;
And worshipp'st at the Temple's inner shrine,
God being with thee when we know it not.

Notes

[12] **Abraham:** in the Old Testament, Abraham was willing to
      sacrifice his son Isaac on God's orders. Abraham stands for
      unswerving faith.
[13] **Temple's inner shrine:** the Temple in the Old Testamant,
      where God was worshipped, was divided into two areas: one
      part where the congregation gathered; and the more sacred
      inner shrine which could only be entered by the priests.

Grasmere in the Lake District:
a nineteenth-century lithograph

EXPLORATIONS

First reading

1. What time of day does
    Wordsworth describe in the first
    five lines of the poem? Choose
    one phrase that you find
    particularly effective. Have you
    ever been moved by a scene in
    nature? Write about your own
    experience.

2. Discuss who or what is 'the
    mighty Being' in line 6. (You
    should find lines 7–8 helpful.)
    What do you feel about this

description—is it vivid, surprising, confusing, or do you have a different reaction?

3. Does the way in which Wordsworth describes the scene in lines 1–8 tell you anything about what he felt at the time? Suggest two words to summarise his reaction.

4. In lines 9–14 Wordsworth tells us about his companion's reaction. How is it different from his own? Do you think that the fact she is a child affects the way she reacts? Does Wordsworth consider one reaction better than the other?

Second reading

5. Wordsworth uses an image of a nun in the opening four lines of the poem. How does he connect it with the sunset? Do you find this a successful connection of ideas? Why?

6. Why do you think Wordsworth referred to the sunset as 'The holy time'? Does the phrase tell you anything about his attitude to nature?

7. What senses does Wordsworth appeal to in this poem? What effect does this have on the overall impact of his description?

Third reading

8. Wordsworth famously wrote that, for him, poetry was stimulated by 'emotions recollected in tranquility'. Consider how the poem shows evidence of this approach.

9. Look again at 'She dwelt among the untrodden ways'. Do you find any similarities in Wordsworth's attitude to nature in the two poems?

10. Find a picture, or paint one yourself, to illustrate this poem.

Skating (extract from The Prelude)

this poem is also prescribed for Ordinary Level exams in 2011 and 2013

And in the frosty season, when the sun
Was set, and visible for many a mile
The cottage windows blazed through twilight gloom,

I heeded not their summons: happy time
It was indeed for all of us — for me   5
It was a time of rapture! Clear and loud
The village clock tolled six, — I wheeled about,
Proud and exulting like an untired horse
That cares not for his home. All shod with steel,
We hissed along the polished ice in games   10
Confederate, imitative of the chase
And woodland pleasures, — the resounding horn,
The pack loud chiming, and the hunted hare.
So through the darkness and the cold we flew,
And not a voice was idle; with the din   15
Smitten, the precipices rang aloud;
The leafless trees and every icy crag
Tinkled like iron; while far distant hills
Into the tumult sent an alien sound
Of melancholy not unnoticed, while the stars   20
Eastward were sparkling clear, and in the west
The orange sky of evening died away.
Not seldom from the uproar I retired
Into a silent bay, or sportively
Glanced sideway, leaving the tumultuous throng,   25
To cut across the reflex of a star
That fled, and, flying still before me, gleamed
Upon the glassy plain; and oftentimes,
When we had given our bodies to the wind,
And all the shadowy banks on either side   30
Came sweeping through the darkness, spinning still
The rapid line of motion, then at once
Have I, reclining back upon my heels,
Stopped short; yet still the solitary cliffs
Wheeled by me — even as if the earth had rolled   35
With visible motion her diurnal round!
Behind me did they stretch in solemn train,
Feebler and feebler, and I stood and watched
Till all was tranquil as a dreamless sleep.

[4]   **heeded not:** paid no attention to
[8]   **exulting:** triumphantly joyful
[11] **Confederate:** allied together
[15] **din:** prolonged loud noise
[16] **Smitten:** struck
[16] **precipices:** sheer cliffs
[19] **tumult:** uproar
[19] **alien:** different
[20] **melancholy:** sadness, depression
[25] **throng:** crowd
[26] **reflex:** reflection
[33] **reclining:** bending back
[36] **diurnal:** daily

EXPLORATIONS

First reading

1. Do you find this piece immediately understandable or rather confusing? Were you carried along by the speed of the language, or did you feel a little overwhelmed? Why do you think Wordsworth chose to write at such a rate?

2. Choose two phrases and two words that you find particularly effective in suggesting a frozen world. Explain why you chose them.

3. Have you ever been skating? Do you feel that Wordsworth successfully conveys a sense of what it is actually like to go skating? Examine the ways he suggests the freedom and speed of movement. Pay particular attention to his choice of words and to the sounds of the words.

4. Discuss the senses that Wordsworth appeals to in the piece. Consider how they contribute to the vividness of the scene.

Second reading

5. In lines 7–9 Wordsworth compares himself to a horse. Discuss the qualities he is trying to suggest by using this image. Do you think that the linking of these two ideas works? Does he use animal imagery elsewhere in the extract? Is it effective?

6. Sounds play a very important part in this poem. Can you suggest a reason for this? Try to remember being outside when there is snow and ice. Is there a particular sound word in the poem that you find especially effective?

7. Can you describe Wordsworth's mood in the poem? Does it remain the same throughout the piece, or can you detect a change? Discuss why his mood is affected.

Third reading

8. Wordsworth seems to feel that children have an instinctive ability to connect with nature. Examine this view in relation to this extract and one of his other poems that you have read.

9. We often tend to idealise memories of our childhood. Has Wordsworth done that here or is this a realistic portrayal of being a child?

10. Wordsworth wrote 'The end of Poetry is to produce excitement in co-existence with an overbalance of pleasure.' Did you feel excitement and pleasure when you read this extract?

To My Sister

It is the first mild day of March:
Each minute sweeter than before,
The redbreast sings from the tall larch
That stands beside our door.

There is a blessing in the air,   5
Which seems a sense of joy to yield
To the bare trees, and mountains bare,
And grass in the green field.

My sister! ('tis a wish of mine)
Now that our morning meal is done,   10
Make haste, your morning task resign;
Come forth and feel the sun.

Edward will come with you; — and, pray,
Put on with speed your woodland dress;
And bring no book: for this one day   15
We'll give to idleness.

No joyless forms shall regulate
Our living calendar:
We from today, my Friend, will date
The opening of the year.   20

Love, now a universal birth,
From heart to heart is stealing,
From earth to man, from man to earth:
— It is the hour of feeling.

One moment now may give us more   25
Than years of toiling reason:
Our minds shall drink at every pore
The spirit of the season.

Some silent laws our hearts will make,
Which they shall long obey: 30
We for the year to come may take
Our temper from to-day.

And from the blessed power that rolls
About, below, above,
We'll frame the measure of our souls: 35
They shall be tuned to love.

Then come, my Sister! come, I pray,
With speed put on your woodland dress;
And bring no book: for this one day
We'll give to idleness.   40

Notes

[11] **make haste:** hurry
[11] **task:** piece of work to be done
[26] **toiling:** hard work
[32] **temper:** mood or mental attitude

EXPLORATIONS

First reading

1. What do you notice about the way Wordsworth uses language in this poem? Is it what you would expect in a piece of poetic writing? Do you like it or not?

2. Can you work out the time of year and the type of weather that has inspired Wordsworth? Support your view by close reference to the poem. Do you think that he would have been equally inspired had the day been wet and windy? Perhaps he might have written a different type of poem — discuss what it might have been like.

3. Why does Wordsworth want his sister to come outside? If you were Dorothy, would this poem persuade you to do as he asks?

4. How, in Wordsworth's view, will a day outside affect the group? Do you agree or disagree with his opinion? Have you ever been positively influenced by a day in the open air?

Second reading

5. Wordsworth twice asks his sister to put on her 'woodland dress'. Can you suggest why he repeated this request? Do you think that there is more to it than simply asking her to change her clothes?

6. In the sixth stanza Wordsworth introduces the idea of 'Love'. Discuss how this connects with the time of year described in the poem. Examine in detail what Wordsworth actually means by his use of the word 'Love'. Would you agree with his interpretation of the word? Why?

7. Wordsworth refers to Time throughout this poem. Consider the different aspects of Time that occur. Does he suggest that there is a fundamental difference in the way that they affect Man?

8. 'We'll give the day to idleness.' Did Wordsworth really believe that the day would be spent in 'idleness'?

Third reading

9. Read 'It is a Beauteous Evening, Calm and Free' again. Are there any similarities between these two poems? Consider in particular the use of language, the senses and the underlying philosophy.

10. Wordsworth frequently uses exclamation marks in his writing. Why do you think he does this? Did you notice them, or are they not very important to the overall effect of his poetry?

A Slumber did my Spirit Seal

A slumber did my spirit seal;
I had no human fears:
She seemed a thing that could not feel
The touch of earthly years.

No motion has she now, no force;   5
She neither hears nor sees;
Rolled round in earth's diurnal course,
With rocks, and stones, and trees.

Notes

[1]   **seal:** close securely, put barriers around
[7]   **diurnal:** daily

First reading

1. What mood do you think Wordsworth is trying to create in this poem? Do the actual sounds of the words help to reinforce the effect? Is there any particular phrase that you feel encapsulates this mood?

2. Wordsworth tries to communicate a particular state in lines 3–6. Try to visualise yourself in this state. Write down any words that occur to you as descriptions of what you feel. Discuss your ideas with a view to choosing the five most successful descriptive words suggested.

3. In the final two lines, Wordsworth uses an image that we have previously met in 'Skating'. What is he describing? Do you find it an effective description? How does it relate to the mood of the piece?

EXPLORATIONS

Second reading

4. Discuss the language used by Wordsworth in this poem. What are your initial impressions of it? Are you more aware of a degree of ambiguity after a second reading? Can you locate the cause of this ambiguity?

5. Examine the opening line of the poem. Explain how you interpret it. Does the fact that it is written in the past tense influence how it is interpreted?

6. In the second line Wordsworth appears to make a simple statement. Discuss how his use of the past tense could affect the meaning it conveys. Is there a further alteration in the meaning of this line when you join it with lines 3–4?

7. Wordsworth changes to the present tense in the second stanza. Discuss the ways in which this adjustment influences your reaction to his description.

Third reading

8. Consider this poem as a whole, interpreting 'she' as referring to 'my spirit'. Can you express, in your own words, what Wordsworth is trying to communicate?

9. Some critics suggest that there are indications that this poem might have been written about Lucy. Re-read 'She Dwelt among the Untrodden Ways'. Does this change your view of the poem?

10. Look at Question 1 again. In the light of your subsequent readings and consideration of the poem, would you alter your answer?

Composed Upon Westminster Bridge

Earth has not anything to show more fair:
Dull would he be of soul who could pass by
A sight so touching in its majesty:
This City now doth, like a garment, wear
The beauty of the morning; silent, bare,   5
Ships, towers, domes, theatres, and temples lie
Open unto the fields, and to the sky;
All bright and glittering in the smokeless air.
Never did sun more beautifully steep
In his first splendour, valley, rock, or hill;   10
Ne'er saw I, never felt, a calm so deep!
The river glideth at his own sweet will:
Dear God! the very houses seem asleep;
And all that mighty heart is lying still!

Notes

[4]   **doth:** does
[11] **Ne'er:** never

Westminster Bridge, London: a contemporary painting

EXPLORATIONS

First reading

1. Do you find the subject of this poem a surprising choice for Wordsworth? Why?

2. Consider Wordsworth's description of the City. Does he successfully convey 'its majesty'? Choose two images that you find especially vivid and explain why they appeal to you.

3. What effect does this scene have on Wordsworth? Why do you think he reacted in this way? Would you have felt the same emotions?

Second reading continued

6. Why do you think Wordsworth wrote this poem in the present tense? Would the overall impact of the piece be altered if it had been written in the past tense? Try changing the tenses.

7. To which of the senses does this poem appeal? Why do you think Wordsworth chose to write it in this way? Would the effect of the description be altered had sounds been added?

Second reading

4. Do you think that Wordsworth was restricted in any way by choosing to write this poem as a fourteen-line sonnet? Was he able to communicate his theme successfully? Would the impact of the piece have been increased or reduced had the poem been longer?

5. Do you feel that Wordsworth suggests that there is a spiritual element to the appreciation of beauty? Is this a valid view? Does the spiritual quality come from the one who appreciates or the object that is being appreciated?

Third reading

8. The Victorian poet Matthew Arnold believed that Wordsworth had a 'healing power'. Can words heal? Do you find any of Wordsworth's poems healing?

The Solitary Reaper

Behold her, single in the field,
Yon solitary Highland Lass!
Reaping and singing by herself;
Stop here, or gently pass!
Alone she cuts and binds the grain,   5
And sings a melancholy strain;
O listen! for the Vale profound
Is overflowing with the sound.

No Nightingale did ever chaunt
More welcome notes to weary bands   10
Of travellers in some shady haunt,
Among Arabian sands:
A voice so thrilling ne'er was heard
In spring-time from the Cuckoo-bird, —
Breaking the silence of the seas   15
Among the farthest Hebrides.

Will no one tell me what she sings? —
Perhaps the plaintive numbers flow
For old, unhappy, far-off things,
And battles long ago: 20
Or is it some more humble lay,
Familiar matter of to-day? —
Some natural sorrow, loss, or pain,
That has been, and may be again?

Whate'er the theme, the Maiden sang   25
As if her song could have no ending;
I saw her singing at her work,
And o'er the sickle bending; —
I listened, motionless and still;
And, as I mounted up the hill,   30
The music in my heart I bore,
Long after it was heard no more.

Grasmere by the Rydal Road: a painting by Francis Towner (1739–1816)

EXPLORATIONS

First reading

1. Discuss the way in which Wordsworth opens this poem with the first stanza. Does it draw you into the poem by the vividness of the descriptions? Or perhaps you find it overdramatic in its language and use of exclamation marks?

2. In the second stanza, Wordsworth describes the quality of the reaper's singing. Do you feel that he was justified in devoting eight lines to this? Was it simply an opportunity for him to show off his descriptive powers?

3. 'Will no one tell me what she sings?'

   Can you explain why Wordsworth asks this question? Does he need to know what the girl was singing about? Would this affect his reaction to the singing? Do you think that it should? Do you need to know what a song is about to enjoy it?

4. In the fourth stanza Wordsworth communicates his reaction to the singing. Do you find it a believable reaction? Have you ever been stopped by a piece of music? Did it stay with you in the way that this song did with Wordsworth?

Second reading

5. There is a sense of immediacy about the first two lines of this poem. Can you explain how Wordsworth achieves this effect? Does it continue through the rest of the piece?

6. Both Wordsworth and the reaper are depicted as being on their own in Nature. Does the way in which each is depicted suggest a difference in their attitude to and relationship with nature?

Third reading

7. This poem describes a scene that comes from a world very different from the one we live in. Does this reduce the relevance of the poem? Is there a time limit on artistic creation?

8. Does the title, 'The Solitary Reaper', suggest the central theme of this poem? Could you suggest a more suitable title?

9. Examine the way in which Wordsworth uses imagery from nature in this poem and two of his other poems. Do you find it a successful technique or simply an overused piece of elaboration?

10. The critic F. R. Leavis commented: 'For Wordsworth solitude is the condition of a contemplative serenity.' Discuss this statement with reference to three of Wordsworth's poems.

The Stolen Boat (extract from The Prelude)

One summer evening (led by her) I found
A little boat tied to a willow tree
Within a rocky cave, its usual home.
Straight I unloosed her chain, and stepping in
Pushed from the shore. It was an act of stealth   5
And troubled pleasure, nor without the voice
Of mountain-echoes did my boat move on;
Leaving behind her still, on either side,
Small circles glittering idly in the moon,
Until they melted all into one track   10
Of sparkling light. But now, like one who rows,
Proud of his skill, to reach a chosen point
With an unswerving line, I fixed my view
Upon the summit of a craggy ridge,
The horizon's utmost boundary; for above   15
Was nothing but the stars and the grey sky.
She was an elfin pinnace; lustily
I dipped my oars into the silent lake,
And, as I rose upon the stroke, my boat
Went heaving through the water like a swan;   20
When, from behind that craggy steep till then
The horizon's bound, a huge peak, black and huge,
As if with voluntary power instinct
Upreared its head. I struck and struck again,
And growing still in stature the grim shape   25
Towered up between me and the stars, and still,
For so it seemed, with purpose of its own
And measured motion like a living thing,
Strode after me. With trembling oars I turned,
And through the silent water stole my way   30
Back to the covert of the willow tree;
There in her mooring-place I left my bark, —
And through the meadows homeward went, in grave
And serious mood; but after I had seen
That spectacle, for many days, my brain   35

Worked with a dim and undetermined sense
Of unknown modes of being; o'er my thoughts
There hung a darkness, call it solitude
Or blank desertion. No familiar shapes
Remained, no pleasant images of trees,   40
Of sea or sky, no colours of green fields;
But huge and mighty forms, that do not live
Like living men, moved slowly through the mind
By day, and were a trouble to my dreams.

Rydal Waterfall: a painting by Joseph Wright (1734–1797)

EXPLORATIONS

First reading

1. What emotions does the young Wordsworth feel as he takes the boat? How does Wordsworth communicate these feelings to you in the first seven lines of the piece?

2.   Consider Wordsworth's emotions in lines 11–20. Describe, in your own words, what he feels.

3.   How does the appearance of the peak affect Wordsworth's actions? Can you locate the words or phrases that suggest his emotional alteration?

4.   Can you explain how Wordsworth felt in the days after this incident? What particular aspect of this experience provoked these feelings? Do you feel that his reaction is understandable or rather overdramatic?

Second reading

5.   Time plays an important part in this piece. Discuss how it is conveyed during and after the incident. Does Wordsworth's emotional state affect his perception of time? Has this ever happened to you?

6.   Discuss how Wordsworth uses the concept of space to suggest his feelings. Can our emotions affect our awareness of space? Can space affect our emotions?

7.   What do you think Wordsworth learned as a result of this experience? Have you ever found yourself in a similar situation? Consider whether such learning experiences are exclusive to the young.

Third reading

8.   Compare this extract with 'Skating', which also comes from *The Prelude*. Are there any similarities between the two? Are they different in any way? This piece comes before 'Skating' in the full work. Is there any sense of this in the extracts themselves?

9.   In many ways the physical activities described in 'The Stolen Boat' and 'Skating' are less important than the emotional changes stimulated by them. Discuss, supporting your view with references from both extracts.

10. Wordsworth described *The Prelude* as 'a poem on my own poetical education'. Consider what lessons he learned, as suggested in 'The Stolen Boat' and 'Skating'. Do you feel that they serve to underpin his later works?

Tintern Abbey

Five years have past; five summers, with the length
Of five long winters! and again I hear
These waters, rolling from their mountain-springs
With a soft inland murmur. — Once again
Do I behold these steep and lofty cliffs,   5
That on a wild secluded scene impress
Thoughts of more deep seclusion; and connect
The landscape with the quiet of the sky.
The day is come when I again repose
Here, under this dark sycamore, and view   10
These plots of cottage-ground, these orchard-tufts,
Which at this season, with their unripe fruits,
Are clad in one green hue, and lose themselves
'Mid groves and copses. Once again I see
These hedge-rows, hardly hedge-rows, little lines   15
Of sportive wood run wild: these pastoral farms,
Green to the very door; and wreaths of smoke
Sent up, in silence, from among the trees!
With some uncertain notice, as might seem
Of vagrant dwellers in the houseless woods,   20
Or of some Hermit's cave, where by his fire
The Hermit sits alone.
These beauteous forms,
Through a long absence, have not been to me
As is a landscape to a blind man's eye: 25
But oft, in lonely rooms, and 'mid the din
Of towns and cities, I have owed to them,
In hours of weariness, sensations sweet,
Felt in the blood, and felt along the heart;
And passing even into my purer mind,   30
With tranquil restoration: — feelings too
Of unremembered pleasure: such, perhaps,
As have no slight or trivial influence
On that best portion of a good man's life,
His little, nameless, unremembered, acts   35

Of kindness and of love. Nor less, I trust,
To them I may have owed another gift,
Of aspect more sublime; that blessed mood,
In which the burthen of the mystery,
In which the heavy and the weary weight   40
Of all this unintelligible world,
Is lightened: — that serene and blessed mood,
In which the affections gently lead us on, —
Until, the breath of this corporeal frame
And even the motion of our human blood   45
Almost suspended, we are laid asleep
In body, and become a living soul:
While with an eye made quiet by the power
Of harmony, and the deep power of joy,
We see into the life of things.   50
If this
Be but a vain belief, yet oh! how oft —
In darkness and amid the many shapes
Of joyless daylight; when the fretful stir
Unprofitable, and the fever of the world,   55
Have hung upon the beatings of my heart —
How oft, in spirit, have I turned to thee,
O sylvan Wye! thou wanderer thro' the woods,
How often has my spirit turned to thee!

And now, with gleams of half-extinguished thought,   60
With many recognitions dim and faint,
And somewhat of a sad perplexity,
The picture of the mind revives again:
While here I stand, not only with the sense
Of present pleasure, but with pleasing thoughts   65
That in this moment there is life and food
For future years. And so I dare to hope,
Though changed, no doubt, from what I was when first
I came among these hills; when like a roe
I bounded o'er the mountains, by the sides   70
Of the deep rivers, and the lonely streams,
Wherever Nature led: more like a man
Flying from something that he dreads than one

Who sought the thing he loved. For Nature then
(The coarser pleasures of my boyish days, 75
And their glad animal movements all gone by)
To me was all in all — I cannot paint
What then I was. The sounding cataract
Haunted me like a passion: the tall rock,
The mountain, and the deep and gloomy wood, 80
Their colours and their forms, were then to me
An appetite; a feeling and a love,
That had no need of a remoter charm,
By thought supplied, nor any interest
Unborrowed from the eye. — That time is past, 85
And all its aching joys are now no more,
And all its dizzy raptures. Not for this
Faint I, nor mourn nor murmur; other gifts
Have followed; for such loss, I would believe,
Abundant recompense. For I have learned 90
To look on Nature, not as in the hour
Of thoughtless youth; but hearing oftentimes
The still, sad music of humanity,
Nor harsh nor grating, though of ample power
To chasten and subdue. And I have felt 95
A presence that disturbs me with the joy
Of elevated thoughts; a sense sublime
Of something far more deeply interfused
Whose dwelling is the light of setting suns,
And the round ocean and the living air, 100
And the blue sky, and in the mind of man:
A motion and a spirit, that impels
All thinking things, all object of all thought,
And rolls through all things. Therefore am I still
A lover of the meadows and the woods, 105
And mountains; and of all that we behold
From this green earth; of all the mighty world
Of eye, and ear, — both what they half create,
And what perceive; well pleased to recognise
In Nature and the language of the sense 110
The anchor of my purest thoughts, the nurse,

The guide, the guardian of my heart, and soul
Of all my moral being.
                                  Nor perchance,
If I were not thus taught, should I the more   115
Suffer my genial spirits to decay;
For thou art with me here upon the banks
Of this fair river; thou my dearest Friend,
My dear, dear Friend; and in thy voice I catch
The language of my former heart, and read   120
My former pleasures in the shooting lights
Of thy wild eyes. Oh! yet a little while
May I behold in thee what I was once,
My dear, dear Sister! and this prayer I make,
Knowing that Nature never did betray   125
The heart that loved her; 'tis her privilege,
Through all the years of this our life, to lead
From joy to joy: for she can so inform
The mind that is within us, so impress
With quietness and beauty, and so feed   130
With lofty thoughts, that neither evil tongues,
Rash judgments, nor the sneers of selfish men,
Nor greetings where no kindness is, nor all
The dreary intercourse of daily life,
Shall e'er prevail against us, or disturb   135
Our cheerful faith, that all which we behold
Is full of blessings. Therefore let the moon
Shine on thee in thy solitary walk;
And let the misty mountain-winds be free
To blow against thee: and, in after years,   140
When these wild ecstasies shall be matured
Into a sober pleasure; when thy mind
Shall be a mansion for all lovely forms,
Thy memory be as a dwelling-place
For all sweet sounds and harmonies; oh! then,   145
If solitude, or fear, or pain, or grief,
Should be thy portion, with what healing thoughts
Of tender joy wilt thou remember me,
And these my exhortations! Nor, perchance —

If I should be where I no more can hear 150
Thy voice, nor catch from thy wild eyes these gleams
Of past existence — wilt thou then forget
That on the banks of this delightful stream
We stood together; and that I, so long
A worshipper of Nature, hither came 155
Unwearied in that service: rather say
With warmer love — oh! with far deeper zeal
Of holier love. Nor wilt thou then forget
That after many wanderings, many years
Of absence, these steep woods and lofty cliffs, 160
And this green pastoral landscape, were to me
More dear, both for themselves and for thy sake!

Notes

[9] **repose:** rest, lie

[20] **vagrant:** wandering

[39] **burthen:** burden

[44] **corporeal:** physical, bodily

[58] **sylvan:** wooded, rural

[62] **perplexity:** puzzlement, confusion

[69] **roe:** small deer

[78] **cataract:** large waterfall

[90] **recompense:** amends

[95] **chasten:** restrain

[98] **interfused:** mixed with

[116] **genial:** cheerful

[135] **prevail:** be victorious

[149] **exhortations:** urgings

[157] **zeal:** fervour

EXPLORATIONS

First reading

1. What was your initial reaction when you saw the length of this poem? Did you find the poem difficult to read once you started, or did Wordsworth draw you along with his language and images? Was your interest sustained throughout the poem? Should a poem be limited in its length? Why?

2. Examine Wordsworth's description of the sweep of the view that is before him. Do you find it effective? Would you find such a scene appealing?

3. How does the view affect Wordsworth? What does the way in which he uses this scene suggest about Wordsworth's attitude to the different worlds he lives in? Do you think that most people have favourite scenes which they evoke as an escape from situations they find difficult? Do you?

Second reading

4. Discuss the changes that take place in Wordsworth's relationship with Nature as he matures. Do you feel that altered relationships are part of the human maturing process? Why?

5. 'A motion and a spirit,
    that impels
   All thinking things, all object
    of all thought,
   And rolls through all things.'

   What do you think Wordsworth is referring to in these lines? Do you think that he is deluding himself into believing that there is a way to understand this 'unintelligible world'?

6. What does Wordsworth's address to his sister, in the final section of the poem, suggest about their relationship? Do you find it surprising that he has someone else with him in this poem? If so, why?

Third reading

7. 'Thy memory be as a dwelling place
   For all sweet sounds and harmonies'

   What role does memory play in Wordsworth's poetry? Does he use the past to go forward? How?

8. Discuss how Wordsworth moves out from himself toward a wider perception. Is this process common to us all? What makes his experience worthy of being studied?

9. With Wordsworth 'an intense intellectual egotism swallows up everything'. (William Hazlitt)

   Wordsworth 'continues to bring joy, peace, strength, exaltation'. (A. C. Bradley)

   Wordsworth shows 'a capricious predilection for incidents that contrast with the depth and novelty of the truths that they are to exemplify'. (Samuel Taylor Coleridge)

   Discuss these opinions on Wordsworth's writing. Do you agree with any of them? Try to summarise your view of Wordsworth in one sentence.

10. Wordsworth commented: 'I have wished to keep the Reader in the company of flesh and blood, persuaded that by so doing I shall interest him.' Did Wordsworth interest you? Why/why not?

3 *Emily Dickinson*
1830–1886

prescribed for Higher Level exams in 2011 and 2014

Emily Dickinson was born and lived all her life in Amherst, Massachusetts in the USA. Her family members were prominent members of the community, lawyers and public representatives. Emily's early years seemed ordinary enough: education at Amherst Academy and Mount Holyoke Female Seminary; trips to Boston, Washington and Philadelphia; and running the family household when her mother became seriously ill. But she seems to have suffered some kind of psychological crisis in her early thirties, which resulted in her withdrawal from society.

She became somewhat eccentric, the 'myth' of Amherst, who didn't meet strangers or visitors and who spoke to friends from behind a half-closed door or shrouded in shadow at the head of the stairs. She produced a great number of rather cryptic poems of a most unusual form. When she died she was found to have left almost two thousand poems and fragments, in which she explored a number of themes including love, pain, absence and loss, doubt, despair and mental anguish, and hope. Hardly any were published in her lifetime, and their true worth and originality were not appreciated for many years.

Note on the Poems

In 1955 an authoritative collection of Dickinson's work, *The Poems of Emily Dickinson*, was prepared by Thomas Johnson. The poems are dated, but as Johnson himself admitted, this is the result of educated guesswork. It is very difficult to be definite, since Dickinson never prepared the poems for publication and did not title them. Each poem below is headed with Johnson's number.

214

I taste a liquor never brewed —
From Tankards scooped in Pearl —
Not all the Vats upon the Rhine
Yield such an Alcohol!

Inebriate of Air — am I —   5
And Debauchee of Dew —
Reeling — thro endless summer days —
From inns of Molten Blue —

When 'Landlords' turn the drunken Bee
Out of the Foxglove's door —   10
When Butterflies — renounce their 'drams' —
I shall but drink the more!

Till Seraphs swing their snowy Hats —
And Saints — to windows run —
To see the little Tippler   15
Leaning against the — Sun —

EXPLORATIONS

First reading

1. If you first approach the poem as a riddle, does this help you to decipher stanzas 1 and 2? For example, can you suggest an answer to any of the following enigmas?

    - How could there be a liquor that wasn't brewed?

    - How are tankards or beer mugs the colour of pearl?

    - 'Inebriate of Air', 'Debauchee of Dew' — who or what might she be? Who or what gets drunk on dew?

    - She is seen staggering from 'inns of Molten Blue' — an unusual colour for an inn as we know it. What or where are the inns?

    Is all revealed in the third stanza? Examine the first two lines. Explain your reading of stanzas 1 and 2.

2. Now explain the central metaphor of the poem.

3. Would you agree that the poet's train of thought becomes more whimsical as the poem progresses?

4. What do the first two stanzas suggest about the speaker's attitude to nature?

Second reading

5. What self-image does the poet attempt to project in this poem? Do you think she sees herself as dissolute, rebellious, assertive, or what? Explain, with reference to phrases or images.

6. It is generally agreed that this is a humorous poem. Comment on some of the methods by which the humour is achieved.

7. Do you think there is a substantial theme beneath the whimsical and humorous surface? Make suggestions.

8. How would you describe the tone of the poem? Refer to words and phrases in the text.

Third reading

9. The literary critic David Porter spoke of a 'tone of ecstatic assurance', reflecting the attitude of the speaker as victor over the pains of life. Would you agree with this?

10. What is your own evaluation of this poem?

'Hope' is the thing with feathers —
That perches in the soul —
And sings the tune without the words —
And never stops — at all —

And sweetest — in the Gale — is heard —   5
And sore must be the storm —
That could abash the little Bird
That kept so many warm —

I've heard it in the chillest land —
And on the strangest Sea —   10
Yet, never, in Extremity,
It asked a crumb — of Me.

EXPLORATIONS

Before reading

1. Consider briefly what part 'hope' plays in your own day-to-day life.

2. If you had to represent it figuratively in a painting or an image, how would you describe it?

First reading

3. How does the poet visualise hope?

4. Examine the analogy in detail. List the qualities or characteristics of hope suggested by each of the images in the first stanza. Pry beneath the obvious. For example, what does 'sings the tune without the words' suggest? What is the effect of that description of hope as the 'thing' with feathers?

5. What aspects of hope are suggested in the second stanza? What does the sound effect of the word 'abash' contribute to this picture? What is the effect of the adjective 'little'?

6. In the third stanza, which qualities of hope are a repetition of suggestions already encountered, and which are new?

7. How do you interpret the last two lines? Do they indicate the strength or a weakness in the virtue of hope? It depends on whether you read the third line as part of the meaning of the previous two or read it with the last line. Experiment with both readings. Is there some ambiguity, and does this show a weakness in the virtue of hope?

Second reading

8. Do you think the bird analogy is successful? Explain your views. What other metaphors for hope could you advance?

9. What insights into the nature of hope did you get from reading this poem?

10. How would you describe the mood of the poem? Suggest ways in which this mood is created in the text.

Third reading

11. What do you notice about the technical features of the poem: punctuation, sentences, capital letters, etc.? What is the effect of these?

12. Would you agree that the extraordinary imagery is one of the best features of this poem? Develop your answer with specific references.

13. Do you find this poem hopeful? Explain your views.

There's a certain Slant of light,
Winter Afternoons —
That oppresses, like the Heft
Of Cathedral Tunes —

Heavenly Hurt, it gives us —   5
We can find no scar,
But internal difference,
Where the Meanings, are —

None may teach it — Any —
'Tis the Seal Despair —   10
An imperial affliction
Sent us of the Air —

When it comes, the Landscape listens —
Shadows — hold their breath —
When it goes, 'tis like the Distance   15
On the look of Death —

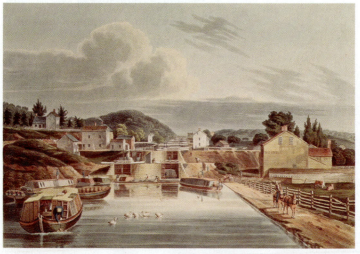

A contemporary painting of a lock on the Erie Canal, completed in 1825, which linked the Great Lakes with the Hudson River in New York State

EXPLORATIONS

1. Try to recall the image of any wintry sunlit afternoon you have experienced. Describe the quality of the sunlight as best you remember it.

First reading

2. On a first reading, what do you notice about the quality of the sunlight described by the poet?

3. Attempt to describe this light. What can we say about it from the descriptive details in the poem? Is it possible to say very much? Explain.

4. Do you notice how we are made aware of the light? Is it described objectively or filtered through the speaker's feelings? Give an example.

Second reading

5. Explore in detail the speaker's attitude to this light. Pay particular attention to the images for what they reveal of the speaker's view. Examine in particular the connotations of similes and metaphors ('like the Heft of Cathedral Tunes', 'the Seal Despair', 'like the Distance | On the look of Death').

Second reading continued

6. What do you think is meant by 'We can find no scar, | But internal difference, | Where the Meanings, are —'?

7. What religious view or philosophy seems to lie behind this poem?

8. How would you describe the tone of the poem? Refer to particular words and phrases. What do you think the sounds of words contribute to the tone? Explain.

Third reading

9. Briefly set down your understanding of the theme of this poem.

10. Outline your general reaction to the poem. What is your evaluation of it as a nature poem?

11. Can you appreciate that the poem might be seen to reflect the poet's deep despair? In your own words, explain the nature of the despair felt by the speaker.

12. Explore the sound effects — echoes, rhymes, alliteration, etc. — used by the poet. Do you think these musical effects might serve to disguise the deep negative feelings in the poem?

13. What questions do you still have about the poem?

280

this poem is also prescribed for Ordinary Level exams in 2011 and 2014

I felt a Funeral, in my Brain,
And Mourners to and fro
Kept treading — treading — till it seemed
That Sense was breaking through —

And when they all were seated,   5
A Service, like a Drum —
Kept beating — beating — till I thought
My Mind was going numb —

And then I heard them lift a Box
And creak across my Soul   10
With those same Boots of Lead, again,
Then Space — began to toll,

As all the Heavens were a Bell,
And Being, but an Ear,
And I, and Silence, some strange Race   15
Wrecked, solitary, here —

And then a Plank in Reason, broke,
And I dropped down, and down —
And hit a World, at every plunge,
And Finished knowing — then —   20

The Dickinson homestead, Amherst, Massachusetts, birthplace of Emily Dickinson and her home for over forty years. She wrote virtually all of her known poetry at the homestead and died there in 1886.

EXPLORATIONS

1. At a first reading, what images in particular hold your attention? What do these images suggest about the subject matter of the poem?

2. List the images suggestive of funerals as they occur throughout the poem. Do these conjure up for you the usual picture of a conventional funeral, or is it somehow different? Comment on any unusual connotations.

3. Where is the speaker in this poem? What suggests this?

Second reading

4. If we read this poem as primarily about the process of dying, what insights about death does it convey?

5. Try a metaphorical reading of the poem. Examine the metaphor in the first line, and then explore the poem as a psychological experience of breakdown. What insights does this reading bring to you?

6. Which view of the poem do you prefer to take? Could we hold both simultaneously?

Third reading

7. Explore the speaker's feelings in the first stanza. What is suggested by the imagery and the repetitions? How do you understand the fourth line?

8. Explore the connotations of the simile 'a Service, like a Drum' in the second stanza. What do the sounds of the words suggest about the speaker's state of mind in this stanza?

9. Explain the speaker's feelings in stanzas 2 and 3.

10. 'As all the Heavens were a Bell, And Being, but an Ear,'

    What image does this conjure up for you and what does it suggest about the speaker's perception of her relationship with the heavens?

11. Is the relationship between the speaker and the universe developed further in the following two lines?

    'And I, and Silence, some strange Race

    Wrecked, solitary, here —'

    Explain your understanding of this. How does the speaker feel about her life, her position here? Read the last line aloud. What does the rhythm, or lack of it, convey?

12. Were you surprised by the actions of the last stanza, or was it predictable? Explain. Do you think it is an effective ending?

13. Experiment with different oral readings of the last line. What implications for meaning have the different readings?

Fourth reading

14. List, briefly, the principal themes and issues you found in the poem.

15. Decide on your own interpretation of the poem, grounding your views in the text.

16. Comment on the effectiveness of the imagery used to convey the ideas.

17. How would you describe the tone of this poem: anguished, oppressed, lonely, helpless, coldly factual, or what? What words, phrases or images do you think best indicate the poet's tone of voice?

18. Explore the writing technique, in particular: the repetitions; the sound effect of words; the truncated phrases; the use of single, isolated words; the effect of capitalisation and the punctuation.

    • What is the effect of 'treading — treading',

    'beating — beating' and other repetitions?

    • What is the effect of the poet's continuous use of 'and'? Examine its use in the last stanza in particular.

    • What is the effect when the dash is used for punctuation? Examine 'Kept beating — beating — till I thought'. What is the effect of the dash at the end of stanzas 4 and 5 in particular? Look at the poet's use of conventional punctuation: what is the effect in line 16? Read it aloud.

    • List the capitalised words. Do they provide a guide through the poem? Trace it.

    • What is the effect of the repeated sounds of words ('drum', 'numb'; 'Soul', 'toll')? Explore the suggestions of the onomatopoeic 'creak'. What do these effects contribute to the creation of the atmosphere in the poem?

19. 'Dickinson treats the most tormented situations with great calm' (Helen McNeil). Would you agree with this statement on the evidence of this poem?

328

A Bird came down the Walk —
He did not know I saw —
He bit an Angleworm in halves
And ate the fellow, raw,

And then he drank a Dew   5
From a convenient Grass —
And then hopped sidewise to the Wall
To let a Beetle pass —

He glanced with rapid eyes
That hurried all around —   10
They looked like frightened Beads, I thought —
He stirred his Velvet Head

Like one in danger, Cautious,
I offered him a Crumb
And he unrolled his feathers   15
And rowed him softer home —

Than Oars divide the Ocean,
Too silver for a seam —
Or Butterflies, off Banks of Noon
Leap, plashless as they swim.   20

EXPLORATIONS

First reading

1. What do you notice about the nature drama unfolding on the walk?

2. Examine the bird's movements. What do they suggest about the creature?

3. Where is the speaker in this picture? When does she enter 'camera shot'? What does she do, and what is the bird's reaction?

Second reading

4. What does the speaker actually see, and what does she create?

5. Examine how Dickinson creates the sense of the bird's flight in the last five lines of the poem. There is no actual description of the flight: rather she proceeds by way of negative comparisons ('then', 'or'). What sense of the experience does she give us? What qualities of bird flight are evoked in this way? Refer to words or phrases in the text.

6. Step back or 'zoom out' from this picture and see the poet watching. What do you think is her attitude to this drama? What does she feel about the scene she is viewing? What words or phrases suggest this?

Third reading

7. What particular insights into the natural world does this poem offer you? Explain, with reference to the text.

8. Do you think Dickinson is being serious or humorous, or a combination of both here? Examine the tone of this poem.

9. 'Dickinson wickedly disturbs a clichéd vision of nature through her ornithological caricature' (Juhasz, Miller and Smith). Comment on this view in the light of your own reading of the poem.

341

After great pain, a formal feeling comes —
The Nerves sit ceremonious, like Tombs —
The stiff Heart questions was it He, that bore,
And Yesterday, or Centuries before?
The Feet, mechanical, go round —   5
Of Ground, or Air, or Ought —
A Wooden way
Regardless grown,
A Quartz contentment, like a stone —
This is the Hour of Lead —   10
Remembered, if outlived,
As Freezing persons, recollect the Snow —
First — Chill — then Stupor — then the letting go —

EXPLORATIONS

Before reading

1. Have you ever experienced severe pain, such as from a broken bone, or appendicitis, or a severe toothache or headache? Try to recollect how you felt as the pain ebbed away and you were free of it for the first moment in a long while. Were you elated or just exhausted, tired, numbed, or what? Recapture how you felt in short phrases or images.

First reading

2. Explore the images in the poem for some indication of the speaker's feeling 'after great pain'.

    - What are the connotations of 'The Nerves sit ceremonious, like Tombs'?
    - What might 'The stiff Heart' indicate?
    - What does the heart's disorientation, in lines 3 and 4, suggest about the strength of the pain?

EXPLORATIONS

- What do the images of the second stanza intimate about the speaker's present mood and condition?

- What does the image 'Hour of Lead' conjure up for you?

- Are the references to snow comforting or threatening? Explain.

Second reading

3. Is there a common thread running through any of these images that might give an overview of the speaker's condition? Consider, for instance, 'The Nerves sit ceremonious', 'The stiff Heart', 'The Feet, mechanical'. Taken together, what do these external physical manifestations reveal of the speaker's inner feelings? What do the natural references to wood, quartz and lead suggest about the speaker's condition?

4. Comment on the poet's own description of this condition as 'a formal feeling'. Is this unusual definition supported by any other evidence from the poem? Explain.

5. Can you express the central concern of this poem in one sentence?

6. Do you find the conclusion of this poem in any way hopeful, or just totally bleak? Explain your reading of it.

Third reading

7. Do you think this poem an effective evocation of the particular feeling? Comment.

8. What do you find most unusual or striking about it?

465

this poem is also prescribed for Ordinary Level exams in 2011 and 2014

I heard a Fly buzz — when I died —
The Stillness in the Room
Was like the Stillness in the Air —
Between the Heaves of Storm —

The Eyes around — had wrung them dry —   5
And Breaths were gathering firm
For that last Onset — when the King
Be witnessed — in the Room —

I willed my Keepsakes — Signed away
What portion of me be   10
Assignable — and then it was
There interposed a Fly —

With Blue — uncertain stumbling Buzz —
Between the light — and me —
And then the Windows failed — and then   15
I could not see to see —

EXPLORATIONS

Before reading

1. Have you ever been present at a death, or read about a deathbed scene, or visited someone who was seriously ill and not expected to live? What did you notice, and what were your thoughts?

First reading

2. What do you notice about the deathbed scene here? What elements do you think might be ordinary or common to any such scene? What would you consider unusual about the scene?

3. Who is the speaker in the poem?

Second reading

4. Comment on the atmosphere in the room. Would you consider it to be emotional or controlled, expectant, frightened, indifferent, or what? What words and phrases suggest this?

5. What is your impression of the onlookers?

6. How does the poet suggest that this is a dramatic moment?

Third reading

7. How is the prospect of death viewed (a) by the onlookers and (b) by the speaker?

8. 'There interposed a Fly'. What is your reaction to the fly, and what do you think might be its significance in the poem? Refer to words or phrases.

9. In general, what understanding of death is conveyed by this

poem? Explore the connotations of phrases such as 'Heaves of Storm', 'that last Onset', 'the King | Be witnessed', 'With Blue— uncertain stumbling Buzz', 'And then the Windows failed'.

10. Do you find the speaking voice effective? Comment on the tone and the style of speech. What part do the phrasing and punctuation play in this?

Fourth reading

11. 'Few poets have dealt with this all-engrossing subject with such intense feeling under such perfect control' (Richard Sewall). Do you find intense feeling and perfect control here?

512

The Soul has Bandaged moments —
When too appalled to stir —
She feels some ghastly Fright come up
And stop to look at her —

Salute her — with long fingers —   5
Caress her freezing hair —

Sip, Goblin, from the very lips
The Lover — hovered — o'er —
Unworthy, that a thought so mean
Accost a Theme — so — fair —   10

The soul has moments of Escape —
When bursting all the doors —
She dances like a Bomb, abroad,
And swings upon the Hours,

As do the Bee — delirious borne —   15
Long Dungeoned from his Rose —
Touch Liberty — then know no more,
But Noon, and Paradise —

The Soul's retaken moments —
When, Felon led along,   20
With shackles on the plumed feet,
And staples, in the Song,

The Horror welcomes her, again,
These, are not brayed of Tongue —

Notes

[1]   **Soul:** psyche or spirit
[3]   **Fright:** a personification of fear or horror
[7]   **Goblin:** a small malevolent spirit
[10] **Accost:** speak to, question
[14] **swings upon the Hours:** an image of childlike play, lasting through all the hours of the day
[16] **his Rose:** the flower with its nectar, source of the bee's energy
[18] **Noon:** the term is used with different connotations in various Dickinson poems; here it probably symbolises the paradise of earthly love. The bee soul escapes from his dungeon, finds fulfilment in the rose, and is transported into an ecstasy of love ('Noon, and Paradise').
[20] **Felon:** a criminal

[21] **the plumed feet:** could suggest freedom of flight, which is in this case curtailed with shackles. In Greek mythology the messenger of the gods, Mercury, had plumed feet. Perhaps 'poetic inspiration' is the theme in question here.

[22] **staples:** metal fastenings, in this case restricting the song

[24] **These:** refers to the soul's 'retaken moments', the capturing horror

EXPLORATIONS

First reading

1. What images, phrases or sounds made most impression on you on a first reading?

2. What is your first impression of the mood or moods of the speaker? What leads you to say this?

3. Is there a narrative line in this poem? Can you trace the sequence of events?

Second reading

4. Explore the following 'thinking points'. Make notes to yourself, to clarify your thinking on them.

   • 'The Soul has Bandaged moments.' How do you visualise this? What does it suggest about the condition of the soul?

   • What does the second line add to our picture of the soul?

   • The soul is named as feminine. How do you perceive

Second reading continued

the scene in lines 3 and 4?

• The situation becomes more threatening in lines 5 and 6. Explain the nature of that threat. What is the impact of the adjective 'freezing'?

• Do you think there is a change of attitude by the speaker in line 7 ('Sip, Goblin')? Explain.

• 'lips | The Lover — hovered — o'er —'. What does 'hovered' mean? What does it suggest about the lover, and the nature of the relationship? Is the use of the past tense significant?

• Do you think lines 9 and 10 refer to the thoughts of the lover or the speaker's present feelings? Could they refer to both? What implications has each interpretation?

• What is suggested about the speaker's state of mind by the first and second stanzas?

- How would you describe the different mood of the third stanza? Do the verbs help create it?

- Is there any suggestion that this mood too is perilous? Explain.

- In the fourth stanza, this new mood is compared to the activities of a bee escaped from captivity. What does this simile convey about the nature of the mood? (Refer to the notes for the significance of 'Noon'.) Explore the effect of the many long vowel sounds in this stanza.

- In the fifth stanza, how does the poet visualise the soul? Do you think this image effective? Explain the mood in this stanza.

- In the fifth stanza, do you think the true horror of captivity is hidden somewhat by the simple repetitive hymn metre and the musical rhyme of lines 2 and 4?

- Is there any community support for the speaker's predicament? What is suggested in the last line about how this mental suffering must be borne? (Note: 'These' refers back to the retaken moments.)

Third reading

5. What are your impressions of the mental state of the speaker? Refer to the text.

6. Explore the appropriateness of the different images and similes Dickinson uses to symbolise the soul.

7. What do you consider to be the main issues and themes explored in this poem? Refer to the text.

8. After some critical thinking, outline a reading you yourself find satisfactory and can substantiate with references to the poem.

Fourth reading

9. What insights into the human condition does this poem offer?

10. 'This poem deals with the intimate aspects of pain and loss.' Comment on the poem in the light of this statement.

11. What part does the music of words — sound effects, metre, rhyme, etc. — play in creating the atmosphere of this poem?

697

I could bring You Jewels — had I a mind to —
But You have enough — of those —
I could bring you Odors from St. Domingo—
Colors — from Vera Cruz —
Berries of the Bahamas — have I —   5
But this little Blaze
Flickering to itself — in the Meadow —
Suits Me — more than those —
Never a Fellow matched this Topaz —
And his Emerald Swing —   10
Dower itself — for Bobadilo —
Better — Could I bring?

Despite her withdrawal from society, Dickinson kept up an active correspondence. Sometimes she sent flowers or gifts with her notes; at other times she sent poems as gifts. She also sent poems as love tokens.

She often used West Indian images as metaphors — for the glories of summer, blooming flowers, poetic success, etc. Rebecca Patterson feels that these images were 'consistently playful rather than intense'.

EXPLORATIONS

First reading

1. In this poem the speaker is presenting a gift. What do you understand about the gift she is describing? Examine lines 6–8 in particular.

2. What do we learn about her attitude to it?

3. Could it be considered a love token? Explain how the poem might be read as a love poem. Do you think this is a credible reading? Explain your own opinion.

Second reading

4. It has been said that Dickinson delighted in making her poems mysterious. For example, she sometimes structured them as riddles. Is there a sense of the mysterious about this poem?

5. What do you think this poem reveals about the writer?

6. Would you consider the tone playful or serious here? Explain your view, with reference to the poem.

986

A narrow Fellow in the Grass
Occasionally rides —
You may have met Him — did you not
His notice sudden is —

The Grass divides as with a Comb —   5
A spotted shaft is seen —
And then it closes at your feet
And opens further on —

He likes a Boggy Acre
A Floor too cool for Corn —   10
Yet when a Boy, and Barefoot —
I more than once at Noon
Have passed, I thought, a Whip lash
Unbraiding in the Sun
When stooping to secure it   15
It wrinkled, and was gone —

Several of Nature's People
I know, and they know me —
I feel for them a transport
Of cordiality —   20

But never met this Fellow
Attended, or alone
Without a tighter breathing
And Zero at the Bone —

Background note

On the other side of the street where
Emily lived was the 'Dickinson Meadow', where she might have encountered the
'narrow Fellow' in a 'Boggy Acre'.

EXPLORATIONS

First reading

You might approach this poem as a sort of literary riddle and explore the clues carried by the connotations and sounds of words and images.

1. Consider the 'narrow Fellow'. What is actually seen of him? Is this enough to identify the creature with any certainty? What does the title lead you to expect?

2. There are incidental indications of his presence. Where are they, and what do they add to our understanding of the 'narrow Fellow'?

3. How do you imagine the speaker? What persona or character does the speaker adopt for this narrative? (See the third stanza.) Do you think this is in any way significant?

Second reading

4. Consider the metaphorical descriptions of the creature. Perhaps the most exciting is 'Whip lash'. What are the connotations of the words? What does the term suggest about the creature? Do these connotations clash with the image of it 'Unbraiding in the Sun'?

5. How did it move when the speaker bent to pick it up?

6. In general, what is your impression of the qualities and nature of this creature?

7. Are there any attempts to make the creature seem less threatening? Refer to the text.

8. What does 'Barefoot' add to the atmosphere of the scene? Who is barefoot? When did this happen?

9. Was the speaker less troubled by this when in her youth? What is the speaker's present or adult reaction to an encounter with the 'narrow Fellow'? Refer to the text. What does 'Zero at the Bone' suggest about her feelings?

Third reading

10. What does the poem convey to us about the writer's attitude or attitudes to nature? Support your ideas with references to the text.

11. Do you think this an effective evocation of a snake? Support your answer with references to the text.

12. Would you agree that there is real fear beneath the apparent casualness of this poem?

Fourth reading

13. 'When she opened her eyes to the real hidden beneath the daily, it was to the peculiarity, awesomeness, and mystery of it' (John Robinson). Would you agree with this interpretation of the poem?

4

Gerard Manley Hopkins
1844–1889

prescribed for Higher Level exams in 2011 and 2013

On Saturday 8 June 1889, at 85 St Stephen's Green, Dublin, a Jesuit priest died of typhoid. None of the other priests who shared the rat-infested building with the odd little man from England could have guessed that he would be commemorated a hundred years later as one of the most important poets in the English language.

Gerard Manley Hopkins was born into a prosperous Anglican family on 28 July 1844 at Stratford in Essex. He was the oldest of nine children. The Hopkins household had a great interest in poetry, drawing, music and architecture. In 1854, Gerard was sent to Highgate School as a boarder. One of his teachers described him as 'a pale young boy, very light and active, with a very meditative and intellectual face'. He was fiercely independent and an outstanding student, winning prizes for poetry and a scholarship to study Classics at Balliol College, Oxford. At Oxford, Hopkins converted to Catholicism and in 1868 he joined the Jesuit Order. He decided to destroy the poems that he had written because he wished to devote his life totally to the service of God, (an act which he described as 'the slaughter of the innocents').

'In my salad days, in my Welsh days'

St Beuno's College, North Wales 1874–1877
Hopkins was sent to St Beuno's College in North Wales to study theology. In 1875, he was encouraged by one of his superiors to write a poem to commemorate the death of five German nuns in a shipwreck. The result was 'The Wreck of the Deutschland', a poem of extraordinary brilliance and originality; in fact, it was so innovative in its use of language and rhythm that no editor would publish it. Undeterred

by the unfavourable reaction, Hopkins continued to write poetry. He corresponded regularly with a friend from his days at Oxford, Robert Bridges. Despite Bridges's dislike for his technical experimentation, Hopkins sensed the importance of his own work. It was Bridges who first published Hopkins's work in 1918, almost thirty years after the poet's death.

The first five poems by Hopkins in this anthology were written in St Beuno's in 1877, between the months of March and August. This was one of the happiest times in the poet's adult life — he called them 'my salad days'. These poems are often referred to as the 'bright sonnets' because of the poet's optimistic mood and obvious delight in the beautiful Clwyd Valley and distant Snowdonia. They contrast starkly with the 'terrible sonnets' which he wrote later.

'The encircling gloom'

Liverpool and Glasgow 1878–1881
After his ordination, Hopkins spent time teaching classics and doing some parish work. Toward the end of 1879, he was sent to work in a parish in Bedford Leigh, near Manchester, and then to St Francis Xavier's in the heart of industrial Liverpool. The poet who had such a love of nature was shocked to see the full impact of England's Industrial Revolution. The population of the city had increased dramatically as a result of immigration from

St Beuno's College in Wales, where Hopkins wrote the first five poems in this chapter

famine-stricken Ireland, and pollution from the factories was unregulated. He found some comfort in the warmth of the local people who made him feel welcome.

One of these local people, a thirty-one-year-old farrier, died from consumption on 21 April 1880. His name was Felix Spencer. A week later, Hopkins wrote the poem 'Felix Randal', which is included in this anthology.

In 1881, Hopkins spent a few months working in St Joseph's Parish in Glasgow. Before he left Scotland, on 28 September he paid a visit to Inversnaid, on the eastern shore of Loch Lomond. William Wordsworth's poem 'To a Highland Girl, | (At Inversnayde, upon Loch Lomond)' may well have prompted this visit. He wasn't very happy with the poem that he composed, 'Inversnaid'. It remained unseen until after his death.

'To seem the stranger lies my lot, my life'

Dublin 1884–89

Hopkins's appointment as Fellow of the Royal University of Ireland and Professor of Greek and Latin Literature at the Catholic University of Ireland was not the accolade one might think. The English Provincial of the Jesuits did not know where to employ the eccentric priest and the President of the University wanted a fellow Jesuit so that he could spend the annual salary of £400 on the upkeep of the college. Thus began the most miserable period in the poet's short life.

> Gerald Hopkins was at an opposite pole to everything around him: literary, political, social etc. (a thorough John Bull incapable of understanding Rebel Ireland). No one took him seriously.
> [Fr Joe Darlington, a colleague of Hopkins in the university.]

To make matters worse, the poet's primary responsibility for the five years he lived in Dublin was correcting examination papers. Alienation and physical exhaustion took its toll on his spiritual wellbeing. He began to suffer from deep depression. The so-called 'terrible sonnets', 'No Worst, there is none' and 'I Wake and Feel the Fell of Dark', were written in 1885 and mark the nadir of his life.

Even though there is evidence of a spiritual recovery, his physical deterioration was hastened by the unsanitary conditions in which he lived. One of his last poems, 'Thou art Indeed Just, Lord' was written on St Patrick's Day 1889, a few months before he died at the relatively young age of forty-four. His final words were, 'I am so happy, I am so happy.' He is buried in Glasnevin Cemetery in Dublin.

God's Grandeur

The World is charged with the grandeur of God.
It will flame out, like shining from shook foil;
It gathers to a greatness, like the ooze of oil
Crushed. Why do men then now not reck his rod?
Generations have trod, have trod, have trod;   5
And all is seared with trade; bleared, smeared with toil;
And wears man's smudge and shares man's smell: the soil
Is bare now, nor can foot feel, being shod.

And, for all this, nature is never spent;
There lives the dearest freshness deep down things;   10
And though the last lights off the black West went
Oh, morning, at the brown brink eastward, springs —
Because the Holy Ghost over the bent
World broods with warm breast and with ah! bright wings.

'The World is charged with the grandeur of God.
It will flame out, like shining from shook foil'

This poem was written while Hopkins was studying in St Beuno's (pronounced 'Bíno') College in North Wales. The poet sent it as a birthday present to his mother on 3 March 1877.

[1]   **charged:** as in electrically charged, suggesting a force rather than a substance

> All things therefore are charged with love, are charged with God, and if we know how to touch them, give off sparks and take fire, yield drops and flow, ring and tell of him.
>
> [Hopkins]

[2]   **foil:** as in tin foil, a leaf of metal often used to set something off by contrast

> Shaken gold foil gives off broad glares like sheet lightning and also, and this is true of nothing else, owing to its zigzag dents and creasings and network of small many-cornered facets, a sort of fork lightning too.
>
> [Hopkins]

[3]   **ooze of oil:** a reference to the harvesting of fruit, compared with:

> Or by a cider-press, with patient look,
> Thou watchest the last oozings hours by hours.
>
> [Keats, 'Ode to Autumn']

[4]   **reck:** heed

[4]   **rod:** authority

[6]   **seared:** withered, scorched

[9]   **spent:** used up, exhausted

[12]   **brink:** brink of daylight

EXPLORATIONS

Before reading

1. Have you ever been startled by the beauty of a natural scene? Do you ever feel that development, 'progress', the work of mankind, is destroying the beauty of the natural world? Discuss these ideas before reading the poem.

First reading

2. All poetry should be experienced 'through the ears' at first. This is especially true of Hopkins's poetry. Read the poem aloud several times. Experiment with the placing of stresses until you find a version that is satisfactory.

3. Pick out a phrase, image or even a word that appeals to you and say why you chose it. (Imagine that you are thinking up a name for a band, e.g. Crushed!)

4. This is the first of Hopkins's so-called 'bright sonnets'. Can you suggest a reason why the poem is considered 'bright'?

Second reading

5. What qualities of the natural world does the poet admire?

6. How does the poet contrast the different manifestations of God's grandeur?

7. At what point does the poet move from admiration to reflection?

8. What, according to the poet, has been the impact of mankind on the natural world?

9. Identify the ways in which mankind is perceived to have affected the physical world.

10. What is the effect of the last word of the image in line 8, 'nor can foot feel, being shod'? What does it suggest about the poet's attitude to human development?

11. How does the mood of the poem change in the sestet?

12. Consider the possible meanings of the line, 'There lives the dearest freshness deep down things'. What word is missing from this statement? The omission of a word from a line is a stylistic device called 'ellipsis'. Hopkins used it frequently. When you have encountered more examples of it, consider its effect.

13. Lines 11 and 12 state in an unusual way that the sun sets and rises again. How does the poet's manner of expressing this idea add greater significance to this mundane event? Does this image have any religious resonance?

14. What is the effect of the 'ah!' in the final line?

Third reading

15. Identify the changes of tone in the poem. Which one is predominant?

16. There is a great sense of energy in the first quatrain. How does the poet generate this energy? Pay close attention to rhythm and sound.

17. How does the second quatrain differ from the first in terms of sound and rhythm?

18. Consider carefully the implications of the final image of the poem. How is the Holy Ghost represented?

Fourth reading

19. How does the poet perceive the relationship between man, God and the natural world?

20. What words or phrases appeal to your senses?

21. How does this poem vary from the standard Petrarchan sonnet?

22. Consider carefully the meaning, the sound and the position of the word 'Crushed'. Would you agree that the poet draws attention to the word? Watch out for other words in later poems that are highlighted by their position in a similar way.

23. What peculiarities of style can you identify in this poem? Pay particular attention to the sound effects.

24. Is there a tension in the poem between the poet who loves beauty and the priest who feels a duty to moralise? Consider the manner in which the poet moves from joy in the contemplation of the natural world to dismay at the way mankind has abused the world, and finally to the assertion that the Holy Ghost will continue to nurture the world. Do you find this movement satisfying?

25. In what way are the poet's concerns relevant to today's world?

26. If you had to recommend this poem to a friend, what aspect or aspects of the poem would you choose to highlight?

As Kingfishers Catch Fire, Dragonflies Draw Flame

As kingfishers catch fire, dragonflies draw flame;
As tumbled over rim in roundy wells
Stones ring; like each tucked string tells, each hung bell's
Bow swung finds tongue to fling out broad its name;
Each mortal thing does one thing and the same: 5
Deals out that being indoors each one dwells;
Selves — goes itself; myself it speaks and spells,
Crying What I do is me: for that I came.

Í say more: the just man justices;
Keeps gráce: that keeps all his goings graces;   10
Acts in God's eye what in God's eye he is —
Christ. For Christ plays in ten thousand places,
Lovely in limbs, and lovely in eyes not his
To the Father through the features of men's faces.

Notes

'All things therefore are charged with love, are charged with God,
and if we know how to touch them give off sparks and take fire,
yield drops and flow, ring and tell of him'.
(Notebooks and Papers of G.M.H.)

[1]   **kingfisher:** a bird with brilliant plumage
[1]   **dragonfly:** an insect
[3]   **tucked:** plucked
[6]   **indoors:** within
[7]   **Selves:** (verb) asserts its own nature, individuality
[9]   **justices:** (verb) acts in a way that promotes justice: 'acts
       in a godly manner, lives fully energised by grace, justness,
       sanctity' (R. V. Schoder SJ).

EXPLORATIONS

Before reading

1. 'I am what I am', a politician once said in self-defence. What do you think he meant? Was it a declaration of apology or defiance? How many of us have the courage to be what we are? Do we express our individuality or hide it behind a veneer of conformity? Is there any other creature or object in existence that possesses such individuality as we do?

First reading

2. Read the poem aloud several times. What sounds dominate?

3. Pick out a phrase or image that you find appealing, intriguing or strange. Explain your choice.

Second reading

4. This poem can be quite difficult to grasp on a first reading. The language itself is not difficult; however, the poet has concentrated his meaning through the use of ellipsis and unusual syntax. It becomes easier to understand when one realises that the same idea is expressed in different ways throughout the octet. Consider

the statement, 'What I do is me: for that I came.' It asserts not only the individuality of all things, but also the notion that everything and everyone has its role in God's creation. With this in mind, attempt an explanation of the first line.

5. Identify the images in the next three lines. What do they have in common?

6. What are all these creatures and things doing?

7. The poet seems to give a sense of destiny or purpose to animate and inanimate objects alike. Identify examples of each. Consider the significance of this idea.

8. Do you agree that there is an extraordinary intensity and sense of conviction to the octet? How is this intensity conveyed?

9. How does the sestet develop the thought in the octet? Would you agree that there is a change of emphasis from the philosophical to the religious?

10. What is your reaction to a statement such as 'the just man justices'? Does it read well? Is it poetic? Can you think of a reason why the poet

should express himself in such a way? Are there any other expressions in the poem which strike you as odd or unusual?

11. In the last three lines, the poet suggests that the 'imprint' of Christ's love is evident in all aspects of God's creation. Everything in existence is unique and has its own essence; but each individual person and thing shares in God's design. The poet sees Christ in 'ten thousand places' and in 'men's faces'. This is the unifying and moral principle that governs the universe. This is how Hopkins sees the Incarnation of Christ. Find out what you can about the word 'incarnation'. It is a very important word if you want to understand the way Hopkins relates to the world.

Third reading

12. How does this poem differ from the previous poem? Would you agree that the nature imagery is employed in a different way in this poem?

13. This poem is believed to have been written as a defence of Scotism against Thomism. The teachings of Duns Scotus advocated the uniqueness of all things and the ability of the senses to perceive what is good and beautiful. In this philosophy there is a moral value to what is beautiful. This point of view has great significance for a priest who was made to doubt the value of poetry by his superiors. Thomas Aquinas, on the other hand, was suspicious of the senses and stressed the importance of reason.

Try to relate these ideas to the poem. What is your own view on this debate, which is sometimes characterised as a debate between the emotions and reason, romance and pragmatism, the heart and the head?

Spring

this poem is also prescribed for Ordinary Level exams in 2011 und 2013

Nothing is so beautiful as Spring —
When weeds, in wheels, shoot long and lovely and lush;
Thrush's eggs look little low heavens, and thrush
Through the echoing timber does so rinse and wring
The ear, it strikes like lightnings to hear him sing;   5
The glassy peartree leaves and blooms, they brush
The descending blue; that blue is all in a rush
With richness; the racing lambs too have fair their fling.

What is all this juice and all this joy?
A strain of the earth's sweet being in the beginning   10
In Eden garden. — Have, get, before it cloy,

Before it cloud, Christ, lord, and sour with sinning,
Innocent mind and Mayday in girl and boy,
Most, O maid's child, thy choice and worthy the winning.

Notes	[2]	**wheels:** an architectural term that describes a design similar to the wheel of a bicycle with spokes radiating from the centre
	[3]	**low heavens:** the eggs mirror the pattern of the clouds against the sky (a dappled effect)
	[4]	**timber:** tree or wood
	[4]	**rinse and wring:** the effect of the bird's song on the ear
	[6]	**leaves and blooms:** these nouns are used as verbs here
	[8]	**fair:** abundant
	[9]	**juice:** possibly meaning the essence or spirit of a thing
	[10]	**strain:** a musical term meaning a remembered melody and/or an inherited quality
	[11]	**cloy:** satiate, fill to the limit, lose its appeal (verb having 'innocent mind' and 'Mayday' as object)
	[12]	**cloud:** verb having 'innocent mind' and 'Mayday' as object

[12] **sour:** verb having 'innocent mind' and 'Mayday' as object

[13] **Mayday:** Hopkins associates May with the purity of Mary, the Blessed Virgin and Mother

[14] **maid's child:** Jesus

EXPLORATIONS

First reading

1. Read the poem aloud several times. Listen carefully to the rhythm or movement of the lines in order to pick up the mood of the poem. Is this a happy or sad poem? Pick out phrases or images that capture the mood of the first verse.

2. Does this poem remind you of 'God's Grandeur' in any way? Discuss the similarities briefly.

Second reading

3. The opening line of the poem is very simple. What is the effect of such a simple beginning? Does it draw you into the poem?

4. Does it surprise you that the poet enthuses about weeds in the second line? What qualities do weeds have that might appeal to the poet? Does his admiration for weeds tell us anything about his personality? How has your attitude to weeds been developed?

Second reading continued

5. What does the poet mean by the phrase 'rinse and wring the ear'? Consider carefully the meanings and associations attached to these two words. Do you think they are unusual words to describe the effect of the bird's song? Suggest a reason for the poet's choice of image.

6. In the previous poem, the poet described how God's grandeur 'will flame out'. Here, he describes the song of the bird striking him 'like lightning'. What effect is the poet creating with these images?

7. Would you agree that there is a great sense of startled delight in the octet? How does the poet achieve this?

8. In the octet, the poet provides us with a rich array of movement, sounds, shapes, textures and colours. Identify each one of them. How does the poet move from weeds to thrush's eggs, to the glassy

pear tree and finally to the descending blue? Would you agree that the movement follows the eye naturally? How does the poet return from the sky to the lambs?

9. What is the tone of the sestet? How does it differ from the octet? Consider the effect of the question in line 9.

10. The poet seems to associate springtime with paradise. But it is only a strain that will soon disappear. Does the poet suggest any reason for this?

11. Do you find the reflection in the sestet satisfying or an intrusion on the wonderful description of spring? Does the complicated syntax (sentence structure) jar the ear after the vibrant octet?

Fourth reading

13. Do you consider this an optimistic or pessimistic poem? Give reasons for your answer.

14. What is the theme of this poem?

15. Do you note any variations in the use of the Petrarchan sonnet?

16. What similarities have you discovered between this poem and 'God's Grandeur' in terms of theme and poetic technique?

17. Which poem do you prefer and why? Do you prefer the poet's descriptions of nature or his meditations on its significance? Or do you find the combination of description and reflection most satisfying?

Third reading

12. Look for examples of the following features: alliteration, assonance, rhyme, ellipsis. Explain how they contribute to the poem.

The Windhover

To Christ our Lord

I caught this morning morning's minion, king-
    dom of daylight's dauphin, dapple-dawn-drawn Falcon, in his riding
    Of the rolling level underneath him steady air, and striding
High there, how he rung upon the rein of a wimpling wing
In his ecstasy! then off, off forth on swing,   5
    As a skate's heel sweeps smooth on a bow-bend: the hurl and gliding
    Rebuffed the big wind. My heart in hiding
Stirred for a bird, — the achieve of, the mastery of the thing!
Brute beauty and valour and act, oh, air, pride, plume, here
    Buckle! And the fire that breaks from thee then, a billion   10
Times told lovelier, more dangerous, O my chevalier!
    No wonder of it: shéer plód makes plough down sillion
Shine, and blue-bleak embers, ah my dear,
    Fall, gall themselves, and gash gold-vermilion.

Hopkins described this poem as 'the best thing I ever wrote'.
Windhover: A kestrel, common in the Clwyd area of Wales.
At St Beuno's College there was a glass case of stuffed birds on which the following inscription was written: 'The Kestrel or Windhover: The commonest and most conspicuous of British falcons remarkable for its habit of remaining suspended in the air without changing position while it scans the ground for its prey.'

[1]   **caught:** caught sight of (an example of ellipsis)

[1]   **minion:** favourite

[2]   **dauphin:** prince, heir apparent to the French throne (to the kingdom of daylight)

[2]   **dapple-dawn-drawn:** a coined adjective meaning 'dappled and drawn out in front of the dawn' or 'dappled and attracted by the dawn'

[4]   **rung upon the rein:** (a) a technical term of the riding school – 'to ring on the rein' is said of a horse that circles at the end of a long rein held by its trainer; (b) 'to ring' in falconry means to rise in spirals.

[4]   **wimpling:** pleated

[6]   **bow-bend:** as the skater forms the figure 8

[6]   **hurl:** normally a verb, here it is a noun meaning the vigorous forward motion

[8]   **achieve:** verb used as noun meaning 'achievement'

[10] **Buckle:** This complex word is crucial to the meaning of the poem. There are several possible interpretations: (a) prepare for action, come to grips, engage the enemy; (b) clasp, enclose, bring together as one; (c) give way, bend, collapse under stress or pressure. Interpretations (a) and (b) can be combined in the image of the chivalric knight putting on his armour in order to do battle. Perhaps the poet is pleading for the qualities mentioned to be united 'here' in his heart.

[10] **fire:** characteristic energy

[11] **chevalier:** a knight (French), a reference to the Christ

[12] **shéer plód:** sheer hard work

[12] **sillion:** a strip of arable land

[14] **gall:** hurt

[14] **gold-vermilion:** a mixture of gold and red colour

EXPLORATIONS

Before reading

1. Some people erroneously regard poetry as a kind of cryptic puzzle to be solved, a sort of verbal Rubik's Cube. If the primary purpose in reading a poem is to 'find the meaning', then surely the poet would have been better employed writing his or her ideas in understandable prose. Clearly, there is more to a poem than 'meaning'. The way in which the 'meaning' is expressed provides the 'beauty' or aesthetic value of a poem. It is possible to enjoy the beauty of a poem without understanding the meaning. Discuss your attitude to poetry in general and how your view of it has been formed.

First reading

2. In a letter to Robert Bridges about this poem, Hopkins invited him to 'Take breath and read it with the ears, as I always wish to be read, and my verse becomes all right.' Read the first eight lines several times and try to get a sense of the rhythm. Pay particular attention to the changes of pace. Do you agree that the

First reading continued

rhythm seems to capture the flight of the bird and that there is a sense of awe and breathlessness as one reaches the end of the octet? How is this achieved?

3. The poet gives a procession of titles to the kestrel 'as in some royal proclamation of medieval pageantry' (Peter Milward SJ). What is the effect of this? How does it lead into the imagery of horse-riding?

4. How does the poet convey the sense that the bird is in complete control of its environment?

5. The poet uses imagery from the world of horse-riding and skating to describe the movement of the bird. Look closely at these images and describe the movements of the bird in your own words. Do you think that the poet's use of imagery is effective in communicating the grace, elegance and energy of the bird?

6. Is there a paradox in the combination of 'hurl' and 'gliding'? Explain.

7. Why is the poet's heart 'in hiding'? Is he afraid, ashamed, humbled, envious? Why might

a student priest feel envious of this magnificent bird in flight? Why does he write 'for a bird' rather than 'for the bird'?

8. The first tercet begins with a list of qualities which the bird embodies. Describe these qualities in your own words.

9. Look at the possible meanings of 'Buckle' and arrive at your own conclusions on its meaning. Does the capitalisation of the word 'and' imply a consequence of 'Buckle'? To what does 'thee' refer? His heart? The bird? Christ? Consider the possibilities.

10. The second part of the tercet is addressed to 'my chevalier'. What connection does the poet see between the windhover and Christ our Lord? Is there a physical similarity between the bird with its outstretched wings and Christ on the Cross? Does the poet see the bird battling against the wind as a symbol of Christ battling against evil? Consider these possibilities.

Second reading

11. The poet uses quite a varied diction in this poem. At the start, the language is regal — 'minion', 'kingdom', 'dauphin'. What other categories of words are used in the poem? Note the contrast between words like 'Buckle', 'plód' and 'minion', 'sillion', 'billion', 'vermilion'. Describe the texture of these words.

12. The second tercet presents the reader with two images of beauty evolving out of what appears to be unpleasant. The drudgery of ploughing the land brings forth a radiant surface. The embers of a dying fire fall from the grate, break open to reveal the glowing interior. What resonances do these images create in the context of the whole poem? Do they connect with the image of Christ on the Cross in any way?

13. Would you agree that there is a passionate intensity to this poem? How is this effect created? Is there a mystical quality to this poem? Discuss your understanding of mysticism.

14. Compare this poem with the previous three poems under the following headings: theme; mood; development of thought; style; and use of the sonnet form. Would you agree that it is quite different in terms of development of thought and use of the sonnet form?

15. Find out what you can about the Spiritual Exercises of St Ignatius Loyola, in particular his 'Meditation on the Kingdom'.

16. Find out what you can about sprung rhythm, inscape and instress.

17. This poem is written in a remarkably original style.

Consider the elements of that style, such as the use of alliteration, assonance, exclamation, ellipsis, inversion, compound adjectives, use of verbs as nouns, sprung rhythm, and rhyme. What is the primary purpose of all these poetic devices? It might be useful to consider their effect.

18. Do the difficulties of interpretation make 'The Windhover' a richer or more frustrating poem? Is it possible to enjoy the parts of the poem without a clear understanding of the whole? Consider this question in relation to poetry in general.

Pied Beauty

Glory be to God for dappled things —
For skies of couple-colour as a brinded cow;
For rose-moles all in stipple upon trout that swim;
Fresh-firecoal chestnut-falls; finches' wings;
Landscape plotted and pieced—fold, fallow, and plough   5
And álltrádes, their gear and tackle and trim.

All things counter, original, spare, strange;
Whatever is fickle, freckled (who knows how?)
With swift, slow; sweet, sour; adazzle, dim;
He fathers-forth whose beauty is past change: 10
Praise him.

Pied: of different colours

[1] **dappled:** irregular patches of different colours. Hopkins was particularly fond of 'dappled' things. It is a word that he used frequently in his writings.

[2] **brinded:** brindled, brownish with streaks of another colour

[3] **rose-mole:** rose-like spots

[3] **stipple:** dotted

[4] **Fresh-firecoal:** In his Journal (17 September 1868), Hopkins refers to 'Chestnuts as bright as coals or spots of vermilion.' (Vermilion is a brilliant red pigment.)

[4] **chestnut-falls:** see 'Fresh-firecoal' above

[5] **fold:** pasture for sheep to graze

[5] **fallow:** unused

[5] **and plough:** planted with crops

[6] **álltrádes . . . tackle:** the variety of trades with their different implements

[7] **counter:** all things that stand in contrast with other things

[7] **spare:** rare

EXPLORATIONS

Before reading

1. Make a class list of 'beautiful things' to see if there is any consensus on what constitutes beauty. Consider the view that 'beauty is in the eye of the beholder'. Is there a social pressure to conform to or agree on a single type of physical beauty? If so, from where does this pressure come? Have you ever considered as beautiful someone whom or something that no one else admires?

First reading

2. This poem seems to be very simple in its message. It is a celebration of 'pied beauty' or the beauty that comes from variety of colour and/or contrast. List all the examples of such beauty to be found in the poem.

3. Are all the poet's illustrations of beauty taken from the natural world? What does the poet mean in line 6 by 'álltrádes, their gear and tackle and trim'?

4. Does his appreciation of variety and contrast extend beyond the mere physical in the last four lines? Do you find it unusual that a priest in the nineteenth century should celebrate 'All things counter, original, spare, strange'? Have you noticed any other aspects of Hopkins's poetry that suggest his unconventionality? Take another look at the descriptive adjectives used in lines 7 and 8.

Second reading

5. How would you describe the tone of this poem?

6. Do you notice a difference between this poem and 'As Kingfishers' on the one hand, and 'God's Grandeur' and 'Spring' on the other?

7. Consider the significance of line 10. Who is 'He'? How is his beauty 'past change'?

8. What is the effect of the brief last line?

Third reading

9. The poem supports the views of the painter John Ruskin, for whom Hopkins had great admiration. Find out what you can about Ruskin's aesthetic theory.

10. The simple opening and conclusion echo the Ignatian mottoes Ad Maiorem Dei Gloriam (AMDG) and Laus Deo Semper (LDS). The poem thus becomes a kind of prayer of praise and a meditation on the glory of God. Consider the efficacy of the poem as a prayer.

11. This is a curtal sonnet, i.e. a sonnet that has been cut short. How has the sonnet been shortened? Why, do you think, did the poet choose to write such a sonnet?

12. This is the last of the five poems on your course that were written during a seven-month period in North Wales. Write a summary of the poet's central concerns in these poems. Make a list of stylistic features that are characteristic of Hopkins's poetry.

Felix Randal

Felix Randal the farrier, O he is dead then? My duty allended,
Who have watched his mould of man, big-boned and hardy-handsome
Pining, pining, till time when reason rambled in it and some
Fatal four disorders, fleshed there, all contended?

Sickness broke him. Impatient, he cursed at first, but mended   5
Being anointed and all; though a heavenlier heart began some
Months earlier, since I had our sweet reprieve and ransom
Tendered to him. Ah well, God rest him all road ever he offended!

This seeing the sick endears them to us, us too it endears.
My tongue had taught thee comfort, touch had quenched thy tears,   10
Thy tears that touched my heart, child, Felix, poor Felix Randal;

How far from then forethought of, all thy more boisterous years,
When thou at the random grim forge, powerful amidst peers,
Didst fettle for the great grey drayhorse his bright and battering sandal!

[1] **farrier:** a blacksmith or horse doctor

[4] **fleshed:** took hold of the flesh

[4] **contended:** competed

[6] **heavenlier:** more focused on the next world

[7] **sweet reprieve and ransom:** Holy Communion

[8] **all road:** in any way (colloquial Lancashire phrase)

[12] **How far from then forethought of:** how far away were the thoughts of death when you were in your prime

[13] **random:** an architectural term, meaning built with rough irregular stones; or it could refer to the untidiness of the forge

[14] **drayhorse:** a horse suitable for pulling heavy loads or dray carts

EXPLORATIONS

Before reading

1. One of the most challenging roles for a priest is to provide comfort to the sick and the dying. He must reconcile the existence of suffering with faith in a loving God. What must it be like to minister to the terminally ill? Does one become indifferent? Does it become a job? How important is faith in the afterlife? Imagine for a moment how you would cope in that role.

First reading

2. Read the poem through several times. Would you agree that the meaning of the poem is relatively easy to grasp?

First reading continued

Write a summary of the thoughts in the poem.

3. The poet provides the reader with a vivid picture of the farrier. What do we learn about his physical appearance and the changes that took place as a result of illness? What do we learn about his personality? Does it undergo any change?

4. How would you describe the relationship between the poet/priest and the farrier? Look at the opening statement and lines 9–11 in particular. Do you see any change or development in the poet's attitude to the farrier?

5. What is the effect of the questions in the first quatrain?

6. The first eight lines of the poem are primarily descriptive. How do the next six lines differ in mood?

7. In the first tercet (lines 9–11) how does the poet convey the idea that his relationship with the farrier was mutually rewarding?

8. In 'The Windhover', the student priest seemed to envy the bird's ability to 'achieve' something. Is there any hint in this poem to suggest that the poet finds satisfaction in his parish work?

9. The second tercet reflects another change of mood. The poet seems to be looking back to a time when the blacksmith was at his physical peak. What is the poet trying to achieve in these lines? How does the ending affect the overall mood of the poem?

10. Suggest reasons why the sandal is described as 'bright and battering'.

Second reading

11. The image of Holy Communion in line 7 ('our sweet reprieve and ransom') is a very rich one. Explore its connotations.

12. What is the effect created by the use of ellipsis (omission of

words in phrases such as 'my duty (is) all ended')?

13. Hopkins tended to use complex syntax in his poetry. The final sentence is a good example. What is the effect of such an unusual arrangement of words? Can you suggest a reason for this arrangement? Try arranging the sentence in a more normal manner and consider the merits of each arrangement.

14. Show how rhythm and imagery combine to create a powerful and triumphant conclusion to the poem.

15. Are there dramatic elements in this poem? Identify them.

Third reading

16. What elements of the sonnet form are recognisable in this poem? How does it differ from a conventional sonnet? How do the innovations contribute to the impact of the poem?

17. Is this a poem about death or a poem about religious faith? Explain your answer.

18. What significance is there in the phrase 'child, Felix, poor Felix Randal'? Does this phrase have a Biblical resonance?

19. Return to your original summary. Would you agree that there is much more to this poem than you thought at first? Elaborate.

20. There is no record of a man named Felix Randal dying in Liverpool around this time, but there is a record for a man called Felix Spencer, who was a farrier. Look up the words 'felix' and 'rand' in the dictionary. Can you suggest a reason why the poet would have changed the man's name in this way?

21. Hopkins writes poetry that appeals to the senses. Discuss.

Inversnaid

this poem is also prescribed for Ordinary Level exams in 2011 and 2013

This darksome burn, horseback brown,
His rollrock highroad roaring down,
In coop and in comb the fleece of his foam
Flutes and low to the lake falls home.

A windpuff-bonnet of fáwn-fróth   5
Turns and twindles over the broth
Of a pool so pitchblack, féll-frówning,
It rounds and rounds Despair to drowning.

Degged with dew, dappled with dew
Are the groins of the braes that the brook treads through,   10
Wiry heathpacks, flitches of fern,
And the beadbonny ash that sits over the burn.

What would the world be, once bereft
Of wet and wildness? Let them be left,
O let them be left, wildness and wet;   15
Long live the weeds and the wilderness yet.

[1] **burn:** A term frequently used by Scottish poets for a small stream. Arklet Water flows from Loch Arklet among the Trossachs and enters Loch Lomond near Inversnaid.

[3] **coop:** an enclosed space; suggests the idea of water trapped in pockets

[3] **comb:** the water combs over the rocks, in contrast to 'coop'

[4] **Flutes:** could describe the flute-like shape (an architectural term) of the water falling and/or the sound made by the waterfall

[5] **fáwn-fróth:** the froth is a fawn colour

[6] **twindles:** a verb coined from an obscure noun, 'twindle' meaning 'twin'. It is a combination of 'dwindle' and 'twitch' and describes the movement of the water.

[6] **broth:** one of the poet's favourite words to describe the seething water, suggestive of a witch's brew

[7] **féll-frówning:** 'Frowning' suggests the gloomy appearance of the scene. 'Fell' can mean a mountain, an animal's hide or 'ruthless'. It could also come from the verb 'to fall' (with theological implications).

[9] **Degged:** sprinkled (Lancashire dialect)

[9] **dappled:** one of the poet's favourite words to describe patches of different (contrasting) colours

[10] **groins:** folds, another architectural term to describe the joints of vaulting in an arched roof or possibly a bodily metaphor

[10] **braes:** steep banks (Scottish term)

[11] **heathpacks:** patches of densely-packed heather

[11] **flitches:** strips cut from a tree, i.e. ragged tufts

[12] **beadbonny ash:** refers to the beautiful (bonny) orange/red berries of the rowan tree or mountain ash

EXPLORATIONS

Before reading

1. Look carefully at the pictures of Inversnaid. Does the place appeal to you? Give reasons for your answer.

2. 'Long live the weeds and the wilderness yet.'

   Do you know any place that remains untouched by human development? Write a brief description of it.

First reading

3. Read the poem aloud several times in the classroom. What sounds are dominant?

4. Choose an image or phrase that appeals because of its sound or association. Explain your choice.

5. In general terms, what sort of scene is evoked by the words in the poem?

Second reading

6. With the aid of the glossary and in your own words, describe the actions and appearance of the water in the first two verses. Does the poet make it easy for you to visualise the scene? How does he do it? Comment on the effect of words such as 'horseback', 'rollrock', 'pitchblack' and 'féll-frówning'.

7. Would you agree that there is a great sense of energy in the first verse? How does the poet achieve this effect? Is the downward movement of the water echoed in the rhythm of the lines?

8. Is there a darkening of mood in the second verse? What words convey the change?

9. In the third verse, the poet describes the terrain through which the stream runs. Describe the scene in your own words. How do the poet's words ('degged', 'groins', 'braes', 'beadbonny') flavour the description?

10. How is the fourth verse different from the previous three? In your own words, explain what aspect of Inversnaid appeals most to Hopkins.

11. Now that your understanding of the poem has deepened, read it aloud again. Would you agree that this is a very simple poem once the difficulties of language are overcome?

12. Would it surprise you to learn that Hopkins once thought of being a landscape painter? Pick out examples of his attention to detail. Use the accompanying photographs to get a sense of the accuracy of his descriptions.

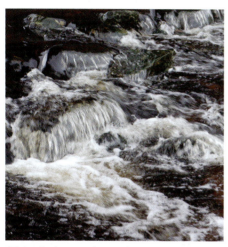

'This darksome burn, horseback brown'

'His rollrock highroad roaring down, In coop and in comb the fleece of his roam' The Falls at Inversnaid

'. . . the grains of the braes that the brook treads through'

'Wiry heathpacks, flitches of fern'

No Worst, there is None

No worst, there is none. Pitched past pitch of grief,
More pangs will, schooled at forepangs, wilder wring.
Comforter, where, where is your comforting?
Mary, mother of us, where is your relief?
My cries heave, herds-long; huddle in a main, a chief-   **5**
woe, world-sorrow; on an age-old anvil wince and sing—
Then lull, then leave off. Fury had shrieked 'No ling-
ering! Let me be fell: force I must be brief'.

O the mind, mind has mountains; cliffs of fall
Frightful, sheer, no-man-fathomed. Hold them cheap   **10**
May who ne'er hung there. Nor does long our small
Durance deal with that steep or deep. Here! creep,
Wretch, under a comfort serves in a whirlwind: all
Life death does end and each day dies with sleep.

Notes

[1] **Pitched past pitch:** to pitch (verb) could mean 'to throw', and 'pitch' (noun) could either mean pitch-black, as in tar, or it could be used in a musical sense. There are other possible combinations of meaning. The sense of the line seems to be that the poet has been cast beyond what are considered to be the normal limits of human suffering.

[2] **forepangs:** previously experienced agonies

[3] **Comforter:** the Holy Spirit

[5] **herds-long:** a long line of cries, like a herd of cattle, huddled together

[6] **wince and sing:** words chosen as much for their sound as their meaning; they suggest the beating of a hammer against an anvil

[7] **Fury:** an avenging spirit sent to punish crime, or possibly the personification of a guilty conscience

[8] **fell:** cruel

[8] **force:** perforce, of necessity

[10]   **no-man-fathomed:** (coinage) no man has fathomed, or explored the depths of this mental abyss

[10,11] **Hold them cheap . . . hung there:** those who . . . anguish it causes

[12]   **Durance:** endurance

EXPLORATIONS

Before reading

1. This is a poem about mental suffering and a struggle with despair. If you have ever experienced such feelings, try to describe them.

First reading

2. When you have read the poem several times, pick out the images or impressions that are most vivid. Discuss these with the rest of the class.

3. Does this poem come as something of a shock after the previous poems? Explain your answer.

Second reading

4. The opening sentence is short and dramatic. Note carefully that the poet uses the superlative 'worst', not the comparative 'worse'. How does this change the meaning?

Second reading continued

5. The second sentence seems to suggest that the agonies that are about to torment him have been 'schooled' by previous agonies and will, therefore, be even more skilled at inflicting pain. How does the poet's expression of this idea surpass this paraphrase? Would you agree that there is an extraordinary intensity in the line?

6. In his address to the Holy Ghost, Hopkins repeats the word 'where'. What is the effect of this repetition? Are there any other examples of this in the poem? What is the cumulative effect of this technique?

7. How does the second quatrain differ from the first? Is it easier or more difficult to comprehend? Give reasons for your answer. Despite the obscurity of the lines, certain impressions are communicated. What are they?

8. How does the poet engage our senses in the octet?

9. In the sestet, the poet suggests that mental torment can feel like hanging on to the edge of a cliff. Is it a good image? Give reasons for your answer.

10. At the end of the poem, Hopkins seems to find some scrap of comfort in the idea that sleep brings the day to a close just as death brings life to a close. What does this 'comfort' say about his state of mind?

Third reading

11. Are we told at any stage in the poem what it is that is causing such anguish? Is the poet concerned more with the experience of suffering than the cause?

12. Do you ever get the feeling that the poet is just feeling sorry for himself? Or is his documentation of suffering a testament to his courage?

13. What variations in the use of the sonnet form are evident in this poem?

14. Consider the overall impact of such poetic devices as alliteration, assonance, ellipsis, repetition, compound words and onomatopoeia.

I Wake and Feel the Fell of Dark

I wake and feel the fell of dark, not day.
What hours, O what black hoürs we have spent
This night! what sights you, heart, saw; ways you went!
And more must, in yet longer light's delay.

    With witness I speak this. But where I say   5
Hours I mean years, mean life. And my lament
Is cries countless, cries like dead letters sent
To dearest him that lives alas! away.

I am gall, I am heartburn. God's most deep decree

Bitter would have me taste: my taste was me; 10

Bones built in me, flesh filled, blood brimmed the curse.

Selfyeast of spirit a dull dough sours. I see

The lost are like this, and their scourge to be

As I am mine, their sweating selves; but worse.

EXPLORATIONS

Before reading

1. Darkness, nightmares and terror, a sense of abandonment, self-disgust — these are the powerful forces at work in this poem. Which of these images do you find most terrifying? Give reasons for your answer.

First reading

2. To what extent is this poem a sequel or continuation to 'No Worst, there is None'?

3. How is the sense of darkness emphasised in the first quatrain?

4. What effect is created by the poet's address to his 'heart'?

5. Does Hopkins use any of the poetic devices found in the previous sonnet?

6. How does the poet create a sense of spiritual desolation? Is it described in abstract terms, or does he create a sense in which it is physical as well as spiritual?

7. To whom are his 'dead letters' sent? Why does he describe them as 'dead'?

8. In the sestet, there is a powerful impression of self-disgust. Identify the images used by the poet to create this effect.

9. Hopkins changed the phrase 'God's most deep decree' to 'God's most just decree' and then changed it back to the original. How do the two phrases differ? What do we learn about the poet's state of mind from this information?

10. Lines 11 and 12 are a kind of definition of self. His physical body is described in gruesome terms; his spirit, instead of

lifting the dough, sours it and makes it worse. What is your reaction to this self-definition? Does it inspire shock or pity?

11. Does the poem end with despair or consolation? Who is 'worse'?

Second reading

12. Are we told why the poet feels such desolation? Does it matter?

13. Pick out examples of the poet's use of inversion (of normal word order). How does this device contribute to the sense of anguish in the poem?

14. Compare this poem with the previous one. (They are usually referred to as 'the terrible sonnets'.) Which of the two is more effective in communicating the poet's suffering? Give reasons for your answer.

Thou Art Indeed Just, Lord, if I Contend

Justus quidemtues, Domine, sidisputemtecum; verumtamen justaloquar ad te: Quare via impiorumprosperatur? etc.

Thou art indeed just, Lord, if I contend
With thee; but, sir, so what I plead is just.
Why do sinners' ways prosper? and why must
Disappointment all I endeavour end?

Wert thou my enemy, O thou my friend,   5
How wouldst thou worse, I wonder, than thou dost
Defeat, thwart me? Oh, the sots and thralls of lust
Do in spare hours more thrive than I that spend,

Sir, life upon thy cause. See, banks and brakes
Now, leavèd how thick! lacèd they are again   10
With fretty chervil, look, and fresh wind shakes

Them; birds build—but not I build; no, but strain,
Time's eunuch, and not breed one work that wakes.
Mine, O thou lord of life, send my roots rain.

Background note

The Latin quotation is taken from Jeremiah 12: 1. The full text is: 'Thou indeed, O Lord, art just, if I plead with thee, but yet I will speak what is just to thee: why doth the way of the wicked prosper: why is it well with all of them that transgress and do wickedly? Thou hast planted them, and they have taken root: they prosper and bring forth fruit. Thou art near in their mouth and far from their reins. And thou, O Lord, hast known me, thou hast seen me, and proved my heart with thee.'

It was customary for a Jesuit priest to repeat the phrase, 'Justus es, Domine, et rectum iudiciumtuum' (You are just, O Lord, and your judgement is right), like a mantra. It signifies an acceptance of God's will, however unpalatable it may seem.

Notes

[7]   **sots:** drunkards
[7]   **thralls:** slaves
[9]   **brakes:** thickets
[11]   **fretty:** fretted or interlaced
[11]   **chervil:** cow parsley
[13]   **eunuch:** castrated male employed in a harem
[13]   **wakes:** comes to life

EXPLORATIONS

Before reading

1. Have you ever felt that life is unfair and that there seems to be no connection between effort and reward? Describe the circumstances and the feeling.

Second reading continued

7. It is difficult to separate the third quatrain from the second. Is this deliberate? What does the poet intend to convey by this arrangement?

First reading

2. Read the poem aloud. Can you hear the sense of hurt, anger and frustration? Identify where you think the feelings are at their most intense.

Second reading

3. The first quatrain takes the words from Jeremiah and arranges them to suit the constraints of the sonnet form. Is there any tension in these lines or is the poet simply repeating the formula from the Bible?

4. Is there a tone of humility or anger in the first quatrain?

5. Is there any evidence in the second quatrain to suggest that the poet's feelings are becoming unmanageable? Look carefully at the metre and syntax.

6. What is the effect of the apostrophes, 'Lord', 'sir', 'O thou my friend', 'O thou lord of life'?

Third reading

8. What is the poet's complaint?

9. Is there a sense of growing anger as the poem progresses? Does it continue to build until the end of the poem?

10. To what extent does the syntax contribute to the expression of tortured innocence?

11. How does the imagery change in the sestet?

12. What sort of relationship exists between the poet and God?

13. What kind of 'work' does the poet want? Does he write as a poet or as a priest? Or both?

14. Hopkins included this poem in a letter to Robert Bridges. He suggested that it be read 'adagio molto' (a musical term meaning very slowly) 'and with great stress'. How would such a reading enhance the impact of the poem?

5 *William Butler Yeats*
1865–1939

prescribed for Higher Level exams in 2011 and 2014

In 1865 William Butler Yeats was born in Dublin to a County Sligo family. His grandfather had been rector of the Church of Ireland at Drumcliff. His father, the portrait painter John Butler Yeats, had married Susan Pollexfen, who belonged to a family of substantial traders and ship-owners from County Sligo. His brother, Jack B. Yeats, was to become one of Ireland's best-known painters. William Yeats was educated intermittently at the Godolphin School in London, the High School in Dublin and the Dublin Metropolitan School of Art.

He was interested in mysticism and the supernatural and developed a great curiosity about Irish mythology, history and folklore. It became one of his life's great passions to develop a distinctive, distinguished Irish literature in English. His first long poem, 'The Wanderings of Oisin' (1889), established the tone of what became known as the 'Celtic Twilight'. His early volumes of poetry reflect his interest in mysticism, theosophy and mythology but also deal with his hopeless love affairs, most notably that with Maude Gonne. In 1889 he had met and fallen in love with her; and though she would not marry him, he remained obsessed with her for most of his life. With Lady Gregory of Coole Park, Gort, County Galway and John Millington Synge he founded the Irish Literary Theatre Society in 1899 and later the Abbey Theatre in 1904.

By the end of the century Yeats had changed his decorative, symbolist style of poetry and began to write in a more direct style. From *The Green Helmet* (1910) onwards he shows a more realistic attitude to love and also begins to write about everyday cultural and political affairs. *Responsibilities* (1914) contains satires on the materialism of Dublin's middle class. Among the major themes of his mature years are the need for harmony in life, the search for perfection in life and art, and the mysteries of time and eternity. These are to be found particularly in the poems of the later volumes, *The Tower* (1928), *The Winding Stair* (1933) and *Last Poems* (1936–1939).

Yeats was made a senator in 1922 and was very active in public life; he supervised the design of the new coinage in 1926. He was awarded the Nobel Prize for Literature in 1923. He died in Rome in 1939, and his body was not brought back to Ireland until after the war, when it was buried in Drumcliff.

The Lake Isle of Innisfree

I will arise and go now, and go to Innisfree,
And a small cabin build there, of clay and wattles made:
Nine bean-rows will I have there, a hive for the honey-bee,
And live alone in the bee-loud glade.

And I shall have some peace there, for peace comes dropping slow,   5
Dropping from the veils of the morning to where the cricket sings;
There midnight's all a glimmer, and noon a purple glow,
And evening full of the linnet's wings.

I will arise and go now, for always night and day
I hear lake water lapping with low sounds by the shore;   10
While I stand on the roadway, or on the pavements grey,
I hear it in the deep heart's core.

Notes

[1] **I will arise . . .:** this has echoes of the return of the Prodigal Son in Luke 15:18 – 'I will arise and go to my father' – so they were the words of another returning emigrant.

[1] **Innisfree:** (in Irish 'Inisfraoich': Heather Island) – a rocky island on Lough Gill, Co. Sligo

[2] **wattles:** rods interlaced with twigs or branches to make a fence

EXPLORATIONS

Before reading

1. Read only the title. What comes into your mind when you read the title?

First reading

2. What do you notice about Yeats's island?

3. What sights and sounds will the poet see and hear? List them.

4. Contrast this island with his present surroundings.

Second reading

5. Do you think that the features of the island mentioned by the poet are the usual sights and sounds of everyday life in the country, or will this place be special? Explain your thinking on this.

6. What kind of space or place is the poet attempting to create? What does that indicate about his needs and philosophy of life or values? Refer to the poem to support your theories.

7. What is the poet's attitude to nature as suggested in the poem? Refer to specific lines and phrases.

Third reading

8. The poet seems almost impelled or driven to go and create this ideal place. Where is the sense of compulsion in the poem and how is it created? Explore the style of language he uses, the syntax, the rhythms of his language and the repeated phrases in order to help you with this.

9. What do you think is the meaning and significance of the last line?

Fourth reading

10. State succinctly what you think the poem is about.

11. What mood do you think the poet creates here and how do the images and the sounds of words contribute to this?

12. Does anything about the poet's vision here appeal to you? Discuss this.

September 1913

What need you, being come to sense,
But fumble in a greasy till
And add the halfpence to the pence
And prayer to shivering prayer, until
You have dried the marrow from the bone?   5
For men were born to pray and save:
Romantic Ireland's dead and gone,
It's with O'Leary in the grave.

Yet they were of a different kind,
The names that stilled your childish play,   10
They have gone about the world like wind,
But little time had they to pray
For whom the hangman's rope was spun,
And what, God help us, could they save?
Romantic Ireland's dead and gone,   15
It's with O'Leary in the grave.

Was it for this the wild geese spread
The grey wing upon every tide;
For this that all that blood was shed,
For this Edward Fitzgerald died,   20
And Robert Emmet and Wolfe Tone,
All that delirium of the brave?
Romantic Ireland's dead and gone,
It's with O'Leary in the grave.

Yet could we turn the years again,   25
And call those exiles as they were
In all their loneliness and pain,
You'd cry, 'Some woman's yellow hair
Has maddened every mother's son':
They weighed so lightly what they gave   30
But let them be, they're dead and gone,
They're with O'Leary in the grave.

Background note

During 1913 Yeats had spent a great deal of energy in support of Lady Gregory's nephew, Sir Hugh Lane, a wealthy art collector, who made a gift to the city of Dublin of an extraordinary collection of modern painting on condition that the city build a suitable gallery. There was a great deal of dispute about the structure, the location and the cost. Yeats was furious at what seemed a mean-spirited, penny-pinching, anti-cultural response to the project.

Notes

[8] **O'Leary:** John O'Leary (1830–1907), a Fenian who was arrested in 1865 and sentenced to twenty years' imprisonment. After a number of years he was released on condition that he went into exile. Returning to Dublin in 1885 he was greatly influential in Yeats's developing views on Irish nationalism.

[17] **the wild geese:** Irish soldiers who were forced into exile after the Williamite victory of the 1690s. They served in the armies of France, Spain and Austria.

[20] **Edward Fitzgerald:** Lord Edward Fitzgerald (1763–1798), one of the leaders of the United Irishmen, who died of wounds received while being arrested.

[21] **Robert Emmet:** leader of the rebellion of 1803

[21] **Wolfe Tone:** Theobald Wolfe Tone (1763–1798), leader of the United Irishmen. Captured and sentenced to death, he committed suicide in prison.

EXPLORATIONS

First reading

Stanza 1

1. 'What need you . . .' The 'you' here refers to the new Irish, relatively prosperous and Catholic middle classes, whom Yeats is addressing. What does he suggest are their main concerns or needs in life?

2. Explore the connotations of the images used in the first five lines, i.e. what is suggested by each of the pictures. List all the suggestions carried by each of the following and discuss them in groups: 'fumble'; 'greasy till'; 'add the halfpence to the pence'; 'add . . . prayer to shivering prayer'; 'dried the marrow from the bone'.

3. As a consequence of your explorations, what do you think is Yeats's attitude to these people? What words do you think best convey the tone?

4. 'For men were born to pray and save'. Does the poet really mean this? If not, what does he mean? How should it be read? Try reading it aloud.

5. (a) Read aloud the last two lines of the stanza as you think the poet would wish it to be read. (b) How is this refrain different from the earlier lines of the stanza? (c) What do you

First reading continued

understand by 'Romantic Ireland' and how does Yeats feel about it?

6. Now read the entire stanza aloud, differentiating between the sections that are sarcastic, bitter or condemnatory and the lines that are wistful, nostalgic or plaintive.

Second reading

Stanza 2

7. 'They' – the romantic generations of heroes – had great power and influence in society. How is this suggested? Explore all the possible suggestions carried by lines 10 and 11.

8. How were they different from the present generation?

9. Is there a suggestion that they were fated to act as they did? Examine line 13.

10. In groups, discuss the best possible way of reading this stanza aloud. Then do it.

Third reading

Stanza 3

11. 'for this . . . For this . . . For this'. Through this repetition Yeats punches out the contrast between past and present. His attitude to the present generation is quite clear by now. But what does this stanza say about his attitude to the heroes of Ireland's past? Explore in detail the suggestions carried by the images.

12. 'All that delirium of the brave'. Discuss what this implies about heroism.

Stanza 4

13. 'All Yeats's sympathy and admiration is with the past generations of heroes.' Discuss this and refer to the text in support of your ideas.

14. 'You'd cry, "Some woman's yellow hair has maddened every mother's son".' What do you think is meant by this?

Fourth reading

15. 'In this poem we find a quite grotesque portrayal of the middle classes in contrast to an unreal and highly romanticised portrayal of past patriots!' Discuss this as an interpretation of the poem.

16. What do you think is the effect of the refrain?

17. Do you think this was a politically risky, even dangerous, poem to publish? Explain.

18. Are you surprised by the passion and strength of feeling here? Outline your reactions.

The Wild Swans at Coole

this poem is also prescribed for Ordinary Level exams in 2011 and 2014

The trees are in their autumn beauty,
The woodland paths are dry,
Under the October twilight the water
Mirrors a still sky;
Upon the brimming water among the stones   5
Are nine-and-fifty swans.

The nineteenth autumn has come upon me
Since I first made my count;
I saw, before I had well finished,
All suddenly mount   10
And scatter wheeling in great broken rings
Upon their clamorous wings.

I have looked upon those brilliant creatures,
And now my heart is sore.
All's changed since I, hearing at twilight,   15
The first time on this shore,
The bell-beat of their wings above my head,
Trod with a lighter tread.

Unwearied still, lover by lover,
They paddle in the cold   20
Companionable streams or climb the air;
Their hearts have not grown old;
Passion or conquest, wander where they will,
Attend upon them still.

But now they drift on the still water,   25
Mysterious, beautiful;
Among what rushes will they build,
By what lake's edge or pool
Delight men's eyes when I awake some day
To find they have flown away?   30

Coole: Coole Park, outside Gort, County Galway and home of Lady Augusta Gregory. She was a friend and benefactor to the poet and collaborated on many of his projects. Yeats regarded Coole Park as a second home and a welcoming refuge and retreat.

[6] **nine-and-fifty swans:** there actually were fifty-nine swans on the lake at Coole Park

[7] **the nineteenth autumn:** Yeats is referring to the summer and autumn of 1897, which was the first time he stayed for a lengthy period at Coole. At that time he was passionately involved with Maude Gonne and in a state of acute nervous exhaustion.

[18] **Trod with a lighter tread:** it is interesting that the poet chooses to recast 1897 as a hopeful and even carefree period, when this was not the case!

EXPLORATIONS

First reading

Stanza 1

1. Notice all the details that draw Yeats's eyes and ears to the scene. Visualise them intently, with your eyes closed, if you can. If you came upon this scene, what would your thoughts be?

2. How would you describe the atmosphere of this scene? What particular images or sounds contribute to this atmosphere? Explain.

Stanza 2

3. Read the second stanza with energy, aloud if possible, and see if you can make the swans come alive.

First reading continued

4. Examine the description of the swans here. (a) What attributes or qualities of these creatures does the poet wish to convey? (b) How are these qualities carried by the language? Look at images, verbs, adverbs, the sounds of words and the structure of the long single sentence.

Second reading

5. In the third stanza the poet introduces a personal note. What does he reveal about himself?

6. In stanzas 3 and 4 he explores the contrasts between the life and condition of the swans and his own life and condition. In your own words, explain the detail of these contrasts.

7. Do you think the poet envies the swans? If so, what exactly does he envy? Refer to phrases and lines to support your thinking.

8. Is this a logical or a poetic argument? Explain.

Third reading

9. If we read the first four stanzas as lamenting the loss of youth, passion and love, what particular loss frightens him in the final stanza? Explain.

10. What general issues or themes does Yeats deal with in this poem?

11. Do you think there is any sense of resolution of the personal issues raised by Yeats in this poem? Does he come to any definite conclusion? Explain your thinking.

12. Examine how the poem is structured stanza by stanza, moving from that very particular local beginning to the general speculation about love in stanza 4, and then opening up into that rather

mysterious ending that seeks to look into the future. What is the effect of this?

13. The poem is built upon a series of antitheses: the swans and the poet; the poet then and the poet now; contrasting moods. Show how these are developed.

14. What do you think the symbolism adds to the poem? Explore the elements of sky and water; trees and paths; great broken rings; and of course the swans themselves.

Fourth reading

15. Would you agree that the poem creates a 'hauntingly evocative description of the swans'? Discuss or write about this.

16. 'Ageing and the diminution of visionary power are bitterly regretted' (Terence Brown).

    Discuss this view of the poem, referring in detail to the text to substantiate your argument.

Coole Park: the home of Lady Gregory, now demolished

The entrance to Coole Park today

An Irish Airman Foresees his Death

this poem is also prescribed for Ordinary Level exams in 2011 and 2014

I know that I shall meet my fate
Somewhere among the clouds above;
Those that I fight I do not hate,
Those that I guard I do not love;
My country is Kiltartan Cross,   5
My countrymen Kiltartan's poor,
No likely end could bring them loss
Or leave them happier than before.
Nor law, nor duty bade me fight,
Nor public men, nor cheering crowds,   10
A lonely impulse of delight
Drove to this tumult in the clouds;
I balanced all, brought all to mind,
The years to come seemed waste of breath,
A waste of breath the years behind   15
In balance with this life, this death.

Notes

An Irish Airman: The speaker in the poem is Major Robert Gregory, the only son of Yeats's friend and mentor Lady Augusta Gregory of Coole Park, near Gort, County Galway. He was a pilot in the Royal Flying Corps in the First World War and at the time of his death, on 23 January 1918, was on service in Italy. It emerged later that he had been accidentally shot down by the Italian allies.

[3]   **Those that I fight:** the Germans
[4]   **Those that I guard:** the English or possibly the Italians
[5]   **Kiltartan Cross:** a crossroads near Robert Gregory's home at Coole Park, Gort, County Galway

EXPLORATIONS

Before reading

1. Read only the title. What do you expect to find in this poem? Imagine what this man's thoughts might be. How might he visualise his death? How might he feel about it? Jot down briefly the thoughts, pictures and feelings you imagine might go through his mind.

First reading

2. Who is the speaker in this poem? If in doubt, consult the note ('An Irish Airman') at the end of the poem.

3. Focus on lines 1 and 2. Are you surprised by how definite he is? Can you suggest any reasons why he might be so definite about his coming death? How would you describe his mood?

4. How do you think the speaker would say these first two lines? Experiment with various readings aloud.

5. Taking the first four lines as a unit, are you surprised that they are spoken by a military man, a pilot? In your own words, describe how he views his situation.

Second reading

6. In lines 5–8 the speaker talks about the people of his home area. How does he feel about them? Does he identify with them in any way? Have the people and the speaker anything in common? How does he think his death will affect their lives? Does he feel they will miss him? Do you think his attitude to them is uncaring, or that he feels unable to affect their lives in any way? Discuss these questions and write down the conclusions you come to, together with the evidence from the text.

7. What do you think is the purpose of his mentioning his Kiltartan countrymen in the context of his explanation? How does it fit in with his reasoning?

8. Lines 9 and 10: in your own words, explain these further reasons that the speaker discounts as having had any influence on his decision to volunteer.

9. What is revealed about the character of the speaker in the lines you have explored so far?

Third reading

10. Lines 11 and 12: here we get to the kernel of his motivation. Examine the language very carefully. 'A lonely impulse of delight': can you understand why he might feel this sense of delight? Explain how you see it. 'Impulse': what does this tell us about the decision? 'A lonely impulse': what does this suggest about the decision and the man? 'Drove': what does this add to our understanding of how he felt and of his decision? 'Tumult in the clouds': in what other context might the words 'tumult' or 'tumultuous' be used? Suggest a few. What does the sound of the word suggest? What does it suggest about the speaker's view of flying?

11. In the light of what you have discovered so far, and in the voice of the speaker, write a letter home, explaining your decision to volunteer as a pilot. Try to remain true to the speaker's feelings as outlined in the poem.

12. Lines 13–16: 'In spite of his hint of excitement earlier, the speaker did not make a rash and emotional decision.' On the evidence of these lines, would you agree with that statement? Write a paragraph.

13. 'The years to come seemed waste of breath . . .
In balance with this life, this death.'
Yet the speaker seemed to want this kind of life very much. Explore how the use of 'breath' and 'death' as rhyming words help to emphasise this.

Fourth reading

14. Having read this poem, what do you find most interesting about the speaker?

15. What appeals to you about the poem? Do you find anything disturbing about it?

16. Thousands of Irishmen fought and died in the British army during the First World War; others could not bring themselves to join that army while Ireland was governed by England. How does the speaker deal with this issue? Is the title significant?

17. As well as being a rhetorical device, the repetition of words and phrases emphasises certain ideas and issues. List the main ideas thus emphasised.

18. What are the principal themes or issues the poem deals with? Write a number of short paragraphs on this.

19. 'The pictures and images are sparsely used but very effective.' Comment on any two images.
20. To whom is this poem being spoken? Read it aloud. Is the tone more appropriate to a letter or to a public statement or speech? Explain your view with reference to phrases or lines in the text.

Easter 1916

I have met them at close of day
Coming with vivid faces
From counter or desk among grey
Eighteenth-century houses.
I have passed with a nod of the head   5
Or polite meaningless words,
Or have lingered awhile and said
Polite meaningless words,
And thought before I had done
Of a mocking tale or a gibe   10
To please a companion
Around the fire at the club,
Being certain they and I
But lived where motley is worn:
All changed, changed utterly: 15
A terrible beauty is born.

That woman's days were spent
In ignorant good-will,
Her nights in argument
Until her voice grew shrill.   20
What voice more sweet than hers
When, young and beautiful,
She rode to harriers?
This man had kept a school
And rode our wingèd horse;   25

This other his helper and friend
Was coming into his force;
He might have won fame in the end,
So sensitive his nature seemed,
So daring and sweet his thought.   30
This other man I had dreamed
A drunken, vainglorious lout.
He had done most bitter wrong
To some who are near my heart,
Yet I number him in the song;   35
He, too, has resigned his part
In the casual comedy;
He, too, has been changed in his turn,
Transformed utterly:
A terrible beauty is born.   40

Hearts with one purpose alone
Through summer and winter seem
Enchanted to a stone
To trouble the living stream.
The horse that comes from the road,   45
The rider, the birds that range
From cloud to tumbling cloud,
Minute by minute they change;
A shadow of cloud on the stream
Changes minute by minute;   50
A horse-hoof slides on the brim,
And a horse plashes within it;
The long-legged moor-hens dive,
And hens to moor-cocks call;
Minute by minute they live: 55
The stone's in the midst of all.

Too long a sacrifice
Can make a stone of the heart.
O when may it suffice?
That is Heaven's part, our part   60
To murmur name upon name,

As a mother names her child
When sleep at last has come
On limbs that had run wild.
What is it but nightfall?   65
No, no, not night but death;
Was it needless death after all?
For England may keep faith
For all that is done and said.
We know their dream; enough   70
To know they dreamed and are dead;
And what if excess of love
Bewildered them till they died?
I write it out in a verse –
MacDonagh and MacBride   75
And Connolly and Pearse
Now and in time to be,
Wherever green is worn,
Are changed, changed utterly:
A terrible beauty is born.   80

Notes

Easter 1916: On Monday 24 April 1916 a force of about 700 republicans, who were members of the Irish Volunteers and the Irish Citizen Army, took over the centre of Dublin in a military revolution and held out for six days against the British army. This was known as the Easter Rising.

[1] **them:** those republicans, in the pre-1916 days

[3] **grey:** built of granite or limestone

[12] **the club:** probably the Arts Club, where Yeats was a founder member in 1907

[17] **That woman:** Constance Gore-Booth (1868–1927) of Lissadell, County Sligo, who married the Polish Count Markiewicz. She became a fervent Irish nationalist and was actively involved in the Fianna and the Citizen Army. She was sentenced to death for her part in the Rising but the sentence was later commuted to penal servitude for life. She was released in 1917 under the general amnesty.

[24] **This man:** Padraig Pearse (1879–1916). Barrister, teacher and poet, he was the founder of St Enda's School and editor of *An Claidheamh Soluis*. He believed that a blood sacrifice was necessary to revolutionise Ireland. A member of the revolutionary IRB and the Irish Volunteers, he was the Commandant General and President of the Provisional Government during Easter week.

[25] **wingèd horse:** Pegasus, the winged horse, was a symbol of poetic vision

[26] **This other:** Thomas MacDonagh (1878–1916), poet and academic who taught at University College Dublin

[31] **This other man:** Major John MacBride, who had fought with the Boers against the British in South Africa and in 1903 married Maude Gonne, the woman Yeats loved. He too was executed for his part in the Rising.

[33] **He had done most bitter wrong:** a reference to rumours of family violence and debauchery

[34] **To some who are near my heart:** Maude Gonne and her daughter

[41–43] **Hearts . . . stone:** 'stone' at its simplest is usually taken to be a symbol for the fanatical heart – i.e. those who devote themselves fanatically to a cause, become hardened and lose their humanness as a result

[67–68] **needless death . . . England may keep faith:** the Bill for Irish Home Rule had been passed in the Westminster Parliament. In 1914, however, it was suspended on the outbreak of World War I, but with the promise that it would be put into effect after the war.

[76] **Connolly:** James Connolly (1870–1916). Trade Union organiser and founder of the Citizen Army, he was military commander of the insurgents in Dublin, Easter 1916.

Explorations

Before reading

1. First reread 'September 1913' and remind yourself how Yeats felt about the Irish middle class of his time.

First reading

Section One

2. Concentrate on the first fourteen lines. These are the same people who feature in 'September 1913'. Yeats is no longer savagely angry but he certainly has no respect for them. Visualise the encounter he describes – time of day; atmosphere; what the poet does; what he says; how he behaves. Share these ideas.

3. (a) What 'polite meaningless words' might he have said? Invent some dialogue for him. (b) As he speaks these 'polite meaningless words', what is he actually thinking? Script his thoughts and the tale or gibe he might tell later.

4. 'Where motley is worn': what does this tell us about how Yeats regarded Ireland at this time?

5. How would you describe the poet's feelings and mood in this first section?

First reading continued

6. The first fourteen lines are transformed by lines 15 and 16 and given a new context. Framed by use of the perfect tense: 'I have met them. I have passed', the impression is given that that was then, this is now. (a) Reread the first section, from this perspective. (b) Do you think Yeats is ashamed of his earlier treatment of these people? Discuss this with reference to lines or phrases in the poem.

7. 'A terrible beauty is born'. Explore all the implications of this phrase.

Second reading

Section Two

8. According to the poet, what are the effects on Constance Markiewicz of fanatical dedication to a political cause?

9. 'This other his helper . . .' In contrast to the portrait of Constance Markiewicz, which is somewhat masculine, this portrait of Thomas MacDonagh is quite feminised. Would you agree? Explain your thinking with reference to words and phrases in the poem.

10. There is great emphasis on change in this section. List all the instances and comment on them.

11. There is a sense that this change or transformation was not something actually effected by these people, but rather something that happened to them.

    'He, too, has been changed in his turn,

    Transformed utterly'

    They were changed by death and by executions. Do you think that Yeats is exploring how ordinary people are changed into heroes, and what is he suggesting? Discuss this.

Third reading

Section Three

12. Here Yeats is fascinated by flux and the process of change. (a) List all the examples he uses. (b) Comment on the atmosphere created here. Is it an appealing picture?

13. In this section he is exploring the paradox that only a stone (the fanatical heart) can alter the flow of a stream, i.e. the course of life. But it can do this only at the expense of losing

humanness. What does this indicate about Yeats's thinking on revolutionary politics?

Fourth reading

Section Four

14. What is your initial impression of the tone of this section? Is the poet weary, worried, confused, giving up; or what? Refer in detail to the text.

15. '. . . our part

    To murmur name upon name'

    How does he see the poet's role here?

16. 'sleep . . . not night but death . . . needless death . . . excess of love | Bewildered them . . .'

    The poet is attempting to think through his confusions and uncertainties here. Trace his thoughts in your own words.

17. Finally, at the end of the poem, Yeats lists out the dead, almost as a sacred act. What is the effect of this for the poet, the reader and those who died?

Fifth reading

18. Yeats had been severely disillusioned by the new Irish Catholic middle class, but he had to rethink this view after

1916. Explain the process of his rethinking as it happens in the poem.

19. 'Despite his sense of awe and admiration for the change brought about, this poem does not represent a totally unqualified approval of revolutionary politics.' Discuss this view of the poem; support your answer with references to the text.

20. Though written in 1916, Yeats did not have this poem published until October 1920. Speculate on his possible reasons. Do you think they were justified?

Maud Gonne: painting by Sarah Purser

The Second Coming

Turning and turning in the widening gyre
The falcon cannot hear the falconer;
Things fall apart; the centre cannot hold;
Mere anarchy is loosed upon the world,
The blood-dimmed tide is loosed, and everywhere   5
The ceremony of innocence is drowned;
The best lack all conviction, while the worst
Are full of passionate intensity.

Surely some revelation is at hand;
Surely the Second Coming is at hand.   10
The Second Coming! Hardly are those words out
When a vast image out of Spiritus Mundi
Troubles my sight: somewhere in sands of the desert
A shape with lion body and the head of a man,
A gaze blank and pitiless as the sun,   15
Is moving its slow thighs, while all about it
Reel shadows of the indignant desert birds.
The darkness drops again; but now I know
That twenty centuries of stony sleep
Were vexed to nightmare by a rocking cradle,   20
And what rough beast, its hour come round at last,
Slouches towards Bethlehem to be born?

Notes

The Second Coming: In its Christian interpretation this refers to the prediction of the second coming of Christ (see Matthew 24). In Yeats's occult and magical philosophy it might also refer to the second birth of the Avatar, or great antithetical spirit, which Yeats and his wife felt certain would be reincarnated as their baby son whose birth was imminent. In fact the child turned out to be a girl, dashing that theory.

[1–2] **Turning . . . falconer:** The bird is rising in ever-widening circles and so making the pattern of an inverted cone or gyre. These lines could be read as the trained bird of prey

Notes

reverting to its wild state or, in a more religious sense, taken to represent Christian civilisation growing further away from Christ (the falconer).

[12] **Spiritus Mundi:** 'The spirit of the world', which Yeats describes as 'a general storehouse of images which have ceased to be a property of any personality or spirit'.

[14] **A shape with lion body and the head of a man:** Instead of the second coming of Christ, Yeats imagines this horrific creature, a sort of Antichrist.

[20] **rocking cradle:** the birth of Christ in Bethlehem began the then two-thousand-year period of Christian history.

EXPLORATIONS

Before reading

1. Read Matthew 24: 1–31 and some of the Book of Revelations, particularly chapters 12, 13, 20 and 21. Discuss these.

First reading

Stanza 1 – Focusing on the Images

2. The trained falcon is released and it circles looking for prey. What do you think might happen if the falcon cannot hear the falconer?

3. What do you see and imagine when you read (a) line 3 and (b) line 4?

4. 'The blood-dimmed tide is loosed'. What does this picture conjure up for you? Do you find it sinister, frightening, or what?

First reading continued

5. Lines 7 and 8 focus on people. What types of people do you think the poet has in mind? Discuss this.

Second reading

6. Taking the first stanza as a whole, what does it communicate about Yeats's view of civilisation as he saw it at that time?

7. 'The first stanza or section is full of the tension of opposites.' Discuss or write about this.

8. In the second section of the poem Yeats is looking for some sufficiently weighty reason which would explain this collapse of civilisation. What occurs to him first?

9. His first short-lived thought is replaced by this 'vast image' that 'troubles' his sight. Read Yeats's description carefully.
(a) Describe what you imagine.
(b) What particular qualities are exhibited by this 'rough beast'?
(c) What particular images or phrases help create the sense of revulsion?

10. Are you shocked by the association with Bethlehem? What is suggested here? Discuss this.

Third reading

11. Yeats is talking about the end of the Christian era, the end of innocence. This is encapsulated particularly in the horrific image of one of the holiest places in

Christianity, Bethlehem, being defiled by this beast. What typically nightmarish elements do you notice in the second section of the poem?

12. In your own words, set out briefly what you think the poem is about.

13. Comment on the power of the imagery.

14. Though this was written primarily as a reaction to events in Europe, can you understand how it might be read as a commentary on the Irish situation of that time? Explain your views.

15. Could the poem be seen as prophetic in any way?

16. What did this poem make you think about? Describe the effect it had on you.

Sailing to Byzantium

I

That is no country for old men. The young
In one another's arms, birds in the trees
– Those dying generations – at their song,
The salmon-falls, the mackerel-crowded seas,
Fish, flesh, or fowl, commend all summer long   5
Whatever is begotten, born, and dies.
Caught in that sensual music all neglect
Monuments of unageing intellect.

II

An aged man is but a paltry thing,
A tattered coat upon a stick, unless   10
Soul clap its hands and sing, and louder sing
For every tatter in its mortal dress,
Nor is there singing school but studying
Monuments of its own magnificence;
And therefore I have sailed the seas and come   15
To the holy city of Byzantium.

III

O sages standing in God's holy fire
As in the gold mosaic of a wall,
Come from the holy fire, perne in a gyre,
And be the singing-masters of my soul.   20
Consume my heart away; sick with desire
And fastened to a dying animal
It knows not what it is; and gather me
Into the artifice of eternity.

IV

Once out of nature I shall never take   25
My bodily form from any natural thing,
But such a form as Grecian goldsmiths make
Of hammered gold and gold enamelling
To keep a drowsy Emperor awake;
Or set upon a golden bough to sing   30
To lords and ladies of Byzantium
Of what is past, or passing, or to come.

Notes

Byzantium: The Roman emperor Constantine, who became a Christian in AD 312, chose Byzantium as his capital city, renaming it Constantinople in 330. Yeats idealised Byzantium, in particular at the end of the fifth century, as the centre of European civilisation – a place where all life was in harmony.

[1]   **That:** Ireland

[4]   **The salmon-falls, the mackerel-crowded seas:** all images of regeneration, new life, energy and plenty

[5]   **commend:** praise, celebrate

[17]   **O sages:** probably refers to the depiction of the martyrs being burned in a fire in a mosaic at the church of San Apollinare Nuovo in Ravenna, which Yeats saw in 1907

[19]   **perne in a gyre:** when Yeats was a child in Sligo he was told that 'pern' was another name for the spool or bobbin on which thread was wound. So the idea of circular movement is carried in the word 'perne', which Yeats constructs here as a verb. A 'gyre' is a revolving cone of time, in Yeats's cosmology. Here, Yeats is asking the sages to journey through the cone of time, to come to him and teach him perfection, teach his soul to sing.

[24]   **artifice of eternity:** artifice is something constructed, created – here a work of art. The word can also have connotations of trickery or sleight of hand. In a certain sense art is outside time and has a sort of eternal quality about it. Yeats asks the sages to gather him into the eternity of art.

[27]   **such a form:** Yeats wrote that he had read somewhere that there existed in the Emperors' Palace in Byzantium 'a tree made of gold and silver, and artificial birds that sang'. Here the golden bird is used as a metaphor for art which is beautiful, perfect and unchanging.

[32]   **Of what is past, or passing, or to come:** though Yeats wished to escape out of the stream of time into the eternity of art, ironically, the golden bird's song is about time.

EXPLORATIONS

First reading

Stanza 1 – Focusing on the Images

The trained falcon is released and it circles.

1.   Read the first stanza carefully for yourself, as many times as you feel necessary. In groups, try out different ways of reading aloud the first sentence. Why do you think it should be read in that way?

2. Notice the perspective. The poet has already left Ireland, either in reality or imagination, and is looking back. (a) What does he remember about the country? (b) Why is it 'no country' for old men?

3. The first stanza portrays the sensuality of life very vividly. Explore how the poet does this. Consider the imagery; the sounds of words; repeated letters, the crowded syntax; the repetitions and rhythms of the sentence, etc.

4. How do you think the poet feels about this teeming fertility? Ostensibly he is renouncing the world of the senses, but do you think he dwells on these scenes a little too much if he dislikes or hates them? Consider phrases such as 'The young | In one another's arms, birds in the trees'; 'commend all summer long'; 'Caught in that sensual music'. Do you think there might be a hint of nostalgia and a sense of loss here? Discuss the tone of the stanza.

5. Yet in the midst of all this energy and life there are the seeds of death. Explain the paradox and word punning in 'dying generations'. Where else, in the first stanza, is there an awareness of time?

6. What does the poet value that he feels is neglected in Ireland?

7. Reread the stanza and list all the reasons you can find for Yeats's departure or withdrawal.

8. Now read aloud the first sentence as you think the poet intended it.

Second reading

Stanza 2

9. In this stanza Yeats asserts that only the soul gives meaning to the human being. (a) Explore the contrast between body and soul here. (b) Do you think that the imagery used is effective? Explain.

10. 'Nor is there . . . own magnificence': (a) Tease out the possible meanings of these two lines. Explore the following reading: the only way the spirit learns to sing (achieves perfection) is by studying monuments created by and for itself, i.e. works of art. In other words, art enriches the soul. (b) Explain why the poet has come to Byzantium.

Third reading

Stanza 3

11. In the third stanza Yeats entreats the sages of the timeless city to teach his soul to sing, i.e. perfect his spirit. But perfection cannot be achieved without pain and sacrifice. Where in the stanza is this notion dealt with?

12. What is the poet's ultimate goal as expressed in the stanza?

13. Byzantium was renowned as the city of religion, philosophy and a highly formalised art. Where are these elements reflected in the second and third stanzas?

Fourth reading

14. In the fourth stanza he wishes that his spirit be transformed into the perfect work of art and so live on, ageless and incorruptible. What do you notice about this piece of art?

15. Do you think Yeats achieves the yearned-for escape from the flux of time into the 'immortality' of art? Consider carefully the irony of the final line.

16. Essentially, what is Yeats writing about in this poem?

17. 'This poem is built around essential contrasts and polarities.' Discuss this with reference to relevant phrases and lines.

18. Can you appreciate Yeats's dilemma as experienced here, as well as his deep yearning?

Mosaic from the church of San Apollinare Nuovo in Ravenna showing a procession of saints carrying crowns, symbols of martyrs. (See the note referring to line 17 in the poem 'Sailing to Byzantium'.)

The Stare's Nest by My Window

Section VI
From 'Meditations in Time of Civil War'

The bees build in the crevices
Of loosening masonry, and there
The mother birds bring grubs and flies.
My wall is loosening; honey-bees,
Come build in the empty house of the stare.   5

We are closed in, and the key is turned
On our uncertainty; somewhere
A man is killed, or a house burned,
Yet no clear fact to be discerned:
Come build in the empty house of the stare.   10

A barricade of stone or of wood;
Some fourteen days of civil war;
Last night they trundled down the road
That dead young soldier in his blood:
Come build in the empty house of the stare.   15

We had fed the heart on fantasies,
The heart's grown brutal from the fare;
More substance in our enmities
Than in our love; O honey-bees,
Come build in the empty house of the stare.   20

Stare's Nest: 'stare' is a term sometimes used in the West of Ireland for a starling.

Meditations in Time of Civil War: this is quite a lengthy poem structured in seven sections. The first was composed in England in 1921; the other sections were written in Ireland during the Civil War of 1922–1923.

[1] **The bees:** there is a possible echo of the bees who were sent by the gods to perform certain tasks in Porphyry's mystical writing. At any rate they may symbolise patient creative endeavour, as distinct from the destructive forces all around.

[14] **That dead young soldier:** this is based on an event that reputedly took place beside Yeats's Galway house, Thoor Ballylee, when a young soldier was dragged down a road, his body so badly battered and mutilated that his mother could only recover his head.

EXPLORATIONS

Before reading

1. Read only the title. What might you expect to find in this poem?

First reading

Stanzas 1–3

2. Examine the detail of the first three lines of stanza 1. Write about what you see: the details, the sounds, the atmosphere.

3. In the actual historical context many big houses of the establishment class were abandoned or evacuated for fear of reprisals. What do you imagine might have been the

First reading continued

poet's thoughts when he first came upon this scene by the window?

4. There are two references to 'loosening' masonry or walls in the first stanza. Do you think these might be significant? Explain.

5. Read the second stanza carefully. What is the atmosphere in the house and what details contribute to this?

6. What single word do you find most powerful in the third stanza? Write about it.

Second reading

7. Tease out the meaning of the fourth stanza, in your own words.

8. Comment on the tones you find in the final stanza and suggest how these are created.

9. How do you think the repeated refrain should be read? Try it.

Third reading

10. Would you agree that Yeats is torn between a bitter disappointment and a desperate hope here? Discuss this.

11. 'The poem captures the atmosphere of war with vivid realism.' Discuss this statement with reference to the text.

12. Explore the music of this piece: the onomatopoeia; the effect of the rhyming; the haunting refrain, etc.

13. 'This poem is really a prayer.' Discuss.

Fourth reading

14. 'This poem could be read as a metaphor for the situation of the poet's traditional class, the Anglo-Irish ascendancy.' Discuss this.

15. How did this poem affect you? Write about it.

In Memory of Eva Gore-Booth and Con Markiewicz

The light of evening, Lissadell,
Great windows open to the south,
Two girls in silk kimonos, both
Beautiful, one a gazelle.
But a raving autumn shears   5
Blossom from the summer's wreath;
The older is condemned to death,
Pardoned, drags out lonely years
Conspiring among the ignorant.
I know not what the younger dreams –   10
Some vague Utopia – and she seems,
When withered old and skeleton-gaunt,
An image of such politics.
Many a time I think to seek
One or the other out and speak   15
Of that old Georgian mansion, mix
Pictures of the mind, recall
That table and the talk of youth,
Two girls in silk kimonos, both
Beautiful, one a gazelle.   20

Dear shadows, now you know it all,
All the folly of a fight
With a common wrong or right.
The innocent and the beautiful
Have no enemy but time;   25
Arise and bid me strike a match
And strike another till time catch;
Should the conflagration climb,
Run till all the sages know.
We the great gazebo built,   30
They convicted us of guilt;
Bid me strike a match and blow.

Background note

Eva Gore-Booth (1870–1926) was a poet and a reader of Eastern philosophy. She became involved in social work for the poor and was a member of the women's suffrage movement.

Constance Gore-Booth (1868–1927) married a Polish poet and landowner, Count Casimir Markiewicz. A committed socialist republican, she became involved in Irish revolutionary movements and joined the Citizen Army. For her part in the Easter Rising she was sentenced to death, but the sentence was commuted to life imprisonment and she was released in the general amnesty of 1917. She was appointed Minister for Labour in the first Dáil Éireann of 1919, the first Irish woman government minister. She took the anti-treaty side in the Civil War.

Notes

[1] **Lissadell:** the County Sligo Georgian mansion referred to below, built in the early part of the nineteenth century and home of the Gore-Booth family. Yeats visited in 1894–1895.

[3] **kimonos:** traditional Japanese long robes

[4] **gazelle:** a small delicately formed antelope. The reference is to Eva Gore-Booth.

[7] **The older:** Constance

[8] **lonely years:** her husband returned to his lands in the Ukraine and she was separated from her children.

[16] **old Georgian mansion:** Lissadell, an image of aristocratic elegance and good taste for Yeats

[21] **Dear shadows:** both women were dead at the time of writing

[30] **gazebo:** the scholar A. N. Jeffares gives three possible meanings: (a) a summer house; (b) a vantage point; and (c) to make a fool of oneself or be conspicuous (in Hibernian English).

EXPLORATIONS

First reading

Lines 1–4

1. Picture the scene in the first four lines – notice all the details. What do you learn about the lifestyle of the people living here?

2. What questions are you prompted to ask by these lines? Formulate at least three. Share your questions.

Explorations

3. (a) Do you think Yeats treasured this memory?
    (b) What do the lines reveal about what Yeats valued or considered important in life?

Lines 5–6

4. Do you think these lines are an effective metaphor for the passage of time or a rather tired one? Discuss this.

Lines 7–13

5. Read these lines, consult the notes and then state briefly, in your own words, how the life paths or careers of these two women have developed.

6. Do you think that Yeats approved of their careers? Explain your view with reference to words and phrases in the text.

Second reading

7. 'Two girls in silk kimonos, both Beautiful, one a gazelle'

    These lines are repeated at the end of the first section. Do you think the refrain here should be spoken in the same tone as lines 3 and 4, or have intervening lines coloured the poet's feeling? Explain your

opinion on this. Read aloud the first section as you think Yeats would want it read.

8. Lines 20–25 carry the kernel of the poet's insight, which he feels certain the spirits ('Dear shadows') of the two sisters will understand. (a) What is this wisdom or insight? (b) Is there a certain weariness of tone here? Explain.

9. What do you understand by Yeats's animated wish at the end of the poem to light a bonfire?

Third reading

10. What are the main issues or themes that Yeats deals with in this poem? Support your view with detailed reference.

11. What could one discern about the poet's philosophy of life from a reading of this poem? Again refer to the detail of the text.

12. Yeats felt that the Anglo-Irish ascendancy class, with their great houses and wealth, had a duty to set an example of graciousness and cultured living. (a) Do you think he felt that Eva and Con had let the

side down? Where and how might this be suggested?

(b) Do you think he may have considered their activities unfeminine?

13. 'The off-rhymes that Yeats employs from time to time give the poem a conversational naturalism and reinforce the theme of imperfection.' Discuss this with reference to the details of the poem.

14. Many of Yeats's poems are about time structured on quite violent contrasts. Do you think this an effective device here? Comment.

15. Think or talk about your personal reactions to this poem. What did it make you think about? What insights did it give you?

Eva Gore-Booth (left) and her sister Constance (Con) Markiewicz

Swift's Epitaph

Swift has sailed into his rest;
Savage indignation there
Cannot lacerate his breast.
Imitate him if you dare,
World-besotted traveller; he
Served human liberty.

Background note

Jonathan Swift (1667–1745) was the most famous Dean of St Patrick's Cathedral, Dublin. Poet, political pamphleteer and satirist, he was the author of such well-known works as: *The Drapier Letters*; *A Modest Proposal*; *A Tale of a Tub*; and *Gulliver's Travels*. Politically conservative, Swift voiced the concerns and values of Protestant Ireland with an independence of mind and a courage that Yeats admired.

This poem is a translation, with some alterations, of the Latin epitaph on Swift's burial stone in St Patrick's, Cathedral, Dublin. Yeats changed the first line and added the adjective 'World-besotted' in the penultimate line.

The original epitaph, which is in Latin, runs as follows:

Here is laid the Body of
JONATHAN SWIFT
Doctor of Divinity,
Dean of this Cathedral Church,
Where savage indignation
can no longer
Rend his heart,
Go traveller, and imitate,
if you can,
This earnest and dedicated
Champion of Liberty.
He died on the 19th day of Oct.,
1745 a.d. aged 78 years.

EXPLORATIONS

First reading

1. What does the first line suggest about Swift's death?

2. What can we learn about Swift's life from this epitaph?

3. What qualities of Swift's do you think Yeats admired?

First reading continued

4. Comment on the tone of the epitaph. Do you think it is unusual? Refer in detail to words and phrases.

Second reading

5. How do Yeats's alterations in lines 1 and 5 (see question 2) change the epitaph?

6. Contrast Swift's original epitaph with Yeats's own epitaph (see page 152).

An Acre of Grass

Picture and book remain,
An acre of green grass
For air and exercise,
Now strength of body goes;
Midnight, an old house   5
Where nothing stirs but a mouse.

My temptation is quiet.
Here at life's end
Neither loose imagination,
Nor the mill of the mind   10
Consuming its rag and bone,
Can make the truth known.

Grant me an old man's frenzy,
Myself must I remake
Till I am Timon and Lear   15
Or that William Blake
Who beat upon the wall
Till Truth obeyed his call;

A mind Michael Angelo knew
That can pierce the clouds,   20
Or inspired by frenzy
Shake the dead in their shrouds;
Forgotten else by mankind,
An old man's eagle mind.

[2–5] **An acre of green grass . . . an old house:** the reference is to Riversdale, a farmhouse with orchards and fruit gardens at the foot of the Dublin mountains in Rathfarnham which in 1932 Yeats leased for thirteen years.

[9] **loose imagination:** unstructured imagination

[11] **rag and bone:** the left-over, discarded bric-à-brac of life. Lines 10–11 might refer to the imagination's everyday, casual focus on life's bric-à-brac.

[15] **Timon:** An Athenian, died in 399 BC, who was satirised by the comic writers of his time for his marked misanthropy or strong dislike of humanity. Shakespeare dramatised the story in *Timon of Athens*.

[15] **Lear:** Shakespeare's King Lear, who couldn't accept old age gracefully, lost his reason and lived wild on the heath.

[16] **William Blake:** (1757–1827) by profession an engraver, Blake is best known for his more accessible poems 'Songs of Innocence' and 'Songs of Experience'. Lesser known is a great body and range of work which shows him as a mystic, apocalyptic visionary, writer of rude verses and an independent thinker who challenged the accepted philosophies and values of his age. He was considered mad by his contemporaries. Yeats admired him greatly and co-edited his *Prophetic Books* in 1893. He also wrote an interpretation of Blake's mythology.

[19] **Michael Angelo:** Michelangelo Buonarroti (1475–1564) was one of the premier figures of the Italian Renaissance – sculptor, architect, painter and poet. Among his most famous creations are the statue of David and the ceiling of the Sistine Chapel in Rome.

EXPLORATIONS

First reading

1. Explore the images and sounds of the first stanza. (a) What do we learn about the condition of the poet? (b) How would you describe the atmosphere created in this stanza? What words and sounds contribute most to that?

2. In the second stanza, despite his age the poet is still thinking of poetry. In your own words, describe his dilemma.

3. Examine the metaphor for the mind used in lines 10 and 11. What do you think of it?

4. Comment on the tones found in stanzas 1 and 2. Do you think there is a sense of emptiness at the end of the second stanza? Explore how the sounds of the words contribute to this.

Second reading

5. 'Grant me an old man's frenzy'. This is a very unusual prayer. Does the remainder of stanza 3 help to explain this intercession? Consult the textual notes and try to outline in your own words what Yeats is actually praying for.

Second reading continued

6. What is the connection that Yeats is making between poetry, madness and truth?

7. There is evidence of a new energy in both language and imagery in stanzas 3 and 4. Comment in detail on this.

8. This extraordinary change or metamorphosis culminates in the final image of 'An old man's eagle mind.' Trace how this conceit (or startling comparison) has been prepared for earlier in the fourth stanza.

Third reading

9. Would you agree that this poem is a most unusual response to the theme of old age?

10. Yeats's theories of creativity (partly inspired by the works of the German philosopher Nietzsche) included the need for continual transformation of the self. Trace the transformation that occurs here.

W. B. Yeats in his later years

Politics

'In our time the destiny of man presents its meanings in political terms'
(Thomas Mann)

How can I, that girl standing there,
My attention fix
On Roman or on Russian
Or on Spanish politics?
Yet here's a travelled man that knows   5

What he talks about,
And there's a politician
That has read and thought,
And maybe what they say is true
Of war and war's alarms,   10
But O that I were young again
And held her in my arms.

Background note

Written in May 1938, this poem was composed as an answer to an article about Yeats that had praised his public language but suggested that he should use it on political subjects.

EXPLORATIONS

First reading

1. In your own words, state the dilemma or conflict that Yeats is experiencing here.

2. 'And maybe what they say is true | Of war'. From the context of the poem, what do you suppose 'they' say? Examine Thomas Mann's epigraph for suggestions.

3. 'That girl standing there'. To whom or to what do you think he might be referring?

Second reading

4. Write about the essential conflicts that are set up here: politics versus love; public life versus private; public devotion versus private satisfaction, etc.

5. 'For all its simplicity of language, this is a very well crafted poem.' Discuss this statement with reference to the text.

6. State what you think this poem is about.

7. 'The vision in this poem is that of an old man.' Argue about this.

From 'Under Ben Bulben'

V

Irish poets, learn your trade,
Sing whatever is well made,
Scorn the sort now growing up
All out of shape from toe to top,
Their unremembering hearts and heads   5
Base-born products of base beds.
Sing the peasantry, and then
Hard-riding country gentlemen,
The holiness of monks, and after
Porter-drinkers' randy laughter;   10
Sing the lords and ladies gay
That were beaten into the clay
Through seven heroic centuries;
Cast your mind on other days
That we in coming days may be   15
Still the indomitable Irishry.

VI

Under bare Ben Bulben's head
In Drumcliff churchyard Yeats is laid.
An ancestor was rector there
Long years ago, a church stands near,   20
By the road an ancient cross.
No marble, no conventional phrase;
On limestone quarried near the spot
By his command these words are cut:
Cast a cold eye   25
On life, on death.
Horseman, pass by!

September 4, 1938

Background note

The final draft of this poem is dated 4 September 1938, about five months before the poet's death. Parts of it were published in 1939. 'Under Ben Bulben' as a whole can be seen as Yeats's poetic testimony, an elegy for himself, defining his convictions and the poetic and social philosophies that motivated his life's work.

Section V: Yeats urges all artists, poets, painters, sculptors to promote the necessary heroic images that nourish civilisation.

Section VI: rounds his life to its close and moves from the mythologies associated with the top of Ben Bulben to the real earth at its foot, in Drumcliff churchyard.

Notes

Section V

[2] **whatever is well made:** note [14] comments on the great tradition of art and letters

[3–6] **Scorn the sort . . . products of base beds:** Yeats had joined the Eugenics Society in London in 1936 and became very interested in its literature and in research on intelligence testing. (Eugenics is the science of improving the human race through selective breeding.)

[11–12] **Sing the lords . . . beaten into the clay:** refers to the Cromwellian settlement of 1652 which evicted the majority of Irish landowners to Clare and Connaught to make room for new English settlers

[13] **centuries:** the centuries since the Norman invasions

[14] **other days:** a reference to the great tradition in European art and letters valued by Yeats. But it could also be a reference to Ireland's literary tradition, particularly of the eighteenth century.

Section VI

[17] **Ben Bulben:** a mountain north of Sligo connected with Irish mythology

[18] **Drumcliff:** at the foot of Ben Bulben, the site of a sixth-century monastery founded by St Colmcille

[19] **ancestor was rector there:** the Revd John Yeats (1774–1846), Yeats's grandfather, was rector there and is buried in the graveyard

[20–21] **a church stands near . . . ancient cross:** as well as the remains of a round tower, there is a high cross and part of an older cross in the churchyard

|Notes|[27]|**horseman:** has echoes of the fairy horseman of folk belief, but might also have associations with the Irish Ascendancy class|

EXPLORATIONS

Section V

First reading

1. Yeats's advice to Irish poets to write about the aesthetically pleasing ('whatever is well made') is quite understandable, but what do you think of his advice on what they should scorn? Consult the textual notes. (a) What exactly is he saying? (b) What is your reaction to this rant?

2. In your own words, what does Yeats consider to be the proper subjects for poetry?

3. What image of 'Irishry' does Yeats wish to celebrate? Do you think he is being elitist and superior?

Second reading

4. Would you agree that this section exhibits an abhorrence for the present at the expense of a romanticised past? Explain your opinion with reference to the details of the verse.

5. This reads like an incantation. What features of poetic

Second reading continued

technique do you think contribute to this? Consider the metre, the rhyming scheme, the choice of diction, etc.

6. Write about the poet's attitude of mind as you detect it from these lines.

7. Professor Terence Brown has written of 'Under Ben Bulben': 'Skill (i.e. poetic) here is complicit with a repulsive politics and a deficient ethical sense.' On the evidence of the extract, would you agree with this?

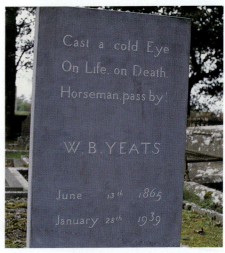

Yeats's grave in Drumcliff churchyard

Section VI

Third reading

8. Yeats visualised the details of his last resting place very carefully. Without checking back, what details of the churchyard can you remember?

9. How would you describe the atmosphere of the churchyard? What details in the verse contribute particularly to this?

Fourth reading

10. What do these lines reveal about the poet, how he sees himself and how he wishes to be remembered?

Fourth reading continued

11. Discuss the epitaph in the last three lines. How does it differ from most epitaphs you have read?

12. The scholar A. N. Jeffares felt that the epitaph embodied Yeats's essential attitude to life and death 'which he thought must be faced with bravery, with heroic indifference and with the aristocratic disdain of the horseman'. Consider this as a possible reading of the lines and write a response to it.

Ben Bulben

6 *Robert Frost*
1874–1963

prescribed for Higher Level exams in 2011 and 2012

Robert Lee Frost was born in San Francisco on 26 March 1874. Following his father's death in 1885, he moved with his younger sister Jeanie and his mother to Lawrence, Massachusetts, where his grandparents lived. Robert entered Lawrence High School in 1888. There he studied Latin, Greek, ancient and European history and mathematics. From high school he went to Dartmouth College and Harvard but left the two colleges without graduating. On 19 December 1895 he married Elinor White, a former classmate. For health reasons he took up farming. In later years he recalled that his favourite activities were 'mowing with a scythe, chopping with an axe and writing with a pen'. He supplemented his income by teaching and lecturing.

Frost devoted his free time to reading the major poets in order to perfect his own writing. Shakespeare, the English Romantics (Wordsworth, Keats and Shelley) and the Victorian poets (Hardy, Kipling and Browning) all influenced his work. The many biblical references in his poems reflect his studies of scripture, while his classical education enabled him to write with confidence in traditional forms. He followed the principles laid down in Wordsworth's 'Preface to the Lyrical Ballads', basing his poetry on incidents from common life described in 'language really used by men'.

Frost and his family emigrated to England in 1912. There he published two collections, *A Boy's Will* (1913) and *North of Boston* (1914). The books were well received and he was introduced into the literary circles in London, where he met W. B. Yeats. After the outbreak of World War I Frost returned to America and wrote his next collection, *Mountain Interval*. This book contains some of his best-known poems, including 'Birches', 'Out, Out –' and 'The Road Not Taken', with their characteristic themes of isolation, fear, violence and death. Frost bought another farm in Franconia, New Hampshire and supported his family by college teaching, readings, lectures, book royalties and reprint fees. In January 1917 he became Professor of English at Amherst, Massachusetts. By 1920 he could afford to move to Vermont and devote himself to apple-farming and writing poetry. In recognition of his work he won the Pulitzer Prize four times, in 1924, 1931, 1937 and 1943.

In contrast to his public life, Frost's personal life was dogged by tragedy. His sister Jeanie was committed to a mental asylum. His daughter Lesley had an emotionally disturbed life and blamed her father for her problems. His favourite child, Marjorie, had a nervous breakdown, developed tuberculosis and died in 1934 aged twenty-nine. Irma, his third daughter, suffered from mental illness throughout her adult life. Elinor, his wife, died of a heart attack on 20 March 1938 and his only son Carol committed suicide in 1940. Frost survived the turbulence of these years with the support of his friend, secretary and manager, Kay Morrison. In his final years, Frost enjoyed public acclaim. He recited 'The Gift Outright' at John F. Kennedy's inauguration, watched on television by over sixty million Americans. He travelled as a celebrated visitor to Brazil, Ireland and Russia. On his eighty-eighth birthday he received the Congressional Gold Medal from President Kennedy and in the same year, 1962, published his final volume, *In The Clearing*. On 29 January 1963, two months before his eighty-ninth birthday, Robert Frost died peacefully in a Boston hospital.

The Tuft of Flowers

this poem is also prescribed for Ordinary Level exams in 2011 and 2012

I went to turn the grass once after one
Who mowed it in the dew before the sun.

The dew was gone that made his blade so keen
Before I came to view the levelled scene.
I looked for him behind an isle of trees;   5
I listened for his whetstone on the breeze.

But he had gone his way, the grass all mown,
And I must be, as he had been, – alone,

'As all must be,' I said within my heart,
'Whether they work together or apart.'   10

But as I said it, swift there passed me by
On noiseless wing a bewildered butterfly,

Seeking with memories grown dim o'er night
Some resting flower of yesterday's delight.

And once I marked his flight go round and round,   15
As where some flower lay withering on the ground.

And then he flew as far as eye could see,
And then on tremulous wing came back to me.

I thought of questions that have no reply,
And would have turned to toss the grass to dry;   20

But he turned first, and led my eye to look
At a tall tuft of flowers beside a brook,

A leaping tongue of bloom the scythe had spared
Beside a reedy brook the scythe had bared.

I left my place to know them by their name,   25
Finding them butterfly weed when I came.

The mower in the dew had loved them thus,
By leaving them to flourish, not for us,

Nor yet to draw one thought of ours to him,
But from sheer morning gladness at the brim.   30

The butterfly and I had lit upon,
Nevertheless, a message from the dawn,
That made me hear the wakening birds around,
And hear his long scythe whispering to the ground,

And feel a spirit kindred to my own;   35
So that henceforth I worked no more alone;

But glad with him, I worked as with his aid,
And weary, sought at noon with him the shade;

And dreaming, as it were, held brotherly speech
With one whose thought I had not hoped to reach.   40

'Men work together,' I told him from the heart,
'Whether they work together or apart.'

Notes

[1]   **to turn the grass:** to toss the cut grass so that it will dry
[3]   **keen:** sharp-edged, eager
[6]   **whetstone:** a stone used for sharpening edged tools
      by friction
[23] **scythe:** a long, curving, sharp-edged blade for
      mowing grass

Explorations

First reading

1. Describe the scene in the first five couplets. What do you see? Who is present? What is he doing?

2. Explore the mood in these opening lines. How does the speaker feel? Do you think you would feel the same way?

3. How does the speaker feel after he discovers the butterfly weed? What words or phrases suggest a change in his mood?

4. According to the poem, why did the mower not cut these flowers?

5. What image or phrases caught your attention, on a first reading? Why?

Second reading

6. In your opinion, what is the 'message from the dawn'?

7. What do you think the poet means when he says 'henceforth I worked no more alone'?

Third reading

8. Briefly outline the themes of this poem.

9. Shifts of mood and tone are marked by the word 'but'. Trace these changes in the poem.

10. The speaker describes the mower as a 'spirit kindred to my own'. In what sense is this true?

Fourth reading

11. Three times in the poem Frost introduces the concept of 'turning'. Examine the changes that occur with each of them.

12. Follow the development of the main ideas. Examine the images that convey these ideas and state whether or not you find them effective.

13. 'Frost rejects ornate, poetic diction, preferring a language that is conversational and relaxed.' Examine Frost's use of language in the poem.

14. 'Frost's decision to write in conventional forms, using traditional rhythms and rhymes and syntax, reflects his belief that poetry should be accessible to the ordinary man.' Assess this poem in the light of the above statement.

Harvesting: painting by Julien Dupré (1851–1910)

Mending Wall

this poem is also prescribed for Ordinary Level exams in 2011 and 2012

Something there is that doesn't love a wall,
That sends the frozen-ground-swell under it,
And spills the upper boulders in the sun;
And makes gaps even two can pass abreast.
The work of hunters is another thing: 5
I have come after them and made repair
Where they have left not one stone on a stone,
But they would have the rabbit out of hiding,
To please the yelping dogs. The gaps I mean,
No one has seen them made or heard them made,   10
But at spring mending-time we find them there.
I let my neighbour know beyond the hill;
And on a day we meet to walk the line
And set the wall between us once again.
We keep the wall between us as we go.   15
To each the boulders that have fallen to each.
And some are loaves and some so nearly balls
We have to use a spell to make them balance:
'Stay where you are until our backs are turned!'
We wear our fingers rough with handling them.   20
Oh, just another kind of out-door game,
One on a side. It comes to little more:
There where it is we do not need the wall:
He is all pine and I am apple orchard.
My apple trees will never get across   25
And eat the cones under his pines, I tell him.
He only says, 'Good fences make good neighbours.'
Spring is the mischief in me, and I wonder
If I could put a notion in his head:
'Why do they make good neighbours? Isn't it   30
Where there are cows? But here there are no cows.
Before I built a wall I'd ask to know
What I was walling in or walling out,
And to whom I was like to give offence.

Something there is that doesn't love a wall,   35
That wants it down.' I could say 'Elves' to him,
But it's not elves exactly, and I'd rather
He said it for himself. I see him there
Bringing a stone grasped firmly by the top
In each hand, like an old-stone savage armed.   40
He moves in darkness as it seems to me,
Not of woods only and the shade of trees.
He will not go behind his father's saying,
And he likes having thought of it so well
He says again, 'Good fences make good neighbours.'   45

EXPLORATIONS

First reading

1. You have been asked to paint a picture based on this poem. Where would you place the wall and the two men? What are the men doing? Are they looking at each other? Describe their postures and their facial expressions. What other details would you include?

2. How are the gaps in the wall created?

3. What do you think the poet means when he describes wall-building as 'just another kind of out-door game'?

4. Outline the arguments Frost uses against building walls.

Second reading

5. In what sense is the neighbour 'all pine and I am apple orchard'?

6. 'He moves in darkness . . .' What forms of darkness overshadow the neighbour?

7. Describe as clearly as possible your image of the neighbour as Frost portrays him.

Third reading

8. Walls unite and divide. How is this illustrated within the poem?

9. 'Good fences make good neighbours.' Do you think the speaker agrees with this proverb? Explain your answer.

10. The neighbour repeats the proverb because 'he likes having thought of it so well'. Why is this comment ironic?

11. What do we learn about the narrator's personality in the poem?

Fourth reading

12. What themes and issues are raised in this poem?

13. How does Frost achieve a sense of mystery in the poem? Are any of the images mysterious or magical? What effect do they have on the poem?

14. Follow the development of the main ideas. Examine the images that convey these ideas and state whether or not you find them effective.

15. This poem is concerned with unity and division, communication and isolation, hope and disappointment. Do you agree? Where are these tensions most obvious? Are they resolved at the end?

16. 'Human nature, not Mother Nature, is the main concern in Frost's poetry.' Would you agree with this statement, based on your reading of this poem?

After Apple-Picking

My long two-pointed ladder's sticking through a tree
Toward heaven still,
And there's a barrel that I didn't fill
Beside it, and there may be two or three
Apples I didn't pick upon some bough.   5
But I am done with apple-picking now.
Essence of winter sleep is on the night,
The scent of apples: I am drowsing off.
I cannot rub the strangeness from my sight
I got from looking through a pane of glass   10
I skimmed this morning from the drinking trough
And held against the world of hoary grass.

It melted, and I let it fall and break.
But I was well
Upon my way to sleep before it fell,   15
And I could tell
What form my dreaming was about to take.
Magnified apples appear and disappear,
Stem end and blossom end,
And every fleck of russet showing clear.   20
My instep arch not only keeps the ache,
It keeps the pressure of a ladder-round.
I feel the ladder sway as the boughs bend.
And I keep hearing from the cellar bin
The rumbling sound   25
Of load on load of apples coming in.
For I have had too much
Of apple-picking: I am overtired
Of the great harvest I myself desired.
There were ten thousand thousand fruit to touch,   30
Cherish in hand, lift down, and not let fall.
For all
That struck the earth,
No matter if not bruised or spiked with stubble,
Went surely to the cider-apple heap   35
As of no worth.
One can see what will trouble
This sleep of mine, whatever sleep it is.
Were he not gone,
The woodchuck could say whether it's like his   40
Long sleep, as I describe its coming on,
Or just some human sleep.

Notes

[7]   **Essence:** scent
[12] **hoary:** white with age (hoarfrost: white particles of
      frozen dew)
[40] **woodchuck:** or groundhog – a burrowing rodent which
      hibernates for half the year

EXPLORATIONS

First reading

1. Imagine the orchard as Frost describes it in the opening lines. What details does he include? How would you describe the scene now the apple-picking is over?

2. Explain in your own words what happened at the drinking trough in the morning.

3. Why had the apple-picker to be so careful with the apples?

4. What connects the woodchuck and the harvester?

Second reading

5. The fruit has been harvested. How does the speaker feel now?

6. What is it that will trouble his sleep?

7. Select your favourite image in the poem and explain your choice.

8. Does the poet successfully capture the sensations of picking apples? Examine his use of images and the language used.

Third reading

9. There are moments of confusion in the poem. Is this deliberate? Why? Refer closely to the text in your answer.

10. In the poem, autumn is seen as a season of abundance rather than a time of decay. How does the poet recreate for the reader the richness of the harvest?

11. A dream-like quality pervades the poem. How is this achieved? Consider the language used, the imagery, descriptions, metre and rhyme.

Fourth reading

12. Frost's language is sensuously evocative and rich in imagery. Discuss his use of tactile, visual and auditory imagery in the poem as a whole.

13. What part do sounds and rhythm play in the creation of the mood in the poem?

14. Briefly explain your personal reaction to 'After Apple-Picking'.

Birches

When I see birches bend to left and right
Across the lines of straighter darker trees,
I like to think some boy's been swinging them.
But swinging doesn't bend them down to stay.
Ice-storms do that. Often you must have seen them   5
Loaded with ice a sunny winter morning
After a rain. They click upon themselves
As the breeze rises, and turn many-colored
As the stir cracks and crazes their enamel.
Soon the sun's warmth makes them shed crystal shells   10
Shattering and avalanching on the snow-crust –
Such heaps of broken glass to sweep away
You'd think the inner dome of heaven had fallen.
They are dragged to the withered bracken by the load,
And they seem not to break; though once they are bowed   15
So low for long, they never right themselves:
You may see their trunks arching in the woods
Years afterwards, trailing their leaves on the ground
Like girls on hands and knees that throw their hair
Before them over their heads to dry in the sun.   20
But I was going to say when Truth broke in
With all her matter-of-fact about the ice-storm
I should prefer to have some boy bend them
As he went out and in to fetch the cows –
Some boy too far from town to learn baseball,   25
Whose only play was what he found himself,
Summer or winter, and could play alone.
One by one he subdued his father's trees
By riding them down over and over again
Until he took the stiffness out of them,   30
And not one but hung limp, not one was left
For him to conquer. He learned all there was
To learn about not launching out too soon
And so not carrying the tree away
Clear to the ground. He always kept his poise   35
To the top branches, climbing carefully

With the same pains you use to fill a cup
Up to the brim, and even above the brim.
Then he flung outward, feet first, with a swish,
Kicking his way down through the air to the ground.   40
So was I once myself a swinger of birches.
And so I dream of going back to be.
It's when I'm weary of considerations,
And life is too much like a pathless wood
Where your face burns and tickles with the cobwebs   45
Broken across it, and one eye is weeping
From a twig's having lashed across it open.
I'd like to get away from earth awhile
And then come back to it and begin over.
May no fate willfully misunderstand me   50
And half grant what I wish and snatch me away
Not to return. Earth's the right place for love:
I don't know where it's likely to go better.
I'd like to go by climbing a birch tree,
And climb black branches up a snow-white trunk   55
Toward heaven, till the tree could bear no more,
But dipped its top and set me down again.
That would be good both going and coming back.
One could do worse than be a swinger of birches.

EXPLORATIONS

Before reading

1. Have you ever climbed a tree? Discuss your experience, explaining where you were, how difficult it was and what skills you needed to climb up and down.

First reading

2. On a first reading, what do you see? Visualise the trees, the ice, the sky and the boy. What sounds can you hear? Are there any other details you should include?

3. What images caught your imagination?

4. How would you describe the general mood of the poem?

Second reading

5. Based on the details given by Frost, describe the character of the boy.

6. Would you agree that the boy is a skilled climber? What details support this point of view?

7. Do you think that the speaker really intends to climb trees again? What makes him long to be a 'swinger of birches' once more?

8. What do you understand by the line 'And life is too much like a pathless wood'?

9. Is the speaker's wish to escape from earth a death wish? Explain your answer.

10. Explain clearly what you think Frost means in the last eight lines of the poem.

Third reading

11. Frost uses the image of girls drying their hair in the sun. Why? How effective is this image?

Third reading continued

12. 'One could do worse than be a swinger of birches'. Does the poet present a convincing argument in support of this claim?

13. How does Frost achieve a conversational tone in the poem? Why does he adopt this voice?

Fourth reading

14. In what way do the boy's actions resemble those of a poet?

15. How does the music in the poem – sounds, metre, etc. – contribute to the atmosphere?

16. Comment on the poet's contrasting use of light and darkness.

17. 'Though much of Frost's poetry is concerned with suffering, he is also capable of capturing moments of unearthly beauty and joy in his work.' Comment on the poem in the light of this statement.

'Out, Out –'

this poem is also prescribed for Ordinary Level exams in 2011 and 2012

The buzz-saw snarled and rattled in the yard
And made dust and dropped stove-length sticks of wood,
Sweet-scented stuff when the breeze drew across it.
And from there those that lifted eyes could count

Five mountain ranges one behind the other   5
Under the sunset far into Vermont.
And the saw snarled and rattled, snarled and rattled,
As it ran light, or had to bear a load.
And nothing happened: day was all but done.
Call it a day, I wish they might have said   10
To please the boy by giving him the half hour
That a boy counts so much when saved from work.
His sister stood beside them in her apron
To tell them 'Supper'. At the word, the saw,
As if to prove saws knew what supper meant,   15
Leaped out at the boy's hand, or seemed to leap –
He must have given the hand. However it was,
Neither refused the meeting. But the hand!
The boy's first outcry was a rueful laugh,
As he swung toward them holding up the hand   20
Half in appeal, but half as if to keep
The life from spilling. Then the boy saw all –
Since he was old enough to know, big boy
Doing a man's work, though a child at heart –
He saw all spoiled. 'Don't let him cut my hand off –   25
The doctor, when he comes. Don't let him, sister!'
So. But the hand was gone already.
The doctor put him in the dark of ether.
He lay and puffed his lips out with his breath.
And then – the watcher at his pulse took fright.   30
No one believed. They listened at his heart.
Little – less – nothing! – and that ended it.
No more to build on there. And they, since they
Were not the one dead, turned to their affairs.

Notes

'Out, Out –': the title is taken from William Shakespeare's
famous tragedy *Macbeth*. 'Out, Out brief candle; life's but a
walking shadow, a poor player that struts and frets his hour
upon the stage, and then is heard no more: it is a tale told
by an idiot, full of sound and fury, signifying nothing.'

[28]   **ether:** an anaesthetic

EXPLORATIONS

First reading

1. Read the poem aloud. What words and phrases made the greatest impact on your ear? What animals are suggested in the opening line? How are these animals evoked?

2. Why does Frost describe the scenery?

3. Frost refers repeatedly to 'they' and 'them'. Who do you think these people are? What is your impression of them?

4. The poem turns on the word 'supper'. What happens? Is it an appropriate word in the context?

5. 'He saw all spoiled'. In what sense is all spoiled?

6. What is the boy's immediate fear? Refer to the poem to support your answer.

Second reading

7. Trace the narrative line in this poem. Were you surprised by the ending? Do you think it is an effective conclusion?

8. Comment on the title. Is it a suitable one? Could you suggest another?

Second reading continued

9. 'Little – less – nothing!' Read this line aloud and comment on the rhythm. What is the effect of the exclamation mark?

Third reading

10. How effectively does the poet evoke the terror felt by the boy? Examine the techniques used by Frost in your answer.

11. Would you describe the poet as a detached or a sympathetic observer? Is he angered by the incident? How do we know? Comment on the tone.

12. How does the poet engage the reader's sympathies for the boy? Examine the details given, the use of emotive language and the comments made throughout the poem.

Fourth reading

13. What themes and issues are explored in the poem?

14. Sound plays an important role in the poem. Examine the use of assonance, alliteration and onomatopoeia in 'Out, Out –'.

15. 'In his poetry, Frost confronts the reader with the harsh realities of life.' Discuss this statement, in the light of your reading of this poem.

16. Identify and discuss some of the distinctive qualities of Frost's style that are evident in this poem.

The Road Not Taken

Two roads diverged in a yellow wood,
And sorry I could not travel both
And be one traveler, long I stood
And looked down one as far as I could
To where it bent in the undergrowth;   5

Then took the other, as just as fair,
And having perhaps the better claim,
Because it was grassy and wanted wear;
Though as for that the passing there
Had worn them really about the same,   10

And both that morning equally lay
In leaves no step had trodden black.
Oh, I kept the first for another day!
Yet knowing how way leads on to way,
I doubted if I should ever come back.   15

I shall be telling this with a sigh
Somewhere ages and ages hence:
Two roads diverged in a wood, and I –
I took the one less traveled by,
And that has made all the difference.   20

A Road through Belvedere, Vermont: painting by Thomas W. Whittredge (1820–1910)

EXPLORATIONS

First reading

1. On a first reading, what do you notice about the setting of the poem? What details made the deepest impression on you? Explain.

2. What is the main focus of the speaker's attention throughout the poem?

3. Why does he choose the second road? Are his reasons convincing?

4. Why will the speaker talk about this moment 'ages and ages hence'?

First reading continued

5. What is the difference referred to by Frost in the last line?

Second reading

6. Comment on the title of the poem. What does it lead you to expect? Does the poem fulfil your expectations?

7. On a surface level the speaker is faced with a choice between two paths. On a deeper level what do the roads symbolise?

8. What is the dominant mood of the poem? What words, phrases and images suggest this mood?

Third reading

9. What images create an autumnal atmosphere in the poem? Why did Frost choose this time of year?

10. What themes or issues can you identify in 'The Road Not Taken'?

11. Do you find the imagery in this poem effective in conveying the theme? Refer to specific images in your answer.

12. The poem opens and closes on a note of regret. Trace the development of thought and mood throughout the poem.

Fourth reading

13. Doubt is replaced by certainty in this poem. Examine the movement from one state to the other.

14. What appeals to you about this poem? Consider the theme, images, sounds, and particular words or phrases, in your answer.

Spring Pools

These pools that, though in forests, still reflect
The total sky almost without defect,
And like the flowers beside them, chill and shiver,
Will like the flowers beside them soon be gone,
And yet not out by any brook or river,   5
But up by roots to bring dark foliage on.

The trees that have it in their pent-up buds
To darken nature and be summer woods –
Let them think twice before they use their powers
To blot out and drink up and sweep away   10
These flowery waters and these watery flowers
From snow that melted only yesterday.

[6] **foliage:** the leaves of a tree or plant

EXPLORATIONS

First reading

1. What do the pools and the flowers have in common?

2. What do you notice about the trees? What characteristic of the trees does the poet focus on, especially in the second stanza? Why?

3. Why should the trees think twice before they drain the pools and overshadow the flowers?

Second reading

4. Outline the argument of the poem. Would you agree that it is condensed with considerable skill? What is the effect of this on the reader?

5. What image made the greatest impression on you? Explain your choice.

6. How important are the sounds of words in creating the atmosphere in this poem?

Third reading

7. What mood is evoked by this scene? How is this mood created?

8. 'The beauty of this poem lies in the aptness of the descriptions and the clarity of the language.' Do you agree? Explain your answer.

Fourth reading

9. Fragility and strength are contrasted in the poem. Where is this contrast most evident? What is the effect? How is this effect achieved?

10. Discuss the techniques Frost uses in this poem to depict the changing nature of the world. Support your answer by quotation or reference.

11. 'Frost is a master of the lyric form, his images are sensuous, his language clear and his tone controlled.' Examine 'Spring Pools' in the light of this statement.

12. Give your personal reaction to the poem.

Acquainted with the Night

I have been one acquainted with the night.
I have walked out in rain – and back in rain.
I have outwalked the furthest city light.

I have looked down the saddest city lane.
I have passed by the watchman on his beat   5
And dropped my eyes, unwilling to explain.

I have stood still and stopped the sound of feet
When far away an interrupted cry
Came over houses from another street,

But not to call me back or say good-bye;   10
And further still at an unearthly height,
One luminary clock against the sky

Proclaimed the time was neither wrong nor right.
I have been one acquainted with the night.

Note

[12] **luminary:** something that gives light, especially a heavenly body

EXPLORATIONS

First reading

1. Describe the scene in your own words.

2. Examine the images used. What do they have in common? Do they provide an insight as to the central idea of the poem?

3. How would you describe the poet's mood?

Second reading

4. What do you think is the main theme of the poem? Explain your answer.

5. Do you think the imagery used is effective in illustrating the theme? Which images are most appropriate, in your opinion?

6. What feelings does the poem arouse in you? How does it do this?

Third reading

7. What do you notice about the verbs in the poem? In what tense is it written? What purpose might this serve?

8. This poem can be read at more than one level. Suggest another reading of 'Acquainted With the Night'.

Fourth reading

9. Note the repetitions in the poem. What effect do they have?

10. How does Frost evoke the atmosphere of the urban landscape?

11. There is a deep sense of isolation in this poem. Do you agree? Where is it most evident, in your opinion?

12. '"Acquainted With the Night" is a tribute to the triumph of the human spirit in the face of adversity, rather than a record of the defeat of the soul at its darkest hour.' Discuss the poem in the light of this statement.

Design

I found a dimpled spider, fat and white,
On a white heal-all, holding up a moth
Like a white piece of rigid satin cloth –
Assorted characters of death and blight
Mixed ready to begin the morning right,   5
Like the ingredients of a witches' broth –
A snow-drop spider, a flower like a froth,
And dead wings carried like a paper kite.

What had that flower to do with being white,
The wayside blue and innocent heal-all?   10
What brought the kindred spider to that height,
Then steered the white moth thither in the night?
What but design of darkness to appall? –
If design govern in a thing so small.

Note

[2] **heal-all:** a common flower, used for medicinal purposes, usually blue or violet in colour

EXPLORATIONS

First reading

1. What do you normally associate with the word 'dimpled'?

2. What images in the octave captured your attention? What do they suggest about the subject matter of the poem?

3. The poet raises several issues in the sestet. What are these issues and what conclusion, if any, does he reach?

4. Jot down the words or phrases that best describe your response to this poem on a first reading.

Provide, Provide

The witch that came (the withered hag)
To wash the steps with pail and rag
Was once the beauty Abishag,

The picture pride of Hollywood.
Too many fall from great and good   5
For you to doubt the likelihood.

Die early and avoid the fate.
Or if predestined to die late,
Make up your mind to die in state.

Make whole stock exchange your own! 10
If need be occupy a throne,
Where nobody can call you crone.

Some have relied on what they knew,
Others on being simply true.
What worked for them might work for you. 15

No memory of having starred
Atones for later disregard
Or keeps the end from being hard.

Better to go down dignified
With boughten friendship at your side 20
Than none at all. Provide, provide!

Notes

[1]   **hag:** an ugly old woman, a witch
[3]   **Abishag:** (I Kings 1:2–4) 'Having searched for a beautiful
      girl throughout the territory of Israel, they found Abishag
      of Shunem and brought her to the king. The girl was of
      great beauty. She looked after the king and waited on
      him . . .'
[12] **crone:** a withered old woman

EXPLORATIONS

Before reading

1.   Read the title only. Jot down
     what you imagine the poem
     is about before reading the
     poem itself.

First reading

2.   The idea that youth rapidly
     fades is introduced in the
     opening stanza. What images
     convey this?

3.   What advice does Frost offer as
     to how to avoid the worst
     aspects of old age?

4. How can one avoid being called a 'crone'?

5. Imagine you are the old woman in the poem. Write your response to 'Provide, Provide'.

Second reading

6. Can memories offer comfort to the old?

7. Has 'boughten friendship' any advantages according to the poet? What is his tone here?

8. What do you think is meant by the title of the poem?

Third reading

9. Is the poem intended to teach us a lesson? Comment on the moral.

10. Do you think Frost is being serious or humorous here? Examine the tone throughout the poem.

Fourth reading

11. Do you think there is an important theme in the poem? Explain your answer.

12. Examine the contrasts in the poem. State what they are and whether or not you think they are effective.

13. Did you enjoy this poem? Why?

14. 'Realism rather than pessimism is a hallmark of Frost's poetry.' Discuss this statement in the light of your reading of this poem.

7 *Patrick Kavanagh*
1904–1967

prescribed for Higher Level exams in 2011 and 2012

Patrick Kavanagh was born on 21 October 1904. He was the fourth child and the eldest son of James and Bridget (née Quinn) born in the townland of Mucker, Inniskeen parish, County Monaghan. From the age of twelve Kavanagh started writing verse and collected it in a copybook. His brother Peter later published this juvenilia in his *Collected Poems*. Kavanagh was keen to use the things around him in his poems, no matter how mundane they might seem to others. Regular trips to Dundalk brought him into contact with literature, especially with the literary journals of the time, such as *Poetry* and the *Irish Statesman*. He entered the joint trades of cobbler and small farmer, like his father before him, but also began to see himself as someone different from the regular farmers. He now began to see himself as a poet.

His first volume of poetry, *Ploughman and Other Poems*, was published in 1936. It contained many of the ideas that would remain central to his poetry for the rest of his life. His poetry in this book examined not only his surrounding area but also poetry itself, the nature of the poet and the creative act. In 1939, Kavanagh made a major change to his life by giving up farming and concentrating on writing as a career, moving to live in Dublin in the process. He wrote a number of regular columns as well as book and film reviews at the time. As well as his poetry he also produced a novel, *Tarry Flynn*. He also ventured into publishing, producing a newspaper called *Kavanagh's Weekly* in 1952. Its stated purpose was 'to introduce the critical constructive note into Irish thought'. Kavanagh put every aspect of Irish life under scrutiny. The newspaper was both loved and hated at the time. Kavanagh himself was put under scrutiny later that year when an article in *The Leader* criticised his work. He sued *The Leader* for libel but lost. Soon after this period, he entered the Rialto hospital with lung cancer. Against great odds, he made a heroic recovery and spent the summer of 1955 regaining his strength on the banks of the Grand Canal in Dublin. He described this period as his 'rebirth'. Kavanagh's health began to decline again in the late 1950s. He returned to journalism. On 19 April 1967 he married Katherine Moloney, whom he had known for a number of years, and on 30 November in that year he died at the age of sixty-three.

Inniskeen Road: July Evening

The bicycles go by in twos and threes –
There's a dance in Billy Brennan's barn tonight,
And there's the half-talk code of mysteries
And the wink-and-elbow language of delight.
Half-past eight and there is not a spot   5
Upon a mile of road, no shadow thrown
That might turn out a man or woman, not
A footfall tapping secrecies of stone.

I have what every poet hates in spite
Of all the solemn talk of contemplation.   10
Oh, Alexander Selkirk knew the plight
Of being king and government and nation.
A road, a mile of kingdom, I am king
Of banks and stones and every blooming thing.

Billy Brennan's barn, Inniskeen, County Monaghan

EXPLORATIONS

First reading

1. What does the 'wink-and-elbow language of delight' mean? Do you think this is an appropriate phrase? Why?

2. Write a dialogue between some of the inhabitants of Billy Brennan's barn.

3. The poet names specific places and people in the poem. What effect does this have?

4. Who was Alexander Selkirk? Why does the poet compare himself to him?

5. Do you think that Kavanagh would forgo being a poet in order to fit in with the crowd? Discuss this.

Second reading

6. The poet uses a good deal of alliteration in the first quatrain. What is the effect of this?

7. Do you see any changes in the language used in the three sections? Would you agree that there are different voices in the poem? Who is the focus of each section?

8. The word 'blooming' has two meanings in the poem. What are they?

Third reading

9. Compare the rhythm of the first quatrain with that of the second. Do you see any major changes? What effect does this have on the development of the poem?

10. Compare the rhythm of the first quatrain with that of the second. Do you see any major changes? How do the vowel sounds contribute to this?

11. Trace the development of thought in the poem over the first and second quatrains and the sestet.

Fourth reading

12. Imagine that the last line of this poem had never been written. How would it change your reading of the whole poem?

13. What is your image of the typical poet? Does Kavanagh, in this poem, fit this?

14. Would you agree with the assertion that 'Kavanagh is a whingeing self-pitying introvert who wants to have his cake and eat it'?

Epic

I have lived in important places, times
When great events were decided: who owned
That half a rood of rock, a no-man's land
Surrounded by our pitchfork-armed claims.
I heard the Duffys shouting 'Damn your soul'   5
And old McCabe stripped to the waist, seen
Step the plot defying blue cast-steel –
'Here is the march along these iron stones'
That was the year of the Munich bother. Which
Was most important? I inclined   10
To lose my faith in Ballyrush and Gortin
Till Homer's ghost came whispering to my mind
He said: I made the *Iliad* from such
A local row. Gods make their own importance.

Notes

[8] **march:** boundary
[9] **Munich bother:** 1939
[11] **Ballyrush and Gortin:** townlands in County Monaghan
[12] **Homer:** a Greek poet
[13] ***Iliad:*** an 'epic' poem by Homer

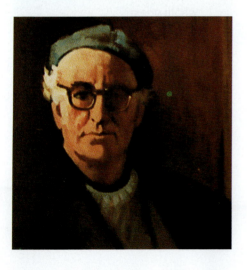

Explorations

Before reading

1. Think about the title. What is an epic? What might you expect the poem to deal with?

First reading

2. What is the argument about? Does it seem important to you? Can you see how it could be important to others?

3. Do the people who are arguing seem to be reasonable? Describe what you imagine them to look like. Write a dialogue that either side might have among themselves.

4. Write a newspaper report on the argument.

5. What does Kavanagh mean by the 'Munich bother'? What does his attitude towards it seem to be?

6. What is his attitude towards the people of the village?

Second reading

7. The first line sounds very portentous. Do you think it is effective?

8. Examine the 'war' imagery that he uses. What does it suggest to you? Write about this.

9. The narrator changes his mind halfway through the poem. What do you notice about this change?

Third reading

10. Comment on the poet's use of irony.

Fourth reading

11. Do you think that the last line summarises the whole poem? In your own words, write about the theme.

12. In an epic poem there is often a hero. Is there one in this poem? Discuss this.

Shancoduff

this poem is also prescribed for Ordinary Level exams in 2011 and 2012

My black hills have never seen the sun rising,
Eternally they look north towards Armagh.
Lot's wife would not be salt if she had been
Incurious as my black hills that are happy
When dawn whitens Glassdrummond chapel.   5

My hills hoard the bright shillings of March
While the sun searches in every pocket.
They are my Alps and I have climbed the Matterhorn
With a sheaf of hay for three perishing calves
In the field under the Big Forth of Rocksavage.   10

The sleety winds fondle the rushy beards of Shancoduff
While the cattle-drovers sheltering in the Featherna Bush
Look up and say: 'Who owns them hungry hills
That the water-hen and snipe must have forsaken?
A poet? Then by heavens he must be poor.'   15
I hear and is my heart not badly shaken?

Notes

[10]	**Rocksavage:**	places in County Monaghan near the poet's father's farm
[11]	**Shancoduff:**	
[12]	**Featherna Bush:**	

EXPLORATIONS

First reading

1. The title of the poem is taken from the name of the place where Kavanagh's family had a farm. It is derived from two Irish words; 'Sean' and 'Dubh'. Do you know what these words mean? If not, find out. What sort of a place would you expect from such a name?

Second reading

2. How does Kavanagh describe this place? Draw a picture or describe the scene in your own words as you imagine it.

3. What is the cattle-drover's attitude to the hills?

4. What is the poet's reaction to this?

Third reading

5. The poet personifies the place. How does he do this? What effect does it have?

6. He names a lot of specific places in the poem, e.g. Glassdrummond, Featherna, Rocksavage. Why does he do this?

7. He repeatedly uses the possessive 'my' when talking about the hills. What does it tell us about the narrator?

8. Do you think the cattle drovers place any value on poetry? Examine their words carefully.

Fourth reading

9. In an earlier version of the poem, Kavanagh used the word 'faith' instead of the word 'heart' in the last line of the poem. Why do you think he made that change? What effect does it have? Do you think that it was a good change to make?

10. In another poem Kavanagh says that 'Naming a thing is the love act and the pledge.' Relate that statement to 'Shancoduff'.

11. 'Shancoduff is a love poem.' Do you agree?

The Great Hunger

I

Clay is the word and clay is the flesh
Where the potato-gatherers like mechanized scare-crows move
Along the side-fall of the hill – Maguire and his men.
If we watch them an hour is there anything we can prove
Of life as it is broken-backed over the Book   5
Of Death? Here crows gabble over worms and frogs
And the gulls like old newspapers are blown clear of the hedges, luckily.
Is there some light of imagination in these wet clods?
Or why do we stand here shivering?
    Which of these men   10
Loved the light and the queen
Too long virgin? Yesterday was summer. Who was itpromised marriage to himself
Before apples were hung from the ceilings for Hallowe'en?
We will wait and watch the tragedy to the last curtain
Till the last soul passively like a bag of wet clay   15
Rolls down the side of the hill, diverted by the angles
Where the plough missed or a spade stands, straitening the way.

A dog lying on a torn jacket under a heeled-up cart,
A horse nosing along the posied headland, trailing
A rusty plough. Three heads hanging between wide-apart   20
Legs. October playing a symphony on a slack wire paling.
Maguire watches the drills flattened out
And the flints that lit a candle for him on a June altar
Flameless. The drills slipped by and the days slipped by
And he trembled his head away and ran free from the world's halter,   25
And thought himself wiser than any man in the townland
When he laughed over pints of porter
Of how he came free from every net spread
In the gaps of experience. He shook a knowing head
And pretended to his soul   30
That children are tedious in hurrying fields of April
Where men are spanging across wide furrows.
Lost in the passion that never needs a wife –

The pricks that pricked were the pointed pins of harrows.
Children scream so loud that the crows could bring   35
The seed of an acre away with crow-rude jeers.
Patrick Maguire, he called his dog and he flung a stone in the air
And hallooed the birds away that were the birds of the years.
Turn over the weedy clods and tease out the tangled skeins.
What is he looking for there?   40
He thinks it is a potato, but we know better
Than his mud-gloved fingers probe in this insensitive hair.

'Move forward the basket and balance it steady
In this hollow. Pull down the shafts of that cart, Joe,
And straddle the horse,' Maguire calls.   45
'The wind's over Brannagan's, now that means rain.
Graip up some withered stalks and see that no potato falls
Over the tail-board going down the ruckety pass –
And that's a job we'll have to do in December,
Gravel it and build a kerb on the bog-side. Is that Cassidy's ass

                                                                                       50
Out in my clover? Curse o' God –
Where is that dog?
Never where he's wanted.' Maguire grunts and spits
Through a clay-wattled moustache and stares about him from the height.
His dream changes again like the cloud-swung wind   55
And he is not so sure now if his mother was right
When she praised the man who made a field his bride.

Watch him, watch him, that man on a hill whose spirit
Is a wet sack flapping about the knees of time.
He lives that his little fields may stay fertile when his own body   60
Is spread in the bottom of a ditch under two coulters crossed in Christ's Name.

He was suspicious in his youth as a rat near strange bread
When girls laughed; when they screamed he knew that meant
The cry of fillies in season. He could not walk
The easy road to his destiny. He dreamt   65
The innocence of young brambles to hooked treachery.

O the grip, O the grip of irregular fields! No man escapes.
It could not be that back of the hills love was free
And ditches straight.
No monster hand lifted up children and put down apes   70
As here
     'O God if I had been wiser!'
That was his sigh like the brown breeze in the thistles.
He looks towards his house and haggard. 'O God if I had been wiser!'
But now a crumpled leaf from the whitethorn bushes   75
Darts like a frightened robin, and the fence
Shows the green of after-grass through a little window,
And he knows that his own heart is calling his mother a liar.
God's truth is life – even the grotesque shapes of its foulest fire.

The horse lifts its head and crashes   80
Through the whins and stones
To lip late passion in the crawling clover.
In the gap there's a bush weighted with boulders like morality,
The fools of life bleed if they climb over.

The wind leans from Brady's, and the coltsfoot leaves are holed with rust, 85
Rain fills the cart-tracks and the sole-plate grooves;
A yellow sun reflects in Donaghmoyne
The poignant light in light in puddles shaped by hooves.
Come with me, Imagination, into this iron house
And we will watch from the doorway the years run back,   90
And we will know that a peasant's left hand wrote on the page.
Be easy, October. No cackle hen, horse neigh, tree sough, duck quack.

Notes

[32] **spanging:** long fast steps
[34] **harrows:** spiked frame for smoothing land
[61] **coulter:** the iron cutter at the front of a ploughshare
[87] **Donaghmoyne:** a townland in County Monaghan

EXPLORATIONS

Before reading

1. What do you think of the title of the poem? Comment on the poet's use of the word 'Great'.

First reading

2. From reading the poem, how do you visualise Patrick Maguire? What age do you think he might be? What do you think he looks like? How does he live, etc.?

3. Write a diary for one day in the life of Patrick Maguire.

4. The poem describes a man and his physical environment. What is the relationship between the two? Describe his environment in your own words.

5. Can you find any indications in the poem of Maguire's attitude to women?

6. Maguire complains about children in the poem. Do you think that this represents his complete attitude toward children?

7. To what extent does Maguire attempt justification for his current position?

Second reading

8. What do you think of the poem's narrator? Is he sympathetic? Is he biased? Is he patronising, etc.?

9. In the fourth verse of the poem, Maguire speaks. Compare the impression that we get of him here with the impression we get from the narrator.

10. 'There is a difference between the life lived and the life wished for.' Do you think that this statement is true for Patrick Maguire? How is this conveyed to us?

Third reading

11. Late autumn is mentioned a number of times throughout the poem. What do you think is the significance of this image?

12. A number of religious metaphors are used in the poem. Explain what each one refers to. What is their overall effect?

13. At the beginning of the poem, the sounds of the words are very harsh. Comment on some of the sounds and words used to give this harsh tone.

Fourth reading

14. Do you think that the poem as a whole could be an allegory for 1930s and 1940s Ireland? Explain your answer.

15. If a similar poem was being written about contemporary Ireland, do you think its concerns would be the same? What would its concerns be? What type of imagery would it use?

16. Do you think that the phrase 'God's truth is life' could be an apt summary of the whole poem?

Fourth reading continued

17. Kavanagh paints a portrait of Patrick Maguire. It has been said that he does not paint a still life but rather uses a 'cinematic technique'. Using examples from the poem, explain what you think is meant by this.

Fifth reading

18. This is part one of a longer poem. Where do you think the poem will go from here?

A Christmas Childhood

this poem is also prescribed for Ordinary Level exams in 2011 and 2012

One side of the potato-pits was white with frost –
How wonderful that was, how wonderful!
And when we put our ears to the paling-post
The music that came out was magical.

The light between the ricks of hay and straw   5
Was a hole in Heaven's gable. An apple tree
With its December-glinting fruit we saw –
O you, Eve, were the world that tempted me

To eat the knowledge that grew in clay
And death the germ within it! Now and then   10
I can remember something of the gay
Garden that was childhood's. Again

The tracks of cattle to a drinking-place,
A green stone lying sideways in a ditch
Or any common sight the transfigured face   15
Of a beauty that the world did not touch.

                            II
My father played the melodion
Outside at our gate;
There were stars in the morning east
And they danced to his music.   20

Across the wild bogs his melodion called
To Lennons and Callans.
As I pulled on my trousers in a hurry
I knew some strange thing had happened.

Outside in the cow-house my mother   25
Made the music of milking;
The light of her stable-lamp was a star
And the frost of Bethlehem made it twinkle.

A water-hen screeched in the bog,
Mass-going feet   30
Crunched the wafer-ice on the pot-holes,
Somebody wistfully twisted the bellows wheel.

My child poet picked out the letters
On the grey stone,
In silver the wonder of a Christmas townland,   35
The winking glitter of a frosty dawn.

Cassiopeia was over
Cassidy's hanging hill,
I looked and three whin bushes rode across
The horizon – the Three Wise Kings.   40

An old man passing said:
'Can't he make it talk' –
The melodion. I hid in the doorway
And tightened the belt of my box-pleated coat.

I nicked six nicks on the door-post   45
With my penknife's big blade –
There was a little one for cutting tobacco.
And I was six Christmases of age.

My father played the melodion,
My mother milked the cows,   50
And I had a prayer like a white rose pinned
On the Virgin Mary's blouse.

Notes

[17,21,43, 49] **melodion:** a small accordion
[37]   **Cassiopeia:** a northern constellation

EXPLORATIONS

Before reading

1. The first part of the poem is an evocation of the poet's memories of his own childhood. What are your memories of Christmas time when you were young?

First reading

2. Do you think that the narrator had a happy childhood? What are his happiest memories?

3. What sort of child do you think he was, according to the evidence in this poem? Discuss this.

4. Why does the narrator compare his village with Bethlehem?

5. What is the relationship between the narrator and nature?

Second reading

6. Show how Kavanagh uses religious imagery throughout the poem. What effect does it have? Does the imagery change as the poem progresses?

7. What type of voice does the narrator use: an adult voice, child's voice or what? Read it aloud.

8. There is awe for the innocence of the past in this poem. Where and how is this conveyed?

Third reading

9. How does Kavanagh make the ordinary seem wondrous and extraordinary?

Fourth reading

10. What is the narrator's standing in relation to everybody else in the poem?

11. What does this poem say about childhood?

Advent

We have tested and tasted too much, lover –
Through a chink too wide there comes in no wonder.
But here in this Advent-darkened room
Where the dry black bread and the sugarless tea
Of penance will charm back the luxury   5
Of a child's soul, we'll return to Doom
The knowledge we stole but could not use.

And the newness that was in every stale thing
When we looked at it as children: the spirit-shocking
Wonder in a black slanting Ulster hill   10
Or the prophetic astonishment in the tedious talking
Of an old fool will awake for us and bring
You and me to the yard gate to watch the whins
And the bog-holes, cart-tracks, old stables where Time begins.

O after Christmas we'll have no need to go searching   15
For the difference that sets an old phrase burning –
We'll hear it in the whispered argument of a churning
Or in the streets where the village boys are lurching.
And we'll hear it among simple decent men too
Who barrow dung in gardens under trees,   20
Wherever life pours ordinary plenty.
Won't we be rich, my love and I, and please
God we shall not ask for reason's payment,
The why of heart-breaking strangeness in dreeping hedges
Nor analyse God's breath in common statement.   25
We have thrown into the dust-bin the clay-minted wages
Of pleasure, knowledge and the conscious hour –
And Christ comes with a January flower.

EXPLORATIONS

Before reading

1. What do you know about 'Advent'? Share ideas.

First reading

2. The first line would suggest that the speaker has experienced a great many of the pleasures of the world. What is the disadvantage of this, as he outlines it in the second line? Explain this in your own words.

3. What is the speaker's personal plan for Advent and what is its purpose? Explore lines 2–6. What phrase do you think best sums up his goal? Discuss this.

4. What change does the speaker hope or expect will follow from this period of penance? Read the remainder of the poem again and list the main changes.

5. What is your understanding of the effect of 'penance'? Is the speaker's understanding different? Discuss this.

6. Who do you think the lover is? What leads you to this conclusion?

Second reading

7. Comment on the religious imagery used in the poem.

8. The poem is made up of two sonnets. Is the tone different in each? How?

9. The poet talks about money throughout the poem. What is wealth to him?

Third reading

10. What does the image of a January flower represent for you?

11. Write about the other images and sounds that the poet finds exciting. Do they have anything in common?

12. What is the poet's attitude to God?

Fourth reading

13. '"Advent" expresses a belief that poetry depends on the poet's attitude to the world.' Do you agree?

14. Picasso said that all artists should strive to reach a state of 'childlikeness'. Based on this poem, do you think Kavanagh would agree?

15. 'This poem is really Kavanagh's manifesto for his own poetry.' Do you agree? Where is this evident?

16. The poem was originally entitled 'Renewal'. Which title do you prefer? Which is the more appropriate?

On Raglan Road

(Air: 'The Dawning of the Day')

On Raglan Road on an autumn day I met her first and knew
That her dark hair would weave a snare that I might one day rue;
I saw the danger, yet I walked along the enchanted way,
And I said, let grief be a fallen leaf at the dawning of the day.

On Grafton Street in November we tripped lightly along the ledge   5
Of the deep ravine where can be seen the worth of passion's pledge,
The Queen of Hearts still making tarts and I not making hay –
O I loved too much and by such by such is happiness thrown away.

I gave her gifts of the mind I gave her the secret sign that's known
To the artists who have known the true gods of sound and stone   10
And word and tint. I did not stint for I gave her poems to say
With her own name there and her own dark hair like clouds over fields of May.

On a quiet street where old ghosts meet I see her walking now
Away from me so hurriedly my reason must allow
That I had wooed not as I should a creature made of clay –   15
When the angel woos the clay he'd lose his wings at the dawn of day.

Note

[1]   **Raglan Road:** a street off Pembroke Road in Ballsbridge, Dublin. Kavanagh lived on Pembroke Road from 1946 to 1958. After that he lived at 19 Raglan Road.

'On Raglan Road on an autumn day'

EXPLORATIONS

First reading

1. What is the relationship between the poet and the dark-haired woman? What was their relationship?
2. What is the poet's attitude to love and courtship?
3. Was there an equal relationship?
4. How does he think he scared her off? What do you think?

Second reading

5. This poem is also a popular song. Are there any elements of the poem that make this obvious?

Third reading

6. Do you think that he's telling the truth when he says that he 'loved too much'?
7. Trace the images of nature in the poem.
8. What effect does he create by putting rhymes in the middle of lines?
9. What part does time play in the poem?

Fourth reading

10. Do you think that the phrase 'it takes two to tango' ever occurred to Kavanagh?
11. Is the poet a misogynist?

The Hospital

A year ago I fell in love with the functional ward
Of a chest hospital: square cubicles in a row
Plain concrete, wash basins – an art lover's woe,
Not counting how the fellow in the next bed snored.
But nothing whatever is by love debarred,   5
The common and banal her heat can know.
The corridor led to a stairway and below
Was the inexhaustible adventure of a gravelled yard.

This is what love does to things: the Rialto Bridge,
The main gate that was bent by a heavy lorry,   10
The seat at the back of a shed that was a suntrap.
Naming these things is the love-act and its pledge;
For we must record love's mystery without claptrap,
Snatch out of time the passionate transitory.

Rialto Hospital

EXPLORATIONS

Before reading

1. What feelings surface when you hear the word 'hospital'? Now what is your immediate reaction to the first line and a half?

First reading

2. What does Kavanagh find beautiful about the hospital?

3. Try to sketch out where things in the poem are physically in relation to each other.

4. The poet thinks that adventure in a 'gravelled yard' could be inexhaustible. Do you agree with him?

5. What do you think the poet means in lines 5 and 6? Discuss your interpretation.

Second reading

6. The tone of the poem is dominated by broad vowel sounds. What effect does this have?

7. What effect do the sounds at the end of the poem have? Describe these sounds.

Third reading

8. According to this poem, what does love do to things?

9. How does the poet use the conventions of the sonnet to make the points that he wants to make?

Fourth reading

10. Do you think that this poem actually does 'record love's mystery without claptrap'?

11. Is Kavanagh's poetic manifesto as shown in this poem put into practice in any of his other poems? If so, where?

12. Is the poet at ease with himself? Share your views on this.

Canal Bank Walk

Leafy-with-love banks and the green water of the canal
Pouring redemption for me, that I do
The will of God, wallow in the habitual, the banal
Grow with nature again as before I grew.
The bright stick trapped, the breeze adding a third   5
Party to the couple kissing on an old seat,
And a bird gathering materials for the nest for the Word
Eloquently new and abandoned to its delirious beat.
O unworn world enrapture me, encapture me in a web
Of fabulous grass and eternal voices by a beech,   10
Feed the gaping need of my senses, give me ad lib
To pray unselfconsciously with overflowing speech
For this soul needs to be honoured with a new dress woven
From green and blue things and arguments that cannot be proven.

The Grand Canal, Dublin

EXPLORATIONS

First reading

1. How does he set the scene?
2. What does Kavanagh want from God?

Second reading

3. How does Kavanagh use sound to express his mood in the first quatrain?
4. What is the relationship between nature and humans in the poem?
5. How important is the image of water in the poem?
6. What tense is the poem set in? Why is this important?
7. How does he use internal rhyme to set his mood and theme?
8. Go through the images by the canal bank – the twig, the couple, etc. – and show how they could relate to the poet's own state.

Third reading

9. The sestet has been described as a hymn. Explain how someone could come to this conclusion.
10. How does the narrator see himself?
11. In order to make sense the reader must often continue on from the end of one line into the next. What is the effect of these 'run-on' lines?
12. Where is God in the poem? How does the poet understand God and His place in the world?

Lines Written on a Seat on the Grand Canal, Dublin

'Erected to the Memory of Mrs Dermot O'Brien'

O commemorate me where there is water,
Canal water preferably, so stilly
Greeny at the heart of summer. Brother
Commemorate me thus beautifully
Where by a lock niagarously roars   5
The falls for those who sit in the tremendous silence
Of mid-July. No one will speak in prose
Who finds his way to these Parnassian islands.
A swan goes by head low with many apologies,
Fantastic light looks through the eyes of bridges –   10
And look! a barge comes bringing from Athy
And other far-flung towns mythologies.
O commemorate me with no hero-courageous
Tomb – just a canal-bank seat for the passer-by.

Notes		
	[8]	**Parnassian:** of Parnassus; a mountain in Greece sacred to Apollo and the muses
	[11]	**Athy:** a town in the Midlands

Patrick Kavanagh's Memorial Seat, Grand Canal, Dublin

EXPLORATIONS

First reading

1. Where exactly is this poem situated? What kind of place do you think it is, from what we are shown in the poem? What makes it so attractive?

2. What mood is the poet in? What words or phrases suggest this?

Second reading

3. There is both movement and stillness in the poem. How does the poet reconcile these?

4. Do you think that Kavanagh is very much aware of his own mortality in this poem? Discuss this.

5. Why does he not want a tomb?

6. What does his preferred form of commemoration suggest about the poet?

Third reading

7. Where does the poet use alliteration and what is its effect?

8. Explore his use of hyperbole. What atmosphere does it help to create in this poem?

9. In the first quatrain he uses 'y' sounds frequently. What do you think is the effect of this?

10. Kavanagh tends to use half-rhymes rather than full rhymes in this poem. Examine these and say what you think is the effect of this technique.

Fourth reading

11. In the poem how does Kavanagh see the place and function of the poet?

12. Do poets deserve commemoration? Does Kavanagh?

8 *Elizabeth Bishop*
1911–1979

prescribed for Higher Level exams in 2013 and 2014

Elizabeth Bishop was born on 8 February 1911 in Worcester, Massachusetts. Her father died when she was eight months old. Her mother never recovered from the shock and for the next five years was in and out of mental hospitals. In 1916 she was institutionalised and separated from her daughter, whom she was never to see again – she died in 1934. Elizabeth was reared for the most part by her grandparents in Great Village, Nova Scotia. The elegy 'First Death in Nova Scotia' draws on some childhood memories. 'Sestina' too evokes the sadness of this period. Yet her recollections of her Nova Scotia childhood were essentially positive and she had great affection for her maternal grandparents, aunts and uncles in this small agricultural village.

She went to boarding school and then attended Vassar College, a private university in New York, from 1930 to 1934. She graduated in English literature (but also took Greek and music), always retaining a particular appreciation for Renaissance lyric poetry and for the works of Gerard Manley Hopkins. It was at Vassar that she first began to publish stories and poems in national magazines and where she met the poet Marianne Moore, who became an important influence on her career as a poet and with whom she maintained a lifelong friendship and correspondence. It was also at Vassar that she formed her first lesbian relationship, and here too, on her own admission, her lifelong problem with alcohol addiction began.

In 1939 she moved to Key West, Florida, a place she had fallen in love with over the previous years. 'The Fish' reflects her enjoyment of the sport of fishing at that time. Key West became

'Cabin with Porthole', a watercolour by Elizabeth Bishop

a sort of refuge and base for Bishop over the next fifteen years. In 1945 she won the Houghton Mifflin Poetry Award. In 1946 her first book of poetry, *North and South*, was published and was well received by the critics. 'The Fish' is among its thirty poems.

The years 1945–1951, when her life was centred on New York, were very unsettled. She felt under extreme pressure in a very competitive literary circle and drank heavily. 'The Bight' and 'The Prodigal' reflect this dissolute period of her life.

In 1951 she left for South America on the first stage of a writer's trip round the world. She was fascinated by Brazil and by Lota Soares, on old acquaintance with whom she began a relationship that was to last until the latter's death in 1967. 'Questions of

Travel' and 'The Armadillo' reflect this period of her life. In 1970 she was appointed poet in residence at Harvard, where she taught advanced verse writing and studies in modern poetry for her first year and, later, poets and their letters. She began to do a good many public readings of her poetry to earn a living. She continued to do public readings, punctuated by spells in hospital with asthma, alcoholism and depression. She died suddenly of a brain aneurysm on 6 October 1979.

Elizabeth Bishop standing with a bicycle in Key West, Florida, c. 1940

The Fish

this poem is also prescribed for Ordinary Level exams in 2013 and 2014

I caught a tremendous fish
and held him beside the boat
half out of water, with my hook
fast in a corner of his mouth.
He didn't fight.   5
He hadn't fought at all.
He hung a grunting weight,
battered and venerable
and homely. Here and there
his brown skin hung in strips   10
like ancient wallpaper,
and its pattern of darker brown
was like wallpaper:
shapes like full-blown roses
stained and lost through age.   15

He was speckled with barnacles,
fine rosettes of lime,
and infested
with tiny white sea-lice,
and underneath two or three 20
rags of green weed hung down.
While his gills were breathing in
the terrible oxygen
– the frightening gills,
fresh and crisp with blood, 25
that can cut so badly –
I thought of the coarse white flesh
packed in like feathers,
the big bones and the little bones,
the dramatic reds and blacks 30
of his shiny entrails,
and the pink swim-bladder
like a big peony.
I looked into his eyes
which were far larger than mine 35
but shallower, and yellowed,
the irises backed and packed
with tarnished tinfoil
seen through the lenses
of old scratched isinglass. 40
They shifted a little, but not
to return my stare.
– It was more like the tipping
of an object toward the light.
I admired his sullen face, 45
the mechanism of his jaw,
and then I saw
that from his lower lip
– if you could call it a lip –
grim, wet, and weaponlike, 50
hung five old pieces of fish-line,
or four and a wire leader
with the swivel still attached,

with all their five big hooks
grown firmly in his mouth.   55
A green line, frayed at the end
where he broke it, two heavier lines,
and a fine black thread
still crimped from the strain and snap
when it broke and he got away.   60
Like medals with their ribbons
frayed and wavering,
a five-haired beard of wisdom
trailing from his aching jaw.
I stared and stared   65
and victory filled up
the little rented boat,
from the pool of bilge
where oil had spread a rainbow
around the rusted engine   70
to the bailer rusted orange,
the sun-cracked thwarts,
the oarlocks on their strings,
the gunnels – until everything
was rainbow, rainbow, rainbow!   75
And I let the fish go.

Note

[40]   **isinglass:** a semi-transparent form of gelatine extracted
        from certain fish and used in making jellies, glue, etc.

EXPLORATIONS

First reading

1. How do you visualise the fish?
    Think of it as a painting or a
    picture. What details strike you
    on a first reading?

2. What is your initial impression of
    the speaker in this poem?

3. Consider in detail the description of the fish. Which elements of the description could be considered objective or factual? Which elements could be seen as purely subjective on the part of the poet? Which are imagined or aesthetic elements in the description?

4. Do you think the poet's re-creation of the fish is a good one? Explain your views.

5. Explore the attitude of the speaker towards the fish, over the entire length of the poem. What changes do you notice, and where?

6. Why do you think she released the fish? Explore the text for possible reasons.

7. Do you think this is an important moment for the poet? What does she learn or discover? Where, in the text, is this suggested?

8. Is the poet excited by this experience? Where, in the text, is this suggested? Comment on the tone of the poem.

9. What issues does this poem raise? Consider what the poem has to say about:
   - our relationship with the natural world
   - the nature of creativity
   - moments of insight and decision
   - other themes hinted at.

10. Do you think the imagery is effective in getting across a real understanding of the fish and an awareness of the poet's mood? Explore any two relevant images and explain how they function.

11. This is quite a dramatic poem. Explain how the dramatic effect is created. Consider such elements as the way the narrative builds to a climax; the ending; the effect of the short enjambed lines; and the speaker's interior debate.

12. What did you like about this poem?

The Bight

(On my birthday)

At low tide like this how sheer the water is.
White, crumbling ribs of marl protrude and glare
and the boats are dry, the pilings dry as matches.
Absorbing, rather than being absorbed,
the water in the bight doesn't wet anything,   5
the color of the gas flame turned as low as possible.
One can smell it turning to gas; if one were Baudelaire
one could probably hear it turning to marimba music.
The little ocher dredge at work off the end of the dock
already plays the dry perfectly off-beat claves.   10
The birds are outsize. Pelicans crash
into this peculiar gas unnecessarily hard,
it seem to me, like pickaxes,
rarely coming up with anything to show for it,
and going off with humorous elbowings.   15
Black-and-white man-of-war birds soar
on impalpable drafts
and open their tails like scissors on the curves
or tense them like wishbones, till they tremble.
The frowsy sponge boats keep coming in   20
with the obliging air of retrievers,
bristling with jackstraw gaffs and hooks
and decorated with bobbles of sponges.
There is a fence of chicken wire along the dock
where, glinting like little plowshares,   25
the blue-gray shark tails are hung up to dry
for the Chinese-restaurant trade.
Some of the little white boats are still piled up
against each other, or lie on their sides, stove in,
and not yet salvaged, if they ever will be, from the last bad storm,   30
like torn-open, unanswered letters.
The bight is littered with old correspondences.

Click. Click. Goes the dredge,
and brings up a dripping jawful of marl.
All the untidy activity continues, 35
awful but cheerful.

EXPLORATIONS

First reading

1. Think of the poem as a painting. Describe it as you see it laid out: background, foreground, centre, left side, right side.

2. What mood is suggested by the scene? Explain.

Second reading

3. In what ways do you think it differs from a chocolate-box painting?

4. Is the reader-viewer encouraged to view the scene in a new and fresh way? Where and how does this happen? Examine the details of the descriptions. What is unusual about them?

Third reading

5. What do you think is the impact of the subtitle, 'On my birthday'? Might it be significant that she marks her birthday in this way, viewing this scene? How might she identify with the scene? From the evidence of the text, what do you think her mood is?

Fourth reading

6. Consider the style of the versification. Concentrate on such aspects as metre, rhyme or the lack of it, the organisation of sentence or sense units, etc. What does the form of the poem contribute to its effectiveness?

7. Would you consider it accurate to suggest that the poem moves along in bursts of poetic intensity, punctuated by more prosaic reflections? Discuss.

At the Fishhouses

Although it is a cold evening,
down by one of the fishhouses
an old man sits netting,
his net, in the gloaming almost invisible,
a dark purple-brown,   5
and his shuttle worn and polished.
The air smells so strong of codfish
it makes one's nose run and one's eyes water.
The five fishhouses have steeply peaked roofs
and narrow, cleated gangplanks slant up   10
to storerooms in the gables
for the wheelbarrows to be pushed up and down on.
All is silver: the heavy surface of the sea,
swelling slowly as if considering spilling over,
is opaque, but the silver of the benches,   15
the lobster pots, and masts, scattered
among the wild jagged rocks,
is of an apparent translucence
like the small old buildings with an emerald moss

growing on their shoreward walls.   20
The big fish tubs are completely lined
with layers of beautiful herring scales
and the wheelbarrows are similarly plastered
with creamy iridescent coats of mail,
with small iridescent flies crawling on them.   25
Up on the little slope behind the houses,
set in the sparse bright sprinkle of grass,
is an ancient wooden capstan,
cracked, with two long bleached handles
and some melancholy stains, like dried blood,   30
where the ironwork has rusted.
The old man accepts a Lucky Strike.
He was a friend of my grandfather.
We talk of the decline in the population
and of codfish and herring   35
while he waits for a herring boat to come in.
There are sequins on his vest and on his thumb.
He has scraped the scales, the principal beauty,
from unnumbered fish with that black old knife,
the blade of which is almost worn away.   40

Down at the water's edge, at the place
where they haul up the boats, up the long ramp
descending into the water, thin silver
tree trunks are laid horizontally
across the gray stones, down and down   45
at intervals of four or five feet.

Cold dark deep and absolutely clear,
element bearable to no mortal,
to fish and to seals . . . One seal particularly
I have seen here evening after evening.   50
He was curious about me. He was interested in music;
like me a believer in total immersion,
so I used to sing him Baptist hymns.
I also sang 'A Mighty Fortress Is Our God'.
He stood up in the water and regarded me   55
steadily, moving his head a little.

Then he would disappear, then suddenly emerge
almost in the same spot, with a sort of shrug
as if it were against his better judgment.
Cold dark deep and absolutely clear,   60
the clear gray icy water . . . Back, behind us,
the dignified tall firs begin.
Bluish, associating with their shadows,
a million Christmas trees stand
waiting for Christmas. The water seems suspended   65
above the rounded gray and blue-gray stones.
I have seen it over and over, the same sea, the same,
slightly, indifferently swinging above the stones,
icily free above the stones,
above the stones and then the world.   70
If you should dip your hand in,
your wrist would ache immediately,
your bones would begin to ache and your hand would burn
as if the water were a transmutation of fire
that feeds on stones and burns with a dark gray flame.   75
If you tasted it, it would first taste bitter,
then briny, then surely burn your tongue.
It is like what we imagine knowledge to be:
dark, salt, clear, moving, utterly free,
drawn from the cold hard mouth   80
of the world, derived from the rocky breasts
forever, flowing and drawn, and since
our knowledge is historical, flowing, and flown.

'Nova Scotia Landscape',
a watercolour by
Elizabeth Bishop

EXPLORATIONS

First reading

1. On a first reading, what do you notice about the setting of the poem? List the things that make an immediate impression on you.

2. Examine in detail what is being described in the first section. What is your impression of the atmosphere of the place?

3. What do you suppose is the writer's attitude to that scene in the first section? Does she find it repulsive, or awe-inspiring, or is she completely unaffected by it? Comment, with reference to the text.

4. What aspect of the scene draws the poet's main focus of attention during the entire poem?

Second reading

5. List all the characteristics or facets of the sea alluded to, or reflected on, by the poet throughout the poem.

6. Do you think she manages to evoke effectively the mysterious power of the sea? Comment.

Third reading

7. Bishop's poetic technique involved (a) detailed description and (b) making the familiar strange or unusual so that we see it afresh. Comment, under these headings, on her description of the sea.

8. How would you assess the mood of this poem? Take into consideration both the landscape and the poet.

9. The poem is written in free verse. What does this contribute to the effect of the poem? What else do you notice about the technique of this poem?

Fourth reading

10. The poem builds to a moment of insight for the poet. Where is this, and what is the insight? Describe, in as much depth as you can, what she comes to learn from the sea.

11. Outline the main issues raised by this poem.

12. Do you find any trace of the personality or feelings of the poet in this poem? Comment.

The Prodigal

this poem is also prescribed for Ordinary Level exams in 2013 and 2014

The brown enormous odor he lived by
was too close, with its breathing and thick hair,
for him to judge. The floor was rotten; the sty
was plastered halfway up with glass-smooth dung.
Light-lashed, self-righteous, above moving snouts,   5
the pigs' eyes followed him, a cheerful stare –
even to the sow that always ate her young –
till, sickening, he leaned to scratch her head.
But sometimes mornings after drinking bouts
(he hid the pints behind a two-by-four),   10
the sunrise glazed the barnyard mud with red;
the burning puddles seemed to reassure.
And then he thought he almost might endure
his exile yet another year or more.

But evenings the first star came to warn.   15
The farmer whom he worked for came at dark
to shut the cows and horses in the barn
beneath their overhanging clouds of hay,
with pitchforks, faint forked lightnings, catching light,
safe and companionable as in the Ark.   20
The pigs stuck out their little feet and snored.
The lantern – like the sun, going away –
laid on the mud a pacing aureole.
Carrying a bucket along a slimy board,
he felt the bats' uncertain staggering flight,   25
his shuddering insights, beyond his control,
touching him. But it took him a long time
finally to make his mind up to go home.

Note

[23] **aureole:** a halo of light around the sun or moon

EXPLORATIONS

Before reading

1. What does the title of the poem lead you to expect?

First reading

2. Were any of your expectations met on reading the poem?

3. How do you see the character in this poem?
   - What is he doing? How does he live?
   - Why is he there?
   - Does he find any satisfaction in his work?
   - What helps him endure his exile?

4. What details of the scene affected you most?

Second reading

5. Examine the final five lines. What do you think the 'shuddering insights, beyond his control' might be? Re-create his thoughts as you imagine them here.

6. Bishop appeals to a range of senses – smell, sight, sound, touch – to re-create the atmosphere of the place. Examine a sample of each type of image and discuss the effect.

7. How would you describe the atmosphere of the place? Is it one of unrelieved misery, or is there some contentment in it? Refer to the text.

8. Examine the poet's attitude to the prodigal. Do you think she is condemnatory, sympathetic, or neutral? Discuss, with reference to the text.

9. What is your own attitude to the prodigal?

Third reading

10. What are the main human issues raised by this poem?

11. Briefly express the theme of the poem.

12. Bishop's poetic technique involved really looking at the detail of her subject matter. Where do you think this works best in 'The Prodigal'?

Questions of Travel

There are too many waterfalls here; the crowded streams
hurry too rapidly down to the sea,
and the pressure of so many clouds on the mountaintops
makes them spill over the sides in soft slow-motion,
turning to waterfalls under our very eyes.   5
– For if those streaks, those mile-long, shiny, tearstains,
aren't waterfalls yet,
in a quick age or so, as ages go here,
they probably will be.
But if the streams and clouds keep travelling, travelling,   10
the mountains look like the hulls of capsized ships,
slime-hung and barnacled.

Think of the long trip home.
Should we have stayed at home and thought of here?
Where should we be today?   15
Is it right to be watching strangers in a play
in this strangest of theatres?
What childishness is it that while there's a breath of life
in our bodies, we are determined to rush
to see the sun the other way around?   20
The tiniest green hummingbird in the world?
To stare at some inexplicable old stonework,
inexplicable and impenetrable,
at any view,
instantly seen and always, always delightful?   25
Oh, must we dream our dreams
and have them, too?
And have we room
for one more folded sunset, still quite warm?

But surely it would have been a pity   30
not to have seen the trees along this road,
really exaggerated in their beauty,
not to have seen them gesturing

like noble pantomimists, robed in pink.
– Not to have had to stop for gas and heard   35
the sad, two-noted, wooden tune
of disparate wooden clogs
carelessly clacking over
a grease-stained filling-station floor.
(In another country the clogs would all be tested.   40
Each pair there would have identical pitch.)
– A pity not to have heard
the other, less primitive music of the fat brown bird
who sings above the broken gasoline pump
in a bamboo church of Jesuit baroque: 45
three towers, five silver crosses.
– Yes, a pity not to have pondered,
blurr'dly and inconclusively,
on what connection can exist for centuries
between the crudest wooden footwear   50
and, careful and finicky,
the whittled fantasies of wooden cages.
– Never to have studied history in
the weak calligraphy of songbirds' cages.
– And never to have had to listen to rain   55
so much like politicians' speeches:
two hours of unrelenting oratory
and then a sudden golden silence
in which the traveller takes a notebook, writes:

'Is it lack of imagination that makes us come   60
to imagined places, not just stay at home?
Or could Pascal have been not entirely right
about just sitting quietly in one's room?

Continent, city, country, society:
the choice is never wide and never free.   65
And here, or there . . . No. Should we have stayed at home,
wherever that may be?'

[45] **baroque:** the style of art that developed in the seventeenth century after the Renaissance, characterised by massive, complex and ornate design

[62] **Pascal:** Blaise Pascal (1623–1662), French mathematician, physicist and philosopher, author of *Pensées*, who commented: 'I have discovered that all human evil comes from this, man's being unable to sit still in a room.'

'Brazilian Landscape', a watercolour by Elizabeth Bishop

EXPLORATIONS

First reading

1. This is a travel poem with a difference. What are the elements found here that one would normally expect of a travel poem, and what elements do you find different or unusual?

2. Follow the traveller's eye. What does she notice in particular about the geography and culture of Brazil?

3. What impression of Brazilian culture do you get? Examine the references in detail.

Second reading

4. Do you think the poet feels comfortable in this place? What is her attitude to what she sees? Do you think she is just the usual tired, grumpy traveller, or what?

Second reading continued

5. One critic has said that Bishop is essentially a poet of the domestic, because she feels estranged in the greater world. Comment on that statement, in the light of your reading of this poem.

6. What bothers her about travel? Jot down your ideas on this.

Third reading

7. List the main issues raised in this poem.

8. What do you notice about the style in which the poem is written? Comment critically on it.

The Armadillo

For Robert Lowell

This is the time of year
when almost every night
the frail, illegal fire balloons appear.
Climbing the mountain height,

rising toward a saint   5
still honored in these parts,
the paper chambers flush and fill with light
that comes and goes, like hearts.

Once up against the sky it's hard
to tell them from the stars –   10
planets, that is – the tinted ones:
Venus going down, or Mars,

or the pale green one. With a wind,
they flare and falter, wobble and toss;
but if it's still they steer between   15
the kite sticks of the Southern Cross,

receding, dwindling, solemnly
and steadily forsaking us,
or, in the downdraft from a peak,
suddenly turning dangerous.   20

Last night another big one fell.
It splattered like an egg of fire
against the cliff behind the house.
The flame ran down. We saw the pair

of owls who nest there flying up   25
and up, their whirling black-and-white
stained bright pink underneath, until
they shrieked up out of sight.

The ancient owls' nest must have burned.
Hastily, all alone,   30

a glistening armadillo left the scene,
rose-flecked, head down, tail down,

and then a baby rabbit jumped out,
short-eared, to our surprise.
So soft! – a handful of intangible ash   35
with fixed, ignited eyes.

Too pretty, dreamlike mimicry!
O falling fire and piercing cry
and panic, and a weak mailed fist
clenched ignorant against the sky!   40

Explorations

First reading

1. Trace the sequence of events in the poem.
2. What images strike you most forcibly?
3. What is your first impression of the location in this poem? How do you imagine it?

Second reading

4. Do you think it would be correct to say that the poet is ambivalent in her attitude to the fire balloons? Discuss.
5. Trace the development of the fire imagery throughout the poem. How does the poet link it with the natural world?
6. Where do you think the poet's sympathies lie in this poem? Explain.

Third reading

7. Examine the poet's outlook on life here. What image of the local people is presented? What view of humanity in general informs this poem? Can you discern a philosophy of life behind it? Note your impressions, however tentative. Then formulate your thoughts in a more organised way.

Third reading continued

8. Would you say the poet is uncharacteristically emotional here? Explain your views.

9. What else do you notice about the style of this poem?

Fourth reading

10. Why do you think this might be considered an important poem?

Sestina

September rain falls on the house.
In the failing light, the old grandmother
sits in the kitchen with the child
beside the Little Marvel Stove,
reading the jokes from the almanac,   5
laughing and talking to hide her tears.

She thinks that her equinoctial tears
and the rain that beats on the roof of the house
were both foretold by the almanac,
but only known to a grandmother.   10
The iron kettle sings on the stove.
She cuts some bread and says to the child,

It's time for tea now; but the child
is watching the teakettle's small hard tears
dance like mad on the hot black stove,   15
the way the rain must dance on the house.
Tidying up, the old grandmother
hangs up the clever almanac

on its string. Birdlike, the almanac
hovers half open above the child,   20
hovers above the old grandmother
and her teacup full of dark brown tears.
She shivers and says she thinks the house
feels chilly, and puts more wood in the stove.

It was to be, says the Marvel Stove.   25
I know what I know, says the almanac.
With crayons the child draws a rigid house
and a winding pathway. Then the child
puts in a man with buttons like tears
and shows it proudly to the grandmother   30

But secretly, while the grandmother
busies herself about the stove,
the little moons fall down like tears
from between the pages of the almanac
into the flower bed the child   35
has carefully placed in the front of the house.

Time to plant tears, says the almanac.
The grandmother sings to the marvellous stove
and the child draws another inscrutable house.

EXPLORATIONS

First reading

1. What is the prevailing atmosphere in this poem? What elements chiefly contribute to this?
2. What are the recurring elements in this poem?

Second reading

3. How do you see the grandmother?
4. How do you see the child here?
5. Is the child completely unhappy? Are there any alleviating soft elements in her life?
6. What do you think is absent from the child's picture of life?

Third reading

7. Do you understand how the poem is constructed? Explain briefly.

8. Trace the progression of the tear imagery throughout the poem, from the reference to September rain in the first stanza. How do you interpret this, in the context of the statement the poet is making about her childhood?

9. Examine the references to her drawings of the house. What do they suggest to you about the child and her environment?

Fourth reading

10. What thoughts does this poem spark off about childhood and about domestic relationships?

11. Do you think Bishop has made a successful re-creation of a child's world? Examine, in particular, the actions and the diction.

12. Would you consider this to be a sentimental poem? The term 'sentimental' can be read neutrally as 'emotional thought expressed in literature' or more negatively as 'showing emotional weakness, mawkish tenderness'. Which, if either, description applies? Discuss.

First Death in Nova Scotia

In the cold, cold parlor
my mother laid out Arthur
beneath the chromographs:
Edward, Prince of Wales,
with Princess Alexandra,   5
and King George with Queen Mary.
Below them on the table
stood a stuffed loon
shot and stuffed by Uncle
Arthur, Arthur's father.   10

Since Uncle Arthur fired
a bullet into him,
he hadn't said a word.
He kept his own counsel
on his white, frozen lake,   15

the marble-topped table.
His breast was deep and white,
cold and caressable;
his eyes were red glass,
much to be desired.   20

'Come,' said my mother,
'Come and say good-bye
to your little cousin Arthur.'
I was lifted up and given
one lily of the valley   25
to put in Arthur's hand.
Arthur's coffin was
a little frosted cake,
and the red-eyed loon eyed it
from his white, frozen lake.   30

Arthur was very small.
He was all white, like a doll
that hadn't been painted yet.
Jack Frost had started to paint him
the way he always painted   35
the Maple Leaf (Forever).
He had just begun on his hair,
a few red strokes, and then
Jack Frost had dropped the brush
and left him white, forever.   40

The gracious royal couples
were warm in red and ermine;
their feet were well wrapped up
in the ladies' ermine trains.
They invited Arthur to be   45
the smallest page at court.
But how could Arthur go,
clutching his tiny lily,
with his eyes shut up so tight
and the roads deep in snow?   50

Notes

[3]   **chromograph:** printed reproduction of a colour photograph

[8]   **loon:** a diver, a kind of bird, noted for its clumsy gait on land

[36]   **Maple Leaf:** national emblem of Canada

[42]   **ermine:** white fur with black spots, from a type of stoat, used in monarchs' robes

EXPLORATIONS

First reading

1. First decide who is speaking. Where and when was the event depicted, and what age is the speaker?

2. What do you find unusual or confusing on a first reading?

3. If we consider the speaker to be a young child, does this help you come to grips with the poem? Reread.

Second reading

4. What is most noticeable about the scene here?

5. What is the atmosphere in the parlour?

6. How do you think the child speaker feels? Discuss.

Third reading

7. Examine the title. Why 'first death'? Discuss the many possible connotations of this.

8. Comment on the use of colour in the poem.

9. Comment on the versification.

Fourth reading

10. Do you think the poet has managed to re-create successfully the young child's experience?

11. Contrast this poem with Séamus Heaney's 'Mid-Term Break'.

12. What did you learn about Elizabeth Bishop from a reading of this poem?

Filling Station

this poem is also prescribed for Ordinary Level exams in 2013 and 2014

Oh, but it is dirty!
—this little filling station,
oil-soaked, oil-permeated
to a disturbing, over-all
black translucency.   5
Be careful with that match!

Father wears a dirty,
oil-soaked monkey suit
that cuts him under the arms,
and several quick and saucy   10
and greasy sons assist him
(it's a family filling station),
all quite thoroughly dirty.

Do they live in the station?
It has a cement porch   15
behind the pumps, and on it
a set of crushed and grease-
impregnated wickerwork;
on the wicker sofa
a dirty dog, quite comfy.   20

Some comic books provide
the only note of color—
of certain color. They lie
upon a big dim doily
draping a taboret   25
(part of the set), beside
a big hirsute begonia.

Why the extraneous plant?
Why the taboret?
Why, oh why, the doily?   30
(Embroidered in daisy stitch
with marguerites, I think,
and heavy with gray crochet.)

Somebody embroidered the doily.
Somebody waters the plant,   35
or oils it, maybe. Somebody
arranges the rows of cans
so that they softly say:
ESSO—SO—SO—SO

to high-strung automobiles.   40
Somebody loves us all.

Explorations

Before reading

1. Think about the title. What do you see?

First reading

2. Describe the atmosphere this poem creates for you. What details appear to you to be significant in creating this? Discuss them.

Second reading

3. Plan the shots you would use if you were making a film of this scene. Describe what you see in each shot, and explain your choice in detail.

4. Is there any progression, development of complexity, etc. in this film? How do you understand it?

5. What do the doily, the taboret and the begonia add to the atmosphere?

Third reading

6. What is it about this scene that fascinates the poet: the forecourt, the domestic details, or something else? Discuss.

7. How do you understand the 'somebody' in stanza 6?

Fourth reading

8. Do you think the poet is discovering a truth, and making a statement about life? If so, what? Discuss this.

9. Write up your own notes on the theme of the poem, the poet's philosophy of life, her poetic method, and the style and tone of the poem.

10. 'The details of Bishop's poems are always compelling but never the whole point.' Discuss, with reference to the text.

11. 'This is a poem that manages to create poignancy and wit simultaneously.' Discuss.

Edward Hopper: 'Gas' (1940), Museum of Modern Art, New York

In the Waiting Room

In Worcester, Massachusetts,
I went with Aunt Consuelo
to keep her dentist's appointment
and sat and waited for her
in the dentist's waiting room.   5
It was winter. It got dark
early. The waiting room
was full of grown-up people,
arctics and overcoats,
lamps and magazines.   10
My aunt was inside
what seemed like a long time
and while I waited I read
the *National Geographic*
(I could read) and carefully   15
studied the photographs:
the inside of a volcano,
black, and full of ashes;
then it was spilling over
in rivulets of fire.   20
Osa and Martin Johnson
dressed in riding breeches,
laced boots, and pith helmets.
A dead man slung on a pole
– 'Long Pig', the caption said.   25
Babies with pointed heads
wound round and round with string;
black, naked women with necks
wound round and round with wire
like the necks of light bulbs.   30
Their breasts were horrifying.
I read it right straight through.
I was too shy to stop.
And then I looked at the cover:
the yellow margins, the date.   35

Suddenly, from inside,
came an oh! of pain
– Aunt Consuelo's voice –
not very loud or long.
I wasn't at all surprised;   40
even then I knew she was
a foolish, timid woman.
I might have been embarrassed,
but wasn't. What took me
completely by surprise   45
was that it was me:
my voice, in my mouth.
Without thinking at all
I was my foolish aunt,
I – we – were falling, falling,   50
our eyes glued to the cover
of the *National Geographic*,
February, 1918.

I said to myself: three days
and you'll be seven years old.   55
I was saying it to stop
the sensation of falling off
the round, turning world
into cold, blue-black space.
But I felt: you are an I,   60
you are an Elizabeth,
you are one of them.
Why should you be one, too?
I scarcely dared to look
to see what it was I was.   65
I gave a sidelong glance
– I couldn't look any higher –
at shadowy gray knees,
trousers and skirts and boots
and different pairs of hands   70
lying under the lamps.
I knew that nothing stranger
had ever happened, that nothing
stranger could ever happen.

Why should I be my aunt,   75
or me, or anyone?
What similarities —
boots, hands, the family voice
I felt in my throat, or even
the *National Geographic*   80
and those awful hanging breasts —
held us all together
or made us all just one?
How — I didn't know any
word for it — how 'unlikely' …   85
How had I come to be here,
like them, and overhear
a cry of pain that could have
got loud and worse but hadn't?

The waiting room was bright   90
and too hot. It was sliding
beneath a big black wave,
another, and another.

Then I was back in it.
The War was on. Outside,   95
in Worcester, Massachusetts,
were night and slush and cold,
and it was still the fifth
of February, 1918.

Date of the poem

It was probably written about 1970 and was published in the *New Yorker* on 17 July 1971. It is the opening poem of her collection *Geography III*, published in 1976.

> **Note**
>
> [21] **Osa and Martin Johnson:** American photographers and explorers; Bishop first saw the Johnsons' jungle film *Baboons* in the winter of 1935

EXPLORATIONS

Before reading

1. What might you expect from this title?

2. Do you remember what it was like as a child to sit in a dentist's waiting-room? Re-create such an experience. Make brief notes for yourself.

First reading

3. In the poem, what elements of the waiting-room experience are all too familiar to you?

4. Who is the speaker in this poem? Assemble as much information, factual and impressionistic, as you can.

Second reading

5. After the familiar, what is encountered by the child?

6. Which event most unnerves her? Can you suggest why she is unnerved?

7. What is the child's reaction to this experience?

Third reading

8. What is your understanding of the experience described in this poem? Comment briefly.

9. What view of women does Bishop project in this poem?

10. Comment on the experience of childhood reflected here.

Fourth reading

11. What themes or issues are raised by this poem? Explain how the poet deals with some of the following:
    - a child's realisation of selfhood
    - the poet's uncomfortable connection with the rest of humanity
    - the variety and strangeness of the world of which one is a part
    - that we are always at risk of being ambushed by the unfamiliar, even in the security of the domestic
    - that the chief lessons of childhood are learning to deal with pain and mortality, and accepting unity in spite of difference
    - any others.

12. What is your own reaction to this poem? Structure your thoughts in the form of questions.

13. Comment on the structure of the poem (five sections) and the type of verse used.

9 *Philip Larkin*
1922–1985

prescribed for higher Level exams in 2012 and 2014

Philip Arthur Larkin was born in Coventry in 1922, the son of Eva Larkin and Sydney Larkin, the city treasurer. He attended King Henry VIII High School, where he was an avid reader and had some poems and humorous prose printed in the school magazine. In 1940 he went to study English at St John's College, Oxford. He is remembered as a shy, introverted person with a speech impediment. He was a prominent member of the Jazz Club and the English Society. As it was wartime, Larkin expected to be called up, but he failed his medical and so managed to spend a full three years at Oxford. Among his contemporaries were John Wain and Kingsley Amis.

In 1943 Larkin was awarded a first-class degree in English language and literature and the same year had three poems included in *Oxford Poetry, 1942–43*. From 1943 to 1946 he was librarian at Wellington, Shropshire, where he reorganised the library and managed to write a good deal. It was here that he first became involved in a relationship with Ruth Bowman.

Some of his poems were included in the anthology *Poetry from Oxford in Wartime*, published in 1945 by Fortune Press, which also brought out Larkin's first collection, *The North Ship*, the same year. In 1946 his first novel, *Jill*,

was published. In September that year he took up a position as assistant librarian at the University College of Leicester. There he met Monica Jones, a lecturer in the English Department, with whom he began a relationship that was to last, on and off, for the rest of his life.

His second novel, *A Girl in Winter*, was published in 1947. In 1948 his father died, and Larkin went back to live with his mother. He became engaged to Ruth Bowman, but the engagement was broken off in 1950. In that year Larkin went to Belfast to become the sub-librarian at Queen's University. He enjoyed living in Belfast, and he wrote a good deal.

In April 1951 Larkin had twenty of his early poems privately printed as *XX Poems*. These included 'Wedding-Wind' and 'At Grass' (both included in his later volume *The Less Deceived*). His emotional life became a bit of a tangle. He developed particular relationships with Patsy Strang and Winifred Arnott, who worked in the library. And Monica Jones came to visit.

In 1955 his collection *The Less Deceived* was published. This included the poem 'Toads', a protest against the daily grind of work. Going for interview for the job of librarian at the University of Hull later that year, Larkin feared the board would have seen his poem as representative of his attitude to his job; but he was appointed and, with brief absences, he spent the rest of his life in this position. Here he met Maeve Brennan.

In 1964 *The Whitsun Weddings* was published, and in 1965 Larkin was awarded the Queen's Gold Medal for Poetry. *All That Jazz*, a selection of his jazz reviews, was published in 1970. He was a visiting fellow at All Souls College, Oxford, for the academic year 1970/71, and he edited *The Oxford Book of Twentieth-Century Verse* (1973).

In 1974 *High Windows* was published, and Larkin bought his first house, opposite the university, where he lived for the rest of his life. His mother died in 1977. In 1982 Monica Jones became ill, and Larkin brought her to live at his home.

Required Writing: Miscellaneous Pieces, 1955–82 was published in 1982. In 1984 Larkin refused the offer of appointment as Poet Laureate. He died on 2 December 1985.

Wedding-Wind

The wind blew all my wedding-day,
And my wedding-night was the night of the high wind;
And a stable door was banging, again and again,
That he must go and shut it, leaving me
Stupid in candlelight, hearing rain,   5
Seeing my face in the twisted candlestick,
Yet seeing nothing. When he came back
He said the horses were restless, and I was sad
That any man or beast that night should lack
The happiness I had.   10
    Now in the day
All's ravelled under the sun by the wind's blowing.
He has gone to look at the floods, and I
Carry a chipped pail to the chicken-run,
Set it down, and stare. All is the wind   15
Hunting through clouds and forests, thrashing
My apron and the hanging cloths on the line.
Can it be borne, this bodying-forth by wind
Of joy my actions turn on, like a thread
Carrying beads? Shall I be let to sleep   20
Now this perpetual morning shares my bed?
Can even death dry up
These new delighted lakes, conclude
Our kneeling as cattle by all-generous waters?

EXPLORATIONS

First reading

1. List what you notice on a first reading of this poem.

2. Who is the speaker?

3. What scene is the speaker describing (a) in the first stanza and (b) in the second stanza?

Second reading

4. How is the woman feeling in the first stanza? What words and phrases indicate her feelings? Explore in detail the nuances and changes of the speaker's mood in the first stanza.

5. What is revealed about her lifestyle in the second stanza? What unanswered questions have you about her and about her circumstances?

6. What is her mood and what are her feelings in the second stanza? How do we know? Does she always express them explicitly, or are we left to interpret her feelings through other means? Explain.

7. Do you think her mood is one of unqualified optimism? Explain.

Third reading

8. Briefly outline Larkin's view of marriage and love as you understand it from this poem.

9. Do you think he is successful at interpreting the woman's viewpoint in this poem? Explain.

10. Do you find the setting appropriate to this theme? Comment.

11. Examine the effectiveness of the imagery. Consider in particular the symbolism of storm and of floods. Explore also what the other images contribute to this poem.

At Grass

The eye can hardly pick them out
From the cold shade they shelter in,
Till wind distresses tail and mane;
Then one crops grass, and moves about
 – The other seeming to look on –   5
And stands anonymous again.

Yet fifteen years ago, perhaps
Two dozen distances sufficed
To fable them: faint afternoons
Of Cups and Stakes and Handicaps,   10
Whereby their names were artificed
To inlay faded, classic Junes –

Silks at the start: against the sky
Numbers and parasols: outside,
Squadrons of empty cars, and heat,   15
And littered grass: then the long cry
Hanging unhushed till it subside
To stop-press columns on the street.

Do memories plague their ears like flies?
They shake their heads. Dusk brims the shadows.   20
Summer by summer all stole away,
The starting-gates, the crowds and cries –
All but the unmolesting meadows.
Almanacked, their names live; they

Have slipped their names, and stand at ease,   25
Or gallop for what must be joy,
And not a fieldglass sees them home,
Or curious stop-watch prophesies:
Only the groom, and the groom's boy,
With bridles in the evening come.   30

A stud farm in England, c. 1950

EXPLORATIONS

First reading

1. On a first reading, what do you notice about (a) the setting or scene, (b) the horses, (c) the time of day, and (d) the general mood of the poem?

Second reading

2. In the first stanza, did you notice the quiet, undramatic opening? How is this achieved? What words or phrases contribute to it? Explain.

Second reading continued

3. Do you find that this poem offers a realistic description of grazing racehorses? Explain, with reference to particular words and phrases.

4. Are there any details that slightly spoil the romantic scene of gently grazing retired horses? Explore this possibility.

5. What elements of a typical race meeting do you think are well caught in stanzas 2 and 3?

Third reading

6. It is as if this scene is viewed from a distance by the poet. Explore how the sense of distance is created in the first three stanzas. What effect has this on the tone of the poem?

7. Explore the poetic use of language in the fourth stanza. (a) What atmosphere do you think is evoked by line 2? (b) Technically, how is the sense of easeful and untraumatic departure communicated in line 3? Examine the sounds of the words. (c) What is suggested to you by 'the unmolesting meadows'? Do you find this phrase in any way startling or slightly disturbing? (d) What part does rhyme play in the creation of atmosphere? (e) Consider the phrase 'their names live; they ...' What do you think is the effect of the punctuation of that phrase and of its particular place in the stanza?

8. How would you describe the atmosphere in stanza 5? Consider the phrases 'have slipped their names' and 'not a fieldglass sees them home' in this context. What is the effect of the poet's presumption that they gallop 'for what must be joy'?

9. Examine the natural, homely, undistressing evocation of death in the last two lines. It comes not as the Grim Reaper but as the unthreatening and completely familiar 'groom' and 'groom's boy'. The long vowels of these words are soothing, and semantically they suggest care, comfort, feeding. Yet the finality of it is not disguised. The inverted word order of the final line emphasises that all activity ends in that final verb. Do you think this portrayal of death is effective and suitable in the context of the poem?

Fourth reading

10. Would you agree that the tone of this poem is unemotional and detached? How is this achieved? Consider the speaking voice (first person, third person, or what?), the sense of distance or perspective, and the effect of the style of description (a succession of brief pictures, often unconnected, like a series of untitled photographs).

11. Comment on the sources and effectiveness of the imagery.

12. What do you particularly like about this poem? Or what do you find less than satisfactory?

Church Going

Once I am sure there's nothing going on
I step inside, letting the door thud shut.
Another church: matting, seats, and stone,
And little books; sprawlings of flowers, cut
For Sunday, brownish now; some brass and stuff   5
Up at the holy end; the small neat organ;
And a tense, musty, unignorable silence,
Brewed God knows how long. Hatless, I take off
My cycle-clips in awkward reverence,

Move forward, run my hand around the font.   10
From where I stand, the roof looks almost new –
Cleaned, or restored? Someone would know: I don't.
Mounting the lectern, I peruse a few
Hectoring large-scale verses, and pronounce
'Here endeth' much more loudly than I'd meant.   15
The echoes snigger briefly. Back at the door
I sign the book, donate an Irish sixpence,
Reflect the place was not worth stopping for.

Yet stop I did: in fact I often do,
And always end much at a loss like this,   20
Wondering what to look for; wondering, too,
When churches fall completely out of use
What we shall turn them into, if we shall keep
A few cathedrals chronically on show,
Their parchment, plate and pyx in locked cases,   25
And let the rest rent-free to rain and sheep.
Shall we avoid them as unlucky places?

Or, after dark, will dubious women come
To make their children touch a particular stone;
Pick simples for a cancer; or on some   30
Advised night see walking a dead one?
Power of some sort or other will go on

In games, in riddles, seemingly at random;
But superstition, like belief, must die,
And what remains when disbelief has gone?　　　　　　35
Grass, weedy pavement, brambles, buttress, sky,
A shape less recognisable each week,
A purpose more obscure. I wonder who
Will be the last, the very last, to seek
This place for what it was; one of the crew　　　　　40
That tap and jot and know what rood-lofts were?
Some ruin-bibber, randy for antique,
Or Christmas-addict, counting on a whiff
Of gown-and-bands and organ-pipes and myrrh?
Or will he be my representative,　　　　　　　　　45

Bored, uninformed, knowing the ghostly silt
Dispersed, yet tending to this cross of ground
Through suburb scrub because it held unspilt
So long and equably what since is found
Only in separation – marriage, and birth,　　　　　50
And death, and thoughts of these – for which was built
This special shell? For, though I've no idea
What this accoutred frowsty barn is worth,
It pleases me to stand in silence here;
A serious house on serious earth it is,　　　　　　55
In whose blent air all our compulsions meet,
Are recognised, and robed as destinies.
And that much never can be obsolete,
Since someone will forever be surprising
A hunger in himself to be more serious,　　　　　60
And gravitating with it to this ground,
Which, he once heard, was proper to grow wise in,
If only that so many dead lie round.

[10] **font:** ornate container, usually of marble or stone and raised on a pedestal, that holds the baptismal water

[13] **lectern:** raised podium or desk from which the reading is done in a church

[15] **'Here endeth':** from the archaic phrase 'Here endeth the Lesson', used at the end of scripture readings

[25] **parchment:** literally animal skin prepared for writing on, here used to signify all church paper, books, and records

[25] **plate:** silver and gold vessels

[25] **pyx:** a container for the consecrated Communion wafers

[30] **simples:** an archaic word for herbs

[41] **tap:** perhaps to strike gently, or to bore a hole containing an internal screw thread

[41] **jot:** to write brief notes; can also mean to bump or jolt. He may be using both 'tap' and 'jot' in their meaning 'to strike gently', referring to the tapping done by experts who examine timbers in old buildings.

[41] **rood-lofts:** screened galleries separating the nave of a church from the choir

[44] **myrrh:** a perfumed gum-resin used in incense

[53] **accoutred:** richly attired

[56] **blent:** archaic form of 'blended'

EXPLORATIONS

First reading

Stanzas 1 and 2

1. This is a first-person narrative poem, so follow the incident with the speaker. See it through his eyes. Step inside the church with him.

   What is to be seen in the first two stanzas? List everything you notice. What picture of the church do you get? Is it in use, is it well cared for, etc.?

2. What do you notice about the speaker – dress, actions, attitude to the place? What sort of character is he? How does he see himself? What words and phrases do you think are most revealing about the character of the speaker? Explain.

EXPLORATIONS

Second reading

Stanzas 3, 4, and 5

3. Is there a change of tone and attitude on the part of the speaker in stanza 3? Explain.

4. Is there a change of style or mode of telling with stanza 3? Explain what you notice.

5. In your own words, trace the speaker's thoughts through stanzas 3, 4, and 5.

Stanzas 6 and 7

6. What value does the speaker see in the institution of the church? Why does he still find himself 'tending to this cross of ground'? Examine the speaker's thought in stanza 6.

7. 'A serious house on serious earth it is' (stanza 7). What do you think the speaker means by 'serious', in the context of this stanza and of the poem as a whole?

Third reading

8. Trace the speaker's shifting attitudes to religion and to the church throughout this poem.

9. Can you state briefly what the poem is about?

10. What appeals to you about it?

11. Comment on Larkin's philosophy as it is revealed in this poem.

Fourth reading

12. Andrew Motion talks about the 'self-mocking, detail-collecting, conversational manner' of this poem. Examine these three aspects of Larkin's style in the poem.

An Arundel Tomb

Side by side, their faces blurred,
The earl and countess lie in stone,
Their proper habits vaguely shown
As jointed armour, stiffened pleat,
And that faint hint of the absurd –   5
The little dogs under their feet.

Such plainness of the pre-baroque
Hardly involves the eye, until
It meets his left-hand gauntlet, still
Clasped empty in the other; and   10
One sees, with a sharp tender shock,
His hand withdrawn, holding her hand.

They would not think to lie so long.
Such faithfulness in effigy
Was just a detail friends would see: 15
A sculptor's sweet commissioned grace
Thrown off in helping to prolong
The Latin names around the base.

They would not guess how early in
Their supine stationary voyage   20
The air would change to soundless damage,
Turn the old tenantry away;
How soon succeeding eyes begin
To look, not read. Rigidly they

Persisted, linked, through lengths and breadths   25
Of time. Snow fell, undated. Light
Each summer thronged the glass. A bright
Litter of birdcalls strewed the same
Bone-riddled ground. And up the paths
The endless altered people came,   30

Washing at their identity.
Now, helpless in the hollow of
An unarmorial age, a trough
Of smoke in slow suspended skeins
Above their scrap of history,   35
Only an attitude remains:

Time has transfigured them into
Untruth. The stone fidelity
They hardly meant has come to be
Their final blazon, and to prove   40
Our almost-instinct almost true:
What will survive of us is love.

Notes

Arundel Tomb: the monument to the Earl and Countess of Arundel in Chichester Cathedral

[7]   **pre-baroque:** the baroque was a style in art predominant about 1600–1720, characterised by massive, complex and ornate design. 'Pre-baroque' suggests a more simple design.

[40]   **blazon:** coat of arms

EXPLORATIONS

Before reading

1. When did you last visit a graveyard, an old church, or a commemorative monument of any kind? Perhaps it was a famous monument like Kilmainham Jail, or just an old church. Visualise it and write brief notes on what you remember; or

2. Discuss your experiences or compose a diary extract on your visit.

EXPLORATIONS

First reading

3. If possible, listen to the poem read aloud. Close your eyes. What do you see in the poem? In discussion, share what you particularly noticed.

Stanzas 1 and 2

4. What is the poet looking at? What absorbs his attention?

5. What specific details attract his attention in stanza 2? How does he feel on seeing this? What words or phrases suggest this?

6. How do you react to this detail? Do you share his attitude?

Second reading

Stanza 3

7. Examine stanza 3. If they could see it, how do you think the earl and countess would view this pose and the detail of the effigy?

8. What does the poet think was the original reason for the detail of the hands? Examine the last two lines of stanza 3.

Stanza 4

9. How is the passage of time evoked in stanza 4? Is it violent or gently insidious? Has the passage of time any social and cultural implications here? Explain.

10. Explore the connotations of 'supine stationary voyage'. What does it suggest to you?

11. If the earl and countess were aware of what has happened up to now and could somehow communicate, what would they say to a visitor to Chichester Cathedral? Choose the view of either figure.

12. Reread stanzas 1 to 4. What do you think is the underlying issue that preoccupies the poet here?

Third reading

Stanzas 5, 6, and 7

13. What pictures or images do you notice in particular in stanza 5? What is the effect of these images?

14. Examine from 'rigidly they' to 'washing at their identity'. If you had a camera to film this section as a sequence of shots, how would you do it? Do you think that shots of contrasting images would create an atmosphere true to the verse? Outline the sequence.

15. What words in stanza 6 best describe the predicament of the earl and countess? Explain.

16. What attitude to life and human enterprise underpins stanza 6, in your opinion?

17. Read the section 'Background' in the Critical Notes. Does this throw any light on your understanding of stanza 7? Attempt to restate the message of stanza 7 in your own words.

Fourth reading

18. Compose extracts from an imaginary diary that Larkin might have written about this event and that show how he was affected by this experience.

19. Briefly, what are the main themes or issues raised by the poem?

20. Larkin concludes with a seemingly positive statement: 'What will survive of us is love.' Is this sentiment justified by the poem as a whole? Review the evidence throughout the poem.

21. How does this poem make you feel, and how does it do that?

22. Briefly compare Larkin's treatment of the possible survival of love against the ravages of time with other poems of a similar theme.

Arundel monument,
Chichester Cathedral

The Whitsun Weddings

That Whitsun, I was late getting away:
    Not till about
One-twenty on the sunlit Saturday
Did my three-quarters-empty train pull out,
All windows down, all cushions hot, all sense   5
Of being in a hurry gone. We ran
Behind the backs of houses, crossed a street
Of blinding windscreens, smelt the fish-dock; thence
The river's level drifting breadth began,
Where sky and Lincolnshire and water meet.   10

All afternoon, through the tall heat that slept
    For miles inland,
A slow and stopping curve southwards we kept.
Wide farms went by, short-shadowed cattle, and
Canals with floatings of industrial froth;   15
A hothouse flashed uniquely: hedges dipped
And rose: and now and then a smell of grass
Displaced the reek of buttoned carriage-cloth
Until the next town, new and nondescript,
Approached with acres of dismantled cars.   20

At first, I didn't notice what a noise
    The weddings made
Each station that we stopped at: sun destroys
The interest of what's happening in the shade,
And down the long cool platforms whoops and skirls   25
I took for porters larking with the mails,
And went on reading. Once we started, though,
We passed them, grinning and pomaded, girls
In parodies of fashion, heels and veils,
All posed irresolutely, watching us go,   30
As if out on the end of an event
    Waving goodbye
To something that survived it. Struck, I leant

More promptly out next time, more curiously,
And saw it all again in different terms: 35
The fathers with broad belts under their suits
And seamy foreheads; mothers loud and fat,
An uncle shouting smut; and then the perms,
The nylon gloves and jewellery-substitutes,
The lemons, mauves, and olive-ochres that   40

Marked off the girls unreally from the rest.
        Yes, from cafés
And banquet-halls up yards, and bunting-dressed
Coach-party annexes, the wedding-days
Were coming to an end. All down the line   45
Fresh couples climbed aboard: the rest stood round;
The last confetti and advice were thrown,
And, as we moved, each face seemed to define
Just what it saw departing: children frowned
At something dull; fathers had never known   50

Success so huge and wholly farcical;
        The women shared
The secret like a happy funeral;
While girls, gripping their handbags tighter, stared
At a religious wounding. Free at last,   55
And loaded with the sum of all they saw,
We hurried towards London, shuffling gouts of steam.
Now fields were building-plots, and poplars cast
Long shadows over major roads, and for
Some fifty minutes, that in time would seem   60

Just long enough to settle hats and say
        I nearly died,
A dozen marriages got under way.
They watched the landscape, sitting side by side
 – An Odeon went past, a cooling tower,   65
And someone running up to bowl – and none
Thought of the others they would never meet
Or how their lives would all contain this hour.

I thought of London spread out in the sun,
Its postal districts packed like squares of wheat: 70

There we were aimed. And as we raced across
    Bright knots of rail
Past standing Pullmans, walls of blackened moss
Came close, and it was nearly done, this frail
Travelling coincidence; and what it held   75
Stood ready to be loosed with all the power
That being changed can give. We slowed again,
And as the tightened brakes took hold, there swelled
A sense of falling, like an arrow-shower
Sent out of sight, somewhere becoming rain.   80

EXPLORATIONS

Before reading

In a television interview in 1981 Larkin explained the genesis of this poem. It had its origins in a journey from Hull to London on Whit Saturday 1955, when Larkin took:

> '. . . a very slow train that stopped at every station and I hadn't realised that, of course, this was the train that all the wedding couples would get on and go to London for their honeymoon; it was an eye-opener for me. Every part was different but the same somehow. They all looked different but they were all doing the same things and sort of feeling the same things. I suppose the train stopped at about four, five, six stations between Hull and London and there was a sense of gathering emotional momentum. Every time you stopped, fresh emotion climbed aboard. And finally, between Peterborough and London when you hurtle on, you felt the whole thing was being aimed like a bullet – at the heart of things, you know. All this fresh, open life. Incredible experience. I've never forgotten it.'

[Quoted by Andrew Motion in *Philip Larkin: A Writer's Life*.]

First reading

1. Where is the speaker in this poem?
2. What is happening?
3. What images or pictures particularly catch your eye?

Second reading

4. Get on the train with the poet and observe what he sees on the journey. List the kinds of things he notices (categories rather than individual sights) and the order in which he sees them.
5. Note the sections you do not understand.
6. What mood is the speaker in at the start of the journey (stanzas 1 and 2)? What words or phrases lead you to this view?

Third reading

7. Is the poet immediately fascinated by the happenings on the station platforms? What is Larkin's initial attitude to the wedding guests? What details strike him in stanzas 3 to 6?
8. When does he make an effort to understand them, to get inside their thinking? Does his attitude change then? Explain.

Third reading continued

9. What is his attitude to the couples? What words or phrases lead you to this conclusion?
10. What do you think is the significance of the weddings for the poet?

Fourth reading

11. From your reading of this poem, what do you conclude about Larkin's views on weddings and marriage?
12. What picture of England emerges from the poem? Examine stanzas 1, 2, 6 and 7 in particular.
13. What has a reading of this poem added to your understanding of Philip Larkin, man and poet?
14. What questions have you about this poem?

MCMXIV

Those long uneven lines
Standing as patiently
As if they were stretched outside
The Oval or Villa Park,
The crowns of hats, the sun   5
On moustached archaic faces
Grinning as if it were all
An August Bank Holiday lark;

And the shut shops, the bleached
Established names on the sunblinds,   10
The farthings and sovereigns,
And dark-clothed children at play
Called after kings and queens,
The tin advertisements
For cocoa and twist, and the pubs   15
Wide open all day;

And the countryside not caring:
The place-names all hazed over
With flowering grasses, and fields
Shadowing Domesday lines   20
Under wheat's restless silence;
The differently-dressed servants
With tiny rooms in huge houses,
The dust behind limousines;

Never such innocence,   25
Never before or since,
As changed itself to past
Without a word – the men
Leaving the gardens tidy,
The thousands of marriages   30
Lasting a little while longer:
Never such innocence again.

MCMXIV: 1914

[15] **twist:** probably a twist of tobacco, i.e. tobacco sold in a rope-shaped piece

[20] **Domesday [pronounced 'doomsday']:** the Domesday Book was the record of the great survey of the lands of England ordered by William the Conqueror in 1086; so this reference communicates an awareness of the country's history and a sense of continuity with the past.

September 1914: a band leads volunteers enlisting in the British army near Waterloo Station, London

EXPLORATIONS

First reading

1. It might be helpful if you were to think of this poem as a picture:

   Centre and foreground: stanza 1
   Right side: stanza 2
   Left side: stanza 3
   Background: stanza 4

   Describe what you see in each part of the picture.

2. Describe the atmosphere in each part of this picture. What words or phrases suggest it?

Second reading

3. Concentrate on stanzas 1 and 4, the central line of the picture. What image of humanity comes across from these sections?

4. Jot down words or phrases that you think best describe the atmosphere in the entire picture (all four stanzas).

5. What questions could you ask about any of the events or scenes in the poem? Do you think the style of the poem encourages you to question and speculate? Explain.

Third reading

6. Examine the attitude or tone of voice of the poet during this poem. Would you describe him as a detached observer, a sympathetic viewer, cynical, nostalgic, or what? Do you think his attitude changes during the course of the poem? Explain your opinion, with reference to the text.

7. What point or points do you think the poet is making in the poem?

8. Compose a new title for the poem and justify it with reference to the body of the text.

9. Do you know any other poems dealing with a similar theme? Which poem do you prefer, and why?

10. Do you find this poem different in any way from the other Larkin poems you have read? Explain, with reference to particular lines or details of poems.

11. 'The grim reality of human suffering and the transience of all things is hidden behind a veneer of nostalgia in "MCMXIV".' Discuss this view of the poem, with suitable reference to the text.

12. 'Despite a naïve, idealistic view of humankind, Larkin shows some awareness of social problems in "MCMXIV".' Explore this opinion of the poem.

13. When asked to select two of his poems for an anthology in 1973, Larkin opted for 'MCMXIV' and 'Send No Money', saying:

    'They might be taken as representative examples of the two kinds of poem I sometimes

think I write: the beautiful and the true . . . I think a poem usually starts off either from the feeling 'How beautiful that is' or from the feeling 'How true that is.' One of the jobs of the poem is to make the beautiful seem true and the true beautiful, but in fact the disguise can usually be penetrated.'

> [James Gibson (editor), *Let the Poet Choose*.]

(a) In what ways do you think 'MCMXIV' might be considered to exemplify the beautiful?

(b) Do you think it makes the beautiful seem true and the true beautiful? Discuss this, with reference to the text.

Ambulances

this poem is also prescribed for Ordinary Level exams in 2012 and 2014

Closed like confessionals, they thread
Loud noons of cities, giving back
None of the glances they absorb.
Light glossy grey, arms on a plaque,
They come to rest at any kerb: 5
All streets in time are visited.

Then children strewn on steps or road,
Or women coming from the shops
Past smells of different dinners, see
A wild white face that overtops   10
Red stretcher-blankets momently
As it is carried in and stowed,

And sense the solving emptiness
That lies just under all we do,
And for a second get it whole,   15
So permanent and blank and true.
The fastened doors recede. Poor soul,
They whisper at their own distress;

For borne away in deadened air
May go the sudden shut of loss   20
Round something nearly at an end,
And what cohered in it across
The years, the unique random blend
Of families and fashions, there

At last begin to loosen. Far   25
From the exchange of love to lie
Unreachable inside a room
The traffic parts to let go by
Brings closer what is left to come,
And dulls to distance all we are.   30

EXPLORATIONS

1. What is happening in this poem?
2. Follow the ambulance through the streets. Describe what you see.
3. What is the reaction of the onlookers?

Second reading

4. Read the first stanza carefully. What is suggested about the ambulances? Consider in particular the connotations of each of the following phrases: 'Closed like confessionals,' 'they thread', 'giving back | None of the glances', 'come to rest', 'All streets in time are visited.'
5. Read the second stanza carefully. What do we learn about the victims? Consider the connotations of 'children strewn', 'a wild white face', 'stowed'.
6. In the third stanza the victims are frightened because they sense the answer to the question of the meaning 'That lies just under all we do'. What is the answer sensed here?
7. In the first three lines of stanza 4, what words or phrases indicate the seriousness of the situation?

Second reading continued

8. What does the use of 'something' and 'it' suggest to you when used to describe the victim?
9. In what sense does the phrase 'begin to loosen' describe death in the poem?
10. The syntax of the last stanza is deliberately scrambled. Why do you think this might be? If you read 'a room | The traffic parts to let go by' as a metaphorical rendering of 'an ambulance', does the sense become clearer?

Third reading

11. What view of death comes from this poem? Support your opinion with reference to the text.
12. How would you describe the poet's attitude to death?
13. What view of life is intimated in this poem?
14. Explain your own response to the poem's philosophy and its view of death.

15. 'The awful ordinariness of death is one of Larkin's chief preoccupations in this poem.' Discuss this statement, with reference to the text.

16. 'The poem becomes a celebration of the values of consciousness' (Andrew Motion). Examine the poem from this perspective.

The Trees

The trees are coming into leaf
Like something almost being said;
The recent buds relax and spread,
Their greenness is a kind of grief.

Is it that they are born again   5
And we grow old? No, they die too.
Their yearly trick of looking new
Is written down in rings of grain.

Yet still the unresting castles thresh
In fullgrown thickness every May.   10
Last year is dead, they seem to say,
Begin afresh, afresh, afresh.

EXPLORATIONS

First reading

1. What do you notice about the trees on a first reading of this poem?

2. What phrases do you find perplexing?

3. Is it your first impression that this is a predominantly sad or a predominantly happy poem?

4. What aspect or quality of the trees does the poet focus on throughout these verses? Explain, with reference to specific words or phrases, etc.

5. 'The trees are coming into leaf | Like something almost being said . . .'

    What does this simile suggest about the process of foliation? From your own experience, do you think this is an accurate observation? Explain.

6. 'Their greenness is a kind of grief.' How could this be? Do you think the 'grief' applies to the trees or to the poet? How do you interpret the line?

7. What have the trees in common with humanity? Is this a source of comfort or of despair to the poet? Explain.

8. What is your reaction to the description of the trees as 'unresting castles'?

9. Trace the poet's mood in each of the stanzas. What words or phrases carry this mood?

10. Explore the relationship between the poet and nature in this poem.

11. What do you think is the essential wisdom or truth of this poem?

12. Would you agree that Larkin's attitude here is one of 'grudging optimism'? Explain your views, with reference to the poem.

13. Read 'The Trees' in conjunction with 'Ambulances'. Do you find the outlook on life in both poems similar or different? Explain. Which poem, in your opinion, exhibits more of a longing for life? Explain.

The Explosion

this poem is also prescribed for Ordinary Level exams in 2012 and 2014

On the day of the explosion
Shadows pointed towards the pithead:
In the sun the slagheap slept.

Down the lane came men in pitboots
Coughing oath-edged talk and pipe-smoke,   5
Shouldering off the freshened silence.

One chased after rabbits; lost them;
Came back with a nest of lark's eggs;
Showed them; lodged them in the grasses.

So they passed in beards and moleskins,   10
Fathers, brothers, nicknames, laughter,
Through the tall gates standing open.

At noon, there came a tremor; cows
Stopped chewing for a second; sun,
Scarfed as in a heat-haze, dimmed.   15

The dead go on before us, they
Are sitting in God's house in comfort,
We shall see them face to face –

Plain as lettering in the chapels
It was said, and for a second   20
Wives saw men of the explosion

Larger than in life they managed –
Gold as on a coin, or walking
Somehow from the sun towards them,

One showing the eggs unbroken.   25

Explorations

First reading

1. On a first reading, what details made the most impression on you?

2. What happens in the poem?

Second reading

3. What do you notice about the village? Examine all details carefully.

4. What information are we given about the miners? Explore details of dress, habit, manner, mood, philosophy, etc.

5. Are there any hints, either in the imagery or the method of narration, that a tragedy was about to happen? Examine stanzas 1 to 4 for any signs of the ominous.

Second reading continued

6. Do you think the poet's description of the explosion is effective? Explain your thinking on this.

7. The fifth stanza marks a division between two quite different halves in this poem. How do the last ten lines differ from the first four stanzas? How would you describe the atmosphere in the last ten lines? What words or phrases contribute to this?

8. What is suggested in stanza 8? What is the effect of the imagery in this stanza?

9. What do you think is the effect of the last line?

10. What does the poet want us to feel in this poem, and how does he achieve this?

11. What statement about life, society and people do you think

the poet is making here? Refer to details in the poem.

12. Is this a poem you might remember five years from now? Why?

Cut Grass

Cut grass lies frail:
Brief is the breath
Mown stalks exhale.
Long, long the death

It dies in the white hours   5
Of young-leafed June
With chestnut flowers,
With hedges snowlike strewn,

White lilac bowed,
Lost lanes of Queen Anne's lace,   10
And that high-builded cloud
Moving at summer's pace.

Note

[10] **Queen Anne's lace:** wild carrot, a plant sometimes used in herbal medicine and reputed to have contraceptive properties

EXPLORATIONS

Before reading

1. From your own experiences, list what you have noticed about a June day in the countryside.

First reading

2. What elements of nature's activity does the poet focus on?

3. Do you find the poet's attitude to the cut grass particularly sensitive? Explain.

4. What is suggested by the image of the 'white hours' of young-leafed June?

5. 'Lost lanes of Queen Anne's lace'. What do you see when you read this line? What atmosphere does it conjure up?

Second reading

6. What exactly is Larkin's main idea about the season, as communicated in this poem? State it briefly in your own words.

7. What part do the sounds of words play in the creation of atmosphere in the poem?

8. 'While the main focus may be on the exuberance of nature in June, we are also aware of the transience of life, the swift passage of time and the changing seasons in this poem.' Comment.

Third reading

9. Do you think this poem is effective? Explain your own reaction to it.

10 *Thomas Kinsella*
1928–

prescribed for Higher Level exams in 2012, 2013 and 2014

Thomas Kinsella was born in Inchicore, Dublin on 4 May 1928 to John Paul and Agnes Casserly Kinsella. His father and grandfather worked in Guinness's Brewery, although his grandfather had retired and was a repairer of shoes when Thomas knew him. His mother's father was an insurance collector. His grandmothers managed small shops: one in Basin Lane, off James's Street; the other in Bow Lane nearby. It was in this intimate world of narrow streets, crowded rooms and close-knit families that he recalls things of importance happening to him for the first time. It was these events that he would later explore through his poetry.

The family moved to Manchester just as the Second World War started. During the war, Thomas came to realise humanity's capacity for destruction. His awareness of the fragile nature of life and relationships never faded, and this awareness appears in many of his poems. The Kinsellas stayed in England for three years and then returned to Ireland, eventually settling in Basin Lane.

Educated at the Model School, Inchicore and the Christian Brothers' O'Connell School, he entered University College Dublin in 1946. While at university, he was offered and accepted a post in the Civil Service. He worked as a civil servant during the day and returned to UCD as a night student. Some of his first poems and stories were published in the college magazine, *St Stephen's*, and in *Comhar*, an Irish language publication.

Kinsella formed significant friendships at this time with the musician and composer Seán Ó Riada and the publisher Liam Miller. Both men had a profound impact on his intellectual and poetic development. Miller, founder of the Dolmen Press, published Kinsella's first pamphlet, *The Starlight Eye* (1952), and his first book-length publication, *Poems* (1956). These were followed by *Another September* (1958), *Moralities* (1960), *Downstream* (1962), *Wormwood* (1966) and *Nightwalker* (1967). His early work deals with issues of love, identity, the self, the precariousness of life and relationships, death, and the act of creation. The exploration of these themes in an urban setting distinguishes him from mainstream Irish poetry in the 1950s and 1960s which was dominated mainly by Patrick Kavanagh.

In December 1955, he married Eleanor Walsh, a radiology student, following her hospitalisation for over a year as she recovered from tuberculosis of the throat. His first collection, *Poems* (1956), was issued as a wedding gift to her. Eleanor appears in his poems in the role of lover, companion, Muse and goddess figure.

Acting on Miller's suggestion, Kinsella began translating Old Irish literature into English, producing versions of *Longes Mac Unsnig* and *The Breastplate of St Patrick* (1954), the *Thirty Three Triads* (1955), the epic narrative *The Tain* (1969), and *An Duanaire 1600–1900: Poems of the Dispossessed* (1981).

In 1965, Kinsella left the Civil Service and became writer-in-residence at Southern Illinois University in the United States. Five years later he moved to Temple University, Philadelphia, as Professor of English, where he taught for almost twenty years, dividing his time between the USA and Ireland.

A director of Dolmen Press and Cuala Press, Kinsella founded his own imprint, Peppercanister, in 1972, to publish pamphlets of his poetry. He produced *Butcher's Dozen* (1972),

Notes From the Land of the Dead and Other Poems (1973) and *One* (1974). The influence of American modernism on his poetry now becomes evident. His extensive reading of poets such as William Carlos Williams, Ezra Pound and Robert Lowell inspired him to move beyond the formal structures of traditional poetry and to write in the looser style of blank verse or free verse. His poetry began to focus on the individual psyche as described in the work of Carl Jung. It turned towards origins and myths, and was strongly influenced by Jungian concepts of structures and archetypes. At the same time, he explored issues relevant to contemporary Ireland and the role of tradition in Irish society.

Kinsella also turned to editing. In 1974, he edited Austin Clarke's *Selected Poems* and *Collected Poems* for Dolmen, and the *New Oxford Book of Irish Verse* in 1986.

In the 1980s, books like *Her Vertical Smile* (1985), *Out of Ireland* (1987) and *St Catherine's Clock* (1987) saw a move from personal poetry to an examination of historical trends. His satirical focus on the contemporary world continued through the late 1980s and 1990s in *One Fond Embrace* (1988), *Personal Places* (1990), *Poems From The Centre City* (1990) and *The Pen Shop* (1996). His *Collected Poems* was published in 2001. *Marginal Economies* and *Reading in Poetry*, a series of readings of notable poems, were both published in 2006. Humanity's capacity for self-destruction, which he had first experienced in Manchester, is the central argument in *Man of War* (2007) and he returns to ways of discovering and understanding in *Belief and Unbelief* (2007).

Kinsella has received many awards, including the Guinness Poetry Award, the Irish Arts Council Triennial Book Award and the Denis Devlin Memorial Award, as well as several Guggenheim Fellowships. He received the Honorary Freedom of the City of Dublin in May 2007.

Thinking of Mr D.

this poem is also prescribed for Ordinary Level exams in 2012, 2013 and 2014

A man still light of foot, but ageing, took
An hour to drink his glass, his quiet tongue
Danced to such cheerful slander.

He sipped and swallowed with a scathing smile,
Tapping a polished toe.   5
His sober nod withheld assent.

When he died I saw him twice.
Once as he used retire
On one last murmured stabbing little tale
From the right company, tucking in his scarf.   10

And once down by the river, under wharf-
Lamps that plunged him in and out of light,
A priestlike figure turning, wolfish-slim,
Quickly aside from pain, in a bodily plight,
To note the oiled reflections chime and swim.   15

Mr D. has been identified as representing Dante Alighieri and Austin Clarke.

Dante Alighieri (1265–1321): Italian poet and satirist from Florence. Involved in politics in Florence, he grew bitter at his treatment by the Florentines. When exiled from the city, he wrote *The Divine Comedy*, which tells of Dante's journey across the river Styx to the realms of the dead. Kinsella's father had a copy of Dante's best known work.

Austin Clarke (1896–1974): Irish poet, playwright and novelist. His early poetry drew heavily on the imagery and mythology of pre-Christian Ireland. His later works protested against social injustice and he added a satirical dimension to his writing.

EXPLORATIONS

First reading

1. What do you learn about the physical appearance of the man in the first six lines? What additional information can you find about him in the rest of the poem?

2. Explain what you think the poet means by the line 'When he died I saw him twice.' In what sense can you 'see' someone who has died?

3. What aspects of the man's character are revealed in this poem? Jot down the words and phrases that give you an insight into his personality.

Second reading

4. Select and comment on any two images that you liked in the poem.

5. From your reading of the poem, do you think that the speaker liked Mr D.? What evidence is there to support your view?

6. Assess the mood of the poem. Is it cheerful, nostalgic, serious, dark or something else? Which mood dominates, in your opinion? Explain your choice.

7. How does the poet establish the mood? Refer to the poem in your answer.

Dick King

In your ghost, Dick King, in your phantom vowels I read
That death roves our memories igniting
Love. Kind plague, low voice in a stubbed throat,
You haunt with the taint of age and of vanished good,
Fouling my thought with losses.   5

Clearly now I remember rain on the cobbles,
Ripples in the iron trough, and the horses' dipped
Faces under the Fountain in James' Street,
When I sheltered my nine years against your buttons
And your own dread years were to come: 10

And your voice, in a pause of softness, named the dead,
Hushed as though the city had died by fire,
Bemused, discovering . . . discovering
A gate to enter temperate ghosthood by;
And I squeezed your fingers till you found again   15
My hand hidden in yours.

I squeeze your fingers:

Dick King was an upright man.
Sixty years he trod
The dull stations underfoot.   20
Fifteen he lies with God.

By the salt seaboard he grew up
But left its rock and rain
To bring a dying language east
And dwell in Basin Lane.   25

By the Southern Railway he increased:
His second soul was born
In the clangour of the iron sheds,
The hush of the late horn.

An invalid he took to wife.   30
She prayed her life away;
Her whisper filled the whitewashed yard
Until her dying day.

And season in, season out,
He made his wintry bed.   35
He took the path to the turnstile
Morning and night till he was dead.

He clasped his hands in a Union ward
To hear St James's bell.
I searched his eyes though I was young,   40
The last to wish him well.

---

[27] **Clangour:** a shrill, sharp, harsh sound
[37] **Union ward:** a home for poor people who were old or sick

EXPLORATIONS

First reading

1. In the opening stanza, what do you learn has happened to Dick King? How do you know?

2. Outline the speaker's fondest memory of him.

3. Write a brief biography of Dick King using only the information given in the poem.

4. What do you learn about Mrs King? Why did the speaker refer to her, in your opinion?

Second reading

5. Explore in detail the relationship between the older man and the boy.

6. Based on your reading of the poem, give your impression of Dick King. Did you like him? Explain your answer.

7. What did you learn about the personality of the boy? Refer to the poem to support your answer.

Third reading

8. If you were asked to read the poem aloud, what tone of voice would you use? Where would it change? Why?

9. Choose one stanza and study the lines carefully. How does the poet create the tone in that stanza?

Fourth reading

10. Examine the rhythm, rhyme and structure of the poem. What do you notice?

11. Is this a poem about the destructive force of death or the enduring power of love and memories?

12. What other themes can you find in this poem? Refer to the poem in your answer.

Mirror in February

this poem is also prescribed for Ordinary Level exams in 2012, 2013 and 2014

The day dawns with scent of must and rain,
Of opened soil, dark trees, dry bedroom air.
Under the fading lamp, half dressed – my brain
Idling on some compulsive fantasy –
I towel my shaven jaw and stop, and stare,   5
Riveted by a dark exhausted eye,
A dry downturning mouth.

It seems again that it is time to learn,
In this untiring, crumbling place of growth
To which, for the time being, I return.   10
Now plainly in the mirror of my soul
I read that I have looked my last on youth
And little more; for they are not made whole
That reach the age of Christ.

Below my window the awakening trees,   15
Hacked clean for better bearing, stand defaced
Suffering their brute necessities,
And how should the flesh not quail that span for span
Is mutilated more? In slow distaste
I fold my towel with what grace I can,   20
Not young and not renewable, but man.

Note

[18] **quail:** to cower, to shrink through fear

Explorations

1. Describe in your own words what is happening in the first stanza.

2. Suggest two different reasons why soil might be 'opened'.

3. Do you think the speaker is surprised by his reflection in the mirror? Does he like what he sees? Explain your answer.

4. What does he learn in the second stanza?

5. Humans age and die while the natural world renews itself. How does the speaker react to this realisation? Do you admire his response? Why?

6. Do you find the ending convincing? Explain your answer.

Second reading

7. Examine the imagery and language used to describe growth and decay. Do you find them effective or stale and overused?

8. How would you describe the mood of the poem? Is it the same throughout? What evidence is there to support your view?

Second reading continued

9. Summarise the theme in a few lines.

10. Study the rhyming scheme. Why did the poet alter it in the final stanza? What is the effect of the change?

Third reading

11. The poem is structured around a series of contrasts. Identify these contrasts and state whether or not you find them interesting.

12. How did this poem affect you? Did it make you think about ageing, death, and the contrast between the human and natural world? How do you feel about the inevitability of death?

Fourth reading

13. This poem is concerned with issues of suffering and endurance. Does it deal with more than this? Refer to the text in your answer.

14. 'Kinsella observes situations, enters them imaginatively and gains an insight into life.' Is this what happens in the poem?

Chrysalides

Our last free summer we mooned about at odd hours
Pedalling slowly through country towns, stopping to eat
Chocolate and fruit, tracing our vagaries on the map.

At night we watched in the barn, to the lurch of melodeon music,
The crunching boots of countrymen – huge and weightless   5
As their shadows – twirling and leaping over the yellow concrete.

Sleeping too little or too much, we awoke at noon
And were received with womanly mockery into the kitchen,
Like calves poking our faces in with enormous hunger.

Daily we strapped our saddlebags and went to experience   10
A tolerance we shall never know again, confusing
For the last time, for example, the licit and the familiar.

Our instincts blurred with change; a strange wakefulness
Sapped our energies and dulled our slow-beating hearts
To the extremes of feeling – insensitive alike   15

To the unique succession of our youthful midnights,
When by a window ablaze softly with the virgin moon
Dry scones and jugs of milk awaited us in the dark,

Or to lasting horror, a wedding flight of ants
Spawning to its death, a mute perspiration   20
Glistening like drops of copper, agonised, in our path.

Note

Chrysalides: plural of chrysalis, the pupa, or torpid state of an insect before it assumes its wings; from the Greek 'Chrysos' meaning 'gold'.

EXPLORATIONS

First reading

1. Do you think that the speaker enjoyed that 'last free summer'? Which aspects of it appealed to you?

2. How did they spend their days and nights? Which activity do you find more attractive?

3. They became insensitive to 'extremes of feeling'. Identify those extremes. What images are used to represent them?

4. Explain in your own words what happened in the final stanza. How do you react to this scene? Do you find it horrible, sad, interesting or something else?

Second reading

5. What were your expectations of the poem when you read the title and footnote? Were you surprised by the poem?

6. Does the title help your understanding of what is happening in the poem? What connects the travellers and the chrysalides?

Third reading

7. Is the poet attempting to describe a series of events or a state of mind? Give reasons for your answer.

8. Trace the development of thought through the poem.

9. How does the poet establish a sense of languor or laziness? Examine the rhythm of the poem and the use of assonance and alliteration.

Fourth reading

10. Comment on the irony of the final stanza.

11. Give your personal response to this poem. Do you like it? What questions does it raise in your mind?

12. 'In his poetry, Kinsella confronts the forces of change and decay that threaten life.' Do you agree with this statement? Refer to the text in your answer.

From Glenmacnass

VI Littlebody

Up on the high road, as far as the sheepfold
into the wind, and back. The sides of the black bog channels
dug down in the water. The white cottonheads
on the old cuttings nodding everywhere.
Around one more bend, toward the car shining in the distance.   5

From a stony slope half way, behind a rock prow
with the stones on top for an old mark,
the music of pipes, distant and clear.

*

I was climbing up, making no noise
and getting close, when the music stopped,   10
leaving a pagan shape in the air.

There was a hard inhale,
a base growl,
and it started again, in a guttural dance.

I looked around the edge   15
 – and it was Littlebody. Hugging his bag
under his left arm, with his eyes closed.

I slipped. Our eyes met.
He started scuttling up the slope with his gear
and his hump, elbows out and neck back.   20

But I shouted:
     'Stop, Littlebody!
I found you fair, and I want my due.'

He stopped and dropped his pipes,
and spread his arms out, waiting for the next move.   25
I heard myself reciting:

'Demon dwarf
with the German jaw,

surrender your purse
with the ghostly gold.'   30

He took out a fat purse,
put it down on a stone
and recited in reply, in a voice too big for his body:

'You found me fair,
and I grant your wishes.   35
But we'll meet again,
when I dance in your ashes.'

He settled himself down once more
and bent over the bag,
        looking off to one side.   40

'I thought I was safe up here.
You have to give the music a while to itself sometimes,
up out of the huckstering

– jumping around in your green top hat
and showing your skills   45
with your eye on your income.'

He ran his fingers up and down the stops,
then gave the bag a last squeeze.
His face went solemn,

his fingertips fondled all the right places,   50
and he started a slow air
        out across the valley.

                         *

I left him to himself.
And left the purse where it was.
I have all I need for the while I have left   55

without taking unnecessary risks.
And made my way down to the main road
with my mind on our next meeting.

Littlebody A mythological figure known in folklore as one of the Little People, the Good Folk, or a leprechaun. Fabled to carry a bag of gold. Tradition states that if you find a leprechaun and do not look away from him he cannot escape until he hands over the gold. The Little People reward kindness but cause mischief to those who anger them. They were associated with making shoes and playing pipes.

[3] **White cottonheads:** bog cotton; a small plant that grows on bogs. The white tuft that forms at the top of the stem resembles cotton wool.

EXPLORATIONS

First reading

1. The poem opens with a realistic description of a hillside. Which lines appealed to you the most?

2. Were you surprised by the appearance of the leprechaun in such a natural setting?

3. What does Littlebody look like? Were any of his features unusual? What do they suggest about him?

4. Give an account in your own words of what happened that day.

Second reading

5. Comment on Littlebody's reaction to the human. Is he fearful, angry, upset, sad?

6. Littlebody gives his reasons for being in that isolated place. What are they? Do you agree with him?

Second reading continued

7. The speaker leaves the bag of gold behind. What prompts him to do this? When will he meet Littlebody again?

Third reading

8. 'Littlebody represents the mythological past, the artist and death.' Where can you find evidence for this claim in the poem?

9. In your opinion, does the poet identify with Littlebody? What do they have in common? Does he sympathise with Littlebody's comment about the music? Refer to the poem in your answer.

10. If you were discussing this poem with Thomas Kinsella, what comments would you make and what questions would you ask?

Tear

I was sent in to see her.
A fringe of jet drops
chattered at my ear
as I went through the hangings.

I was swallowed in chambery dusk.   5
My heart shrank
at the smell of disused
organs and sour kidney.

The black aprons I used to
bury my face in   10
were folded at the foot of the bed
in the last watery light from the window

(Go in and say goodbye to her)
and I was carried off
to unfathomable depths.   15
I turned to look at her.

She stared at the ceiling
and puffed her cheek, distracted,
propped high in the bed
resting for the next attack.   20

The covers were gathered close
up to her mouth,
that the lines of ill-temper still
marked. Her grey hair

was loosened out like a young woman's   25
all over the pillow,
mixed with the shadows
criss-crossing her forehead

and at her mouth and eyes,
like a web of strands tying down her head   30
and tangling down toward the shadow
eating away the floor at my feet.

I couldn't stir at first, nor wished to,
for fear she might turn and tempt me
(my own father's mother)   35
with open mouth

– with some fierce wheedling whisper –
to hide myself one last time
against her, and bury my
self in her drying mud.   40

Was I to kiss her? As soon
kiss the damp that crept
in the flowered walls
of this pit.

Yet I had to kiss.   45
I knelt by the bulk of the death bed
and sank my face in the chill
and smell of her black aprons.

Snuff and musk, the folds against my eyelids,
carried me into a derelict place   50
smelling of ash: unseen walls and roofs
rustled like breathing.

I found myself disturbing
dead ashes for any trace
of warmth, when far off   55
in the vaults a single drop

splashed. And I found
what I was looking for
– not heat nor fire,
not any comfort,   60

but her voice, soft, talking to someone
about my father: 'God help him, he cried
big tears over there by the machine
for the poor little thing.' Bright

drops on the wooden lid   65
for my infant sister.
My own wail of child-animal grief
was soon done, with any early guess

at sad dullness and tedious pain
and lives bitter with hard bondage.   70
How I tasted it now –
her heart beating in my mouth!

She drew an uncertain breath
and pushed at the clothes
and shuddered tiredly.   75
I broke free

and left the room
promising myself
when she was really dead
I would really kiss.   80

My grandfather half looked up
from the fireplace as I came out,
and shrugged and turned back
with a deaf stare to the heat.

I fidgeted beside him for a minute   85
and went out to the shop.
It was still bright there
and I felt better able to breathe.

Old age can digest
anything: the commotion   90
at Heaven's gate – the struggle
in store for you all your life.

How long and hard it is
before you get to Heaven,
unless like little Agnes   95
you vanish with early tears.

---

[2]   **jet:** a black coloured mineral, used to make beads and ornaments

[95] **little Agnes:** Kinsella's baby sister

EXPLORATIONS

First reading

1. The young boy was 'sent in' to see his grandmother. Why is he reluctant to visit her? How does he feel?

2. Describe the old woman in detail. What does her appearance suggest about her?

3. 'And I found what I was looking for.' What does he find? Do her words give you a different picture of the old woman?

First reading continued

4. Examine the child's reaction to his experience. Does he feel relief, sadness, guilt, confusion, or something else? Are his feelings understandable?

Second reading

5. Do you agree with the conclusion he reaches in the final stanzas? Explain your answer.

6. Choose the image you find most effective in this poem. Give reasons for your choice.

7. How many references to tears can you find? How do they affect the mood?

8. Imagine you are an artist. Choose four colours you would use to paint a picture inspired by this poem. Justify your choice.

Third reading

9. The poem contrasts two deaths: one in the past, the other about to happen. What do they have in common? How are they different?

10. Examine the words and phrases that suggest light and darkness. Discuss the emotions associated with each.

11. Atmosphere plays an important role in this poem. How would you describe the atmosphere? What details appear to you to be significant in creating it? Describe its effect on you.

Fourth reading

12. In your opinion, does the poet make an important discovery about life and death as a result of this experience? If so, what is it?

13. Identify three themes raised in this poem and explain how the poet deals with them.

14. Outline your response to this poem.

Hen Woman

The noon heat in the yard
smelled of stillness and coming thunder.
A hen scratched and picked at the shore.
It stopped, its body crouched and puffed out.
The brooding silence seemed to say 'Hush . . .'   5

The cottage door opened,
a black hole
in a whitewashed wall so bright

The eyes narrowed.
Inside, a clock murmured 'Gong . . .'   10

(I had felt all this before.)

She hurried out in her slippers
muttering, her face dark with anger,
and gathered the hen up jerking
languidly. Her hand fumbled.   15

Too late. Too late.

It fixed me with its pebble eyes
(seeing what mad blur).
A white egg showed in the sphincter;
mouth and beak opened together;   20
and time stood still.

Nothing moved: bird or woman,
fumbled or fumbling – locked there
(as I must have been) gaping.

                    *

There was a tiny movement at my feet,   25
tiny and mechanical; I looked down.
A beetle like a bronze leaf
was inching across the cement,
clasping with small tarsi
a ball of dung bigger than its body.   30

The serrated brow pressed the ground humbly,
lifted in a short stare, bowed again;
the dung-ball advanced minutely,
losing a few fragments,
specks of staleness and freshness.   35

                    *

A mutter of thunder far off
– time not quite stopped.

I saw the egg had moved a fraction:
a tender blank brain
under torsion, a clean new world.   40

As I watched, the mystery completed.
The black zero of the orifice
closed to a point
and the white zero of the egg hung free,
flecked with greenish brown oils.   45

It fell and turned over slowly.
Dreamlike, fussed by her splayed fingers,
it floated outward, moon-white,
leaving no trace in the air,
and began its drop to the shore.   50

                        *

I feed upon it still, as you see;
there is no end to that which, not understood,
may yet be hoarded in the imagination,
in the yolk of one's being, so to speak,
there to undergo its (quite animal) growth,   55

dividing blindly, twitching, packed with will,
searching in its own tissue
for the structure in which it may wake.
Something that had – clenched in its cave –
not been now as was: an egg of being.   60

Through what seemed a whole year it fell
– as it still falls, for me, solid and light,
the red gold beating in its silvery womb,
alive as the yolk and white of my eye.
As it will continue to fall, probably, until I die, 65
through the vast indifferent spaces
with which I am empty.

                        *

It smashed against the grating

and slipped down quickly out of sight.
It was over in a comical flash.   70
The soft mucous shell clung a little longer,
then drained down.

She stood staring, in blank anger.
Then her eyes came to life, and she laughed
and let the bird flap away.   76

'It's all the one.
There's plenty more where that came from!'

EXPLORATIONS

1. Where is the poem set? What figures are present? Jot down other details you noticed on a first reading.

2. What aspects of the scene draw the speaker's attention in the first section?

3. In your opinion, why was the beetle introduced into the scene? What effect does it have?

4. What happened to the hen and the egg? How did the woman react? Did her response surprise you? Why?

5. How does the speaker 'feed upon it still'? Explain what you think he means by that line.

6. Examine how the sense of tension is created. What details heighten the tension? Look at the language and punctuation used.

7. Read the poem carefully again. Is the final line an anti-climax or is the poet making a point about life? If so, what is it, in your opinion?

8. The image of the egg is linked to all references to enclosed spaces within the poem. What are these spaces?

9. The poem deals with a number of important processes: fertilisation, the cycle of life, and the movement towards and away from light. Where are these most evident? Which is the most important, in your opinion, or are they all treated equally?

10. The poet and the reader are both present as witnesses to the event. Are there other similarities between the poet and the reader in this poem?

11. The central focus of the poem is the role of the imagination and the power of memory. Do you agree? Refer to the poem in your answer.

12. Archetypal images, such as the woman, egg, beetle, and cave, add immeasurably to richness of this poem. Take each image and jot down a list of ideas associated with it. Now discuss the effect of these universal images on your appreciation of the poem.

His Father's Hands

I drank firmly
and set the glass down between us firmly.
You were saying.

My father
Was saying.   5

His fingers prodded and prodded,
marring his point. Emphas-
emphasemphasis.

I have watched
his father's hands before him   10

cupped, and tightening the black Plug
between knife and thumb,
carving off little curlicues
to rub them in the dark of his palms,

or cutting into new leather at his bench,   15
levering a groove open with his thumb,
insinuating wet sprigs for the hammer.

He kept the sprigs in mouthfuls
and brought them out in silvery
units between his lips.   20

I took a pinch out of their hole
and knocked them one by one into the wood,
bright points among hundreds gone black,
other children's – cousins and others, grown up.

Or his bow hand scarcely moving,   25
scraping in the dark corner near the fire,
his plump fingers shifting on the strings.

To his deaf, inclined head
he hugged the fiddle's body

whispering with the tune
with breaking heart
whene'er I hear
in privacy, across a blocked void,

the wind that shakes the barley.
The wind . . .
round her grave . . .

on my breast in blood she died . . .
But blood for blood without remorse
I've ta'en . . .

Beyond that.

*

Your family, Thomas, met with and helped
many of the Croppies in hiding from the Yeos
or on their way home after the defeat
in south Wexford. They sheltered the Laceys
who were later hanged on the Bridge in Ballinglen
between Tinahely and Anacorra,

From hearsay, as far as I can tell
the Men Folk were either Stone Cutters
or masons or probably both.
      In the 18
and late 1700s even the farmers
had some other trade to make a living.

They lived in Farnese among a Colony
of North of Ireland or Scotch settlers left there
in some of the dispersions or migrations
which occurred in this Area of Wicklow and Wexford
and Carlow. And some years before that time
the Family came from somewhere around Tullow.

Beyond that.

*

Littered uplands. Dense grass. Rocks everywhere,
wet underneath, retaining memory of the long cold.
First, a prow of land

chosen, and wedged with tracks;
then boulders chosen
and sloped together, stabilised in menace.   65

      I do not like this place.
I do not think the people who lived here
were ever happy. It feels evil.
Terrible things happened.
I feel afraid here when I am on my own.   70

           *

Dispersals or migrations.
Through what evolutions or accidents
toward that peace and patience
by the fireside, that blocked gentleness . . .

That serene pause, with the slashing knife,   75
in kindly mockery,
as I busy myself with my little nails
at the rude block, his bench.

The blood advancing
– gorging vessel after vessel –   80
and altering in them
one by one.

Behold, that gentleness already
modulated twice, in others;
to earnestness and iteration;   85
to an offhandedness, repressing various impulses.

           *

Extraordinary . . . The big block – I found it
years afterward in a corner of the yard
in sunlight after rain
and stood it up, wet and black: 90
it turned under my hands, an axis
of light flashing down its length,
and the wood's soft flesh broke open,
countless little nails
squirming and dropping out of it.   95

[11] **plug:** tobacco

[17] **sprigs:** nails with no head

[25] **bow hand:** hand used to pull the bow across a violin

[42] **Croppies:** popular name for the Irish who fought in the 1798 Rebellion

[42] **Yeos:** Yeomen – a volunteer cavalry force in the British Army who fought against the Irish, comprised mainly of gentlemen and wealthy farmers

[45–6] **Ballinglen, Tinahely, Anacorra:** places in County Wicklow

[53] **Farnese:** a farming area owned by the Coolattin estate

[58] **Tullow:** a town in County Carlow

EXPLORATIONS

First reading

1. How did the grandfather use his hands? What does this indicate about his personality?

2. Give a brief account of what you learn about the family.

3. Kinsella believes the past is important. Do you agree with him?

4. How does he feel in the hills? What does that suggest about the past?

Second reading

5. What point is he making in the fourth section? How can the violent past lead to such 'peace and patience'?

6. The poet describes the discovery of the block as 'extraordinary'. Comment on his use of this word.

Third reading

7. Based on your reading of the poem, describe Kinsella's relationship with his grandfather.

8. Kinsella uses the words 'block' and 'blocked' several times. Discuss the contexts in which he uses the words. How does it change their meaning?

9. What did you learn about the personality of the poet from reading this poem?

Fourth reading

10. The block symbolises masculine and feminine principles, as it fertilises and gives birth. It also represents growth and decay. Where else in the poem are there references to the life cycle and to

evolution? How does this change your understanding of the poem?

11. Kinsella describes insignificant and ordinary events and gives them a sense of otherness. Do you agree?

12. Decay and rebirth are twin concerns in Kinsella's work. Comment on this statement in the light of your reading of this poem.

From Settings

Model School, Inchicore

Miss Carney handed us out blank paper and marla,
old plasticine with the colours
all rolled together into brown.

You started with a ball of it
and rolled it into a snake curling   5
around your hand, and kept rolling it
in one place until it wore down into two
with a stain on the paper.

We always tittered at each other
when we said the adding-up table in Irish   10
and came to her name.
               *

In the second school we had Mr Browne.
He had white teeth in his brown man's face.

He stood in front of the blackboard
and chalked a white dot.   15

     'We are going to start
     decimals.'

     I am going to know
     everything.
              *

One day he said: 20
'Out into the sun!'
We settled his chair under a tree
and sat ourselves down delighted
in two rows in the greeny gold shade.

A fat bee floated around   25
shining amongst us
and the flickering sun
warmed out folded coats
and he said 'History . . . !'
                        *

When the Autumn came   30
and the big chestnut leaves
fell all over the playground
we piled them in heaps
between the wall and the tree trunks
and the boys ran races   35
jumping over the heaps
and tumbled into them shouting.
                        *

I sat by myself in the shed
and watched the draught
blowing the papers   40
around the wheels of the bicycles.

Will God judge
        our most secret thoughts and actions?
God will judge
        our most secret thoughts and actions   45
and every idle word that man shall speak
he shall render an account of it
on the Day of Judgement.
                        *

The taste
of ink off   50
the nib shrank your
mouth.

EXPLORATIONS

First reading

1. Do you remember playing with plasticine? Do you recall the smell, the colours and how it felt to touch?

2. From your reading of this poem, do you think that the speaker enjoyed school? How did he feel about learning?

3. What is he doing in the bicycle shed? How is this section different from the others?

4. Explain what you think he means in the final four lines.

Second reading

5. What type of child was he, according to the evidence in the poem?

6. The snake is an ancient symbol of fertility. In what ways will the child's mind become fertile?

7. How many references to writing and writing materials can you find in this poem? Why are they present, in your opinion?

Third reading

8. This is a sensual poem. Identify the words and phrases that appeal to the senses. How do they add to your enjoyment of the poem?

9. The ordinary is packed with potential. Do you think that Kinsella makes this point in the poem? Give reasons for your answer.

10. Did you like this poem? Why or why not?

Fourth reading

11. The poem moves from a description of innocence to a reflection on accountability. Comment on this statement in the light of your reading of the poem.

12. Trace the progress of thought in the poem from the white dot of beginnings, through history, to the Day of Judgement.

From The Familiar

VII

I was downstairs at first light,
looking out through the frost on the window
at the hill opposite and the sheets of frost
scattered down among the rocks.

The cat back in the kitchen.   5
Folded on herself. Torn and watchful.

*

A chilled grapefruit
– thin-skinned, with that little gloss.
I took a mouthful, looking up along the edge of the wood

at the two hooded crows high in the cold   10
talking to each other,
flying up toward the tundra, beyond the waterfall.

*

I sliced the tomatoes in thin discs
in damp sequence into their dish;
scalded the kettle; made the tea,   15

and rang the little brazen bell.
And saved the toast.
        Arranged the pieces

in slight disorder around the basket.
Fixed our places, one with the fruit   20
and one with the plate of sharp cheese.

*

And stood in my dressing gown
with arms extended
over the sweetness of the sacrifice.

Her shade showed in the door.   25

Her voice responded:

'You are very good. You always made it nice.'

---

[12]   **tundra:** cold region in the northern hemisphere, near the
       Arctic ice sheet. It is thinly populated and there is very
       little vegetation because of the extreme cold.

EXPLORATIONS

First reading

1. Imagine the poem is based on the opening sequence in a film. Describe the scene: the setting, the props, the characters and the actions.

2. What daily ritual is the speaker performing? What makes it special?

3. How does the woman respond? How do you think the speaker felt at that moment?

4. Do the crows and the humans share anything in common? What is it, in your opinion?

Second reading

5. Based on your reading of this poem, describe the relationship between the two people.

6. Would you describe this as a love poem? Give reasons for your answer.

Third reading

7. How important is the landscape and weather in establishing the atmosphere? Compare the atmosphere outside with the atmosphere in the house. What similarities and differences do you find?

8. Is the mood the same as the atmosphere in this poem? Give reasons for your answer.

9. Examine the use of religious imagery in the poem. Where is it most evident? Does it remind you of a religious ceremony? Which one? Why do you think that the poet decided to describe the ritual of making breakfast in these terms?

Fourth reading

10. The imposition of order is central to this poem. Do you agree? Examine the actions of the speaker and the structure of the poem.

11. Is there a connection between making breakfast and writing a poem? How are the two activities similar? Refer to the poem in your answer.

12. 'This poem is a celebration of fidelity and togetherness.' Give your response to this statement.

From Belief and Unbelief

Echo

He cleared the thorns
from the broken gate,
and held her hand
through the heart of the wood
to the holy well.   5

They revealed their names
and told their tales
as they said that they would
on that distant day
when their love began.   10

And hand in hand
they turned to leave.
When she stopped and whispered
a final secret
down to the water.   15

Notes

Echo: a repetition of a sound. A nymph, in Greek mythology, who loved her own voice. She was punished by Hera, who took away her voice, except in repetition of another's shouted words. She fell in love with Narcissus, a vain young man, who rejected her, and she fled to lonely glens, pining away for love, until only her voice remained.

EXPLORATIONS

Before reading

1. Jot down the symbols that you find in the poem. Suggest meanings for them. What do they add to your understanding of the poem?

2. There is a sense of revelation and openness in the second stanza. Do you agree? Where is it most evident?

First reading

3. What is your interpretation of the final lines? Do you think that he overheard the whisper? Did they share the secret? Was she hiding something from him? Was it the end of secrets between them?

Second reading

4. They enter, stay, leave, and stop. Which action is the most significant, in your opinion? Explain your answer.

5. Based on your reading of the poem, describe their relationship.

Third reading

6. Is this poem like a fairytale? Give reasons for your answer.

7. Trace the development of thought in the poem.

8. Comment on the title of the poem. Do you find it appropriate? Suggest another title that you think would be suitable.

Fourth reading

9. There is a sense of incompleteness in the poem. What is the poet suggesting about relationships and processes?

10. This is a poem that conceals as well as reveals. In your opinion, why did the poet choose to adopt this approach to his material?

Adrienne Rich
1929–

prescribed for Higher Level exams in 2011, 2012 and 2013

Adrienne Rich was born in Baltimore, USA on 16 May 1929, the elder of two daughters. Her father, Arnold, was a doctor and a pathology professor at Johns Hopkins University, while her mother, Helen, had been a talented pianist and composer before devoting herself to raising her two daughters.

Adrienne was a bright child and was educated at home by her parents prior to entering the school system. It was her father who was to have the greater influence on her. Indeed, it was under his guidance that she began to write poetry. As she developed, Rich was to experience a sense of conflict as she tried to break away from her father's influence both in her writing and in her life.

In 1951 Adrienne graduated from Radcliffe College with an excellent degree. In the same year she received the Yale Younger Poets award for her first book of poetry. In 1953 she married a Harvard economist, Alfred Conrad, and had three sons. Adrienne continued to write, but she felt increasingly unhappy with the direction of her life. The 1960s were a time of great political upheaval in the United States and both Rich and her husband became involved with movements for social justice, with her interest focusing on the women's movement.

Her experiences as a lesbian and a feminist led her to develop an empathy with all those groups in society who are considered less equal, and her poetry became increasingly politicised as she sought to give a voice to those who are not normally heard. Although Rich has won many prizes for her writing, in 1997 she declined the National Medal for the Arts from the then President, Bill Clinton, saying, 'A president cannot meaningfully honour certain token artists while the people at large are so dishonoured.'

Adrienne Rich published her latest book of poems, *Telephone Ringing in the Labyrinth: Poems 2004–2006*, at the age of seventy-eight.

Aunt Jennifer's Tigers

this poem is also prescribed for Ordinary Level exams in 2011, 2012 and 2013

Aunt Jennifer's tigers prance across a screen,
Bright topaz denizens of a world of green.
They do not fear the men beneath the tree;
They pace in sleek chivalric certainty.

Aunt Jennifer's fingers fluttering through her wool   5
Find even the ivory needle hard to pull.
The massive weight of Uncle's wedding band
Sits heavily upon Aunt Jennifer's hand.

When Aunt is dead, her terrified hands will lie
Still ringed with ordeals she was mastered by.   10
The tigers in the panel that she made
Will go on prancing, proud and unafraid.

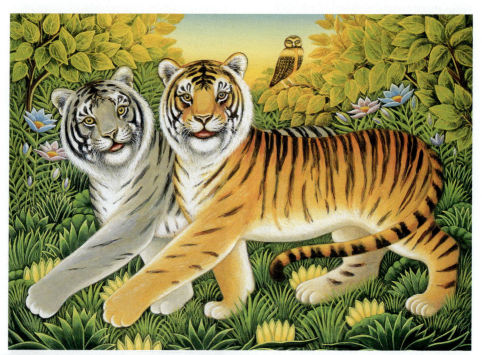

Frances Broomfield: Tyger/Tyger

Notes

[1] **prance:** to spring forward on back legs with front legs raised; to walk arrogantly

[2] **topaz:** a yellow/gold gem

[2] **denizens:** inhabitants

[4] **chivalric:** courtly, knightly

[10] **ordeals:** painful or horrifying experiences

EXPLORATIONS

First reading

1. Imagine that you are a director preparing to film this scene. Using the clues given in the poem, write the instructions that you would give to (a) the set designer, regarding how the sets should look; and (b) the cameraman/woman, describing the camera shots that he/she should use.

2. Divide a copy page into two short columns. Put the heading 'Tigers' at the top of one column and 'Aunt Jennifer' at the top of the second. Put the answers to the following questions side by side in the relevant columns. Leave a one-line gap after each pair of answers:
(a) What verbs are associated with the tigers in the first and third stanzas? What verbs are associated with Aunt Jennifer in the second and third stanzas?
(b) What colours are associated with the tigers in the first stanza? What colours are associated with Aunt Jennifer in the second stanza?
(c) What emotions are associated with the tigers in the first and third stanzas? What emotions are associated with Aunt Jennifer in the second and third stanzas?

3. *Class Discussion:* (a) Discuss the differences between the two lists of verbs in Question 2. (b) Is there a feeling of power in one list and powerlessness in the other? (c) Can you decide who was having more fun in life – the tigers or Aunt Jennifer? Give reasons for your decision.

4. *A. Paired Discussion:* The colour yellow/gold is suggested in connection with the tigers and Aunt Jennifer. Using the list you made in Question 2 (a), discuss the following questions: (a) Are there any differences in the way the colour is used with the tigers and with Aunt Jennifer?
(b) Consider the colours that appear alongside the yellow/gold in each case. Do they change how you see the yellow/gold?

B. *Individual Writing:* Using the points that arose in the discussion, answer the following question. How does Rich use colour to convey that the tigers have very different lives from Aunt Jennifer's?

5. *Group Discussion:* (a) Using your lists of emotions from Question 2, discuss the mood created in the images of the tigers and the mood created in the descriptions of Aunt Jennifer. (b) Would you rather be with the tigers or with Aunt Jennifer? Why?

7. A. *Class Discussion:* (a) Discuss the different ways in which the male figures interact with the tigers and with Aunt Jennifer. (b) What is the poet's attitude to the male figures in the poem? (c) Do you think that this is a fair attitude, bearing in mind that Rich wrote this poem as a woman living in the early 1950s?

B. *Individual Writing:* Using the points that arose in the discussion, answer the following question. How are men portrayed in this poem?

Second reading

6. A. *Paired Discussion:* (a) Do you find it surprising that Aunt Jennifer was the creator of the tiger screen? Why? (b) Can you suggest what might have driven Aunt Jennifer to make this screen? (c) What do you think she was trying to say?

B. *Paired Writing:* With one of you as Aunt Jennifer and one as a reporter, write an interview with Aunt Jennifer about her tiger screen.

Third reading

8. (a) Can you explain the theme of the poem? (b) Do you agree or disagree with the attitude expressed in the theme? Give reasons for your answer.

9. Physically, the tigers are suggested as whole bodies, while Aunt Jennifer is represented only by her hands. How does Rich use this method to reveal the differing lives of Aunt Jennifer and the tigers?

10. 'Power lies at the heart of this poem.' Discuss this statement, using references from the poem to support your views.

The Uncle Speaks in the Drawing Room

this poem is also prescribed for Ordinary Level exams in 2011, 2012 and 2013

I have seen the mob of late
Standing sullen in the square,
Gazing with a sullen stare
At window, balcony, and gate.
Some have talked in bitter tones,   5
Some have held and fingered stones.

These are follies that subside.
Let us consider, none the less,
Certain frailties of glass
Which, it cannot be denied,   10
Lead in times like these to fear
For crystal vase and chandelier.

Not that missiles will be cast;
None as yet dare lift an arm.
But the scene recalls a storm   15
When our grandsire stood aghast
To see his antique ruby bowl
Shivered in a thunder-roll.

Let us only bear in mind
How these treasures handed down   20
From a calmer age passed on
Are in the keeping of our kind.
We stand between the dead glass-blowers
And murmurings of missile-throwers.

[7]	**follies:** foolish activities	
[16]	**aghast:** dismayed	

C. Johnson-Wahl: 'Sunset, Waverly Place'

EXPLORATIONS

First reading

1. *Class Discussion:* (a) What image does the word 'mob' suggest to you? (b) How would you describe the mood of the mob in the first stanza? (c) Pick out two words that really help you to understand their mood.

2. 'These are follies that subside.' (a) What does this line tell you about the uncle's attitude to the mob?

   'Not that missiles will be cast'. (b) Do you think the uncle truly believes what he is saying? (c) Is he really as calm and confident as the two quotations in this question suggest? Refer to the second and third stanzas to support your view.

3. *A. Group Discussion:* The uncle is concerned about the 'crystal vase and chandelier'. Would you be concerned about items such as these if your house were under threat of attack?

   B. Individual Writing: Using the points that arose in the discussion, answer the following question. What do the uncle's reactions reveal about the type of person he is?

4. *A. Paired Discussion:* (a) Is it significant that the uncle speaks in 'the drawing room'? (b) Would the effect be the same if the uncle were in the kitchen or the bedroom? Why/why not?

B. *Individual Writing:* Using the points that were discussed, answer the following question. Imagine that you were visiting the house when this incident occurred. Write a letter to your friend describing what happened and how you felt about it all.

Second reading

5. (a) What do the 'crystal vase and chandelier' and the 'ruby bowl' suggest about the uncle's lifestyle? (b) Pick out any other words in the poem that give further clues about the type of house that the uncle lives in. (c) How do you think the mob feel about the way that he lives?

6. *Class Discussion:* (a) What qualities do 'the mob' in the first stanza and the 'thunder-roll' in the third stanza have in common? (b) Might they have similar effects on the glass objects? (c) How are the 'glass-blowers' in the final stanza different from them?

7. (a) What does the final stanza tell us about the uncle's attitude to the glass objects? (b) Pick out the key phrases that you feel reveal his attitude. (c) Do you agree with his opinion? Why?

Third reading

8. Individual Writing: (a) This poem comes from Rich's book entitled *A Change of World*. How could this poem be seen as representing a possible 'change of world'? (b) What could (i) the uncle, (ii) the glass objects and (iii) the mob represent in this context? You might like to share your thoughts with the class when you have finished.

9. A. *Group Discussion:* Where do you think Rich's sympathies lie: with the uncle or with the mob? Refer to the poem to support your viewpoint.

    B. *Individual Writing:* Using the points that were discussed, answer the following question. How does the poem reveal Rich's loyalties?

10. 'In "The Uncle Speaks in the Drawing Room" and "Aunt Jennifer's Tigers", Rich skilfully uses everyday language to create poems that are both elegant and vivid.' Discuss this statement with regard to her use of (a) rhyme and rhythm, alliteration, assonance and onomatopoeia; (b) clear and effective images.

Storm Warnings

The glass has been falling all the afternoon,
And knowing better than the instrument
What winds are walking overhead, what zone
Of gray unrest is moving across the land,
I leave the book upon a pillowed chair
And walk from window to closed window, watching
Boughs strain against the sky

And think again, as often when the air
Moves inward toward a silent core of waiting,
How with a single purpose time has traveled
By secret currents of the undiscerned
Into this polar realm. Weather abroad
And weather in the heart alike come on
Regardless of prediction.

Between foreseeing and averting change
Lies all the mastery of elements
Which clocks and weatherglasses cannot alter.
Time in the hand is not control of time,
Nor shattered fragments of an instrument
A proof against the wind; the wind will rise,
We can only close the shutters.

I draw the curtains as the sky goes black
And set a match to candles sheathed in glass
Against the keyhole draught, the insistent whine
Of weather through the unsealed aperture.
This is our sole defense against the season;
These are the things that we have learned to do
Who live in troubled regions.

5

10

15

20

25

Notes

[11] **undiscerned:** unperceived by thought or senses
[14] **prediction:** forecast
[15] **averting:** preventing
[23] **sheathed:** enclosed, protected by
[25] **aperture:** gap

K. F. Nordstrom: 'Storm Clouds'

EXPLORATIONS

Before reading

1. How do you feel about storms: the wind, rain, thunder and lightning? Are you afraid of them or do you feel exhilarated by them? Take one minute and write a list of all the words that come into your head when you think of the word 'Storms'. Don't try to control the words or leave out words that seem to have no sensible connection. When the minute is up, review your list. You could use it as a basis for a short descriptive piece of writing, either in prose or poetry, about your perception of 'Storms'.

First reading

2. *Group Discussion:* (a) What do you think of Rich's description of a developing storm? (b) Are there any similarities between her poem and your written piece? (c) Did any of her images or phrases express something of what you felt about storms? If so, try to explain what she was able to express for you.

First reading continued

3. 'Weather abroad
   And weather in the heart alike come on
   Regardless of prediction.'
   (a) What thoughts does the impending storm trigger in Rich? (b) Do you feel that the connection she makes actually works? Why?

4. *Class Discussion:* The third stanza outlines the level of power that we humans have in the face of impending storms, be they emotional or meteorological. How effective does Rich think our power is? Choose one phrase or one image from this stanza that you feel clearly conveys this view.

5. *Individual Writing:* (a) In your own words, outline the actions that Rich takes in the final stanza. (b) Do these actions actually succeed in keeping the storm out of her house?

6. Examine the structure of this poem and compare it to 'Aunt Jennifer's Tigers' and 'The Uncle Speaks in the Drawing Room'. (a) What similarities do you notice between the three poems? (b) What would you consider to be the main difference? (c) Can you suggest why Rich altered her approach to structure in this way?

7. *Class Discussion:* (a) What does the weather suggest to you about Rich's emotions?
   (b) How do you interpret her actions of closing the curtains and lighting the candles?
   (c) Can you think of another poem by Rich where a woman contains her emotions?

Third reading

8. 'Rich uses language in this poem with the skill of a sculptor. Rhythm and metre, metaphor, assonance and alliteration have all been chiselled into a smoothly flowing form.' Discuss this statement using quotations to illustrate your points.

9. A lyric poem is one in which a single speaker communicates a mood, an attitude or a state of mind to the reader. A lyric poem does not seek to tell a story, but rather to express an individual feeling or thought. Consider whether 'Storm Warnings' could be described as a lyric. Support your arguments with relevant quotations and references.

10. 'These are the things that we have learned to do
    Who live in troubled regions.'
    Taking any three of Rich's poems, discuss how she conveys her view that women have learned to do certain 'things' in order to 'live in troubled regions'.

11. Review the short descriptive piece that you wrote on 'Storms'. (a) Does it suggest anything about your emotional state? (b) Having read Rich's poem, would you like to add anything to it or are you happy with your work?

Living in Sin

She had thought the studio would keep itself;
no dust upon the furniture of love.
Half heresy, to wish the taps less vocal,
the panes relieved of grime. A plate of pears,
a piano with a Persian shawl, a cat   5
stalking the picturesque amusing mouse
had risen at his urging.
Not that at five each separate stair would writhe
under the milkman's tramp; that morning light
so coldly would delineate the scraps   10
of last night's cheese and three sepulchral bottles;
that on the kitchen shelf among the saucers
a pair of beetle-eyes would fix her own –
envoy from some village in the moldings . . .
Meanwhile, he, with a yawn,   15
sounded a dozen notes upon the keyboard,
declared it out of tune, shrugged at the mirror,
rubbed at his beard, went out for cigarettes;
while she, jeered by the minor demons,
pulled back the sheets and made the bed and found   20
a towel to dust the table-top,
and let the coffee-pot boil over on the stove.
By evening she was back in love again,
though not so wholly but throughout the night
she woke sometimes to feel the daylight coming   25
like a relentless milkman up the stairs.

[1] **studio:** studio flat/apartment: a flat with a room used as an artist's studio, a one-roomed flat

[3] **heresy:** contrary to doctrine or what is normally accepted

[6] **picturesque:** beautiful, as in a picture

[10] **delineate:** draw

[11] **sepulchral:** like a tomb, gloomy

[14] **moldings:** mouldings, strips of decorative wood

[26] **relentless:** persistent

EXPLORATIONS

First reading

1. *Class Discussion:* (a) Have you ever heard the phrase 'living in sin' before? (b) What do you understand it to mean? (c) In the 1950s and 1960s this phrase suggested a relationship that was rather shocking, yet exciting, because the couple were not married. Do you think the phrase has lost its impact nowadays?

2. A. *Paired Discussion:* (a) What picture of the studio does the girl have in her imagination in lines 4–7? (b) What is the studio like in reality?

   B. *Individual Writing:* Using the points that arose in the discussion, imagine that you are the girl in the poem. Describe how you feel about the studio in which you are living.

3. Consider the description of the man in lines 15–18. (a) Does he seem like a man who would tempt a woman to 'live in sin'? Why? (b) From the clues in these lines, describe him in your own words.

4. *Group Discussion:* (a) How does the woman spend her time when she first gets up? (b) Consider the phrase 'jeered by the minor demons'. Does it help you to understand what urges the woman to do these things?

5. A. *Class Discussion:* (a) Why do you think that it is she who tidies up the 'studio' while he does not? (b) Do you think that this is a realistic portrayal of male/female behaviour? Why?

   B. *Presentation to the Class:* Using the points that were discussed, write and present a short speech on the following topic: 'Women are too concerned with housework, while men are not concerned enough.'

6. 'By evening she was back in love again,'.

   (a) Can you suggest what might make the woman fall in love again with the man as the day progresses? (b) This line implies a happy ending to the poem. Do you think that there is, indeed, a happy ending? Why?

Second reading

7. *Paired Writing:* Imagine that either the man or the woman writes to a 'Problem Page' in a magazine about their relationship. With one of you writing as the man/woman and the other writing as the 'agony aunt/uncle', write the letters that you think would pass between the two. You might like to read your work out to the class so as to see some different approaches to the situation.

8. What do you think that Rich is trying to communicate about love in the poem? Do you agree with her? Refer to the poem in your answer.

Third reading

9. *A. Group Discussion:* (a) The woman's decision to tidy the studio is a significant one. How could it be seen as a metaphor for women in society? (b) Is Rich suggesting that women are trained, or forced, by society to behave in a certain way?

   B. Individual Writing: Using the points that arose in the discussion, explain in your own words the themes of this poem. Use quotations to support your points.

10. Rich wrote this poem in the 1950s. Do you think that the message the poem carries is relevant in the twenty-first century?

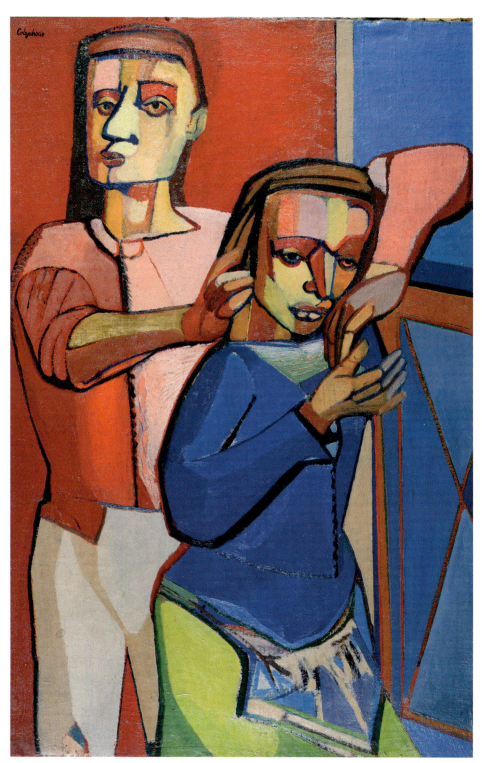

'Lovers' by Robert Colquhoun (1914–62)

The Roofwalker

– for Denise Levertov

Over the half-finished houses
night comes. The builders
stand on the roof. It is
quiet after the hammers,
the pulleys hang slack.   5
Giants, the roofwalkers,
on a listing deck, the wave
of darkness about to break
on their heads. The sky
is a torn sail where figures   10
pass magnified, shadows
on a burning deck.

I feel like them up there:
exposed, larger than life,
and due to break my neck.   15
Was it worth while to lay –
with infinite exertion –
a roof I can't live under?
– All those blueprints,
closings of gaps,   20
measurings, calculations?
A life I didn't choose
chose me: even
my tools are the wrong ones
for what I have to do.   25
I'm naked, ignorant,
a naked man fleeing
across the roofs
who could with a shade of difference
be sitting in the lamplight   30
against the cream wallpaper
reading – not with indifference –
about a naked man
fleeing across the roofs.

Denise Levertov 1923–1997: poet who was born in England but moved to America after she married. Feminism and activism became important elements in her writing. She developed a style in which the thinking process was reflected in line and image.

EXPLORATIONS

Before reading

1. Have you ever walked along a high narrow wall, or a narrow track on a hillside, or across a bridge where you felt uncomfortable about your situation? Take a moment to remember, then write a short passage describing your feelings.

First reading

2. *A. Class Discussion:* (a) What mood is created in the first section of the poem? (b) How do you think the builders feel about being up on the roof?

   B. Individual Writing: Using the points that were discussed, answer the following question. Imagine that you are one of the builders. Using the information in the first section of the poem, describe in your own words your thoughts and feelings at this time.

First reading continued

3. *A. Paired Discussion:*

   'Giants, the roofwalkers, on a listing deck'

   (a) The speaker imagines the builders on something other than a roof. Can you explain what it is? (b) What does this imagery tell you about the speaker's attitude to the builders?

   B. Individual Writing: Using the points that were discussed, answer the following question. Choose one image that you find particularly vivid from the first section and explain in your own words what it helps you to 'see'.

4. 'I feel like them up there: exposed, larger than life, and due to break my neck.'

   (a) In what way do these lines signal a change in the speaker's attitude towards the roofwalkers? (b) Do you think that she is afraid, or worried, or both?

5. *Class Discussion:* (a) How does the speaker feel about her life? (b) Pick out one image or phrase that you think clearly suggests these feelings. (c) Do you think she has put a lot of effort into trying to make this life work? Why?

6. *Individual Writing:* Remembering the piece that you wrote before reading this poem, and using your work for Questions 3 and 4, write a short piece expressing what you would say to this woman if you met her.

Second reading

7. 'I'm naked, ignorant,

   a naked man fleeing

   across the roofs'

   (a) What emotions do you feel when you read these lines? (b) What do you think the word 'fleeing' suggests about the man's actions? (c) Does this image help you to understand how the speaker feels, or do you find it confusing?

8. *Class Discussion:* Read lines 30–34. (a) What mood is created in this final image? (b) Do you find the mood surprising, given the feelings that the speaker expressed earlier on in the poem?

(c) Is the speaker actually 'sitting in the lamplight', or is she just imagining the scene?

9. A. *Class Discussion:* (a) Do you think the speaker would be truly happy if she could manage to change and sit in a room with 'cream wallpaper'? (b) Which phrases or images reveal her realisation that, even if she changed, she would not be happy in such a situation?

   B. *Individual Writing*: Using your work on Questions 7, 8 and 9, answer the following: (a) Can you explain the final 13 lines of this poem in your own words? (b) Do you find the final 13 lines of this poem a successful conclusion to the piece? Give reasons for your viewpoint.

Third reading

10. A. *Group Discussion:* (a) How is the appearance of this poem different from poems such as 'Aunt Jennifer's Tigers' and 'Storm Warnings'? (b) What effect does this appearance have on the way you read the poem? (c) Can you suggest why Rich decided to try a new approach with this poem?

B. *Individual Writing:* Using the points that were discussed, answer the following question. 'When we read "The Roofwalker", it is as if we are inside Rich's head listening to her thoughts.' Discuss, with reference to the poem.

11. Choose two poems that you feel show Rich's efforts to use her 'tools' of writing to the best of her ability. In your answer, examine her use of everyday language, images, rhyme, rhythm, assonance and alliteration.

Our Whole Life

Our whole life a translation
the permissible fibs

and now a knot of lies
eating at itself to get undone

Words bitten thru words   5

meanings burnt-off like paint
under the blowtorch

All those dead letters
rendered into the oppressor's language

Trying to tell the doctor where it hurts   10
like the Algerian
who has walked from his village, burning

his whole body a cloud of pain
and there are no words for this

except himself   15

Notes	[2]	**permissible:** allowable
	[8]	**dead letters:** undelivered letters
	[9]	**oppressor:** one who governs harshly and cruelly

EXPLORATIONS

Before reading

1. Have you ever been somewhere where you and your family did not speak the language and had difficulty making yourself understood? Or did you find the first days in Irish college very difficult because you could not understand or be understood? Recount your experience to the class.

First reading

2. Did this poem remind you in any way of the experiences that were described in the Before reading exercise?

3. *A. Class Discussion:* Rich uses the word 'translation' in the opening line of the poem. (a) Look it up in a dictionary and write down the definitions given. (b) Suggest situations where you might be involved in translating words. (c) How are the 'fibs', 'lies' and 'meanings' connected to the act of 'translation'?

First reading continued

B. Individual Writing: Using the points that arose in the discussion, answer the following question. What aspects of language is Rich concerned with in lines 1–7 of this poem?

4. *A. Group Discussion:*
'All those dead letters rendered into the oppressor's language'.

(a) Imagine that you had sent letters to someone and they had never been delivered; how would you feel? (b) Do you think that Rich is suggesting similar emotions by using the phrase 'dead letters' here? (c) Think back to Ireland's past. How did the Irish people feel when they were forced to speak English? (d) Do you think that Rich uses the phrase 'the oppressor's language' to convey similar feelings?

B. Individual Writing: Using the points that were discussed, answer the following question. In your own words, describe the emotions that Rich is trying to communicate in the two lines quoted above.

5. Imagine that you are the Algerian in lines 10–15. Write a short passage expressing your feelings and thoughts as you go through the experience that Rich describes. You might like to share your work with the class.

6. *Class Discussion:* Using your work for Questions 3, 4 and 5, discuss the following: (a) Can you see any connections between your three answers? (b) Do you think that Rich is happy with the language she uses? (c) What clues in the poem lead you to your conclusion?

Second reading

7. *A. Class Discussion:* Rich uses the phrase 'the oppressor's language'. (a) Has the 'oppressor' figure appeared in any of Rich's other poems that you have studied? (b) Can you sum up how this 'oppressor' figure is portrayed? (c) In the light of this, whom do you think the 'Our' in the first line of the poem refers to?

B. *Individual Writing:* Using the points that arose in the discussion, answer the following question. What is Rich trying to say in this poem about the language that women use?

8. *A. Class Debate:* Write a short speech either for or against the motion: 'The English language is a male-centred language.'

9. *Individual Writing:* (a) In your own words, explain the theme of this poem. (b) What is your reaction to this theme?

Third reading

10. How do you feel about the way Adrienne Rich portrays the male figure in her poetry? Use references from at least four of her poems to support your viewpoint.

11. Rich uses the 'stream of consciousness' approach in this poem to suggest the way in which her thoughts and feelings spontaneously develop. Using references from this poem and one other poem by Rich, discuss the advantages and disadvantages of such an approach.

Trying to Talk with a Man

this poem is also prescribed for Ordinary Level exams in 2011 and 2012

Out in this desert we are testing bombs,

that's why we came here.

Sometimes I feel an underground river
forcing its way between deformed cliffs
an acute angle of understanding   5
moving itself like a locus of the sun
into this condemned scenery.

What we've had to give up to get here—
whole LP collections, films we starred in
playing in the neighborhoods, bakery windows   10
full of dry, chocolate-filled Jewish cookies,
the language of love-letters, of suicide notes,
afternoons on the riverbank
pretending to be children

Coming out to this desert   15
we meant to change the face of
driving among dull green succulents
walking at noon in the ghost town
surrounded by a silence

that sounds like the silence of the place   20
except that it came with us
and is familiar
and everything we were saying until now
was an effort to blot it out—
Coming out here we are up against it   25

Out here I feel more helpless
with you than without you
You mention the danger

and list the equipment
we talk of people caring for each other   30
in emergencies—laceration, thirst—
but you look at me like an emergency

Your dry heat feels like power
your eyes are stars of a different magnitude
they reflect lights that spell out: EXIT   35
when you get up and pace the floor

talking of the danger
as if it were not ourselves
as if we were testing anything else.

---

[4]   **deformed:** misshapen
[5]   **acute angle:** an angle less than 90°
[6]   **locus:** the defined motion of a point
[17]   **succulents:** thick, fleshy plants
[31]   **laceration:** torn flesh

James Doolin: 'The Indian Shafts Valley'

EXPLORATIONS

First reading

1. (a) What is your reaction to the opening two lines of the poem? (b) Did they make you want to read the rest of the poem? Why?

2. *Individual Writing:* (a) In your own words, describe the scene that you imagine from the clues in lines 1–7 and lines 15–19. (b) How would you feel in such an environment? You might like to share your thoughts with the class.

3. *Class Discussion:* (a) What sort of environment did the people live in before they came to the desert? (b) Are there any indications in the poem as to why they left this world for the desert?

4. *A. Group Discussion:* (a) Examine lines 1–7 and 15–19, where Rich describes the desert. What do you notice about her use of punctuation in these lines? (b) Now look at lines 8–14. What do you notice about the punctuation in these lines? (c) Why do you think she changes her use of punctuation?

   B. Individual Writing: Using the points that were discussed, answer the following question. How does Rich use punctuation to strengthen her descriptions in this poem?

Second reading

5. *Paired Discussion:*

   'surrounded by a silence

   that sounds like the silence of the place

   except that it came with us . . .'

   (a) Can you explain the two types of silence that Rich is referring to here? (b) Why do you think there is silence between the two people?

6. *Class Discussion:* (a) What do the couple do in response to the silence? (b) Why do you think they react in this way?

   Individual Writing: Based on the behaviour you considered in Questions 5 and 6, do you think the couple are happy or unhappy together? Use quotations from the poem to prove your viewpoint.

7. 'Out here I feel more helpless with you than without you'. (a) What do these lines tell you about how the speaker feels when she is with her partner? (b) Does the title of the poem make it easier for you to understand why she feels 'helpless'? (c) Can you now suggest what the theme of this poem is?

8. *A. Class Discussion:* (a) Do the last 12 lines of the poem indicate a happy or unhappy ending for the couple?

B. *Individual Writing:* Using the points that were discussed, answer the following question. Do you find the conclusion to the poem a satisfactory one? Support your opinion by reference to the poem.

Third Reading

9. This poem is based on two areas of imagery: (a) the testing of bombs in the desert; (b) the nature of the couple's relationship. Trace how Rich weaves the two together in order to convey the theme of this poem. Before you answer

this question you might find it helpful to set out the relevant points in two columns, following the method we used for 'Aunt Jennifer's Tigers'.

10. The lyric poem is one in which a single speaker communicates a mood, an attitude or a state of mind to the reader. Discuss the following statement with reference to 'Trying to Talk with a Man' and one other poem: 'Rich takes the lyric poem and gives it a political twist so that the single speaker communicates not only about herself, but also about the society that she lives in.'

Diving into the Wreck

First having read the book of myths,
and loaded the camera,
and checked the edge of the knife-blade,
I put on
the body-armor of black rubber   5
the absurd flippers
the grave and awkward mask.
I am having to do this
not like Cousteau with his
assiduous team   10
aboard the sun-flooded schooner
but here alone.

There is a ladder.
The ladder is always there
hanging innocently   15
close to the side of the schooner.
We know what it is for,
we who have used it.
Otherwise
it's a piece of maritime floss   20
some sundry equipment.

I go down.
Rung after rung and still
the oxygen immerses me
the blue light   25
the clear atoms
of our human air.
I go down.
My flippers cripple me,
I crawl like an insect down the ladder   30
and there is no one
to tell me when the ocean
will begin.

First the air is blue and then
it is bluer and then green and then   35
black I am blacking out and yet
my mask is powerful
it pumps my blood with power
the sea is another story
the sea is not a question of power   40
I have to learn alone
to turn my body without force
in the deep element.

And now: it is easy to forget
what I came for   45
among so many who have always
lived here
swaying their crenellated fans
between the reefs
and besides   50
you breathe differently down here.

I came to explore the wreck.
The words are purposes.
The words are maps.
I came to see the damage that was done   55
and the treasures that prevail.
I stroke the beam of my lamp
slowly along the flank
of something more permanent
than fish or weed   60

the thing I came for:
the wreck and not the story of the wreck
the thing itself and not the myth
the drowned face always staring
toward the sun   65
the evidence of damage
worn by salt and sway into this threadbare beauty
the ribs of the disaster

curving their assertion
among the tentative haunters. 70

This is the place.
And I am here, the mermaid whose dark hair
streams black, the merman in his armored body
We circle silently
about the wreck 75
we dive into the hold.
I am she: I am he

whose drowned face sleeps with open eyes
whose breasts still bear the stress
whose silver, copper, vermeil cargo lies 80
obscurely inside barrels
half-wedged and left to rot
we are the half-destroyed instruments
that once held to a course
the water-eaten log 85
the fouled compass

We are, I am, you are
by cowardice or courage
the one who find our way
back to this scene 90
carrying a knife, a camera
a book of myths
in which
our names do not appear.

[1] **myths:** legends, folklore
[9] **Cousteau:** Jacques-Yves Cousteau, famous for his underwater films and TV programmes. He worked tirelessly to increase public awareness of the oceans.
[10] **assiduous:** hard-working
[11] **schooner:** a type of ship
[20] **maritime:** connected with the sea
[20] **floss:** thread
[21] **sundry:** various pieces
[48] **crenellated:** lacy, with irregular edges
[56] **prevail:** triumph, exist
[67] **threadbare:** worn, ragged
[69] **assertion:** statement
[70] **tentative:** cautious, uncertain
[80] **vermeil:** a bright, beautiful red, as in vermilion

EXPLORATIONS

Before reading

1. Rich's poems work on a number of interwoven levels and this can sometimes cause confusion, particularly in a longer poem such as this. For this poem, use an A4 or double copy page. Rule out five equal columns. Use the following five headings: 'Setting'; 'Activity'; 'Emotional Setting'; 'Emotional Activity'; 'Political Messages'. As you answer the questions, fill in the appropriate columns with points summarising your thinking. In this way, the interrelationship between the layers should become clearer.

First reading

2. *A. Class Discussion:* This discussion will help you to fill in the 'Setting' and 'Activity' columns in Question 1.
(a) Where is this poem set?
(b) What is the speaker going to do? (c) What preparations does she make? (d) What does she use to move down to the water? (e) Is her journey down the ladder an easy one or does it take a lot of effort? (f) Is there anyone with her?

B. Individual Writing: Using the answers that arose out of your discussion, begin to fill in the columns headed 'Setting' and 'Activity' in point form.

3. *A. Class Discussion:* This discussion will help you to fill in the 'Setting' and 'Activity' columns. (a) What does the diver have to learn to do in the water? (b) Why does she go to the wreck? (c) How do you imagine the wreck from the description in the poem? (d) Who does the diver meet at the wreck?

   B. Individual Writing: Using the answers you discussed, finish filling in the columns headed 'Setting' and 'Activity' in point form.

Second reading

4. *A. Class Discussion:* This discussion will help you to fill in the 'Emotional Setting' column in Question 1. (a) How do you think the diver feels as she prepares for the dive? (b) Consider what her checking of the knife edge and putting on the 'body-armor' convey about the emotional setting of the poem. (c) Read lines 22–37 and consider her emotions during these experiences.

   B. Individual Writing: Using the answers that arose out of your discussion, fill in the column headed 'Emotional Setting' in point form.

5. *Class Discussion:* This discussion will help you to fill in the 'Emotional Activity' column in Question 1. (a) How does the diver's mood change when she learns how to move in 'the deep element'? (b) What are her feelings when she reaches the wreck? (c) How does she feel when she meets the mermaid and merman? (d) What is her mood in the final eight lines of the poem, when she becomes one with the mermaid and merman?

   B. Individual Writing: Using the answers that arose out of your discussion, fill in the column headed 'Emotional Activity' in point form.

6. *Class Discussion:* This discussion will help you to fill in the final column, 'Political Messages'. This poem tells of a heroic quest for treasure in an old wreck and the transformation that occurs to the heroine when she succeeds in her quest. (a) Consider what the quest represents: is the diver trying to learn something about being a woman, or is she questioning 'the book of myths' that contain all the accepted inequalities of our society? (b) What do you think the treasure represents: is it

self-knowledge, or knowledge about why men have most of the power in society? (c) What might the wreck represent: the diver's own unsatisfactory life as a woman, or the outdated rules of society that reinforce inequality? (d) What could her transformation into an androgynous figure (partly male, partly female) represent: the achievement of true personal power through surviving all the injustices, or could it stand for society, doomed to destruction because it is based on inequality?

B. Individual Writing: Using the answers that arose out of your discussion, fill in the column 'Political Messages' in point form.

Third reading

7. *A. Paired Discussion:* Referring back to the relevant columns should prove helpful. (a) How does the physical setting at the beginning of the poem influence the diver's emotional setting? (b) What effects do the physical activities in which the diver engages have on her emotional activities?

B. Individual Writing: Using the answers that arose out of your discussion, answer the following question. Trace how the diver's emotions change as she goes through the different experiences described in the poem. Use quotations to support your points.

8. *A. Group Discussion:* Referring back to the relevant column should prove helpful. (a) What message does this poem communicate about Rich's attitude to being a woman? (b) What message is conveyed about the society that Rich lived in?

B. Individual Writing: Using the answers that arose out of your discussion, explain in your own words the major themes of this poem.

9. 'Rich has the ability to create images that are stunningly vivid.' Discuss this statement, using quotations from 'Diving into the Wreck' and two other poems by Rich that you have studied.

10. 'The words are purposes.

The words are maps.'

Consider how Rich conveys her belief that language traps people in inequality, with reference to two of her poems on your course.

From a Survivor

The pact that we made was the ordinary pact
of men & women in those days

I don't know who we thought we were
that our personalities
could resist the failures of the race   5

Lucky or unlucky, we didn't know
the race had failures of that order
and that we were going to share them

Like everybody else, we thought of ourselves as special

Your body is as vivid to me   10
as it ever was: even more

since my feeling for it is clearer:
I know what it could and could not do

it is no longer
the body of a god   15
or anything with power over my life

Next year it would have been 20 years
and you are wastefully dead
who might have made the leap
we talked, too late, of making   20

which I live now
not as a leap
but a succession of brief, amazing movements

each one making possible the next

Note

Rich wrote this poem to her husband, Alfred Conrad, who committed suicide in 1970

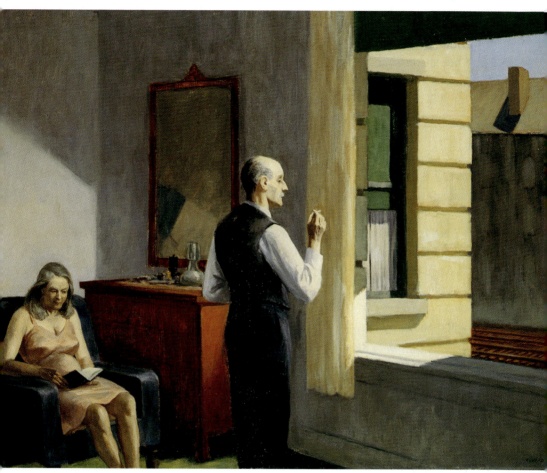

Edward Hopper: 'Hotel by the Railroad'

EXPLORATIONS

Before reading

1. Have you ever been a bridesmaid or a groomsman at a wedding? What can you remember about the day? How did the couple who were getting married feel about their wedding? Did the experience make you feel positive or negative about getting married?

EXPLORATIONS

2. (a) From your first reading of the poem, can you suggest a phrase that sums up Rich's feelings for her late husband? (b) Do you find some of the feelings expressed in this poem surprising when set against the other poems on your course? Why?

3. *A. Class Discussion:* (a) Can you explain what the 'ordinary pact' was that Rich made with her husband? (b) Look up the word 'pact' in the dictionary and note the definitions of the word. (c) Do you think that it is a good word to describe the marriage of a man and a woman? Why?

   B. Individual Writing: Using the points that were discussed, answer the following question. What does Rich's use of the word 'pact' to describe marriage suggest about her attitude to this connection between men and women?

4. *Class Discussion:* (a) What do you think she means by the phrase 'the failures of the race'? (b) Can you suggest a connection between the 'pact' and these 'failures'?

5. (a) How does Rich's attitude towards her husband's body change during their marriage? (b) Do you think that such a change is natural in a long-term relationship? Why? (c) In your opinion, would such a change make the couple's love stronger or weaker? Give reasons for your answer.

6. Adrienne Rich believes that 'Young readers need to learn that a poem is not a letter, or a diary entry, it's a crafted work which may begin in a personal experience but always evolves into something else if it has any value as art at all.' As the poem develops, what themes does Rich draw out of her starting point of 'personal experience'? You may find it helpful to consider some of the themes that you have already encountered in her work.

7. *Class Discussion:* (a) Can you suggest what the 'leap' in lines 19 and 22 might represent? (b) Do Rich's other poems give you any indication of what this 'leap' might involve?

8. 'but a succession of brief, amazing movements

   each one making possible the next'

   (a) Why do you think that Rich does not use a full stop at the end of the poem? (b) What do these final lines suggest to you about Rich's attitude to her life? (c) Is there a connection between these lines and the poem's title?

9. *Group Discussion:* Rich uses very little punctuation in this poem. (a) Read the poem aloud as it is and listen to it carefully. (b) Put in the correct punctuation and read the poem again. (c) What effect does the added punctuation have on the way the poem is read? (d) Which version do you prefer, the unpunctuated or the punctuated one? Why?

10. *Class Presentation:* Prepare a piece for presentation to the class either agreeing or disagreeing with the statement: 'Rich has a depressingly negative view of male/female relationships.' Use quotations from at least three of her poems to support your argument.

11. Survival is an important concept in Rich's poetry. With reference to two of her poems featuring women who are successful survivors and two of her poems featuring women who are unsuccessful survivors, explain the factors that Rich believes make women successful or unsuccessful survivors.

Power

Living   in the earth-deposits   of our history

Today a backhoe divulged   out of a crumbling flank of earth
one bottle   amber   perfect   a hundred-year-old
cure for fever   or melancholy   a tonic
for living on this earth   in the winters of this climate   5

Today I was reading about Marie Curie:
she must have known she suffered   from radiation sickness
her body bombarded for years   by the element
she had purified
It seems she denied to the end   10
the source of the cataracts on her eyes
the cracked and suppurating skin   of her finger-ends
till she could no longer hold   a test-tube or a pencil

She died   a famous woman   denying
her wounds   15
denying
her wounds   came   from the same source as her power

---

[2]   **backhoe:** a mechanical digger
[2]   **flank:** side of the body between ribcage and hip
[4]   **melancholy:** a thoughtful sadness
[6]   **Marie Curie** (1867–1934): discovered the radioactive
      elements plutonium and radium that are used in medicine
      today. First person to win two Nobel prizes. Died of
      leukaemia caused by exposure to high levels of radiation.
[11] **cataracts:** condition where the lens of the eye becomes
      opaque so that light cannot pass through
[12] **suppurating:** oozing pus

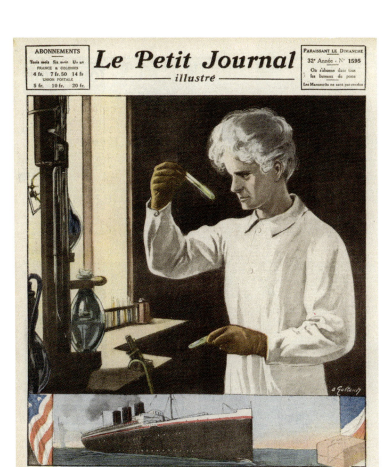

ABONNEMENTS

Trois mois Six mois Un an
FRANCE & COLONIES
4 fr.   7 fr. 50   14 fr
UNION POSTALE
5 fr.   10 fr.   20 fr.

Le Petit Journal
illustré

PARAISSANT LE DIMANCHE

32ᵉ Année · Nᵒ 1595

On s'abonne dans tous les bureaux de poste

Les Manuscrits ne sont pas rendus

Mme CURIE dans son Laboratoire

Après les jours glorieux qu'elle vient de vivre en Amérique, où elle a reçu, avec mille témoignages d'admiration, le gramme de radium offert par les Femmes américaines, l'illustre chimiste a repris son existence laborieuse dans la paix de son Laboratoire.

Marie Curie depicted in a French magazine in 1921

EXPLORATIONS

First reading

1. *Class Discussion:* (a) What is your reaction to the way that this poem is arranged on the page? (b) Did this arrangement encourage or discourage you from reading the poem? Why?

2. *A. Paired Discussion:* (a) What is the discovery that triggers the poet's thoughts? (b) What senses does Rich appeal to in her description of this discovery in lines 2–5? (c) Why do you think the bottle was thrown away with its contents apparently unused?

   B. Paired Writing: Using the points that were discussed, answer the following question. You are visiting Rich when she discovers the bottle. With one of you writing as Rich and the other as yourself, write out the conversation you have.

3. Do you find the first five lines of this poem interesting or confusing? Give reasons for your opinion.

6. *Group Discussion:* (a) Do you find the movement of the poem from describing the discovery of the 'bottle' to writing about Marie Curie confusing? (b) Might the idea of a 'cure' connect the two images in some way?

Second reading

4. The poet's thoughts move on to the woman scientist Marie Curie. (a) What effects did Curie's work have on her life? (b) Would you like to live a life such as Marie Curie's? Why?

5. *A. Class Discussion:* (a) How does Marie Curie react to the 'radiation sickness'? (b) Can you suggest any reasons for her behaviour? (c) As a woman, Curie was very unusual in the male-dominated scientific world. Do you think that this factor played a part in her denial of her sickness?

   B. Individual Writing: Using the points that arose in the discussion, answer the following question. Imagine that you are interviewing Marie Curie for a newspaper. Using your work on this question and Question 4, write out the questions you would ask her and the answers she might give.

Third reading

7. (a) Obviously, Curie had physical wounds from the radiation sickness, but could she have also been 'wounded' by the society in which she lived? In what ways? (b) Why would Rich be unhappy about Curie denying the fact that, as a woman, society inflicted 'wounds' on her?

8. Do you find Rich's use of the 'stream of consciousness' method successful in 'Power', or is it all rather confusing? Use quotations from the poem to support your opinion.

9. Compare 'Power' with 'Aunt Jennifer's Tigers'. Which poem do you prefer? Give reasons for your preference.

10. Consider how Rich explores the concept of 'Power' in three of the poems you have studied. Use quotations to support your answer.

12 *Sylvia Plath*
1932–1963

prescribed for Higher Level exams in 2012, 2013 and 2014

Sylvia Plath was born in Boston, Massachusetts on 27 October 1932, to Aurelia Schober Plath and Otto Plath, professor of biology and German at Boston University. In l940 Otto died after a long illness, a tragedy which haunted Sylvia throughout her life. From a young age, Sylvia wanted above all else to be a writer. Already writing at the age of five, she had her first poem published in the children's section of the *Boston Herald* at the age of eight. She was a brilliant high school student, consistently earning A grades, and also led a busy social life. She had a number of stories and poems published – and also got many rejection slips; this pattern recurred throughout her writing life. In 1950 she entered the prestigious women's university, Smith College, Massachusetts.

In 1952 Plath was selected to work as one of twenty 'guest editors' with *Mademoiselle* magazine in New York City. On her return to Wellesley, she suffered a serious bout of depression for which she was given electric shock treatment. However, this seems to have deepened her depression and she attempted suicide in August, leading to a four-month spell in a psychiatric hospital. She resumed her studies in Smith College in January 1953,

graduating with honours in 1955, and winning a Fulbright scholarship to study in Cambridge, England. There she met Ted Hughes, a young English poet, whom she married in June 1956.

Sylvia and Ted worked and wrote in the US for two years and returned to London in December l959. 'Black Rook in Rainy Weather' and 'The Times Are Tidy' date from this period. Her first book, *The Colossus and Other Poems*, was published in February 1960, but received disappointing reviews. April 1960 saw the birth of their daughter, Frieda. The following year they moved to Devon where their son, Nicholas, was born in January 1962. Throughout this time, Sylvia was writing poetry (including 'Morning Song', 'Finisterre',

'Mirror', 'Pheasant' and 'Elm'), some of which was published in magazines in Britain and the USA. Her semi-autobiographical novel, *The Bell Jar*, was published in 1963.

Shortly after Nicholas's birth, Ted and Sylvia separated. She remained in Devon, caring for her children and writing, despite poor health and recurring depression. She completed most of the poems which made up her second book, *Ariel* (published posthumously), among them 'Poppies in July' and 'The Arrival of the Bee Box'. In mid-December 1962, she moved to London with her children. The poems she wrote at this time include 'Child', written on 28 January 1963. However, unable to cope with the many difficulties facing her, she took her own life on 11 February 1963. Since her death her writing has received wide acclaim, including the prestigious Pulitzer Prize, an award rarely bestowed posthumously.

Black Rook in Rainy Weather

On the stiff twig up there
Hunches a wet black rook
Arranging and rearranging its feathers in the rain.
I do not expect a miracle
Or an accident   5

To set the sight on fire
In my eye, nor seek
Any more in the desultory weather some design,
But let spotted leaves fall as they fall,
Without ceremony, or portent.   10

Although, I admit, I desire,
Occasionally, some backtalk
From the mute sky, I can't honestly complain:
A certain minor light may still
Lean incandescent   15

Out of kitchen table or chair
As if a celestial burning took
Possession of the most obtuse objects now and then –
Thus hallowing an interval

Otherwise inconsequent   20
By bestowing largesse, honour,
One might say love. At any rate, I now walk
Wary (for it could happen
Even in this dull, ruinous landscape); sceptical,
Yet politic; ignorant   25

Of whatever angel may choose to flare
Suddenly at my elbow. I only know that a rook
Ordering its black feathers can so shine
As to seize my senses, haul
My eyelids up, and grant   30

A brief respite from fear
Of total neutrality. With luck,
Trekking stubborn through this season
Of fatigue, I shall
Patch together a content   35

Of sorts. Miracles occur,
If you care to call those spasmodic
Tricks of radiance miracles. The wait's begun again
The long wait for the angel,
For that rare, random descent.   40

Notes

[2]   **rook:** crow
[8]   **desultory:** without method, disjointed
[10] **portent:** omen of some possibly calamitous event
[15] **incandescent:** glowing, brilliant
[19] **hallowing:** making sacred
[21] **largesse:** generously given present
[25] **politic:** prudent
[31] **respite:** brief period of relief

EXPLORATIONS

Before reading

1. What picture does the title create for you? Does it suggest a particular mood?

First reading

2. The poem is set against a very definite landscape: read the poem and describe the scene as accurately as you can. Build your picture from the poet's words and phrases.

3. What does the narrator seem to be doing in this poem? What thoughts does this lead to?

4. Describe the atmosphere the poem creates for you. What details are most important in setting this atmosphere?

Second reading

5. There is an abrupt change between lines 3 and 4. What is it?

6. The narrator claims that 'I do not expect . . . nor seek . . .' (lines 4–10). What does she neither expect nor seek?

7. What does she 'admit' to desiring? How does she convey the idea that it may not be possible to get what she desires?

Second reading continued

8. Can you find other places in the poem where she makes a statement, and then qualifies it – 'neutralises' it? What do such statements tell us about the narrator's frame of mind?

9. The 'minor light' of line 14 'may' have an extraordinary effect: read lines 14–22 carefully and explain this effect in your own words.

10. Can you explain how the 'rook | Ordering its black feathers can . . . grant | A brief respite' to the speaker? A brief respite from what?

11. In the final lines, she is waiting for the 'rare, random descent' of the angel. What might the angel bring? What examples of this has she already given?

12. The angel's 'rare, random descent' is a metaphor: what do you think it represents? Look at references to other heavenly phenomena before answering.

Third reading

13. Comment on the effect of the repetition of the sound 'rain' in line 3.

14. Look through the poem again, and pick out words connected with darkness and light. Compare the images or words used. Can you find any pattern?

15. The narrator does not 'seek . . . design' in things around her. How does the language reflect that lack of design, the accidental nature of what happens? A good starting point might be to identify the words associated with time or chance.

16. There is a mixture of the everyday/earthly and the extraordinary/miraculous here. How is this effect achieved? You might find it helpful to contrast concrete descriptions with references to the sacred.

Fourth reading

17. Examine the rhyme scheme. What pattern do you find? What is the effect of this careful sound pattern?

18. Write a note on the style of the poem, looking at tone, language, imagery, structure.

19. Throughout her life, Plath was preoccupied with the conflict between her ambitions to be a poet and the expectations of a society which defined women as home-makers. Reread this poem with this in mind. Would you agree that this could be one theme of the poem? Are there other possibilities? Write about what you consider to be the main themes of this poem.

The Times Are Tidy

Unlucky the hero born
In this province of the stuck record
Where the most watchful cooks go jobless
And the mayor's rôtisserie turns
Round of its own accord.   5

There's no career in the venture
Of riding against the lizard,
Himself withered these latter-days
To leaf-size from lack of action:
History's beaten the hazard.   10

The last crone got burnt up
More than eight decades back
With the love-hot herb, the talking cat,
But the children are better for it
The cow milks cream an inch thick.   15

EXPLORATIONS

Before reading

1. Think back to folk tales or legends you have read or heard involving knights in armour, witches and monsters. What can you remember about their world, the adventures described?

2. Jot down whatever comes into your mind when you hear the word 'tidy'.

3. The poem puts two eras side by side. What can you learn from the poem about each of them?

4. Which era sounds more appealing to you? Why? Which does the author seem to favour? Refer to the poem to support your impression.

5. Try to mentally recapture the effect of listening to a stuck record. What do you think the poet is telling you about 'this province' when she uses this image? Do you think this links in any way with 'tidy'?

6. The poem was written about a particular phase in American political life. Suggest then what the 'mayor's rôtisserie' might represent. Who might the 'cooks' be?

7. We are told that the jobless cooks are the 'most watchful': why then are they jobless? By choice? Because they have been sacked?

8. What mythical creature does the lizard resemble? Think of medieval knights and the creatures they did battle with. What is there in this stanza to show that the poet intends this connection to be made?

9. In what way has 'history' beaten the hazard?

10. What association exists between the crone and the 'love-hot herb', the 'talking cat' and the 'cream an inch thick'?

11. What do the crone, the hero and the lizard have in common? How does their absence affect the 'times'?

12. Most of the poem focuses on what this age has lost: the last two lines suggest a gain. What is this? Do you think the poet is being serious here, or is she being ironic? Explain your answer.

13. Two eras are contrasted in the poem. How do they differ? Be precise – refer to the text for each point you make.

14. Choose the image(s) you consider to be most effective. Explain your choice.

15. Keeping in mind the title, the images used and the comparisons made, write a note on the tone of the poem.

General question

16. 'This poem is an ironic commentary on an era of smug, self-satisfied complacency in American life.' Discuss this statement, referring to imagery, language and tone.

Morning Song

Love set you going like a fat gold watch.
The midwife slapped your footsoles, and your bald cry
Took its place among the elements.

Our voices echo, magnifying your arrival. New statue.
In a drafty museum, your nakedness   5
Shadows our safety. We stand round blankly as walls.

I'm no more your mother
Than the cloud that distils a mirror to reflect its own slow
Effacement at the wind's hand.

All night your moth-breath   10
Flickers among the flat pink roses. I wake to listen:
A far sea moves in my ear.

One cry, and I stumble from bed, cow-heavy and floral
In my Victorian nightgown.
Your mouth opens clean as a cat's. The window square   15

Whitens and swallows its dull stars. And now you try
Your handful of notes;
The clear vowels rise like balloons.

EXPLORATIONS

Before reading

1. Look at the title of this poem: jot down the ideas you associate with both words. What mood do they evoke?

First reading

2. Stanzas 1–3 centre on the infant taking her place in the world. How do others respond to her? Which emotions come across most clearly?

3. How do you understand the image of the baby as a 'New statue' taking its place in a 'drafty museum'? How does nakedness 'shadow' the safety of the onlookers? (There are a number of possibilities.)

4. Explain in your own words what happens in stanzas 4–6. Do you find the description realistic?

Second reading

5. What emotions does the opening line suggest to you? Look at the first word, the image, the rhythm. Do you think it is an effective opening line? Why?

Second reading continued

6. Identify the noises named in the poem. Name the source of each sound. Who is listening to them? What impression do they create? How do they contribute to the texture of the poem?

Third reading

7. This poem is rich in vivid imagery and word-pictures. Identify these.

8. Say what each image or word-picture suggests about the baby, about the mother, about the world they inhabit. How is this suggested? Refer to the language, the juxtaposition of images, the associations implied.

9. Explain the cloud/mirror/wind image used in stanza 3. What does the comparison suggest about the narrator's feelings about motherhood?

General questions

10. 'Morning Song' is a tender evocation of a simple, daily event. Examine how the writer conveys the mood of tenderness, while avoiding sentimentality.

11. Compare this poem with 'Child' in terms of theme, tone, language and imagery.

Which of the two poems do you prefer? Why?

Finisterre

This was the land's end: the last fingers, knuckled and rheumatic,
Cramped on nothing. Black
Admonitory cliffs, and the sea exploding
With no bottom, or anything on the other side of it,
Whitened by the faces of the drowned.   5
Now it is only gloomy, a dump of rocks –
Leftover soldiers from old, messy wars.
The sea cannons into their ear, but they don't budge.
Other rocks hide their grudges under the water.

The cliffs are edged with trefoils, stars and bells   10
Such as fingers might embroider, close to death,
Almost too small for the mists to bother with.
The mists are part of the ancient paraphernalia –
Souls, rolled in the doom-noise of the sea.
They bruise the rocks out of existence, then resurrect them.   15
They go up without hope, like sighs.
I walk among them, and they stuff my mouth with cotton.
When they free me, I am beaded with tears.

Our Lady of the Shipwrecked is striding toward the horizon,
Her marble skirts blown back in two pink wings.   20
A marble sailor kneels at her foot distractedly, and at his foot
A peasant woman in black
Is praying to the monument of the sailor praying.
Our Lady of the Shipwrecked is three times life size,
Her lips sweet with divinity.   25
She does not hear what the sailor or the peasant is saying –
She is in love with the beautiful formlessness of the sea.

Gull-colored laces flap in the sea drafts

Beside the postcard stalls.

The peasants anchor them with conches. One is told: 30

'These are the pretty trinkets the sea hides,

Little shells made up into necklaces and toy ladies.

They do not come from the Bay of the Dead down there,

But from another place, tropical and blue,

We have never been to.   35

These are our crêpes. Eat them before they blow cold.'

EXPLORATIONS

Before reading

1. What kind of landscape/seascape do the place names 'Finisterre' and 'land's end' suggest? How do you visualise it – the colours, shapes, sounds, weather, etc.?

First reading

Stanza 1

2. Read stanza 1. What overall picture do you form of the scene? What words or images do you find most striking? Is the personification effective?

3. How is language used to create the impression of an attack, a battle? Does this description of a headland create a familiar picture for you?

Stanza 2

4. What does stanza 2 describe? How does it connect with stanza 1? Notice how language and imagery are used to create links.

5. What qualities do you usually associate with mist? Which of these qualities does this mist share? What other qualities does the narrator attribute to it? Do these add anything new?

6. What is your impression of the atmosphere in this place? How is it created?

Second reading

Stanza 3

7. Describe in your own words the scene depicted in stanza 3. What connection is there with the first two stanzas?

8. The perspective in this stanza has changed: the poet is showing us things from a different angle. How is this indicated?

9. This stanza tells a little story within the poem. Tell it in your own words.

Stanza 4

10. The stalls in stanza 4 are suggested through a few precise details: look at the description – can you picture them?

11. This stanza differs remarkably from the preceding stanzas. In what way?

12. Identify the ideas/words/images which link stanza 4 with the earlier stanzas. Explain the connection.

13. We now learn that the bay is named the 'Bay of the Dead': does the name fit, in your opinion? Why do you think the poet did not name it until the end of the poem?

Third reading

14. Comment on the effect of the image in lines 1 and 2. How is this image developed in the rest of this stanza and in stanza 2?

15. Stanza 3 opens with a description of the monument. Contrast the 'I' of stanza 2 with Our Lady of the Shipwrecked. What is the impact of the contrast? What is the narrator's attitude to Our Lady?

16. Comment on the language used to describe the scene – the details given, the intentions or qualities attributed to each figure. Where does the narrator fit into this scene? What does she seem to be saying about prayer?

17. The author broadens the scope of the poem through the stall-keeper's comments, which reflect quite a different response to the bay. How? What is the effect of the wider canvas?

18. How does the final line strike you? Would you agree that there is a slightly ironic note here? What effect does this have on your reading of the poem?

General questions

19. Write a note on the tone of the poem. Be aware of the gradual change in tone, reflected in the language and imagery; note

the differences between the narrator's attitude, and that of the other figures in the poem.

20. Trace the progress of thought from the opening line to the end of the poem. Focus on how the author moves from the inner thoughts of the narrator to a more objective view. Note where the changes occur.

21. Plath once commented: '. . . a poem, by its own system of illusions, can set up a rich and apparently living world within its particular limits.' Write about 'Finisterre' in the light of this comment, looking at her choice of words, images, sound effects and point of view.

Coastal landscape at Finisterre

Mirror

I am silver and exact. I have no preconceptions.
Whatever I see I swallow immediately
Just as it is, unmisted by love or dislike.
I am not cruel, only truthful –
The eye of a little god, four-cornered.   5
Most of the time I meditate on the opposite wall.
It is pink, with speckles. I have looked at it so long
I think it is a part of my heart. But it flickers.
Faces and darkness separate us over and over.

Now I am a lake. A woman bends over me,   10
Searching my reaches for what she really is.
Then she turns to those liars, the candles or the moon.
I see her back, and reflect it faithfully.
She rewards me with tears and an agitation of hands.
I am important to her. She comes and goes.   15
Each morning it is her face that replaces the darkness.
In me she has drowned a young girl, and in me an old woman
Rises toward her day after day, like a terrible fish.

Note

[11]   **reaches:** stretch of water, depths

EXPLORATIONS

Before reading

1. Think for a minute about a mirror. Write down quickly all the words, ideas and associations that come to mind.

First reading

2. Listen to this poem a number of times. What is it saying?

3. Write a note on the form of the poem: number of stanzas, number of lines, etc.

4. Pick out all the 'I' statements. How many are there? What effect do they have?

5. Identify the qualities the mirror claims to possess. What overall impression is created by these attributes?

6. Notice the position of the words 'a little god': they are at the exact centre of stanza 1. Can you suggest why the poet placed them just there?

7. What impression is created by the description of 'the opposite wall'?

8. In stanza 2, the mirror states that it is now 'a lake': what similarities are there between a lake and a mirror? What differences are there? How does this new image expand the mirror image?

9. Why do you think the narrator describes the candles and the moon as 'liars'?

10. What might cause the woman's tears and agitation? How does this point broaden the scope of the poem?

11. The mirror/lake contains three phases of the woman's life: what are these?

Second reading

12. The focus – the point of view – changes between stanzas 1 and 2. How has the centre of consciousness changed? What is the effect of this?

13. Write a note about what you think the 'terrible fish' might be.

14. 'I am important to her': this is a very strong statement. How could a mirror be important to her? What do you think the mirror may represent to the narrator? (Try to move beyond the most obvious points.)

Third reading

15. Compare the opening lines (1–3) with the final lines. Trace the progress of thought through the poem, showing how the narrator moves from the opening statement to the conclusion. Note the changes in tone which occur.

16. The poem concludes on a note of desperation. How is this prepared for in the poem as a whole?

17. Do you agree that the narrator has 'no preconceptions' as stated in line 1? What evidence can you find to support your opinion? Look especially at phrases like 'I think', 'those liars', etc.

18. While the poem is unrhymed, Plath uses a variety of sound effects. Identify some of these, and say what effect they create.

General questions

19. Many writers and artists use the mirror as a symbol – for example, of the self, the alter ego, the 'dark side of the soul'. Reread the poem with this idea in mind. How does it colour

your reading of the poem? Does it fit the poem?

20. It has been argued that in this poem Plath is addressing the conflict between what a woman was expected to be (smooth, unruffled, reflecting the image the world wanted to see), and her true nature (struggling to be heard, seen for what it is: the 'terrible fish'). Reread the poem in the light of this comment, and write your response.

Pheasant

You said you would kill it this morning.
Do not kill it. It startles me still,
The jut of that odd, dark head, pacing

Through the uncut grass on the elm's hill.
It is something to own a pheasant,   5
Or just to be visited at all.

I am not mystical: it isn't
As if I thought it had a spirit.
It is simply in its element.

That gives it a kingliness, a right.   10
The print of its big foot last winter,
The tail-track, on the snow in our court –

The wonder of it, in that pallor,
Through crosshatch of sparrow and starling.

Is it its rareness, then? It is rare.   15
But a dozen would be worth having,
A hundred, on that hill – green and red,
Crossing and recrossing: a fine thing!

It is such a good shape, so vivid.
It's a little cornucopia.   20
It unclaps, brown as a leaf, and loud,

Settles in the elm, and is easy.
It was sunning in the narcissi.
I trespass stupidly. Let be, let be.

EXPLORATIONS

First reading

1. The poem opens very abruptly: it plunges the reader right into the narrator's preoccupation. What is this? Why do you think she repeats the word 'kill'?

2. Lines 3 and 4 present a graphic picture. What scene is evoked?

3. The speaker's attitude toward the pheasant is clearly signalled in lines 5 and 6. What is it? Can you find any further echo of this feeling in the poem?

4. In stanzas 4 and 5 the poet pictures the pheasant: how does she underline its difference from the other birds that visit her yard?

5. Stanza 7 moves back to the present: the pheasant's 'clap' draws her attention. What was it doing before it flew up into the elm?

6. She loves the colour, the shape, the sound of the pheasant. Identify where each of these is praised.

Second reading

7. In verse 3 the narrator explains why she feels so honoured by the visit of the pheasant: identify what 'it is' and what 'it isn't' that touches her. Why do you think she tells us that she is 'not mystical'?

8. In what sense is she trespassing? What does this word suggest about her attitude to the pheasant?

9. How do the final words link back to the opening statement and request? Do you feel the narrator has got her way at the end? Explain.

Second reading continued

10. What is the tone/mood of the poem? Use the text to support your points, paying attention to the narrator's relationship with 'you'.

General question

11. Plath describes the pheasant as 'vivid'. The same word could apply to this poem: it is strong, vigorous and sinewy. Write about this quality of the poem. Look at language – verbs, nouns, adjectives – as well as imagery, structure, rhythm and rhyme.

Elm

For Ruth Fainlight

I know the bottom, she says. I know it with my great tap root:
It is what you fear.
I do not fear it: I have been there.

Is it the sea you hear in me,
Its dissatisfactions?   5
Or the voice of nothing, that was your madness?

Love is a shadow.
How you lie and cry after it
Listen: these are its hooves: it has gone off, like a horse.

All night I shall gallop thus, impetuously,   10
Till your head is a stone, your pillow a little turf,

Echoing, echoing.

Or shall I bring you the sound of poisons?
This is rain now, this big hush.
And this is the fruit of it: tin-white, like arsenic.   15
I have suffered the atrocity of sunsets.
Scorched to the root
My red filaments burn and stand, a hand of wires.

Now I break up in pieces that fly about like clubs
A wind of such violence   20
Will tolerate no bystanding: I must shriek.

The moon, also, is merciless: she would drag me
Cruelly, being barren.
Her radiance scathes me. Or perhaps I have caught her.

I let her go. I let her go   25
Diminished and flat, as after radical surgery.
How your bad dreams possess and endow me.

I am inhabited by a cry.
Nightly it flaps out
Looking, with its hooks, for something to love.   30

I am terrified by this dark thing
That sleeps in me;
All day I feel its soft, feathery turnings, its malignity.

Clouds pass and disperse.
Are those the faces of love, those pale irretrievables?   35
Is it for such I agitate my heart?

I am incapable of more knowledge.
What is this, this face
So murderous in its strangle of branches? –

Its snaky acids hiss.   40
It petrifies the will. These are the isolate, slow faults
That kill, that kill, that kill.

[15] **arsenic:** lethal poison
[18] **filaments:** thread-like conductors of electrical current
[24] **scathe:** to hurt or injure, especially by scorching
[35] **irretrievables:** cannot be recovered or won back

EXPLORATIONS

First reading

1. Listen to the poem a number of times. What sounds are most striking? Which words stay in your mind? Jot down your impressions.

2. What attitude does 'I' seem to adopt towards 'you' in stanza 3?

3. Stanzas 5–8 introduce rain, sunset, wind and moon: how is each one presented? How do they affect 'I'?

4. What change seems to occur in 'I' in stanzas 9–14? Can you identify at what point the change began?

5. Would you agree that the latter half of the poem powerfully conveys a nightmare world? Which images and phrases are most effective in building this impression?

Second reading

6. 'Elm' opens on a confident, objective note, as if the narrator is quite detached from 'you'. How is this achieved?

7. Trace the references to love in the poem. How does the narrator view love? Is it important to her?

8. There are several references to violence, both physical and mental. Select those you consider most powerful. What is the source of the violence?

9. Compare the force of love with the force of evil. Which comes across as the more powerful? Explain how this is achieved.

Third reading

10. Plath uses many rich and powerful images. The central image is the elm, the 'I' persona. (a) Trace the elm's feelings, mood through the poem. (b) What do you think the elm may symbolise to the

poet? In answering this, reflect on the tone, the utter weariness, the feelings of anguish, the growing terror and the role 'you' plays in generating these feelings.

11. The moon is another important image in the poem. Reread the stanzas describing it (8, 9, 13). What qualities are attributed to it? What do you think it symbolises? Can you explain the seeming contradictions?

Fourth reading

12. The poet uses rich sound effects throughout the poem. Note where she uses rhyme, assonance, repetition, cacophony and soft sounds. How do these affect the reader/listener?

13. The poem opens with a calm confident voice, a sense of control: 'I know . . . | I do not fear . . .'. It closes on a note of hysterical despair, total loss of control: 'It petrifies the will. These are the isolate, slow faults | That kill, that kill, that kill.' Trace the change through the poem. Describe how this transformation is achieved.

General questions

14. 'Plath infuses this poem with a strong sense of vulnerability pitted against destructive energy.' What is your response to this statement? Use detailed reference to the poem in support of each point you make.

15. '"Elm" is a powerful urgent statement spoken by a narrator who has been abandoned by the person she loves.' Discuss this view of the poem.

16. 'This poem has the surreal quality of a nightmare in which the smallest objects seem fraught with hidden significance.' Discuss how this effect is achieved, basing each point you make on specific reference to the poem.

Poppies in July

this poem is also prescribed for Ordinary Level exams in 2012, 2013 and 2014

Little poppies, little hell flames,
Do you do no harm?

You flicker. I cannot touch you.
I put my hands among the flames. Nothing burns.

And it exhausts me to watch you   5
Flickering like that, wrinkly and clear red, like the skin of a mouth.

A mouth just bloodied.
Little bloody skirts!

There are fumes that I cannot touch.
Where are your opiates, your nauseous capsules?   10

If I could bleed, or sleep! –
If my mouth could marry a hurt like that!

Or your liquors seep to me, in this glass capsule,
Dulling and stilling.

But colorless. Colorless.   15

Notes

[10] **opiates:** narcotics, drugs which induce sleep, dull feelings
[10] **nauseous:** causing vomiting or illness

EXPLORATIONS

1. Imagine a poppy: what qualities do you associate with it? Think of colour, texture and shape.

First reading

2. The poem opens with a question. What does it suggest to you?

3. Describe what the narrator is doing in this poem. What thoughts are triggered by her actions?

4. Identify the words associated with fire in lines 1–6. What is the narrator's feeling about this fire/these poppies? What does fire symbolise? Do you see any of these qualities reflected here?

5. Which qualities of the poppies might make the narrator think of a mouth?

6. What could 'bloody' a mouth? Do any of the other words suggest violence?

7. Lines 9–13 focus on another aspect of poppies: what is this?

8. Looking at the various descriptions of the poppies, try to explain the author's attitude to them.

Second reading

9. What feelings does the narrator convey in this poem? Say how each feeling is suggested, referring to specific words and images.

10. There is a strong contrast between lines 1–8 and lines 9–15. How is this effected? Look at how words, images and tone contribute to the contrast.

11. The narrator seems to imply an answer to the question posed in stanza 1. How does she answer it?

Third reading

12. While there is no end rhyme in this poem, the poet uses quite intricate sound effects, including repetition. Trace these, noting the effect they have.

13. Write a paragraph about the poet's use of colour in the poem, noting how she moves from the vividness of the early stanzas to the final repeated 'colorless'. What might the loss of colour say about the narrator's feelings?

14. The poem moves from the outside world to the inner world of the narrator. Chart this movement through the poem. How does she connect one to the other?

Fourth reading

15. Do you consider the intensity of the feeling conveyed is consistent with a simple description of poppies?

What underlying emotion do you think might cause such intense anguish? Discuss this point, referring to the text in support of your arguments.

16. In both 'Poppies in July' and 'Elm', Plath takes a simple natural object and invests it with intense feelings, creating a metaphor for personal suffering – the inner struggle to come to terms with an overwhelming problem. Write a comparison of the two poems.

The Arrival of the Bee Box

this poem is also prescribed for Ordinary Level exams in 2013 and 2014

I ordered this, this clean wood box
Square as a chair and almost too heavy to lift.
I would say it was the coffin of a midget
Or a square baby
Were there not such a din in it.   5

The box is locked, it is dangerous.
I have to live with it overnight
And I can't keep away from it.
There are no windows, so I can't see what is in there.
There is only a little grid, no exit.   10

I put my eye to the grid.
It is dark, dark,
With the swarmy feeling of African hands
Minute and shrunk for export,
Black on black, angrily clambering.   15

How can I let them out?
It is the noise that appals me most of all,
The unintelligible syllables.
It is like a Roman mob,
Small, taken one by one, but my god, together!   20

I lay my ear to furious Latin.
I am not a Caesar.
I have simply ordered a box of maniacs.
They can be sent back.
They can die, I need feed them nothing, I am the owner.   25

I wonder how hungry they are.
I wonder if they would forget me
If I just undid the locks and stood back and turned into a tree.
There is the laburnum, its blond colonnades,
And the petticoats of the cherry.   30

They might ignore me immediately
In my moon suit and funeral veil.
I am no source of honey
So why should they turn on me?
Tomorrow I will be sweet God, I will set them free.   35

The box is only temporary.

Notes

[22]   **Caesar:** Roman emperor
[28]   **turned into a tree:** a reference to the Greek myth of
       Daphne, who was chased by Apollo. She pleaded with the
       gods to help her escape, and they changed her into a tree.
[32]   **moon suit and funeral veil:** protective clothing worn by
       beekeepers

EXPLORATIONS

First reading

1. Stanza 1 gives the background to the arrival of the bee box and the narrator's reaction. Which feeling is most obvious? Have you ever felt this way about bees, wasps . . .?

2. How does she seem to relate to the bees in stanzas 3–5?

3. Stanza 5 concludes with the statement 'They can die'. Do you actually believe she means this? How does she undermine her statement? Be precise.

4. How does she propose to escape the bees' wrath if she releases them?

5. She describes her clothing as a 'moon suit': what ideas does this image suggest?

6. Comment on the contradiction between 'I am no source of honey' and 'I will be sweet God'. Note the play on words – what is the tone of these lines? How can she be 'sweet God' to the bees?

7. What happens in this poem? What part does the 'I' of the poem play in the event?

Second reading

8. The language used to describe the bee box is strong, suggesting something sinister and dangerous. Select the words or images that help to create this impression.

9. There is a contradiction between the image of a coffin and the intense life within the box. Which idea – death or life – is implied with more strength in the rest of the poem? Be precise.

10. In stanza 3, the writer creates a graphic metaphor for the bees and their sound. Identify these and note the common link between them. What do they tell us about the narrator?

11. In stanzas 4 and 5, the bees have become a metaphor for the narrator's words. Explain the image, trying to convey some of the feeling she captures. What relationship is suggested between the narrator and her words in these two stanzas?

12. The image of turning into a tree is associated with the Greek myth of the god Apollo and Daphne: she turned into a tree to escape his attentions. What does this association say about the narrator's attitude to the bees?

13. Write a detailed description of the changes in the narrator's attitude between stanza 1 and stanza 7.

14. The final line stands alone, separated from the rest of the poem which is arranged in five-line stanzas. What does the line suggest? How does it colour the reader's response to the poem as a whole?

Third reading

15. Plath makes extensive use of internal rhyme, assonance and word play. One example is 'square as a chair'. Here, 'chair' suggests the homely and ordinary, while 'square' implies honest, straightforward, exact. The rhyme almost echoes the box's shape – its regularity and squareness. Identify other examples of sound effects and word-play in the poem. Comment on their use.

16. This poem moves between the real and familiar world, and the symbolic. Can you identify what is real and ordinary, what happens on the surface?

17. On the symbolic level, what is suggested by the poem? Look at the metaphors used for the bee box, the bees, the 'I' persona. Be aware of the feelings conveyed throughout.

18. There is a touch of dark humour, self-mockery, running through the poem. Where is this most obvious? What effect does it have on the reader?

Fourth reading

19. What do you consider to be the central theme of the poem? In answering, refer to the writer's tone and the images used. Look also at your answers to Questions 16 and 17.

Child

this poem is also prescribed for Ordinary Level exams in 2012, 2013 and 2014

Your clear eye is the one absolutely beautiful thing.
I want to fill it with color and ducks,
The zoo of the new

Whose names you meditate –
April snowdrop, Indian pipe,   5
Little

Stalk without wrinkle,
Pool in which images
Should be grand and classical

Not this troublous   10
Wringing of hands, this dark
Ceiling without a star.

EXPLORATIONS

First reading

1. Read this poem aloud and listen to its lyrical tone. What is your first impression of the speaker's feeling for her child? Try to imagine the speaker and child – what image do you see?

2. What pictures does she create for the child's 'eye'?

3. Which words here remind you of childlike things? What mood is usually associated with these?

4. How do you interpret the final stanza? Does it affect your reading of the rest of the poem?

Second reading

5. What feelings does the narrator display toward the child in the opening stanzas?

6. Does the narrator's focus remain consistent through the poem? Where do you think the change occurs? Look at the verb tenses used when answering this.

7. How is the adult/narrator/ mother contrasted with the child?

Third reading

8. What is the effect of line 1 on the reader? Examine how this is achieved.

9. Write a paragraph showing how this contrasts with the final lines. Look at language, imagery, tone.

10. The language of the poem is fresh, clear and simple. What is the effect of this?

11. Write a note about the impressions created by this poem for you.

13 *Seamus Heaney*
1939–

prescribed for Higher Level exams in 2012 and 2014

Seamus Heaney was born on 13 April 1939 on the family farm at Mossbawn, near Bellaghy, County Derry. From 1945 to 1951 he attended Anahorish primary school; in the period 1951–57 he was educated at St Columb's College in Derry and during the period 1957–61 at Queen's University, Belfast, where he achieved a first-class degree in English language and literature. In 1961 and 1962 he took a teacher training diploma at St Joseph's College of Education in Belfast. In 1966 he was appointed lecturer in English at Queen's University.

Heaney's first volume of poetry, *Death of a Naturalist*, was published in 1966. Filled mostly with the characters, scenes, customs, flora and fauna of the countryside that formed him, this volume, which includes 'Twice Shy' and 'Valediction', explores Heaney's cultural and poetic origins. *Door in the Dark*, Heaney's second volume, was published in 1969. While the first collection dealt mainly with childhood, coming of age, and the poet's relationship with the somewhat heroic figure of his father, *Door in the Dark* deals with more adult relationships. A few poems, such as 'The Forge', hark back to the style of the first volume in the celebration of local skills and in the poet's discovery in them of metaphors for his own craft. But the poet's Irish focus broadens out from local considerations to a more general awareness of geography, history and archaeology in such poems as 'Bogland'.

Heaney's third volume of poetry was published in 1972. The year 1969 had seen riots, bombs and sectarian killings. The Provisional IRA became a powerful force and the British army was deployed on the streets. Yet Heaney hardly ever addresses these contemporary political issues directly; instead he makes a journey back into the past of prehistoric humankind. In 'The Tollund Man' Heaney finds an oblique way of examining the sacrificial killings, the power of religion and the deadly demands of myth in our society. Heaney spent the academic year 1970–71 as guest lecturer at the University of California in Berkeley and found it difficult to settle back into life in Northern Ireland when he returned, a transition he described as 'like putting an old dirty glove on again'. He found the daily ritual of roadblocks, arrests, vigilante patrols, explosions and killings deeply disturbing. Heaney decided that it was time to leave Belfast and devote himself entirely to his writing. He resigned his post as lecturer in English at Queen's University and moved with his family to a cottage at Glanmore, County Wicklow, during the summer of

1972, determined to go it alone as a poet and freelance writer.

Heaney's fourth volume of poetry, *North*, was published in 1975: in Part I he ranges over three thousand years of European civilisation, from the myths of Classical Greece to nineteenth-century Irish history, examining stories of conquest, cultural conflict and deeds of violence. A sequence of six poems entitled *Singing School* was published in 1972. The year 1969 had seen marked milestones in his development as a poet and member of his tribe: the Northern Catholic. In 'A Constable Calls', part of the *Singing School* sequence, he recalls, from a child's perspective, his fear of an alien law. This collection of conflict poems is prefaced by two totally different poems: two peaceful poems outside the stream of history and time recalling the security of childhood, the holistic nature of the old ways of life, the peacefulness of the countryside, and the stability and certainty provided by family love and values. These two poems are 'Mossbawn: Two Poems in Dedication', of which the first is 'Sunlight'.

Field Work, Heaney's fifth collection, was published in 1979. It includes 'The Skunk' and 'The Harvest Bow'. *Seeing Things,* published in 1991, in some ways sees a return to Heaney's early concerns. It deals with personal vision and personal history rather than with politics or historical issues. 'Lightenings VIII' was published in this collection. A further collection, *The Spirit Level*, was published in 1996.

In 1988 Heaney was elected professor of poetry at the University of Oxford, and in 1995 his lectures were published as *The Redress of Poetry*. Also in 1995 he was awarded the Nobel Prize for Literature.

The Forge

CD 2
Track 1

All I know is a door into the dark.
Outside, old axles and iron hoops rusting;
Inside, the hammered anvil's short-pitched ring,
The unpredictable fantail of sparks
Or hiss when a new shoe toughens in water.   5
The anvil must be somewhere in the centre,
Horned as a unicorn, at one end square,
Set there immovable: an altar
Where he expends himself in shape and music.
Sometimes, leather-aproned, hairs in his nose,   10
He leans out on the jamb, recalls a clatter
Of hoofs where traffic is flashing in rows;
Then grunts and goes in, with a slam and flick
To beat real iron out, to work the bellows.

EXPLORATIONS

Before reading

1. Read the title only. Jot down all the images that come into your head of what you might expect to see in the forge.

First reading

2. What do you actually see in this picture of the forge?

3. Where is the speaker standing in this poem? Do you think this might be significant? Why? What can he see? What can he not see?

Second reading

4. What can we say about the smith from his appearance and manner? Refer to the text.

5. How do you think the smith views his work? Read lines 13 and 14 again.

6. How does the poet view the smith's work? Read lines 6–9 again.

7. What do you think is the poet's theme here?

8. Could the poem be read in a symbolic way, i.e. as dealing with a subject other than the surface one of the work of a blacksmith? If so, how?

9. Comment on the appropriateness of the imagery in this poem.

10. Would you agree with the following criticism by James Simmons?

    '"The Forge" . . . is shapely and vivid at first but fails to stand as a metaphor for the creative act. It becomes a cliché portrait of the village smithy. The smith has hairs in his nose and remembers better times. He retreats from the sight of modern traffic to beat real iron out, to work the bellows.'

    Give your opinion on both the metaphor and the portrait of the village forge.

11. Comment on the style of language used. Is it poetic, prosaic, conversational, or what?

12. Do you think Heaney brings a sense of concrete realism to his art? Comment, with reference to the text.

13. What elements of the poem do not work very well for you? Explain, with reference to the text.

Bogland

For T. P. Flanagan

We have no prairies
To slice a big sun at evening —
Everywhere the eye concedes to
Encroaching horizon,

Is wooed into the cyclops' eye   5
Of a tarn. Our unfenced country
Is bog that keeps crusting
Between the sights of the sun.

They've taken the skeleton
Of the Great Irish Elk   10
Out of the peat, set it up
An astounding crate full of air.

Butter sunk under
More than a hundred years
Was recovered salty and white.   15
The ground itself is kind, black butter

Melting and opening underfoot,
Missing its last definition
By millions of years.
They'll never dig coal here,   20

Only the waterlogged trunks
Of great firs, soft as pulp.
Our pioneers keep striking
Inwards and downwards,

Every layer they strip   25
Seems camped on before.
The bogholes might be Atlantic seepage.
The wet centre is bottomless.

[5]   **cyclops:** in Greek mythology a Cyclops was one of a race of one-eyed giants

[6]   **tarn:** a small mountain lake

'Boglands' (for Seamus Heaney), an oil painting by T. P. Flanagan

EXPLORATIONS

First reading

1. Explain the contrast between the prairies and the Irish landscape, as described in the first two stanzas.

2. Where else in the poem is this cultural contrast referred to?

3. What properties of bogland are dwelt on in stanzas 3–6?

4. Who do you see as the speaking voice in this poem?

Second reading

5. What queries are raised in your mind by a further reading? List at least three.

Second reading continued

6. What do you think this poem is about?

Third reading

7. If we accept that the bog is a metaphor for Irishness, what is the poet saying on this theme? Refer to the text to substantiate your views.

8. Comment on the tone of this poem. Do you think the poet is pessimistic, excited, neutral, nostalgic, or what? Refer to the text.

9. Do you think this poem asks you to think in a different way

about what it means to be Irish? Explain.

10. Consider the following critical comment made by another poet, James Simmons: 'As a man and poet in his life and philosophy Heaney is not geared to progress and reform. He wants to wallow and look back. He is going through a door into the dark, inward and downward, a kind of Jungian ground he will call it.' Which elements of this criticism do you think are justified? Do you think

any element is unwarranted? Justify your comments with reference to the text.

Fourth reading

11. What questions would you like to ask Seamus Heaney about this poem?

12. In the form of headings, or a flow chart, or a spider diagram, bring together your ideas on the theme and imagery of this poem.

The Tollund Man

CD 2
Track 3

I
Some day I will go to Aarhus
To see his peat-brown head,
The mild pods of his eye-lids,
His pointed skin cap.

In the flat country nearby   5
Where they dug him out,
His last gruel of winter seeds
Caked in his stomach,

Naked except for
The cap, noose and girdle,   10
I will stand a long time.
Bridegroom to the goddess,

She tightened her torc on him
And opened her fen,

Those dark juices working   15
Him to a saint's kept body,

Trove of the turfcutters'
Honeycombed workings.
Now his stained face
Reposes at Aarhus.   20

                    II
I could risk blasphemy,
Consecrate the cauldron bog
Our holy ground and pray
Him to make germinate

The scattered, ambushed   25
Flesh of labourers,
Stockinged corpses
Laid out in the farmyards,

Tell-tale skin and teeth
Flecking the sleepers   30
Of four young brothers, trailed
For miles along the lines.

                    III
Something of his sad freedom
As he rode the tumbril
Should come to me, driving,   35
Saying the names

Tollund, Grauballe, Nebelgard,
Watching the pointing hands
Of country people,
Not knowing their tongue.   40

Out there in Jutland
In the old man-killing parishes
I will feel lost,
Unhappy and at home.

EXPLORATIONS

First reading

1. Listen to a reading of part I. What do you see? What words or phrases make images for you?

2. Now read it. Describe the poet's subject. What details do you find most interesting? Why?

3. Identify the speaker in the poem. Identify the 'he' and 'she' referred to.

4. Explain the incident described. What do you think happened?

Second reading

5. Now read part I again. What is still unclear?

6. Read part II. What is the poet writing about here, and when do you think it occurred?

7. What do you think is the connection between part II and part I?

Third reading

8. What is happening in part III?

9. How does the poet feel? Read the second-last stanza aloud. Listen to the sounds of the words. Picture the scene in your mind.

10. Explain why you think the poet feels 'lost, unhappy and at home'.

Fourth reading

11. Examine the parallels and contrasts between Tollund Man and modern people as Heaney pictures them in this poem.

12. Is the poem making a political statement? If so, what?

13. Discuss the political imagery in this poem.

14. Make brief notes on the themes dealt with in this poem.

15. Comment on the variety of imagery used throughout the poem.

16. Do you think Heaney manages to create a feeling of sympathy for Tollund Man? How does he manage to achieve this?

17. Michael Parker described this poem as 'a potent combination of historical analogy and myth and intense emotion which exhibits the depth of Heaney's religious nature'. Discuss this analysis, substantiating your view by reference to the text.

Sunlight

There was a sunlit absence.
The helmeted pump in the yard
heated its iron,
water honeyed

in the slung bucket   5
and the sun stood
like a griddle cooling
against the wall

of each long afternoon.
So, her hands scuffled   10
over the bakeboard,
the reddening stove

sent its plaque of heat
against her where she stood
in a floury apron   15
by the window.

Now she dusts the board
with a goose's wing,
now sits, broad-lapped,
with whitened nails   20

and measling shins:
here is a space
again, the scone rising
to the tick of two clocks.

And here is love   25
like a tinsmith's scoop
sunk past its gleam
in the meal-bin.

Explorations

First reading

1. What is described here?
2. What details stand out on a first reading?

Second reading

3. Think of the poem as a picture in two panels: the yard and the kitchen. (a) Study the detail of each scene, and discuss the significance of each piece of detail. What era is evoked by the detail? (b) Examine the portrait of Mary Heaney. What kind of person is she? (c) Describe the atmosphere created in each scene, and explain how it is created.

Third reading

4. This is the opening poem in a volume that deals for the most part with violence, conflict and conquest. Does this surprise you? Explain.

5. In that context, what do you think is the significance of the poem? What does this poem suggest about the poet's values and attitudes to living?

6. Do you think there is any significance in the change from past tense to present tense that occurs from stanza 5 onwards?

7. Explain your own reaction to this poem.

A Constable Calls

this poem is also prescribed for Ordinary Level exams in 2012 and 2014

His bicycle stood at the window-sill,
The rubber cowl of a mud-splasher
Skirting the front mudguard,
Its fat black handlegrips

Heating in sunlight, the 'spud'   5
Of the dynamo gleaming and cocked back,
The pedal treads hanging relieved
Of the boot of the law.

His cap was upside down
On the floor, next his chair.   10
The line of its pressure ran like a bevel
In his slightly sweating hair.

He had unstrapped
The heavy ledger, and my father
Was making tillage returns   15
In acres, roods, and perches.

Arithmetic and fear.
I sat staring at the polished holster
With its buttoned flap, the braid cord
Looped into the revolver butt.   20

'Any other root crops?
Mangolds? Marrowstems? Anything like that?'
'No.' But was there not a line
Of turnips where the seed ran out

In the potato field? I assumed   25
Small guilts and sat
Imagining the black hole in the barracks.
He stood up, shifted the baton-case

Further round on his belt,

Closed the domesday book,
Fitted his cap back with two hands,
And looked at me as he said goodbye.

A shadow bobbed in the window.
He was snapping the carrier spring
Over the ledger. His boot pushed off
And the bicycle ticked, ticked, ticked.

30

35

EXPLORATIONS

First reading

1. What descriptive details of the bicycle did you notice as you read this poem? Did they seem to you in any way significant?

2. What details of the policeman's description did you think significant? What type of character is suggested by these details?

Second reading

3. What do you think is the boy's attitude to the bicycle, as described in the poem? Where and how is this attitude communicated to the reader?

4. What is the relationship between the participants in this encounter: the policeman, the boy and his father? Examine the imagery and dialogue and the actions of those involved.

Third reading

5. Can you understand how the boy feels? Explain.

6. Do you think the poem faithfully represents how a child might actually feel in this situation? Examine your own experiences to test the truth of the poem.

7. Outline the main themes of this poem, as you understand them.

8. From your reading of this poem, would you agree that one of Heaney'sstrengths as a poet is his ability to create realistic descriptions in minute detail?

Fourth reading

9. What is your evaluation of this poem's truth and significance?

The Skunk

Up, black, striped and damasked like the chasuble
At a funeral mass, the skunk's tail
Paraded the skunk. Night after night
I expected her like a visitor.

The refrigerator whinnied into silence.   5
My desk light softened beyond the verandah.
Small oranges loomed in the orange tree.
I began to be tense as a voyeur.

After eleven years I was composing
Love-letters again, broaching the word 'wife'   10
Like a stored cask, as if its slender vowel
Had mutated into the night earth and air

Of California. The beautiful, useless
Tang of eucalyptus spelt your absence.
The aftermath of a mouthful of wine   15
Was like inhaling you off a cold pillow.

And there she was, the intent and glamorous,
Ordinary, mysterious skunk,
Mythologized, demythologized,
Snuffing the boards five feet beyond me.   20

It all came back to me last night, stirred
By the sootfall of your things at bedtime,
Your head-down, tail-up hunt in a bottom drawer
For the black plunge-line nightdress.

EXPLORATIONS

First reading

1. What images do you notice in particular? What sounds or smells? How would you describe the atmosphere?

2. The poem is set in two separate places, at two different times. Where is that division reflected in the stanzas? What are the two distinct times and places?

3. What image is associated with both locations? Explain the connection.

Second reading

4. How would you describe the poet's mood or state of mind in the first five stanzas?

5. What part does the skunk play here? What are your reactions to this analogy?

6. What is the poet saying in stanza 5?

Third reading

7. Examine the nature of the poet's relationship with his wife, as it comes across in this poem.

Fourth reading

8. Examine the sensuous language in this poem.

9. What does the imagery contribute to the effectiveness of the poem?

10. Do you think the transmutation of wife and skunk works well?

11. What exactly is the poet saying about love and relationships?

Fifth reading

12. Give a considered response to the following evaluation of the poem by the critic Neil Corcoran:

    '"The Skunk"' is characteristic of these marriage poems, which are one of the highest points of Heaney's career: tender without being cosy, personal without being embarrassingly self-revealing. They are poems of a deeply disinterested maturity, managing an intensely difficult tone: honest and quite without self-regard.'

    Deal separately with each point.

The Harvest Bow

As you plaited the harvest bow
You implicated the mellowed silence in you
In wheat that does not rust
But brightens as it tightens twist by twist
Into a knowable corona,   5
A throwaway love-knot of straw.

Hands that aged round ashplants and cane sticks
And lapped the spurs on a lifetime of game cocks
Harked to their gift and worked with fine intent
Until your fingers moved somnambulant: 10
I tell and finger it like braille,
Gleaning the unsaid off the palpable.

And if I spy into its golden loops
I see us walk between the railway slopes
Into an evening of long grass and midges,   15
Blue smoke straight up, old beds and ploughs in hedges,
An auction notice on an outhouse wall —
You with a harvest bow in your lapel,

Me with the fishing rod, already homesick
For the big lift of these evenings, as your stick   20
Whacking the tips off weeds and bushes
Beats out of time, and beats, but flushes
Nothing: that original townland
Still tongue-tied in the straw tied by your hand.

The end of art is peace   25
Could be the motto of this frail device
That I have pinned up on our deal dresser—
Like a drawn snare
Slipped lately by the spirit of the corn
Yet burnished by its passage, and still warm.   30

Harvest Bow: a knot woven from wheat straw, a symbol of a fruitful harvest, embodying the spirit of the corn

[5] **corona:** halo of light round the sun

[10] **somnambulant:** sleep-walking (here, performing unconsciously, as in sleep)

[12] **palpable:** capable of being touched, felt, or readily perceived

A harvest bow from Ulster

EXPLORATIONS

First reading

1. As you read, visualise the poem in your mind's eye. What colours predominate? Which images strike you in particular? How do you imagine the setting?

Second reading

2. 'As you plaited the harvest bow' — who do you think is the 'you' addressed in the poem: a person older or younger than the poet, living in the town or in the country? What type of person?

3. Where is the poem set? Are there a number of settings in it? Examine the imagery again.

4. Examine the time frames in the poem. Is it set in the present or the past, or both? Read the verses in the order 5, 1, 2, 3, 4. Does this help to clarify which is the present, which is the recent past, and which are distant memories?

5. In your own words, briefly reconstruct the narrative.

Third reading

6. Trace the various references to the harvest bow that are scattered throughout the poem. Examine each image and say what it suggests to you about the significance of the bow.

7. How does the poet regard the bow? Is it important to him? What does it enable him to do?

8. How do you think the father viewed the bow?

9. How does the poet regard his father? Examine the images used about him and the tone of the utterances referring to him.

10. If the father was a better communicator, what do you think he might have said in stanza 4?

Fourth reading

11. What do you imagine he might mean by the motto 'The end of art is peace'?

12. What lines, phrases or images are still unclear to you? Discuss interpretations.

13. What does the poem reveal about Heaney's attitude to his rural heritage?

14. What does the poet feel about the value of art and poetry in society?

Fifth reading

15. What is your own reaction to 'The Harvest Bow'? Does it say anything of significance to you?

16. What questions would you like to ask the poet if you could?

The Underground

this poem is also prescribed for Ordinary Level exams in 2012 and 2014

There we were in the vaulted tunnel running,
You in your going-away coat speeding ahead
And me, me then like a fleet god gaining
Behind you before you turned to a reed

Or some new white flower japped with crimson   5
As the coat flapped wild and button after button
Sprang off and fell in a trail
Between the Underground and the Albert Hall.

Honeymooning, mooning around, late for the Proms,
Our echoes die in that corridor and now   10
I come as Hansel came on the moonlit stones
Retracing the path back, lifting the buttons

To end up in a draughty lamplit station
After the trains have gone, the wet track
Bared and tensed as I am, all attention   15
For your step following and damned if I look back.

Notes

The Underground: the underground train system in London
[3]   **fleet:** fleet of foot, swift, nimble
[5]   **japped:** possibly means varnished or lacquered

Classical myths and fairy tale allusions and references:

[4]   **before you turned to a reed:** this is a reference to the classical myth of Pan and Syrinx. The nymph Syrinx was being pursued by the god Pan and in order to preserve her virginity she appealed to the river nymphs for help. Just as Pan reached for her she was transformed into a bed of reeds, which he was left clutching. He made his music pipes from these reeds and called them syrinx in memory of her.

[11]   **Hansel:** refers to a Grimms' fairy tale about two inseparable children, Hansel, a woodcutter's son, and Gretel, a young girl found in the forest. The family fell on bad times and were starving so the wife persuaded the father to abandon the children in the forest. But Hansel marked the trail with pebbles so they found their way home.

[16]   **damned if I look back:** refers to the classical myth of Orpheus and Eurydice. In Greek legend Orpheus was a Thracian poet and a very skilled musician. When his wife Eurydice died, he travelled down to the underworld, the kingdom of the dead, and by his music persuaded King Pluto to free her. However, this was on the condition that Orpheus would not look back until they reached the earth. Just as they came towards the light at the mouth of the tunnel, because of his love for Eurydice, Orpheus could not prevent himself glancing back to look at her face. She immediately vanished down to Hades again. Because he loved her too much Orpheus lost her forever.

EXPLORATIONS

Before reading

1.   Make a list of all the connotations, real and imaginary, that occur to you about the word 'underground'.

First reading

2.   In your own words, describe what happens in this poem.

3.   What details in particular catch your eye?

4.   How would you describe the atmosphere?

First reading continued

5.   Retell the narrative from the woman's perspective.

Second reading

6.   Do you think the speaker is as carefree as you might expect him to be on his honeymoon? Develop your ideas on this.

7.   If this is a love poem, what is it saying about love?

8.   Do you think the setting is appropriate to a love poem? Explain. What would you like to ask the poet about this?

Postscript

And some time make the time to drive out west
Into County Clare, along the Flaggy Shore,
In September or October, when the wind
And the light are working off each other
So that the ocean on the one side is wild   5
With foam and glitter, and inland among stones
The surface of a slate-grey lake is lit
By the earthed lightning of a flock of swans,
Their feathers roughed and ruffling, white on white,
Their fully grown headstrong-looking heads   10
Tucked or cresting or busy underwater.
Useless to think you'll park and capture it
More thoroughly. You are neither here nor there,
A hurry through which known and strange things pass
As big soft buffetings come at the car sideways   15
And catch the heart off guard and blow it open.

EXPLORATIONS

First reading

1. (a) Have you ever seen flashes
    of scenery on a car journey that
    you can still remember, even
    though you only saw them for a
    moment? (b) Does this poem in
    any way remind you of your
    experience?

Second reading

2. This poem is set in County
    Clare in 'September or
    October'. What images are
    there in lines 3–7 that help you
    to picture what County Clare is
    like at this time of year?

3. 'The surface of a slate-grey
    lake is lit

    By the earthed lightning of a
    flock of swans,

    Their feathers roughed and
    ruffling, white on white'

Can you suggest why Heaney describes the swans as 'earthed lightning'? You might find it helpful to consider the colour and texture of the lake and the swans.

4. Do you find Heaney's description of the swans a realistic one? Why? Use quotations from the poem to support your answer.

5. Heaney decided not to use any full stops until line 11 of this poem. (a) What effect does this have on the way that you read the poem? (b) Does the effect that he is trying to create have anything to do with the fact that he is describing a car journey?

6. 'You are neither here nor there,

    A hurry through which known and strange things pass'

    What do you think Heaney is trying to suggest about travelling in a car when he uses the phrases 'neither here nor there' and 'A hurry through'?

Third reading

7. What do the final two lines of the poem reveal about how the glimpses of the scenery affected Heaney?

8. From your readings of the poem, can you work out how Seamus Heaney feels about County Clare? You will find it useful to consider the tone, or the emotion, of his words.

9. (a) Why do you think Heaney decided to give this poem the title 'Postscript'? (b) Do you think that it is a successful title, or can you suggest another title that you would consider more suitable?

10. Imagine that you have been asked to prepare a short film to be shown as Seamus Heaney reads this poem. Describe the images that you would show and the camera angles that you would use to capture how you 'see' this poem.

A Call

this poem is also prescribed for Ordinary Level exams in 2012 and 2014

'Hold on,' she said, 'I'll just run out and get him.
The weather here's so good he took the chance
To do a bit of weeding.'

So I saw him
Down on his hands and knees beside the leek rig,   5
Touching, inspecting, separating one
Stalk from the other, gently pulling up
Everything not tapered, frail and leafless,
Pleased to feel each little weed-root break,
But rueful also . . .   10

Then found myself listening to
The amplified grave ticking of hall clocks
Where the phone lay unattended in a calm
Of mirror glass and sunstruck pendulums . . .

And found myself then thinking: if it were nowadays,   15
This is how Death would summon Everyman.

Next thing he spoke and I nearly said I loved him.

Notes

[16]   **Everyman:** the main character in a famous English morality
       play of the early sixteenth century. When Everyman is
       summoned by Death he invites all his acquaintances
       (who include Kindred, Good Deeds, Goods, Knowledge,
       Beauty and others) to go with him, but only Good Deeds
       agrees to go.

Explorations

Before reading

1. When you last made a phone call to a house landline and someone went away to get whoever you were trying to reach, what thoughts went through your mind as you waited? Share the results in groups.

First reading

2. What thoughts were going through the poet's mind as he waited?

3. The poet has a very clear visual image of his father. What aspects of the man does he highlight?

4. Re-read the section describing the hallway as the speaker waits. (a) If you close your eyes and picture the scene, what do you see and hear? (b) What thoughts come to your mind? (c) How would you describe the atmosphere in the hallway? Refer to words and images to support your answer.

5. Now read the next two lines. Does it come as a complete surprise that the poet is thinking about death? Explain your thinking.

First reading continued

6. (a) Suggest some possible reasons why the poet did not say he loved his father. (b) Do you think he might now regret that?

Second reading

7. What are the main ideas/issues dealt with in this poem?

8. (a) Do you think it was important to write about these issues? Explain your thinking. (b) Do you think he does it well? What aspects or sections do you find particularly effective? Explain.

9. There is some ambiguity about the title. Suggest a couple of different ways in which the title might be understood.

10. Phone a friend. Listen, think and write it up.

Tate's Avenue

Not the brown and fawn car rug, that first one
Spread on sand by the sea but breathing land-breaths,
Its vestal folds unfolded, its comfort zone
Edged with a fringe of sepia-coloured wool tails.

Not the one scraggy with crusts and eggshells   5
And olive stones and cheese and salami rinds
Laid out by the torrents of the Guadalquivir
Where we got drunk before the corrida.

Instead, again, it's locked-park Sunday Belfast,
A walled back yard, the dust-bins high and silent   10
As a page is turned, a finger twirls warm hair
And nothing gives on the rug or the ground beneath it.

I lay at my length and felt the lumpy earth,
Keen-sensed more than ever through discomfort,
But never shifted off the plaid square once.   15
When we moved I had your measure and you had mine.

Notes

[3] **vestal:** chaste, virginal. Vesta was the Roman goddess of
hearth and home and vowed to chastity.
[4] **sepia-coloured:** brown-coloured
[6] **salami:** a kind of sausage
[7] **Guadalquivir:** a river in Spain
[8] **corrida:** bullfight

Explorations

First reading

1. Make a list of the images you remember after a first reading. Are they all of a similar kind or are there differences or contrasts?

2. Examine the experience described in the first stanza. Do you think it was a happy experience? Explain your thinking, making reference to the text.

3. Do you think that experience was enjoyable? Explain your thinking, referring to the poem.

Second reading

4. Now read the fourth stanza and describe the experience there.

5. The third stanza gives a rationale for the difference of experience. Examine this closely and from the evidence here, describe what it may have been like to live in 'locked-park Sunday Belfast'.

6. Using the contrasting romantic experiences on rugs, the poet is making a point about ways of life and cultural differences. In groups discuss what these might be and write up the opinions in a coherent form.

The Pitchfork

Of all implements, the pitchfork was the one
That came near to an imagined perfection:
When he tightened his raised hand and aimed with it,
It felt like a javelin, accurate and light.

So whether he played the warrior or the athlete   5
Or worked in earnest in the chaff and sweat,
He loved its grain of tapering, dark-flecked ash
Grown satiny from its own natural polish.

Riveted steel, turned timber, burnish, grain,
Smoothness, straightness, roundness, length and sheen.   10
Sweat-cured, sharpened, balanced, tested, fitted.
The springiness, the clip and dart of it.

And then when he thought of probes that reached the farthest,
He would see the shaft of a pitchfork sailing past
Evenly, imperturbably through space,   15
Its prongs starlit and absolutely soundless –

But has learned at last to follow that simple lead
Past its own aim, out to an other side
Where perfection – or nearness to it – is imagined
Not in the aiming but the opening hand.   20

EXPLORATIONS

Before reading

1. Talk to a farmer or go online. Find out all you can about the uses of a pitchfork.

2. If possible, see if you can find a pitchfork to examine in detail. Hold it, weigh it, handle it, try using it. Or examine a picture of one. Think about its uses.

First reading

3. What does the farmer in the poem love about the pitchfork? Examine the text in detail and write three paragraphs on the qualities of a good pitchfork.

4. Apart from its value as an agricultural implement, what else does the pitchfork contribute to the life and consciousness of the farmer?

Second reading

5. Consider the final stanza and, in pairs or groups, share your thoughts or possible meanings.

6. This poem is taken from a volume entitled *Seeing Things*. Explore the different kinds of 'seeing' that occur in this poem.

7. What does this poem say about farmers and farming? Write about it.

The annals say: when the monks of Clonmacnoise
Were all at prayers inside the oratory
A ship appeared above them in the air.

The anchor dragged along behind so deep
It hooked itself into the altar rails 5
And then, as the big hull rocked to a standstill,

A crewman shinned and grappled down the rope
And struggled to release it. But in vain.
'This man can't bear our life here and will drown,'

The abbot said, 'unless we help him.' So 10
They did, the freed ship sailed, and the man climbed back
Out of the marvellous as he had known it.

EXPLORATIONS

First reading

1. On a first reading, what do you notice about this narrative? What do you find exciting or arresting or amusing?

2. 'This man can't bear our life here and will drown'. Explore the significance of this statement.

3. 'The man climbed back | Out of the marvellous as he had known it.' Imagine the incident as seen from the point of view of the crewman. Tell it.

Second reading

4. What is real here and what is fabulous or imaginary?

5. What do you see as the point of the anecdote? Is it making a statement about poetry, about imagined reality, about knowledge? Explain your thinking.

6. Comment on the form or structure of the poem.

7. What do you notice about the style of the language? Do you find it effective for this poem?

8. Do you like this poem? Elaborate.

14 *Derek Mahon*
1941–

prescribed for Higher Level exams in 2013 and 2014

Derek Mahon is a retiring man who shuns publicity and literary politics. Born in 1941, he was the only child of a Church of Ireland family. He grew up in Glengormley, a north-side suburb of Belfast. His father worked in the Harland and Wolff shipyard, where the Titanic was built, and his mother in the Flax Spinning Company. His earliest memories are of the bomb raids on Belfast during the Second World War. He spent much of his school holidays cycling, often to the seaside town of Portrush and sometimes even to Donegal. He was a choirboy in St Peter's Church, and says that this experience fostered his interest in language. While at school he discovered poetry but that did not deter him from being, in his own words, a

'fairly nifty' scrum half. Cinema also attracted him, especially war movies and *A Night to Remember*, a film about the *Titanic*. He attended Royal Belfast Academical Institution, a grammar school. When he failed the eyesight test for the Merchant Navy he entered Trinity College, Dublin, where he studied French, English and Philosophy, and began writing poetry in earnest. Later he studied at the Sorbonne in Paris.

On leaving university Mahon earned a living from freelance journalism and teaching, as well as radio and television work. For years his humorous, insightful literary reviews in *The Irish Times* attracted a regular following. In addition to Dylan Thomas, the first modern poets he encountered were Robert Graves, W. B. Yeats and Louis MacNeice (another Northern Irish poet). He claims a cultural affinity with Dublin-born writer Samuel Beckett that relates to their shared Protestantism and mordant humour. Other poets he admires include the Americans Robert Lowell, Elizabeth Bishop and Hart Crane. French and Russian poetry also interest him, and he has been awarded numerous prizes for his translations.

He has lived in Canada, the USA, London, Kinsale in County Cork and briefly in Northern Ireland. His relationship with his home place is complex. He found it impossible to settle there, yet admits to feelings of guilt for having abandoned it. He recognises that his middle-class, urban background is uninspiring and, unlike its rural counterpart, has little mythology or symbolism to nurture his imagination. His raw materials are the unresolved tensions and ironies of harsh, intolerant Belfast. If he does have a hidden myth, it is what Terence Brown describes as 'the Protestant Planter's historical myth of conquest, and careful, puritan self-dependence frozen to vicious, stupid bigotry'.

Mahon has rejected the idea that poetry should be socially or politically relevant. Poetry 'may appear to be about history or politics or autobiography, but [it] is essentially an artistic activity', he wrote. He believes that it is about shape and form, about taking the formless and making it interesting. Notice the spareness of his poems: the few, precise details; the limited palette of colour; the controlled tone; the unyielding landscape; all fastidiously chosen. That technical virtuosity is matched by inspiration. 'You need soul, song and formal necessity,' he has written. Yet he recognises that a life spent pursuing perfect form and technique carries the danger of isolating the poet from his or her fellow humans.

His interest in form is evident in his versions of classic dramas. He has adapted French plays by Molière and Racine as well as Euripides' *The Bacchae*. You will encounter Mahon's early poetry in the selection here – the most recent poem included was published in 1985. In later poems he has adopted a less tense and less minimalist style, using a more relaxed and contemporary conversational idiom – characterised by an informal candour, longer lines and playful lists. The autobiographical, intimate form of the verse letter, in particular, attracts him. Nowadays Mahon lives in Dublin and is a member of Aosdána, an elected group of Irish artists who receive pensions from the state. He has two adult children.

Grandfather

CD 2
Track 9

this poem is also prescribed for Ordinary Level exams in 2013 and 2014

They brought him in on a stretcher from the world,
Wounded but humorous; and he soon recovered.
Boiler-rooms, row upon row of gantries rolled
Away to reveal the landscape of a childhood
Only he can recapture. Even on cold   5
Mornings he is up at six with a block of wood
Or a box of nails, discreetly up to no good
Or banging round the house like a four-year-old –

Never there when you call. But after dark
You hear his great boots thumping in the hall   10
And in he comes, as cute as they come. Each night
His shrewd eyes bolt the door and set the clock
Against the future, then his light goes out.
Nothing escapes him; he escapes us all.

Notes

[3]   **gantries:** overhead structures with a platform supporting a
      travelling crane, an essential tool of shipbuilding
[11] **cute:** attractive, or shrewd, cunning or crafty

EXPLORATIONS

First reading

1. Who is the subject of the poem?
2. Where did grandfather work?
3. Describe grandfather's working life and contrast it with his present-day activities.

Second reading

4. Describe grandfather's conduct.
5. Do you think that the members of his community would approve of his behaviour?

6. Note the adjectives used to describe grandfather. What do they suggest about his personality?

7. Outline his bedtime ritual.

8. What do the first two lines of the poem tell us about the old man?

Third reading

9. How does he relate to the outside world?

10. What is the speaker's attitude towards grandfather? What evidence is there to support your view?

11. Why do you think that grandfather is described as 'cute'?

12. What is revealed about his attitude to the future?

13. Describe the mood of the poem. Is it serious, playful, dark, or a combination of these and other moods?

14. Look at the three prepositions in the first line, 'in', 'on' and 'from'. What do they convey about grandfather's relationship with the world?

15. Comment on the diction of the poem.

Fourth reading

16. Would you consider this a nostalgic poem? Why?

17. What is the effect of the repetition in the poem? Examine these examples: 'row upon row of gantries rolled'; '. . . he is up at six with a block of wood | Or a box of nails, discreetly up to no good'; 'You hear his great boots thumping in the hall | And in he comes, as cute as they come.'

18. In what ways might grandfather be a role model for the speaker of the poem?

19. What values are underwritten and questioned in this poem?

20. What characteristics of the sonnet do you discern in this poem? How does it differ from the Shakespearean sonnet? You might take account of the rhyming scheme, the irregular use of the iambic pentameter (the metre most common to the sonnet), the 'turn' or volta.

21. Examine the treatment of time in this poem. Consider, for example, the implicit contrast between the old man and the speaker, two generations younger. Think about the childhood memories to which only he has access. Note the poem's treatment of seasonal change and the ebb and flow of days. What does the future hold for grandfather?

Day Trip to Donegal

We reached the sea in early afternoon,
Climbed stiffly out; there were things to be done,
Clothes to be picked up, friends to be seen.
As ever, the nearby hills were a deeper green
Than anywhere in the world, and the grave   5
Grey of the sea the grimmer in that enclave.

Down at the pier the boats gave up their catch,
A writhing glimmer of fish; they fetch
Ten times as much in the city as here,
And still the fish come in year after year –   10
Herring and mackerel, flopping about the deck
In attitudes of agony and heartbreak.

We left at eight, drove back the way we came,
The sea receding down each muddy lane.
Around midnight we changed-down into suburbs   15
Sunk in a sleep no gale-force wind disturbs.
The time of year had left its mark
On frosty pavements glistening in the dark.

Give me a ring, goodnight, and so to bed . . .
That night the slow sea washed against my head,   20
Performing its immeasurable erosions –
Spilling into the skull, marbling the stones
That spine the very harbour wall,
Muttering its threat to villages of landfall.

At dawn I was alone far out at sea   25
Without skill or reassurance – nobody
To show me how, no promise of rescue –
Cursing my constant failure to take due
Forethought for this; contriving vain
Overtures to the vindictive wind and rain.   30

Derek Mahon   409

[6]   **enclave:** a part of one state surrounded by another. It can also mean a group of people who are culturally, intellectually or socially distinct from those surrounding them.

[29]   **vain:** both meanings, proud and conceited, and worthless and futile, apply here

[30]   **vindictive:** vengeful, spiteful, unforgiving

EXPLORATIONS

First reading

1. Generally, what kind of experiences are day trips?

2. Discuss the significance of the title of this poem.

3. What does the speaker see on the pier?

4. Where does the speaker go in stanza three?

5. Briefly paraphrase each stanza.

Second reading

6. The encounter with the sea has a profound effect on the speaker. What is it about the sea that makes it so profoundly different from the land?

7. What is the most telling image in the poem for you?

8. Note where the plural 'we' gives way to the singular 'I'. What does this shift convey?

9. Discuss the contrasts that abound in this poem. In addition to the oppositions of land and sea already mentioned, you might consider the antitheses of suburban and rural landscape, isolation and camaraderie, night and day. Note the contrast in stanza four between the desultory goodbyes and the experience that follows.

10. Having read the poem, do you detect an irony in the term 'day trip'?

Third reading

11. How is the speaker's thinking and feeling altered by the sight of the dying fish?

12. Describe the movement in the poem.

13. Alliteration is widely used in this poem – for example, in stanza one there is an accumulation of 'gr' sounds: 'green | . . . grave | Grey . . .

grimmer'. Find other examples of alliteration in the poem. Why is this and how effective is it?

14. Consider some of the distinctive features of stanza three. Comment on sentence length, the change of setting, the pace of the third line and how this is achieved.

15. What does the speaker mean when he says he is 'far out to sea'?

Fourth reading

16. In what ways could the erosion of the sea be compared to the effects of history?

17. What change is brought about in the speaker as a result of his day trip?

18. What political significance might be read into the greenness of Donegal, the fact that the speaker sees it as an enclave, and the grim greyness of its sea?

After the Titanic

CD 2
Track 11

this poem is also prescribed for Ordinary Level exams in 2013 and 2014

    They said I got away in a boat
And humbled me at the inquiry. I tell you
    I sank as far that night as any
Hero. As I sat shivering on the dark water
    I turned to ice to hear my costly   5
Life go thundering down in a pandemonium of
    Prams, pianos, sideboards, winches,
Boilers bursting and shredded ragtime. Now I hide
    In a lonely house behind the sea
Where the tide leaves broken toys and hatboxes   10
    Silently at my door. The showers of
April, flowers of May mean nothing to me, nor the
    Late light of June, when my gardener
Describes to strangers how the old man stays in bed
    On seaward mornings after nights of   15
Wind, takes his cocaine and will see no one. Then it is
    I drown again with all those dim
Lost faces I never understood, my poor soul
    Screams out in the starlight, heart
Breaks loose and rolls down like a stone.   20
    Include me in your lamentations.

Notes

Titanic: the *Titanic* was a ship built in Belfast. It was completed in 1912 and was described as 'the latest thing in the art of shipbuilding'. The word 'titanic' has come to mean colossal, and indeed, the ship was immense. That it was built in Belfast placed the city at the very leading edge of the Industrial Revolution. However, it sank dramatically when it collided with an iceberg on its maiden voyage to America, with the loss of 1,500 lives, the greatest tragedy in maritime history. This catastrophe has entered the global imagination as a major disaster, and was a mortal blow to the self-confidence of the age.

[1] **They said I got away in a boat:** the speaker of the poem is Bruce Ismay (1892–1937), manager of the White Star Line for which the *Titanic* sailed. He was one of the relatively few men to have escaped from the sinking *Titanic*, and he was strongly criticised for failing to help the drowning passengers.

[6] **pandemonium:** chaos, confusion, turmoil. In John Milton's poem 'Paradise Lost' it is the place of all demons.

[7] **winches:** plural of a windlass, the crank of a wheel or axle (singular is 'winch')

[8] **ragtime:** a type of jazz music, a syncopated musical rhythm developed by American black musicians in the 1890s and usually played on the piano

[15] **seaward:** going or facing toward the sea

[16] **cocaine:** a drug used as both a local anaesthetic and a stimulant

[21] **lamentations:** at one level, 'Include me in your lamentations' is the plea of the poem's speaker, Bruce Ismay, for inclusion in the community's mourning of the victims of the *Titanic* disaster. However, it is also a reference to the Old Testament book containing five poems that comprise the Lamentations of Jeremiah.

Workers leaving Belfast Shipyard in 1911 with the half-finished Titanic *in the background*

EXPLORATIONS

First reading

1. What does the title suggest to you?

2. Describe the persona that speaks in this poem.

3. Why and at what inquiry was he humbled?

4. How does the speaker spend his time?

5. What does he remember of the *Titanic* disaster?

Second reading

6. What has the persona of the poem in mind when he refers to his 'costly life'?

7. How would you describe his mood?

8. How does the speaker convey his isolation?

9. 'Prams, pianos, sideboards, winches,

   Boilers bursting and shredded ragtime.'

   Describe the effect of this list.

10. In what way is the speaker's suffering indicated?

11. How does he deal with the pain?

Third reading

12. How would you describe the diction of the following three lines? '. . . my poor soul | Screams out in the starlight, heart | Breaks loose and rolls down like a stone.' What effect does this style have on the reader?

13. In your opinion, what causes the greatest distress to Ismay?

14. What does the speaker finally demand of his listeners?

15. In your opinion, should the persona Ismay be included in the mourning?

Fourth reading

16. '. . . Then it is | I drown again with all those dim | Lost faces I never understood . . .'

    What does the speaker mean by these three lines?

17. Is there a resemblance between his response to the catastrophe and that of society to its victims?

18. How does Ismay deal with the tragedy of the *Titanic*, the burden of the episode in history in which he is implicated?

Ecclesiastes

God, you could grow to love it, God-fearing, God-
    chosen purist little puritan that,
for all your wiles and smiles, you are (the
    dank churches, the empty streets,
the shipyard silence, the tied-up swings) and   5
    shelter your cold heart from the heat
of the world, from woman-inquisition, from the
    bright eyes of children. Yes, you could
wear black, drink water, nourish a fierce zeal
    with locusts and wild honey, and not   10
feel called upon to understand and forgive
    but only to speak with a bleak
afflatus, and love the January rains when they
    darken the dark doors and sink hard
into the Antrim hills, the bog meadows, the heaped   15
    graves of your fathers. Bury that red
bandana and stick, that banjo; this is your
    country, close one eye and be king.
Your people await you, their heavy washing
    flaps for you in the housing estates –   20
a credulous people. God, you could do it, God
    help you, stand on a corner stiff
with rhetoric, promising nothing under the sun.

Notes

Ecclesiastes: the title of an Old Testament book of the Bible, but also a person who addresses an assembly, a preacher

[2]   **purist:** a person who scrupulously advocates rigid precision and formality, especially in the field of language or art

[2] **puritan:** in its historical meaning, the term refers to a member of a group of English Protestants who regarded the Reformation as incomplete and refused to subscribe to the established church, that is, the Church of Ireland or the Church of England. They sought to simplify and regulate forms of worship. However, a puritan is also a distinct character type, a person who practises extreme strictness in matters of religion and morals. The term could be applied in both senses to the person addressed in the poem.

[5] **the tied-up swings:** It was customary for many local authorities in Northern Ireland to close public parks on Sundays.

[9] **zeal:** fervour and earnestness in furthering a cause; uncompromising partisanship; fanaticism; indefatigable enthusiasm

[10] **locusts and wild honey:** in the Bible, this was often the only food available to penitents who fasted in the desert.

[13] **afflatus:** a divine creative impulse; inspiration

[16–17] **red | bandana . . . stick . . . banjo:** emblems of non-conformity, wanderlust and art

[18] **close one eye:** closing one eye may sharpen the focus, but it restricts the range of vision and is a metaphor for narrow-mindedness.

[21] **credulous:** gullible

[23] **rhetoric:** the discipline, or art, of persuasive writing or speaking. It often implies exaggeration or insincerity.

EXPLORATIONS

First reading

1. What does the word 'Ecclesiastes' mean?

2. Where is the poem set?

3. Who is the speaker in this poem?

4. Describe the ecclesiastes to whom this poem is addressed. What kind of person is he or she?

5. Describe the place in which this preacher's community lives.

Second reading

6. Is the title a good one? Why?

7. What does the preacher promise his or her people?

8. Find some positive and negative images of Belfast in this poem.

9. Find some references to the Bible and to religion in this poem.

10. Are the speaker and the ecclesiastes one and the same person? Why do you think that?

11. What colours predominate in this poem?

12. What kind of atmosphere pervades the place described?

13. What groups of people tend to wear black and why?

Third reading

14. Discuss the mood of the poem.

15. What tone does the speaker use?

16. Why must the ecclesiastes leave behind the 'red | bandana . . . stick . . . banjo'?

17. What is the effect of the repetition of the word 'God'?

18. In what does the preacher take pleasure?

Fourth reading

19. Explore some of the rhetorical devices employed in the poem. These might include the declamatory tone, the fluency and formality, the repetitions of sentence structure and the amplitude of the first two sentences.

20. Discuss the irony of this poem. At whom is it directed?

21. Can you identify any parallels between the preacher depicted here and the poet-speaker?

22. Show how the first and last sentences of the poem are similar. Consider the sentence structure, the sentiments expressed and the repetition of words. What purpose does this form serve?

As It Should Be

We hunted the mad bastard
Through bog, moorland, rock, to the starlit west
And gunned him down in a blind yard
Between ten sleeping lorries
And an electricity generator.　　　　　　　　　5

Let us hear no idle talk
Of the moon in the Yellow River;
The air blows softer since his departure.

Since his tide-burial during school hours
Our children have known no bad dreams.　　　　　10
Their cries echo lightly along the coast.

This is as it should be.
They will thank us for it when they grow up
To a world with method in it.

Notes

[1]　**We hunted the mad bastard:** the persona of the poem is a spokesman for the Irish Free State, which condones the murder of the revolutionary, the dreamer.

[3]　**blind:** in this case, walled up, closed at one end; also lacking foresight and understanding

[5]　**an electricity generator:** a machine for converting mechanical energy into electrical energy

[7]　**the moon in the Yellow River:** this is the title of a play by Denis Johnston written in 1931. Johnston took the phrase from Ezra Pound's image of a drunken poet, Li-Po, who grasped at illusory ideals and was drowned while trying 'to embrace the moon in the yellow river'. The play's story is set in Ireland in 1927, and one of the new Irish State's projects intended to modernise the country is a hydroelectric scheme. When a revolutionary called Blake tries to blow up its generator, Lanigan, an officer of the Free State, shoots him. In this poem, a revolutionary is

shot among lorries beside an electricity generator, monuments to progress. Material improvement comes at a price, in this case brutal murder.

[9] **tide-burial:** the body is cast into the water and carried away on the tide

[14] **method:** implies orderliness, regular habits, procedure, pattern, system.

EXPLORATIONS

First reading

1. On what incident is this poem based?
2. In what part of the country was the fugitive pursued?
3. Would it be easy to hide in bog, moorland or rock?
4. Where was he found?
5. What did his pursuers do when they found him?

Second reading

6. How did they dispose of his body?
7. Whom does the 'we' of the poem represent?
8. Why does the speaker say that the children no longer have bad dreams?

Third reading

9. What is the effect of the obscenity in the first line?

Third reading continued

10. What image of themselves do the speakers present in the first stanza?
11. What values do the speakers wish to pass on to their children?
12. Show how the poem suggests that violence is implicated in the fabric of the state from its foundation.
13. Describe the speaker's tone.

Fourth reading

14. Comment on the variations in line and stanza length.
15. What is it that the speakers wish to suppress? With what will they replace it?
16. Compare the ironic tone of this poem with that of other poems by Mahon.
17. In what sense are the speakers making history?
18. Examine this poem's links to other literary works.

A Disused Shed in Co. Wexford

Let them not forget us, the weak souls among the asphodels.
– Seferis, Mythistorema

(for J.G. Farrell)

Even now there are places where a thought might grow –
Peruvian mines, worked out and abandoned
To a slow clock of condensation,
An echo trapped for ever, and a flutter
Of wild flowers in the lift-shaft,   5
Indian compounds where the wind dances
And a door bangs with diminished confidence,
Lime crevices behind rippling rain-barrels,
Dog corners for bone burials;
And in a disused shed in Co. Wexford,   10

Deep in the grounds of a burnt-out hotel,
Among the bathtubs and washbasins
A thousand mushrooms crowd to a keyhole.
This is the one star in their firmament
Or frames a star within a star.   15
What should they do there but desire?
So many days beyond the rhododendrons
With the world waltzing in its bowl of cloud,
They have learnt patience and silence
Listening to the rooks querulous in the high wood.   20

They have been waiting for us in a foetor
Of vegetable sweat since civil war days,
Since the gravel-crunching, interminable departure
Of the expropriated mycologist.
He never came back, and light since then   25
Is a keyhole rusting gently after rain.

Spiders have spun, flies dusted to mildew
And once a day, perhaps, they have heard something –
A trickle of masonry, a shout from the blue
Or a lorry changing gear at the end of the lane.   30
There have been deaths, the pale flesh flaking
Into the earth that nourished it;
And nightmares, born of these and the grim
Dominion of stale air and rank moisture.
Those nearest the door grow strong –   35
'Elbow room! Elbow room!'
The rest, dim in a twilight of crumbling
Utensils and broken pitchers, groaning
For their deliverance, have been so long
Expectant that there is left only the posture.   40

A half century, without visitors, in the dark –
Poor preparation for the cracking lock
And creak of hinges; magi, moonmen,
Powdery prisoners of the old regime,
Web-throated, stalked like triffids, racked by drought   45
And insomnia, only the ghost of a scream
At the flash-bulb firing-squad we wake them with
Shows there is life yet in their feverish forms.
Grown beyond nature now, soft food for worms,
They lift frail heads in gravity and good faith.   50

They are begging us, you see, in their wordless way,
To do something, to speak on their behalf
Or at least not to close the door again.
Lost people of Treblinka and Pompeii!
'Save us, save us,' they seem to say,   55
'Let the god not abandon us
Who have come so far in darkness and in pain.
We too had our lives to live.
You with your light meter and relaxed itinerary,
Let not our naive labours have been in vain!'   60

asphodels: a type of lily. It has been represented in literature as an immortal flower growing in the fields of Elysium, the place where, in Greek mythology, the blessed go after death.

Seferis: George Seferis (1900–71), a Greek poet and ambassador to Britain, whose poetry draws on Greek mythology.

J. G. Farrell: This poem had its source in Farrell's novel *Troubles*. Farrell, a good friend of Mahon, was drowned while fishing in 1979. 'I'd read *Troubles* and I was convinced that there was a shed in it, with mushrooms,' Mahon has written. 'But when I went back and re-read it, the shed with the mushrooms was missing. I must have imagined it.'

[6]   **compounds:** large open enclosures for housing workers

[14] **firmament:** the sky

[17] **rhododendrons:** evergreen shrubs with large flowers that grow profusely in some parts of Ireland

[20] **querulous:** complaining, fractious

[21] **foetor:** stench

[22] **civil war days:** This is probably a reference to the civil war fought in Ireland in 1922–23. It began when some members of nationalist movements rejected the treaty that brought an end to the War of Independence fought with Britain. Although the actual death toll was not high, it left a legacy of bitterness and a lasting influence on the shape of party politics in Ireland. J. G. Farrell's novel *Troubles*, which inspired this poem, is set in civil war Ireland.

[24] **expropriated mycologist:** an expert on fungi or mushrooms who has been dispossessed, especially one whose property has been taken away by the state

[43] **magi:** the 'wise men' who brought gifts to the infant Jesus; the plural of 'magus', a word that means a sorcerer; also priests in ancient Persia

[43] **moonmen:** they are moonmen because they have been denied the light of the sun for so long.

[45] **triffids:** monstrous, lethal plants from outer space that can propel themselves about, originally in John Wyndham's science fiction novel, *The Day of the Triffids*. This book describes the contrast between a comfortable setting and a sudden invasion that is a metaphysical catastrophe. The term has now come to describe any hostile plant.

[45] **racked by drought:** tortured by thirst

[46] **insomnia:** sleeplessness

[54] **Treblinka:** a Nazi concentration camp in Poland where Jews were put to death during the Second World War

[54] **Pompeii:** a city in south-east Italy which was buried after Mount Vesuvius erupted in 79 BC.

[59] **itinerary:** a detailed route, often mapped out for tourists by travel consultants

EXPLORATIONS

First reading

1. Name some of the places where 'a thought might grow'.

2. Describe in detail the mushrooms' surroundings.

3. How have they spent their existence?

4. Describe the horrors endured by the forgotten mushrooms in stanza four.

5. How long have they been behind locks?

6. Describe the effect of their confinement on the mushrooms.

7. How do they respond to the garish light of 'the flash-bulb firing-squad'?

Second reading

8. What is distinctive about the places 'where a thought might grow'?

9. What is the mushrooms' plea?

10. How do the mushrooms communicate?

11. Discuss the title of the poem.

Third reading

12. What is the significance of the opening phrase 'Even now'?

13. Describe the tone, or range of tones, of this poem. How does the poem represent the strong emotions aroused by the plight of the abandoned?

14. Why do you think Mahon chose to nominate mushrooms as his central characters?

15. Why does the poet delay before introducing the mushrooms, on which the poem is centred?

16. What is the effect of the rhetorical question 'What should they do there but desire'?

17. What does the poet mean when he writes 'the world waltzing in its bowl of cloud'?

18. Discuss who or what you think the 'expropriated mycologist' represents.

Fourth reading

19. How does Mahon achieve the effect of time passing in stanzas two and three?

20. Identify the specific historic references in the poem and discuss their significance.

21. What is the speaker's reaction to the plight of the mushrooms?

22. Would the liberation of the mushrooms resolve all their difficulties? Does being part of history offer a solution to the agonies described in the poem?

23. In what way is this poem a meditation on the legacy of war?

24. What difficulties confront the speaker of this poem? You might refer to the problem of speaking on behalf of the voiceless, representing them rather than enabling them to speak for themselves.

25. Show how this poem depicts the manner in which the powerful abandon and ignore the helpless.

26. What in your opinion, is significant about the epigram and dedication?

27. How do the themes of this poem relate to those in other poems by Mahon that you have read?

28. Consider the use of the past tense in 'We too had our lives to live' (stanza six).

29. Does this poem suggest that Mahon is 'through with history', as he has twice suggested in other poems? What evidence is there to support your opinion?

30. In what ways is the speaker of the poem involved in the present exploitation of the victims of history?

31. Show how Mahon achieves a local and global context. What does this double focus suggest?

The Chinese Restaurant in Portrush

Before the first visitor comes the spring
Softening the sharp air of the coast
In time for the first seasonal 'invasion'.
Today the place is as it might have been,
Gentle and almost hospitable. A girl   5
Strides past the Northern Counties Hotel,
Light-footed, swinging a book-bag,
And the doors that were shut all winter
Against the north wind and the sea-mist
Lie open to the street, where one   10
By one the gulls go window-shopping
And an old wolfhound dozes in the sun.

While I sit with my paper and prawn chow mein
Under a framed photograph of Hong Kong
The proprietor of the Chinese restaurant   15
Stands at the door as if the world were young,
Watching the first yacht hoist a sail
– An ideogram on sea-cloud – and the light
Of heaven upon the hills of Donegal.

Notes

Portrush: a seaside town in north Antrim, to which the young Mahon would cycle at weekends

[12] **wolfhound:** this is perhaps an oblique reference to the bloody Ulster cycle of heroic tales. When the young mythical champion Cuculann killed a wolfhound owned by Culann, a blacksmith, he replaced the animal as Culann's guardian, and became known as the hound of Ulster. In one of his exploits, he single-handedly defended Ulster from the army of Queen Maeve of Connaught. Here the hound is sleeping, suggesting that ancient aggressions are temporarily laid aside.

[18] **ideogram:** a character symbolising or representing the idea of a thing without indicating the sequence of sounds in its name. Ideograms are used in Chinese writing.

Explorations

First reading

1. To what 'invasion' does the poem's persona refer?

2. Why is the word 'invasion' placed in quotation marks?

3. What is meant by 'the gulls go window-shopping'?

4. What does the speaker find attractive about Portrush on this particular day?

5. Where is the restaurateur's home?

6. How is Donegal depicted?

Second reading

7. In stanza two, what does the speaker see and what does the restaurateur see?

8. Put yourself in the persona's position in stanza two, seated in the restaurant. Sketch the scene described in that stanza.

9. How do the seasons affect Portrush?

Third reading

10. How does the poet achieve the optimistic, upbeat tone of the first stanza?

11. Comment on the humour in this poem. You might refer to the title, the name of the hotel, the 'almost hospitable' place, the 'invasion', and the dozing wolfhound. You might also consider the humorous rhyming of 'Hong Kong' with 'restaurant' and 'young'. What is the effect of this humour?

Fourth reading

12. What does the poet mean by 'as if the world was young'? You might relate the statement to Mahon's preoccupation with the horrors perpetrated by humans throughout history.

13. What statement does the poem make about the nature of home?

14. In what ways is this a visual poem?

Rathlin

A long time since the last scream cut short –
Then an unnatural silence; and then
A natural silence, slowly broken
By the shearwater, by the sporadic
Conversation of crickets, the bleak   5
Reminder of a metaphysical wind.
Ages of this, till the report
Of an outboard motor at the pier
Shatters the dream-time and we land
As if we were the first visitors here.   10

The whole island a sanctuary where amazed
Oneiric species whistle and chatter,
Evacuating rock-face and cliff-top.
Cerulean distance, an oceanic haze –
Nothing but sea-smoke to the ice-cap   15
And the odd somnolent freighter.
Bombs doze in the housing estates
But here they are through with history –
Custodians of a lone light which repeats
One simple statement to the turbulent sea.   20

A long time since the unspeakable violence –
Since Somhairle Buí, powerless on the mainland,
Heard the screams of the Rathlin women
Borne to him, seconds later, upon the wind.
Only the cry of the shearwater   25
And the roar of the outboard motor
Disturb the singular peace. Spray-blind,
We leave here the infancy of the race,
Unsure among the pitching surfaces
Whether the future lies before us or behind.   30

Church Bay, Rathlin Island

Notes

Rathlin: an island off the north Antrim coast. It attracted settlers from the Bronze Age to the Middle Ages. Its landscape is magnificent, with masses of basalt columns, similar to those in the Giant's Causeway, contrasting with chalk cliffs. It contained a fortified castle in the late Middle Ages. Robert the Bruce hid there in 1306, in a cave, and learnt persistence and patience from the spiders he saw ceaselessly repairing their webs. There is now a national nature reserve on the island.

[4] **shearwater:** a long-winged seabird of the puffin family

[4] **sporadic:** intermittent, occasional

[6] **metaphysical wind:** the term 'metaphysical' relates to the philosophy of being and knowing, the philosophy of mind, abstract or subtle talk. The sounds of Rathlin are reminders or echoes of speech. There is a pun on the word 'wind'. The wind creates a sound on Rathlin that is reminiscent of human conversation, but 'wind' can also mean idle, pointless talk.

[9] **dream-time:** in Australian Aboriginal mythology, dream-time is also called the 'alcheringa', the golden age when the first ancestors were created.

[12] **Oneiric:** relating to dreams

[14] **Cerulean:** deep blue like a clear sky

[16] **somnolent:** sleepy, drowsy

[18] **through with history:** This phrase also occurs in another poem by Mahon, 'The Last of the Fire Kings'.

[19] **a lone light:** There is a lighthouse on the nature reserve in the east of the island.

[22–23] **Somhairle Buí . . . | . . . Rathlin women:** Probably refers to Sorley Boy MacDonnell (1505?–1590). He was a Scots-Irish chieftain whose lands stretched from the glens of Antrim across the Mull of Kintyre to include Islay and Kintyre in Scotland. Queen Elizabeth's marshal in Ireland, the eighteenth Earl of Essex, was determined to subdue him in 1575. Expecting a battle, Somhairle 'put most of his plate [silver], most of his children, and the most of the children of his gentlemen with their wives' in a fortified castle on the island of Rathlin. On Essex's orders, they were all massacred, with Somhairle, almost frantic with despair, witnessing the carnage from the mainland. In all, five or six hundred people perished (not only women, as Mahon suggests, but men and children too), either in the castle or hunted down and butchered as they sought shelter on the rugged island.

[29] **pitching:** sloping; intense; in motion; unstable

EXPLORATIONS

First reading

1. What kind of place is Rathlin?

2. How does the speaker arrive on the island?

3. What does the first line suggest to you about Rathlin's past?

4. Why was the silence first 'unnatural' and then 'natural'?

5. Who or what inhabits the island now?

6. What effect does the arrival of the speaker's boat have on the island?

7. Paraphrase the description of Rathlin and its setting found in the first six lines of stanza two.

Second reading

8. What does the speaker mean by 'dream-time' in stanza one?

9. Why is the violence done to Somhairle MacDonnell's family described as 'unspeakable'?

10. What is the 'one simple statement' that the birds repeat to the sea?

11. Why, in your opinion, is the opening phrase 'A long time' repeated at the beginning of the last stanza?

Third reading

12. Explain the phrase 'here they are through with history'.

13. What is the effect of the accumulation of terms such as 'oneiric', 'haze', 'sea-smoke' and 'somnolent' in stanza two?

14. Comment on the juxtaposition of the 'somnolent freighter' and the 'dozing bombs' at the centre of stanza two.

Fourth reading

15. What link does the speaker forge between the brutal murder of the MacDonnell tribe in Elizabethan times and the troubles raging in Northern Ireland as the poem was written?

16. Explore the treatment of time in this poem. You might refer to dream-time, historical time and the future. You might compare and contrast the timescale of Rathlin with that of the inhabitants of the housing estates.

17. Examine Mahon's use of rhyme, partial or slant rhyme, feminine rhyme and half-rhyme in this poem.

18. What might the speaker mean when he claims he is 'Unsure . . . | Whether the future lies before us or behind'?

Antarctica

(for Richard Ryan)

this poem is also prescribed for Ordinary Level exams in 2013 and 2014

'I am just going outside and may be some time.'
The others nod, pretending not to know.
At the heart of the ridiculous, the sublime.

He leaves them reading and begins to climb,
Goading his ghost into the howling snow;   5
He is just going outside and may be some time.

The tent recedes beneath its crust of rime
And frostbite is replaced by vertigo:
At the heart of the ridiculous, the sublime.

Need we consider it some sort of crime,   10
This numb self-sacrifice of the weakest? No,
He is just going outside and may be some time –

In fact, for ever. Solitary enzyme,
Though the night yield no glimmer there will glow,
At the heart of the ridiculous, the sublime.   15

He takes leave of the earthly pantomime
Quietly, knowing it is time to go.
'I am just going outside and may be some time.'
At the heart of the ridiculous, the sublime.

Antarctica: the Antarctic is the south polar region. This poem relates to an incident that took place during Captain Robert Scott's expedition to Antarctica in 1911–12. His plan was to be the first to reach the South Pole. After much hardship and mismanagement, he and three others, including Captain Lawrence Oates (1880–1912), attained their goal, only to find that an expedition led by a Norwegian, Roald Amundsen, had succeeded just three weeks before them. Scott's return journey was dogged by misfortune. One member suffered a bad fall and died a fortnight later. Oates's frostbitten feet became gangrenous and he begged the others to abandon him. They refused. To avoid being a burden he walked out into the night, to his certain death, with the words 'I am just going outside and may be some time.' The other three struggled to within a mere eleven miles of their base camp, but then a blizzard struck. Their bodies were found in a tent eight months later.

Richard Ryan: an Irish diplomat and poet, author of a poem on the American army's massacre of Vietnamese people at My Lai

Scott and his team finding Amundsen's tent at the South Pole, 18 January 1912

Captain Lawrence Oates

Notes

[3]   **sublime:** exalted, grand, noble, awe-inspiring, lofty, majestic

[5]   **goading:** urging on

[7]   **rime:** frost formed from cloud or fog; poets sometimes use the word 'rime' to describe the glittery frost often seen on plants on clear, still days

[8]   **frostbite:** damage to body tissue exposed to freezing temperatures. Severe cases lead to gangrene, which causes the body tissue to die.

[8]   **vertigo:** dizziness, a whirling sensation, a tendency to lose one's balance

[13] **enzyme:** an enzyme causes a living organism to change but is not changed itself. In scientific terms, it is a protein that acts as a catalyst in a specific biochemical reaction.

EXPLORATIONS

1. Why do you think the poem is called 'Antarctica'? What images does Antarctica conjure up?

2. Who is the speaker of the first line?

3. Who are 'The others' referred to in the second line?

4. Summarise the story told in the first three stanzas.

5. Why does the persona in the poem 'go outside'?

6. What will happen to him when he leaves the tent?

7. What is the rhyming pattern in this poem?

8. How does the speaker of the poem view Oates's act?

9. What conclusion does the speaker come to about Oates's action?

10. How would you describe the tone?

11. How does Mahon achieve this tone?

12. Consider the last line of each stanza. What pattern do you notice?

13. What is the effect of the caesura after 'for ever' in stanza five?

14. In what ways do the last three stanzas differ from the first three? How does the last stanza differ from the others?

15. The persona of the poem calls Oates a 'solitary enzyme'. What is the effect of using a scientific term to describe a human being?

16. What is meant by 'the earthly pantomime'?

17. Discuss the run-on line or enjambment in the last stanza.

18. Do you agree with the speaker that Oates's suicidal act is both ridiculous and sublime? Why?

The kind of rain we knew is a thing of the past –
deep-delving, dark, deliberate you would say,
browsing on spire and bogland; but today
our sky-blue slates are steaming in the sun,
our yachts tinkling and dancing in the bay   5
like racehorses. We contemplate at last
shining windows, a future forbidden to no one.

Notes

Kinsale: a town in County Cork, nowadays a thriving seaside
tourist resort and a fishing port. Kinsale is important from
the point of view of the history of Ulster and Ireland because
in the battle fought there in 1601, Queen Elizabeth's soldier,
Mountjoy, routed the Ulster chieftains Hugh O'Neill and
Hugh O'Donnell. This defeat signalled the end of Gaelic rule
in Ireland. Ulster, which had been the province most
resistant to English rule, was colonised by Scots and English
settlers and eventually became the most anglicised. Kinsale
is therefore the site of failure, a post-historical place.

[3]   **browsing on:** feeding on; also randomly surveying or
skimming

EXPLORATIONS

First reading

1. Describe Kinsale as depicted in this poem.

2. Describe the rain.

3. When the rain stops, how does the landscape change?

Second reading

4. Here the rain has negative implications. With what is it associated, do you think?

5. The yachts are described as 'tinkling and dancing . . . | like racehorses'. Compare and contrast this image with the description of the rain.

6. Do you think the imagery is effective in getting across an awareness of the poet's mood?

7. 'Tinkling' is an unusual verb to describe the sound of yachts. Why do you think Mahon uses it?

Third reading

8. Notice that 'past' rhymes with 'at last'. Does this echo reinforce the sense of relief that the past is over?

9. What events from the past might the poet have in mind in this poem? The title of the poem points us in a particular direction.

10. The first person plural 'we' is used twice in the poem. Is that significant?

11. In what ways are the rain and the past alike?

12. Why do you think that Mahon set this poem in Kinsale and not in any other seaside town in Ireland?

Fourth reading

13. How would looking through shining windows affect the way we see the world?

14. How does the poet suggest that while he is optimistic, there is no certainty about the future?

15. The speaker contemplates shining windows, but does not look through them or see reflections in them. Is that significant?

15

Eavan Boland
1944–

prescribed for Higher Level exams in 2011 and 2012

Eavan Boland was born in Dublin in 1944, daughter of the painter Frances Kelly and the diplomat Frederick Boland. She was educated at Holy Child Convent, Killiney, and Trinity College, Dublin. For some years she lectured at Trinity College in the English Department, before becoming a literary journalist, chiefly with *The Irish Times* but also with RTÉ, where she produced award-winning poetry programmes for radio. She married the novelist Kevin Casey, exchanging the Dublin literary scene for family life in the suburbs where she wrote prolifically.

New Territory (1967) was her first volume of poetry. Her second volume, *The War Horse* (1975), deals with the Northern Ireland 'Troubles' and with the way violence encroaches on our domestic lives. The poem 'Child of Our Time' is taken from this volume. Her third volume, *In Her Own Image* (1980), explores the darker side of female identity, 'woman's secret history'; it deals with real but taboo issues such as anorexia, infanticide, mastectomy, menstruation and domestic violence. The fourth collection, *Night Feed* (1982), celebrates the ordinary, everyday domestic aspect of woman's identity. The fifth volume, *The Journey* (1986), and the sixth, *Outside History* (1990), consider the image of women

in Irish history as illustrated in painting and in literature – a tale of exploitation and repression, of being marginalised and kept from the centre of influence. The seventh collection, *In a Time of Violence* (1994), deals specifically with Irish national and historical issues such as the Famine, agrarian violence and the Easter Rising. It also focuses on the theme of women as mothers and the relationship between mothers and daughters. The poem 'This Moment' is taken from this volume.

The place of the woman writer in Irish literature, mythology and history is a prominent theme in Boland's poetry and other writings. Her pamphlet *A Kind of Scar* (1989) examines this issue. Her collection of autobiographical prose, published in 1995, is entitled *Object Lessons: The Life of the Woman and the Poet in Our Time*. In 1980 she was joint founder of Arlen House, a feminist publishing company.

The War Horse

This dry night, nothing unusual
About the clip, clop, casual
Iron of his shoes as he stamps death
Like a mint on the innocent coinage of earth.
I lift the window, watch the ambling feather   5
Of hock and fetlock, loosed from its daily tether
In the tinker camp on the Enniskerry Road,
Pass, his breath hissing, his snuffling head
Down. He is gone. No great harm is done.
Only a leaf of our laurel hedge is torn –   10
Of distant interest like a maimed limb,
Only a rose which now will never climb
The stone of our house, expendable, a mere
Line of defence against him, a volunteer
You might say, only a crocus, its bulbous head   15
Blown from growth, one of the screamless dead.
But we, we are safe, our unformed fear
Of fierce commitment gone; why should we care
If a rose, a hedge, a crocus are uprooted
Like corpses, remote, crushed, mutilated?   20
He stumbles on like a rumour of war, huge
Threatening. Neighbours use the subterfuge
Of curtains. He stumbles down our short street
Thankfully passing us. I pause, wait,
Then to breathe relief lean on the sill   25
And for a second only my blood is still
With atavism. That rose he smashed frays
Ribboned across our hedge, recalling days
Of burned countryside, illicit braid:
A cause ruined before, a world betrayed.   30

[4]   **mint:** place where money is coined

[6]   **hock:** joint on horse's leg corresponding to the human ankle

[6]   **fetlock:** tuft of hair above and behind the horse's hoof

[27]   **atavism:** resemblance to remote ancestors; in this instance the horse's violation of the domestic garden stirs race memories of English colonial violence and the destruction of Irish homesteads

[29]   **braid:** anything plaited or interwoven, such as hair or ribbon, or the gold and silver thread decoration on uniforms; it might refer to rebel uniforms

Genesis of the poem: this poem stems from an incident when the front garden of Boland's new house in the suburbs was invaded a number of times by a stray horse, presumed to belong to local Travellers. Perhaps the horse had lived there when the site was open fields.

EXPLORATIONS

First reading

1. On a first reading, what do you see? Visualise the night, the garden, the atmosphere, the animal. What sounds are there in this scene?

2. At one level, this horse is made real to the reader. How is this realised? What words best convey the shape, size, movement, etc. of the animal to us? Explore sounds of words as well as visual images. What is your first impression of the horse?

3. Do you think this horse carries a sense of menace or threat? Examine the first four couplets especially. Explore the imagery, the sounds of words and the rhythm of the piece in coming to a conclusion.

4. How is the fragility of the domestic garden conveyed to us? What words or images suggest this?

Second reading

5. What do you notice about the speaker's reactions to this intrusion? Do they change as the poem progresses? Make specific references to the text.

6. (a) Could this piece be read as a political poem, with the horse as a symbol of violence? What evidence do you find in the poem for this reading?

Second reading continued

(b) At a symbolic level, what is being suggested here about the nature of violence?

Third reading

7. How do you read the poem? What themes do you find it deals with, and what levels of meaning do you notice?

The Famine Road

CD 2
Track 20

'Idle as trout in light Colonel Jones
these Irish, give them no coins at all; their bones
need toil, their characters no less.' Trevelyan's
seal blooded the deal table. The Relief
Committee deliberated: 'Might it be safe,   5
Colonel, to give them roads, roads to force
from nowhere, going nowhere of course?'

     one out of every ten and then
     another third of those again
     women – in a case like yours.   10

Sick, directionless they worked; fork, stick
were iron years away; after all could
they not blood their knuckles on rock, suck
April hailstones for water and for food?
Why for that, cunning as housewives, each eyed –   15
as if at a corner butcher – the other's buttock.
     anything may have caused it, spores,
     a childhood accident; one sees
     day after day these mysteries.

Dusk: they will work tomorrow without him.　　　　20
They know it and walk clear. He has become
a typhoid pariah, his blood tainted, although
he shares it with some there. No more than snow
attends its own flakes where they settle
and melt, will they pray by his death rattle.　　　　25
　　　You never will, never you know
　　　but take it well woman, grow
　　　your garden, keep house, good-bye.
'It has gone better than we expected, Lord
Trevelyan, sedition, idleness, cured　　　　30
in one; from parish to parish, field to field;
the wretches work till they are quite worn,
then fester by their work; we march the corn
to the ships in peace. This Tuesday I saw bones
out of my carriage window. Your servant Jones.'　　　　35
　　　Barren, never to know the load
　　　of his child in you, what is your body
　　　now if not a famine road?

Notes

Famine Road: in the Great Famine of 1845–48 the potato crop failed and the people were left destitute and starving. Among the relief works organised to allow the hungry to earn money was road construction; but these roads were rarely meant to be used and often ended uselessly in bog or field. So the famine road might be read as a symbol of unfulfilled lives that go nowhere.

[1]　**Colonel Jones:** Lieutenant-Colonel Jones was one of the officers in charge of relief works around Newry. There exists a letter from him to Trevelyan reporting on work carried out during the winter of 1846; this may be the source of the exchange here.

[3]   **Trevelyan:** Charles Trevelyan was a senior British civil servant, Assistant Secretary to the Treasury, in charge of relief works in Ireland at the outbreak of the Great Famine in 1845. At first his approach was dominated by the laissez-faire (non-intervention) policy popular at the time, and he was concerned that the Irish might be demoralised by receiving too much government help. Later he came to realise that they would not survive without it; but he never really warmed to the Irish, speaking of 'the selfish, perverse and turbulent character of the people'.

[4–5]   **Relief Committee:** committees that organised local schemes to try to alleviate the starvation

[22]   **pariah:** outcast

[30]   **sedition:** conduct or language directed towards the overthrow of the state

[33–4] **corn to the ships:** despite the starvation, normal commerce was carried on, and corn was exported as usual, though grain carts now needed protection against the local population

EXPLORATIONS

First reading

1. Read aloud Trevelyan's letter in the first three lines of the poem. How do you think it should sound? Consider the tone. What is Trevelyan's attitude? What words or phrases convey his attitude particularly well? What do Trevelyan's gestures add to the tone of this? Read it as you think he would say it.

2. Read aloud the Relief Committee's speech to Colonel Jones, as you imagine it said. Pay attention to the tone of 'might it be safe' and 'going nowhere of course.'

3. Read stanzas 3 and 5 (beginning 'Sick' and 'Dusk', respectively). What do you notice about the relief work and the condition of the people?

4. Consider Colonel Jones's letter to Trevelyan ('It has gone better . . .'). What does it reveal about the writer – his priorities, his attitude to the Irish, his awareness of the famine, etc.? Is there evidence of sympathy, or of superiority and indifference? Consider phrases such as 'the wretches . . .', 'fester by their work', 'march . . . in peace.' What is the effect of the hollow rhyme 'bones – Jones'? Read the letter aloud as you think he might say it.

Second reading

5. In the third stanza, how is the desperate bleakness of the people's situation conveyed? What image in particular conveys the depth of their degradation? Explain your thinking.

6. Illness isolates and degrades human beings. How is this portrayed in the fifth stanza? Consider the effect of the imagery and the sounds of words.

Third reading

7. Now explore the woman's story (stanzas 2, 4, 6 and 8). (a) Who is speaking in the first three stanzas? Which words suggest that? (b) Consider the tone, and read these three aloud. (c) Who speaks the last stanza? How does the speaker feel? Which words best convey the feelings?

8. Write an extract from that woman's diary, as she might compose it, following that meeting. Fill it with the thoughts you imagine going through her head as she listened to the consultant.

Fourth reading

9. What statement do you think this poem makes on the status of women?

10. Explain the comparisons implied in the poem between the experience of women and the treatment of the famine people. Do you find it enlightening? Explain.

11. In her writings, Boland has often expressed concern that history is sometimes simplified into myth.

    'Irish poets of the nineteenth century, and indeed their heirs in this century, coped with their sense of historical injury by writing of Ireland as an abandoned queen or an old mother. My objections to this are ethical. If you consistently simplify women by making them national icons in poetry or drama you silence a great deal of the actual women in that past, whose sufferings and complexities are part of that past, who intimately depend on us, as writers, not to simplify them in this present.'

    [From the interview in *Sleeping with Monsters*]

    Do you think 'The Famine Road' shows an awareness of the real complexity of actual lives from history? Explain, with reference to the text.

12. What sense of national identity or Irishness comes across from 'The Famine Road'?

Child of Our Time

CD 2
Track 21

For Aengus

this poem is also prescribed for Ordinary Level exams in 2011 and 2012

Yesterday I knew no lullaby
But you have taught me overnight to order
This song, which takes from your final cry
Its tune, from your unreasoned end its reason;
Its rhythm from the discord of your murder   5
Its motive from the fact you cannot listen.

We who should have known how to instruct
With rhymes for your waking, rhythms for your sleep,
Names for the animals you took to bed,
Tales to distract, legends to protect   10
Later an idiom for you to keep
And living, learn, must learn from you dead,

To make our broken images, rebuild
Themselves around your limbs, your broken
Image, find for your sake whose life our idle   15
Talk has cost, a new language. Child
Of our time, our times have robbed your cradle.
Sleep in a world your final sleep has woken.

Background note
This poem was inspired by a press photograph showing a firefighter carrying a dead child out of the wreckage of the Dublin bombings in May 1974.

EXPLORATIONS

First reading

1. If you hadn't read the title or the last three lines, what might suggest to you that the poem was written to a child? Examine stanzas 1 and 2.

2. The speaker acknowledges that it was the child's death that prompted her to compose this poem ('you have taught me overnight to order | This song'). How does she feel about the child's death in the first stanza? Examine the words and phrases describing the death: 'your final cry', 'your unreasoned end', and 'the discord of your murder'. What do these phrases tell us about the way the poet views the death?

3. In the second stanza notice that the main clause consists of the first word and the final five words in the stanza: 'We . . . must learn from you dead'. The rest of the stanza is in parenthesis and relates to 'we', presumably adult society. (a) In what way has adult society failed, according to the poet? (b) What particular aspect of childbearing and education does the poet focus on? (c) 'Later an idiom for you to keep | And living, learn'. In your own words, what do you think is meant by this? ('Idiom' here means style of expression.)

4. In the third stanza the child's body is described poetically as 'your broken image'. What does this picture suggest to you?

5. What do you think she has in mind when she says that we need to (a) rebuild 'our broken images . . . around your limbs' and (b) 'find . . . a new language'?

6. Does the speaker find any ray of hope for the society in which this calamity occurred? Refer to the text of the third stanza.

Second reading

7. Consider this poem as an elegy, a meditation on death. What ideas on that subject are explored or suggested?

8. Can this be read as a public or political poem? Explain, with reference to the text.

9. Concerning the poet's feelings, do you find here a sense of personal sorrow or community guilt and sorrow? Explain your thinking.

Third reading

10. The poem might be seen as a mixture of dirge and lullaby. What elements of dirge or of lullaby do you find? Consider the theme, the choice of language, the imagery, the repetitions, etc.

The Black Lace Fan My Mother Gave Me

**CD 2
Track 22**

It was the first gift he ever gave her,
buying it for five francs in the Galeries
in pre-war Paris. It was stifling.
A starless drought made the nights stormy.

They stayed in the city for the summer.   5
They met in cafés. She was always early.
He was late. That evening he was later.
They wrapped the fan. He looked at his watch.
She looked down the Boulevard des Capucines.

She ordered more coffee. She stood up.   10
The streets were emptying. The heat was killing.
She thought the distance smelled of rain and lightning.

These are wild roses, appliquéd on silk by hand,
darkly picked, stitched boldly, quickly.
The rest is tortoiseshell and has the reticent,   15
clear patience of its element. It is

a worn-out, underwater bullion and it keeps,
even now, an inference of its violation.
The lace is overcast as if the weather
it opened for and offset had entered it.   20

The past is an empty café terrace.
An airless dusk before thunder. A man running.
And no way now to know what happened then –
none at all – unless, of course, you improvise:

The blackbird on this first sultry morning,   25
in summer, finding buds, worms, fruit,
feels the heat. Suddenly she puts out her wing –
the whole, full, flirtatious span of it.

EXPLORATIONS

First reading

1. The black lace fan was a present from the poet's father to her mother and was passed on later to the speaker. How do you visualise the fan? What assistance does the poem give us? Examine the details in stanza 4.

2. How do you visualise the scene, the background, the atmosphere of the evening as the woman waits? Look at the details.

3. What do you notice about the man in the poem? What else would you like to know about him: why is he always late? Is the gift a peace offering or a genuine love token? What does he really feel for her? Can any of these questions be answered from the poem?

4. What do you notice about the woman? Examine the details. What do they suggest about how she is feeling, etc.? While remaining faithful to the text, jot down what you imagine are the thoughts inside her head as she waits.

5. Do you think this was a perfectly matched and idyllic relationship? What is suggested by the poem? Explain.

Second reading

6. How does the poet think of the fan? Does she see it as more than just the usual love token, a symbol in the sensual ritual? Explore in detail her imaginative apprehension of the fan in stanza 5. For example, what is meant by 'it keeps . . . an inference of its violation' and 'the lace is overcast as if the weather . . . had entered it'?

7. How do you think the final stanza relates to the rest of the poem? Does the mating display of the blackbird add anything to the connotations of the keepsake?

8. How do you think you would regard the first present from a lover? Were you at all surprised by the fact that the mother in this poem gave away the fan? Explain your thinking.

9. Do you think the poet views the keepsake solely in a romantic or in an erotic way? How do you think she sees it?

10. Examine what the poet herself says (in *Object Lessons*) about the symbol. What does this add to your own thinking on the subject?

'I make these remarks as a preliminary to a poem I wrote about a black lace fan my mother had given me, which my father had given her in a heatwave in Paris in the thirties. It would be wrong to say I was clear, when I wrote this poem, about disassembling an erotic politic. I was not. But I was aware of my own sense of the traditional erotic object – in this case the black fan – as a sign not for triumph and acquisition but for suffering itself. And without having words for it, I was conscious of trying to divide it from its usual source of generation: the sexualised perspective of the poet. To that extent I was writing a sign which might bring me close to those emblems of the body I had seen in those visionary years, when ordinary objects seemed to warn me that the body might share the world but could not own it. And if I was not conscious of taking apart something I had been taught to leave well alone, nevertheless, I had a clear sense of – at last – writing the poem away from the traditional erotic object towards something which spoke of the violations of love, while still shadowing the old context of its power. In other words, a back-to-front love poem.'

Third reading

11. What does the poem say to you about love and time?

12. In your own words, outline the themes you find in this poem.

13. What images appeal to you particularly? Explain why you find them effective.

14. Comment on the use of symbolism in this poem.

Fourth reading

15. 'The past is an empty café terrace.

    An airless dusk before thunder. A man running.

    And no way now to know what happened then –

    none at all – unless, of course, you improvise'

    In a brief written description, improvise the sequel to the 'empty café terrace' and 'A man running' as you imagine it. Keep faith with the spirit of the poem.

The Shadow Doll

They stitched blooms from the ivory tulle
to hem the oyster gleam of the veil.
They made hoops for the crinoline.

Now, in summary and neatly sewn –
a porcelain bride in an airless glamour –   5
the shadow doll survives its occasion.

Under glass, under wraps, it stays
even now, after all, discreet about
visits, fevers, quickenings and lusts

and just how, when she looked at   10
the shell-tone spray of seed pearls,
the bisque features, she could see herself

inside it all, holding less than real
stephanotis, rose petals, never feeling
satin rise and fall with the vows   15

I kept repeating on the night before –
astray among the cards and wedding gifts –
the coffee pots and the clocks and

the battered tan case full of cotton
lace and tissue-paper, pressing down, then   20
pressing down again. And then, locks.

Shadow Doll: this refers to the porcelain doll modelling the proposed wedding dress, under a dome of glass, sent to the nineteenth-century bride by her dressmaker

[1]   **tulle:** soft, fine silk netting used for dresses and veils

[2]   **oyster:** off-white colour

[12] **bisque:** unglazed white porcelain used for these models

[14] **stephanotis:** tropical climbing plant with fragrant white flowers

A porcelain dress doll in satin and lace (England, c. 1887)

EXPLORATIONS

1. The function of the doll is explained above; but what does the title 'shadow doll' suggest to you?

2. What do you notice about the model dress?

3. 'A porcelain bride in an airless glamour' – what does this suggest to you about the poet's view of the doll?

4. Do you think the poet understands the doll's significance in more general terms, as an image of something, a symbol? If so, of what?

Second reading

5. What image of woman is portrayed by the doll? Explore stanza 3 in particular.

Second reading continued

6. How does this image contrast with the poet's experience of her own wedding? Explore stanzas 5, 6, and 7.

7. The speaker's reality is more appealing, despite the clutter; but has she anything in common with the 'shadow doll'?

Third reading

8. What does the poem say to you about the image of woman? Refer to the text to substantiate your ideas.

9. Explore the significance of colour in this poem.

10. 'In the main, symbol and image carry the main themes of this poem.' Comment, with reference to the text.

White Hawthorn in the West of Ireland

I drove West
in the season between seasons.
I left behind suburban gardens.
Lawnmowers. Small talk.

Under low skies, past splashes of coltsfoot,   5
I assumed
the hard shyness of Atlantic light
and the superstitious aura of hawthorn.

All I wanted then was to fill my arms with
sharp flowers,   10
to seem, from a distance, to be part of
that ivory, downhill rush. But I knew,

I had always known
the custom was
not to touch hawthorn.   15
Not to bring it indoors for the sake of

the luck
such constraint would forfeit –
a child might die, perhaps, or an unexplained
fever speckle heifers. So I left it   20

stirring on those hills
with a fluency
only water has. And, like water, able
to re-define land. And free to seem to be –

for anglers,   25
and for travellers astray in
the unmarked lights of a May dusk –
the only language spoken in those parts.

Eavan Boland   453

[5]   **coltsfoot:** wild plant with yellow flowers

EXPLORATIONS

First reading

1. In this migration, what is the speaker leaving behind her? From what little is said in the first stanza, what do you understand of her attitude to life in suburbia?

2. How does her state of mind alter as she drives west? Explore stanzas 2 and 3. How does this experience contrast with life in suburbia?

3. According to the poem, what is the significance of hawthorn in folklore?

First reading continued

4. Water, too, is a deceptive source of hidden energies. What is the poet's thinking on this? Explore stanzas 6 and 7.

Second reading

5. 'The speaker's attitude to the hawthorn is a combination of passionate, sensuous attraction balanced by a degree of nervous respect.' Would you agree? Substantiate your views with reference to the text.

Second reading continued

6. What do you think this poem reveals about the speaker?

7. What statement is the poet making about our modern way of life?

Third reading

8. List the themes or issues raised by this poem.

9. What is your personal reaction to this poem?

Outside History

CD 2
Track 25

There are outsiders, always. These stars –
these iron inklings of an Irish January,
whose light happened

thousands of years before
our pain did: they are, they have always been   5
outside history.

They keep their distance. Under them remains
a place where you found
you were human, and

a landscape in which you know you are mortal.   10
And a time to choose between them.
I have chosen:

out of myth into history I move to be
part of that ordeal
whose darkness is   15

only now reaching me from those fields,
those rivers, those roads clotted as
firmaments with the dead.

How slowly they die
as we kneel beside them, whisper in their ear.   20
And we are too late. We are always too late

EXPLORATIONS

First reading

1. Boland's argument is that Irish history has been turned into myth and therefore rendered false and remote from real lives. Do you think the image of the stars is an effective metaphor for historical myths? Examine the attributes of the stars as suggested in the first two stanzas.

2. In contrast, what aspects of real, lived history are emphasised in this poem?

Second reading

3. The poet chooses to turn her back on myth, and this choice brings her, and the reader, face

Second reading continued

to face with the unburied dead of history. Does she find this an easy choice? Explore her feelings on this. What words, phrases, gestures, etc. indicate her feelings?

4. What do you think she means by the last line of the poem? Explore possible interpretations.

Third reading

5. On the evidence of this poem as a whole, what is the poet's attitude to the historical past?

6. Comment on the effectiveness of the imagery.

This Moment

CD 2
Track 26

this poem is also prescribed for Ordinary Level exams in 2011 and 2012

A neighbourhood.
At dusk.

Things are getting ready
to happen
out of sight.   5

Stars and moths.
And rinds slanting around fruit.

But not yet.

One tree is black.
One window is yellow as butter.   10

A woman leans down to catch a child
who runs into her arms
this moment.

Stars rise.
Moths flutter.   15
Apples sweeten in the dark.

EXPLORATIONS

First reading

1. What do you see in this scene? List the items.
2. What senses, other than sight, are involved, or hinted at?
3. Do you think this scene unusual, or very ordinary? Explain. What do you think the poet is celebrating here?
4. Yet there is a hint of the mysterious about the scene. Where and what do you think is suggested?

Second reading

5. What do you think is the most significant image in the poem? How does the poet draw attention to its importance?

6. Do you notice any sense of dramatic build-up in the poem? Examine the sequence of ideas and images.
7. Explore the imagery. What do the images contribute to the atmosphere? What is suggested, for example, by 'one window is yellow as butter' and by 'apples sweeten in the dark'?

Third reading

8. What is the key moment in this poem all about?
9. What do you think the poem is saying about nature?
10. Do you think it is making a statement about the experience of women? Explain your ideas.

Love

this poem is also prescribed for Ordinary Level exams in 2011 and 2012

Dark falls on this mid-western town
where we once lived when myths collided.
Dusk has hidden the bridge in the river
which slides and deepens
to become the water   5
the hero crossed on his way to hell.

Not far from here is our old apartment.
We had a kitchen and an Amish table.
We had a view. And we discovered there
love had the feather and muscle of wings   10
and had come to live with us,
a brother of fire and air.

We had two infant children one of whom
was touched by death in this town
and spared; and when the hero   15
was hailed by his comrades in hell
their mouths opened and their voices failed and
there is no knowing what they would have asked
about a life they had shared and lost.

I am your wife.   20
It was years ago.
Our child is healed. We love each other still.
Across our day-to-day and ordinary distances
we speak plainly. We hear each other clearly.

And yet I want to return to you   25
on the bridge of the Iowa river as you were,
with snow on the shoulders of your coat
and a car passing with its headlights on:

I see you as a hero in a text –
the image blazing and the edges gilded –   30

and I long to cry out the epic question
my dear companion:
Will we ever live so intensely again?
Will love come to us again and be
so formidable at rest it offered us ascension   35
even to look at him?

But the words are shadows and you cannot hear me.
You walk away and I cannot follow.

EXPLORATIONS

First reading

1. The poem is occasioned by a return visit to 'this mid-western town' in America where they had once lived. Which lines refer to present time and which refer to that earlier stay?

2. 'When myths collided' – what do you think this might refer to?

3. Explore the mood of the opening stanza. How is it created, and does it fit in with the mythical allusions? Explain.

4. On a first reading, what issues do you notice that preoccupy the poet?

Second reading

5. The second stanza contains some memories of the speaker's previous visit. What was important to her?

Second reading continued

6. What insights about love are communicated in the second stanza? What is your opinion of the effectiveness of the imagery used?

7. The poet uses allusions from myth to create an awareness of death in the third stanza. What insights on death are communicated to you by this very visual presentation? Do you think this is an effective way of recording the speaker's feelings? Explain your view.

8. Explore the speaker's feelings for her husband at the present time, and contrast them with past emotions. Is she content? What does she yearn for?

Third reading

9. Overall, what does this poem have to say about love? What does she think is important?
10. What other themes do you find are dealt with?
11. What has the poem to say about women's experience?

Third reading continued

12. What do the mythical allusions contribute to the poem?
13. Comment on the effectiveness of the imagery.

The Pomegranate

CD 2
Track 28

The only legend I have ever loved is
the story of a daughter lost in hell.
And found and rescued there.
Love and blackmail are the gist of it.
Ceres and Persephone the names.   5
And the best thing about the legend is
I can enter it anywhere. And have.
As a child in exile in
a city of fogs and strange consonants,
I read it first and at first I was   10
an exiled child in the crackling dusk of
the underworld, the stars blighted. Later
I walked out in a summer twilight
searching for my daughter at bed-time.
When she came running I was ready   15
to make any bargain to keep her.
I carried her back past whitebeams
and wasps and honey-scented buddleias.
But I was Ceres then and I knew
winter was in store for every leaf   20
on every tree on that road.

Was inescapable for each one we passed.
And for me.
It is winter
and the stars are hidden.   25
I climb the stairs and stand where I can see
my child asleep beside her teen magazines,
her can of Coke, her plate of uncut fruit.
The pomegranate! How did I forget it?
She could have come home and been safe   30
and ended the story and all
our heart-broken searching but she reached
out a hand and plucked a pomegranate.
She put out her hand and pulled down
the French sound for apple and   35
the noise of stone and the proof
that even in the place of death,
at the heart of legend, in the midst
of rocks full of unshed tears
ready to be diamonds by the time   40
the story was told, a child can be
hungry. I could warn her. There is still a chance.
The rain is cold. The road is flint-coloured.
The suburb has cars and cable television.
The veiled stars are above ground.   45
It is another world. But what else
can a mother give her daughter but such
beautiful rifts in time?
If I defer the grief I will diminish the gift.
The legend will be hers as well as mine.   50
She will enter it. As I have.
She will wake up. She will hold
the papery flushed skin in her hand.
And to her lips. I will say nothing.

Pomegranate: the fruit of a North African tree, the size and colour of an orange. In classical mythology it was associated with the underworld.

[5] **Ceres and Persephone:** Ceres in Roman mythology (identified with Demeter in Greek mythology) was the goddess of corn and growing vegetation, an earth goddess. Her daughter by Zeus, Persephone, was carried off to the underworld by Hades. Ceres wandered over the earth in mourning, vainly searching. In grief she made the earth barren for a year. She resisted all entreaties by the gods to allow the earth back to fertility. Eventually Zeus sent his messenger to persuade Hades to release Persephone, which he did, but not before he had given her a pomegranate seed to eat. This fruit was sacred to the underworld, and so Persephone was condemned to spend one-third of each year there with Hades, only appearing back on earth each spring, with the first fertility.

EXPLORATIONS

First reading

1. The poet says: '. . . the best thing about the legend is | I can enter it anywhere.' When did she first encounter it and why did she find it relevant to her life?

2. At what other times and in what ways did the legend run parallel to her own situation?

3. How closely do you think the poet identifies with the myth? What evidence is there for this?

Second reading

4. What does the poem tell us about the poet's relationship with her daughter?

5. What does the legend contribute to that relationship?

6. What do you think the poet has in common with Ceres?

7. Where and how do the time zones of past and present fuse and mingle? What does this suggest about the importance of myth in our lives?

8. What statement do you think this poem is making about the significance of legend to ordinary lives? Refer to the text.

9. What truths about human relationships are discovered in this poem?

10. Examine the different motifs in the imagery – fruit, darkness, stars, stone, etc. What do these strands of imagery contribute to the atmosphere and the themes?

11. What effect did reading this poem have on you?

16 Ordinary Level

Explanatory Note

Candidates taking the Ordinary (Pass) Level Examination have a choice of questions when dealing with prescribed poems.

Ordinary Level candidates can answer either:
1. A question on one of the poems by a Higher Level poet prescribed for that year *or*
2. A question from a list of other prescribed poems.

1. The poems by Higher Level poets that may also be studied by Ordinary Level candidates are listed below. Candidates are advised to check which of these poems are prescribed for the year in which they are sitting their examination. (See Course Overview pages iv–vii.)

William Shakespeare	Sonnet 18 Shall I compare thee . . .	6
	Sonnet 60 Like as the waves . . .	12
	(both poems prescribed for exams in 2013)	
William Wordsworth	She Dwelt among the Untrodden Ways	26
	It is a Beauteous Evening, Calm and Free	28
	Skating (from *The Prelude*)	30
	(all three poems prescribed for exams in 2011 and 2013)	
Emily Dickinson	I felt a Funeral, in my Brain	60
	I heard a Fly buzz – when I died	67
	(both poems prescribed for exams in 2011 and 2014)	
Gerard Manley Hopkins	Spring	87
	Inversnaid	100
	(both poems prescribed for exams in 2011 and 2013)	
W. B. Yeats	The Wild Swans at Coole	118
	An Irish Airman Foresees His Death	122
	(both poems prescribed for exams in 2011 and 2014)	

2. The alternative poems that Ordinary Level candidates may choose are contained on pages 467–586. Candidates should check which of these poems are prescribed for the year in which they are sitting their examinations. (See Course Overview pages iv–vii)

Ordinary Level:
Alternative Poems

George Herbert (1593–1633)

George Herbert came from an aristocratic family in the Welsh Border country. An outstanding scholar, he was educated at Westminster and at Trinity College, Cambridge, where he was Public Orator from 1619 to 1627. His initial hopes of a political appointment were not fulfilled. In 1630 he was ordained a priest in the Anglican ministry and became rector of Bemerton, near Salisbury. None of his poetry was published during his lifetime but when he knew that he was dying he sent a collection of his verse to his friend George Ferrar with the advice to 'publish or burn' depending on his judgement of the poems. The collection was published under the title 'The Temple'.

The Collar

prescribed for exams in 2011 and 2014

I struck the board and cry'd, 'No more.
               I will abroad!
    What? shall I ever sigh and pine?
My lines and life are free; free as the rode,
    Loose as the winde, as large as store.   5
        Shall I be still in suit?
    Have I no harvest but a thorn
    To let me bloud, and not restore
    What I have lost with cordiall fruit?

Sure there was wine $\quad$ 10
Before my sighs did drie it; there was corn
Before my tears did drown it.
Is the yeare onely lost to me?
Have I no bayes to crown it,
No flowers, no garlands gay? All blasted? $\quad$ 15
All wasted?
Not so, my heart; but there is fruit,
And thou hast hands.
Recover all thy sigh-blown age
On double pleasures; leave thy cold dispute $\quad$ 20
Of what is fit, and not. Forsake thy cage,
Thy rope of sands,
Which pettie thoughts have made, and made to thee
Good cable, to enforce and draw,
And be thy law, $\quad$ 25
While thou didst wink and wouldst not see.
Away; take heed;
I will abroad.
Call in thy deaths head there; tie up thy fears.
He that forbears $\quad$ 30
To suit and serve his need,
Deserves his load.
But as I rav'd and grew more fierce and wilde
At every word,
Methoughts I heard one calling, *Child!* $\quad$ 35
And I reply'd, *My Lord*.

---

[20] **double pleasures:** by throwing off the restraints he feels and enjoying new experiences

[20] **dispute:** debate

[23] **pettie:** petty, minor, insignificant

[29] **deaths head:** human skull as an emblem of mortality

EXPLORATIONS

First reading

Lines 1 to 16

1. How would you describe the poet's feelings in these lines? Choose images and lines that you think best catch the poet's feelings and discuss what they suggest about his mood.

2. Are there any hints to suggest possible reasons for his bleak state of mind? Discuss this.

Second reading

Lines 17 to 32

3. How does the poet's mood change in this section?

4. What advice does he give himself in his effort to break free and rebel? In your own words, list the sequence of his thoughts.

Third reading

5. What happens in the last four lines? Is this unexpected?

Third reading continued

6. On a rereading of the poem, list everything of which the poet feels himself deprived.

7. The collar can be read as a symbol of religious and moral restraint. What other images in the poem portray freedom and restraint? Are these images linked?

Fourth reading

8. What do you think the poet is rebelling against?

9. Do you find this a dramatic poem? What makes it so ?

10. Metaphysical poets are renowned for being clever and witty in their use of words and images. What evidence of this do you find here?

11. Can you sympathise with the poet here? Discuss your feelings about his feelings.

12. Write about the view 'that this poem discusses an issue that affects every human life'.

John Milton (1608–1674)

John Milton was born in London of well-to-do parents who appear to have given him a good basic education, especially in music and literature. He attended St Paul's School and later graduated with BA and MA degrees from Cambridge. Milton was appointed 'Latin secretary of the council of state' by Oliver Cromwell in 1649, because of his fluency in Latin, the language of diplomacy at that time. He wrote extensively on religious and political matters as well as writing poetry in Latin and English. His eyesight, which had been failing for some time, failed him completely when he was aged forty-four. From then on he dictated his work to his secretaries and family members. In his masterpiece, the epic *Paradise Lost*, which was published in 1667, he attempted 'to justify the ways of God to men'. The restoration of the monarchy briefly threatened Milton with execution for regicide, and brought an end to his political career in 1660. Having been granted a royal

pardon he retired to concentrate on writing and published the sequel to *Paradise Lost*, called *Paradise Regained*, and, in 1671, a drama called *Samson Agonistes*. A revised volume of his collected poetry appeared the following year. Milton died of gout in 1674.

When I Consider

prescribed for exam in 2013

When I consider how my light is spent,
E're half my days, in this dark world and wide,
And that one Talent which is death to hide,
Lodg'd with me useless, though my Soul more bent
To serve therewith my Maker, and present   5
My true account, least he returning chide,

Doth God exact day-labour, light deny'd,
I fondly ask; But patience to prevent
That murmur, soon replies, God doth not need
Either man's work or his own gifts, who best   10
Bear his milde yoak, they serve him best, his State
Is Kingly. Thousands at his bidding speed
And post o're Land and Ocean without rest:
They also serve who only stand and waite.

Notes

[3]   **Talent:** gift, faculty, also a unit of currency in New
       Testament times
[4]   **bent:** determined
[8]   **fondly:** foolishly
[11]   **yoak:** yoke, burden

EXPLORATIONS

First reading

1. What is Milton saying about his blindness in the opening three lines? How do you imagine 'this dark world'?

2. Does Milton take the parable of the Talents seriously? What is the implication of 'which is death to hide'?

3. What does Milton's soul incline to do? What does this tell us about him?

4. 'Doth God exact day-labour, light deny'd'. What is your understanding of this line? What does the question tell us about Milton's attitude to God?

5. What does 'Patience' reply to the question posed in the first eight lines? According to Milton, does God need man's work? Does he need man's gifts?

6. According to Milton, how do people best serve God? How can God be served passively?

Second reading

7. Read the poem aloud. What do you notice about its sounds and rhythm? How many full stops appear in the text? Does this affect how you read the poem? What tone of voice should you adopt?

8. Comment on the financial terminology: 'spent'; 'Talent'; 'Lodg'd'; 'account'. What is Milton saying with this choice of words?

9. How do you see John Milton on the evidence of the poem? What kind of person do you think he was? Does he display any self-pity or sense of injustice? What comment would you make on how he deals with his disability?

10. How would you summarise the octet?

11. Describe how Milton resolves his difficulties in the sestet. Do you find his conclusion convincing?

12. How does Milton feel towards God in the poem? What words and images convey his emotions?

Third reading

13. Examine how images of light and darkness are used in the first eight lines. Do you consider such imagery to be appropriate?

14. How is the majesty of God conveyed in the final six lines?

15. Would you agree that this poem's language has a biblical quality? What words or phrases would you highlight for comment?

16. What do you think of Milton's portrayal of God? Is this interpretation of God one you are comfortable with?

17. How would you describe the mood of the final line? Has the conclusion been anticipated in the poem?

18. Write a paragraph giving your personal response to the poem.

Percy Bysshe Shelley (1792–1822)

The son of an English country gentleman, Shelley was educated at Eton and Oxford, where he spent a rebellious and unhappy youth. Revolutionary in thought, he was anti-religious and anti-monarchy and wrote and spoke publicly on the need for radical social and political reforms. He felt it was the role of the poet to be prophetic and visionary. He lived a fairly unconventional family life, much of it in Italy, where the Shelleys seemed dogged by illness and death. It was here that he wrote some of his best-known poems, such as 'Stanzas Written in Dejection Near Naples', 'Ode to the West Wind', 'Ode to a Skylark', and 'Prometheus Unbound'.

Ozymandias

prescribed for exam in 2012

I met a traveller from an antique land
Who said: Two vast and trunkless legs of stone
Stand in the desert . . . Near them, on the sand,
Half sunk, a shattered visage lies, whose frown,
And wrinkled lip, and sneer of cold command,   5
Tell that its sculptor well those passions read
Which yet survive, stamped on these lifeless things,
The hand that mocked them, and the heart that fed:
And on the pedestal these words appear:
'My name is Ozymandias, king of kings: 10
Look on my works, ye Mighty, and despair!'
Nothing beside remains. Round the decay
Of that colossal wreck, boundless and bare
The lone and level sands stretch far away.

Ozymandias: another name for the Pharaoh Rameses II of Egypt (thirteenth century BC, whose great tomb at Thebes was shaped like a sphinx. It was the great historian Diodorus the Sicilian who first referred to it as the tomb of Ozymandias.

[1] **antique:** ancient

[4] **visage:** face

[8] **The hand that mocked:** the hand that imitated, referring to the hand of the sculptor

[8] **the heart that fed:** the king's heart which gave life to these qualities and passions that were captured in stone by the sculptor

EXPLORATIONS

First reading

1. The poem is in the form of a narrative or story told by a traveller who had been to 'an antique land'. What suggestions and pictures does this phrase conjure up for you?

2. What did the traveller actually see, as reported in lines 2–4? What is your first reaction to this scene: interesting, pathetic, grotesque, or what? Why do you think he might consider this worth reporting?

3. Where is this scene? What impressions of the land do we get?

4. Does the poet tell us the name of the place? Why do you think this is?

Second reading

5. What do we learn of the king from this sculpture: his qualities, character traits, etc.?

6. Do you think Shelley appreciates the sculptor's skill? Explain.

7. Relate lines 4–8 in your own words and as simply as possible.

Third reading

The sestet, etc.

8. What was your own reflection on reading the words on the pedestal?

9. Explore the final two and a half lines. What do you see? Really look. What atmosphere is created here? What statement do you think is being made?

10. What do you think this poem is saying about human endeavour and about power? Explain with reference to specific phrases, etc.

11. Consider the imagery. Do you think the imagery appropriate to the theme? Explain. What pictures do you find most effective?

Fourth reading

12. How does the poet make use of irony to communicate his theme? Do you find this effective?

13. Would you agree that this poem embodies Shelley's view that the poet should really be a kind of prophet or wise person in society? Discuss this with reference to the text.

14. What features of the sonnet do you notice in the poem? Do you think it is a good sonnet?

15. Do you think this poem was worth reading? Why, or why not?

Thomas Hardy (1840–1928)

Thomas Hardy, a major poet and novelist, was born in Dorset on 2 June 1840. A sickly child, he did not attend school until he was eight years old. He made rapid progress and learned Latin, French and German. The Bible was his main focus of attention; he taught in Sunday school and considered taking holy orders. After leaving school he went to work for an ecclesiastical architect in Dorchester in 1859, and three years later he left for London to further his career. He was influenced by Darwin, Mill and Huxley and became an agnostic, in contrast with his earlier religious enthusiasm. Hardy pursued his interest in writing as a career and in 1871 published his first novel, *Desperate Remedies*. In 1872 *Under the Greenwood Tree* was published, and this was followed by *A Pair of Blue Eyes* in 1873. His first major success, *Far From the Madding Crowd* (1874), allowed him to become a full-time writer and to contemplate marriage.

He met Emma Gifford on a working visit to Cornwall in 1870 and they married four years later. The marriage was initially happy but came under increasing strain. Emma considered Hardy her social inferior and resented his literary success. Her conventional attitudes were offended by the subject matter of *Tess of the D'Urbervilles* (1891), and especially *Jude the Obscure* (1896) which she tried to have suppressed. This final novel received so much adverse critical reaction on moral grounds that Hardy gave up the novel as a form and concentrated on his first love, poetry. Hardy's first volume of poetry, *Wessex Poems*, was published in 1898 when he was 58 years old. He went on to publish over 900 poems. When Emma died in 1912 Hardy was stricken by intense remorse. He was moved to write a remarkable series of love poems based on the early days of their relationship and the places he associated with Emma. Nevertheless, in 1914 he married Florence Dugdale, with whom he had enjoyed a relationship since 1905. When Thomas Hardy died in 1928 his cremated ashes were buried under a spade full of Dorset earth at Westminster Abbey. His heart was, according to his wishes, buried in

Stinford with his first wife, Emma. Hardy published eight volumes of poetry and fourteen novels. He is remarkable for the variety of his themes and his range of poetic styles.

When I Set Out for Lyonnesse

prescribed for exam in 2012

When I set out for Lyonnesse,
A hundred miles away,
The rime was on the spray,
And starlight lit my lonesomeness
When I set out for Lyonnesse   5
A hundred miles away.

What would bechance at Lyonnesse
While I should sojourn there
No prophet durst declare,
Nor did the wisest wizard guess   10
What would bechance at Lyonnesse
While I should sojourn there.

When I came back from Lyonnesse
With magic in my eyes,
All marked with mute surmise   15
My radiance rare and fathomless,
When I came back from Lyonnesse
With magic in my eyes!

Notes

Lyonnesse: this was the name of his first wife Emma Gifford's house. In legend it is the home of King Arthur and Merlin the magician.

[3]   **rime:** frost; an accumulation of ice

[7]   **bechance:** happen

[8]   **sojourn:** stay for a time

[9]   **durst:** dared

EXPLORATIONS

First reading

1. Briefly tell the story in the poem.

2. 'With magic in my eyes,' how is the sense of magic built up in the poem?

3. What do we know about the speaker? How do you visualise him? Is information deliberately kept from the reader to enhance the sense of mystery?

4. In medieval romance poems the hero is frequently on a quest where he must overcome hardship. What is the hero of this poem on a quest for? Explain your answer.

Second reading

5. What details help to convey the poet's 'lonesomeness' in stanza 1?

6. What is the effect of the archaic language such as 'bechance' and 'durst' in stanza 2? What does such diction contribute to the poem?

7. How do you think the final stanza relates to the rest of the poem? Has it been prepared for in the earlier stanzas?

8. How does the speaker's state of mind alter as he travels? Refer to the text in your answer.

Third reading

9. Does the knowledge that this poem was written against the background of a marriage that later failed affect how you view the poem?

10. Hardy wrote of Cornwall, 'the place is pre-eminently the region of dream and mystery'. What does 'Lyonnesse' suggest to you? Do you think of it as a place or state of mind?

11. The poem has many features of the traditional ballad. Comment on the subject matter and Hardy's use of simple diction, archaic words, repetition, rhyme and musical sound effects.

Fourth reading

12. Does the poem fit in with the view of Thomas Hardy's work you have gained from reading the other poems on your course? Explain your answer.

13. What does this poem say to you about love? How would you rate 'When I Set Out for Lyonnesse' as a love poem?

14. 'When I Set Out for Lyonnesse' is remarkable for the way in which the poet has been able to transmute autobiographical details into a medieval romance. Discuss.

William Carlos Williams

(1883–1963)

The early poetic work of William Carlos Williams shows the influence of two of the major poets of the twentieth century, Ezra Pound and T. S. Eliot. However, he eventually felt limited by this, and searched for an authentic American expression in poetry. He found this in writing about commonplace objects and the lives of ordinary people. In this way, he managed to bring out the significance of people and things we might otherwise take for granted. He has proved an inspiration for some major poets, in particular Ginsberg. His output includes stories and plays as well as his five well-known books of poetry.

This is Just to Say

prescribed for exam in 2014

I have eaten
the plums
that were in
the icebox

and which   5
you were probably
saving
for breakfast

Forgive me
they were delicious   10
so sweet
and so cold

EXPLORATIONS

Before reading

1. Imagine that you have just eaten a large, and very delicious, bar of chocolate that your best friend had been saving to eat at lunchtime. Write a short note to explain what happened and to apologise for what you have done.

   You might like to read aloud some of the notes written by the class and to discuss the various approaches taken.

First reading

2. (a) While you were reading 'This is Just to Say', did you notice any differences between the poem and your piece of writing? (b) Which of the two pieces do you think works better as an explanation and an apology? Give reasons for your answer.

3. (a) In your own words, summarise the main point that Williams makes in each of the three stanzas of this poem. (b) Do you think that he has the points in the best sequence in order to gain forgiveness, or would you rearrange the sequence?

First reading continued

4. Williams breaks up his message into very short phrases written on separate lines with no punctuation. Experiment with reading this poem aloud to see what effect this has on: (a) the pace, or speed, that should be used when reading this poem; and (b) the tone of voice.

Second reading

5. Williams rarely uses capital letters in his poetry, so there are only two capital letters employed in this poem: 'I' and 'Forgive'. (a) Why do you think he decided to use capital letters for these particular words? (b) Do these words help you to explain what the theme of this poem is? Explain your answer.

6. 'Forgive me

   they were delicious

   so sweet

   and so cold'

   Alliteration is when two or more words close together begin with the same letter. (a) Can you pick out Williams's use of alliteration in this stanza? (b) In what ways does his use of alliteration help you to imagine how the plums tasted? (c) Why do you think he emphasises how 'delicious' the plums were in his message?

Third reading

7. Which one of the following statements do you think best describes Williams's motivation for writing this poem?

(a) He wanted to leave a note reminding the person to buy more plums.

(b) He felt guilty about eating the plums but was too embarrassed to speak to the person who had put the plums in the 'icebox'.

(c) He wanted to show the person who had put the plums in the 'icebox' that he was genuinely sorry by leaving the poem as a gift to make up for the missing plums.

8. (a) If you received this poem would you forgive Williams? Why? (b) Write a short reply to Williams explaining how you feel.

9. Williams said of his poetry, 'I try to say it straight, whatever is to be said.' In what ways could this poem be said to be a 'straight' piece of writing? You might like to consider: (a) the language that he uses; (b) the form of the poem; and (c) the theme.

10. This poem, including the title, consists of thirty-three words. (a) Do you think that this piece is too short to be a poem? (b) In your view, what turns a piece of writing into a poem? Is it the language, the use of rhyme, the emotions expressed or something else?

Louis MacNeice (1907–1963)

Frederick Louis MacNeice, a British and Irish poet and playwright, was born in Belfast in 1907 and educated in England at Marlborough and Oxford. He lectured in classics in England and the United States before joining the BBC in 1941, where he produced programmes for the famous Features Department until his death in 1963. Among his numerous collections of poetry were: *Letters from Iceland* (1937), with W. H. Auden; *Autumn Journal* (1939); *Plant and Phantom* (1941); *Visitations* (1957); and *The Burning Perch* (1963).

Meeting Point

prescribed for exam in 2012

Time was away and somewhere else,
There were two glasses and two chairs
And two people with the one pulse
(Somebody stopped the moving stairs):
Time was away and somewhere else.   5

And they were neither up nor down;
The stream's music did not stop
Flowing through heather, limpid brown,
Although they sat in a coffee shop
And they were neither up nor down.   10

The bell was silent in the air
Holding its inverted poise –
Between the clang and clang a flower,
A brazen calyx of no noise:
The bell was silent in the air.   15

The camels crossed the miles of sand
That stretched around the cups and plates;
The desert was their own, they planned
To portion out the stars and dates:
The camels crossed the miles of sand.   20

Time was away and somewhere else.
The waiter did not come, the clock
Forgot them and the radio waltz
Came out like water from a rock:
Time was away and somewhere else.   25

Her fingers flicked away the ash
That bloomed again in tropic trees:
Not caring if the markets crash
When they had forests such as these,
Her fingers flicked away the ash.   30

God or whatever means the Good
Be praised that time can stop like this,
That what the heart has understood
Can verify in the body's peace
God or whatever means the Good.   35

Time was away and she was here
And life no longer what it was,
The bell was silent in the air
And all the room one glow because
Time was away and she was here.   40

---

[8]   **limpid:** clear
[12] **poise:** calm, dignified manner
[14] **brazen:** made of bronze
[14] **calyx:** outer leaves that protect the flower bud

EXPLORATIONS

Before reading

1. Have you ever noticed that when two people are in love they seem to exist 'in a world of their own'? How do you think that feels? Do they notice the world around them as much? How do friends react to this? Jot down some thoughts on the topic.

First reading

2. Read the entire poem twice or, preferably, listen to it being read. If you were an observer of this scene in the coffee shop: (a) What exactly would you see? Make a list and discuss in pairs or groups. (b) What exactly would you hear? Again, make a list and compare.

3. Do you think they are very much in love? Explain your view.

Second reading

4. 'Time was away and somewhere else'. (a) What does this suggest about the relationship? (b) Do you notice this reference to time anywhere else in the poem? What is the effect of this?

5. Read the third stanza carefully. What is happening here? Would it help to draw it? (a) Suggest possible meanings. (b) Do you think the image is clever? Explain your thoughts on this. (c) What do you think the poet is saying about love and time?

Third reading

Focus on stanzas four to six

6. In the poet's imagination, the coffee shop is transformed. How does the imagined scene fit in with the idea of being in love?

7. What do you think the poet is suggesting here about the power of love? Discuss this.

8. Do you think any images work particularly well? Explain your ideas.

Fourth reading

9. Do you think the poet is really grateful for this moment? What suggests this?

10. Suggest a meaning for: 'God . . . be praised . . . That what the heart has understood | Can verify in the body's peace'. In groups, discuss possible meanings.

Fourth reading continued

11. Would you agree that, although it is simple, the final stanza says all that needs to be said about love? Explain your opinions on this.

Fifth reading

12. Try reading the poem aloud or listen to it read well.

    (a) What do you notice about: the rhythm/beat of the lines; the repeated sounds within words; the pattern of end rhymes?

Fifth reading continued

    (b) What effect do these techniques have on you, the listener?

13. Which images do you think work best in this poem? Explain.

14. List all the possible points this poem is making about love. These are the themes.

15. Do you think this is a good love poem? Is it too romantic, too unreal, or does it catch the experience well?

16. Read 'Moonshine' by Richard Murphy and compare the two poems.

W. H. Auden (1907–1973)

Wystan Hugh Auden was born in York on 21 February 1907 and educated at Oxford and Berlin. He is considered one of the most important English poets of the 1930s, writing on political and social themes. A prolific poet, he wrote in a variety of verse forms, composing both humorous and serious poetry. 'Funeral Blues', originally a song in one of his plays, is taken from the volume *Another Time* (1940), which contains many of his best-known poems, such as 'September 1939' and 'Lullaby'. Auden spent much of his life in the United States, becoming an American citizen in 1946.

Funeral Blues

prescribed for exam in 2011

Stop all the clocks, cut off the telephone,
Prevent the dog from barking with a juicy bone,
Silence the pianos and with muffled drum
Bring out the coffin, let the mourners come.

Let aeroplanes circle moaning overhead   5
Scribbling on the sky the message He Is Dead,
Put the crêpe bows round the white necks of the public doves,
Let the traffic policemen wear black cotton gloves.

He was my North, my South, my East and West,
My working week and my Sunday rest,   10
My noon, my midnight, my talk, my song;
I thought that love would last for ever: I was wrong.

The stars are not wanted now: put out every one;
Pack up the moon and dismantle the sun;
Pour away the ocean and sweep up the wood.   15
For nothing now can ever come to any good.

EXPLORATIONS

First reading

1. What images grab your attention?

2. What do you think is happening in this poem?

3. Do you find it unusual in any way? Explain.

Second reading

4. The first two stanzas create the atmosphere of a funeral. What sights and sounds of a funeral do you notice?

5. It used to be the custom that clocks were stopped in a house where a death had occurred: as well as marking the time of death, this signified that time stood still for the grieving family. Do you think that the signs of mourning have been carried to extremes in the first two stanzas? Examine the actions called for.

6. How do you think the first stanza should be read: in a low, defeated tone, or semi-hysterical, or what? Read it aloud.

7. Read the second stanza aloud.

8. Do you think there might be a change of tone from the third stanza on? Read aloud stanzas 3 and 4.

9. Are you sympathetic to the speaker in this poem?

Third reading

10. What does the third stanza suggest about the relationship between the speaker and the person mourned? Examine each line in detail for the kernel of truth behind the clichés.

11. How do you understand the speaker's state of mind, particularly in the last verse?

12. Do you take this poem to be a serious statement about loss and bereavement, or do you find it exaggerated and 'over the top'? Explain your opinion. Do you think it could be read as a satire, that is, a poem ridiculing, in this case, the public outpouring of emotion at the funerals of famous people? Read the poem again.

Fourth reading

13. What do you think the poem is saying?

14. Look at the imagery again. How does it fit in with what the poem is saying?

15. Find out what you can about blues music and lyrics. What elements of a blues song do you find in the poem?

16. What do you like about this poem?

William Stafford (1914–1993)

William Stafford was born in Kansas in 1914. Although the family suffered financially during the American Depression, Stafford's parents consistently encouraged their three children to develop an independently moral view of life, through reading and discussion.

This tendency towards independence led the teenage Stafford to embark on a camping trip, during which he developed a close spiritual connection with the natural world: 'The earth was my home; I would never feel lost while it held me'. Later, as a conscientious objector during the Second World War, he refused to fight but did work in areas such as fire-fighting and building roads.

In 1948, he began teaching at Lewis and Clark College, Oregon, a position that he retained until his retirement, despite travelling widely to share his work with others. It was not until he was in his forties that his first anthology of poetry, *Traveling Through the Dark* was published, which subsequently won the 1963 National Book Award. Until his death in 1993, Stafford maintained the daily habit of rising at four in the morning to write poetry because he found it 'a confirming, satisfying activity to do'.

Traveling through the Dark

prescribed for exams in 2012 and 2013

Traveling through the dark I found a deer
dead on the edge of the Wilson River road.
It is usually best to roll them into the canyon:
that road is narrow; to swerve might make more dead.

By glow of the tail-light I stumbled back of the car   5
and stood by the heap, a doe, a recent killing;

she had stiffened already, almost cold.
I dragged her off; she was large in the belly.

My fingers touching her side brought me the reason –
her side was warm; her fawn lay there waiting,   10
alive, still, never to be born.
Beside that mountain road I hesitated.

The car aimed ahead its lowered parking lights;
under the hood purred the steady engine.
I stood in the glare of the warm exhaust turning red;   15
around our group I could hear the wilderness listen.

I thought hard for us all – my only swerving –,
then pushed her over the edge into the river.

Note

[3]   **canyon:** a deep and narrow opening running between hills

EXPLORATIONS

First reading

1. (a) Based on the clues in the first and second stanzas, describe in your own words how you picture 'the Wilson River road'. (b) Would you like to   drive along it in the dark? Why/why not? Use references from the poem to support your view.

2. (a) What reason does the poet give for saying about the dead deer, 'It is usually best to roll them into the canyon'? (b) Do you agree with his attitude? Why?

3. (a) What does the poet discover that causes him to hesitate in the third stanza? (b) Can you understand why he pauses? Explain your answer.

4. (a) Were you shocked when you read the final line of the poem? If so, why? (b) Would you have preferred the poem to end in another way? Describe the ending that you would prefer.

5. The poet's emotions change a number of times during his experience on Wilson River road. (a) Go through the poem and trace the emotions that he feels. (b) Based on what you have learned about his feelings, would you consider the poet to be a kind or unkind person? Give reasons for your answer.

6. How does the poet use the senses of sight, touch and hearing in order to make this scene more vivid and easy to imagine? Use references from the poem in your answer.

7. Although this scene takes place at night Stafford still includes some colours in his poem. (a) What colours appear in the poem? (b) Why do you think he refers only to these colours in the poem?

8. It has been suggested that, in this poem, Stafford portrays his view of the relationship between the world of nature, represented by the deer, and the world of technology, represented by the car. What do you think this poem says to us about this relationship?

9. Although this poem is written in everyday, conversational language, Stafford uses words and phrases that have layers of meaning. (a) Discuss the different meanings the word 'still' can have in the following lines:

   'her fawn lay there waiting, alive, *still*, never to be born.'

   (b) Consider, in a similar way, how the title of the poem, 'Traveling through the Dark', can be interpreted in a number of ways.

10. Imagine that you live on Wilson River road and you are very concerned about the dangers posed both to people and to deer by the driving conditions in this area at night. Write a letter to the local newspaper trying to persuade the readers that something has to be done to improve the situation.

Dylan Thomas (1914–1953)

Dylan Thomas was born in Swansea, South Wales, where his father was an English teacher. After attending the local grammar school he went to work as a journalist on a local newspaper, the *South Wales Daily Post*. In 1934 he went to London, where he worked as a journalist and reviewer, as well as doing other jobs for newspapers and magazines. During the Second World War he worked as a scriptwriter for the BBC and a number of film companies. In the post-war years he began broadcasting, featuring his own poems and stories. Thomas published four volumes of poetry and two prose works. His 'play for voices' *Under Milk Wood*, which evokes the spirit of a Welsh village from early morning to night, was published after his death. Thomas said of his poetry, 'I wrote my poems for the glory of God and the love of man.'

He married Caitlin Macnamara in 1937, and after much wandering eventually settled in Wales in 1949. He went to America on a lecture and poetry reading tour the following year and made a great deal of money. Unfortunately Thomas found life as a literary celebrity a strain, which he relieved by heavy drinking. In 1953 he died in America after a heavy drinking bout.

Do Not Go Gentle into that Good Night

prescribed for exams in 2013 and 2014

Do not go gentle into that good night,
Old age should burn and rave at close of day;
Rage, rage against the dying of the light.

Though wise men at their end know dark is right,
Because their words have forked no lightning they   5
Do not go gentle into that good night.

Good men, the last wave by, crying how bright
Their frail deeds might have danced in a green bay,
Rage, rage against the dying of the light.
Wild men who caught and sang the sun in flight,   10
And learn, too late, they grieved it on its way,
Do not go gentle into that good night.

Grave men, near death, who see with blinding sight
Blind eyes could blaze like meteors and be gay,
Rage, rage against the dying of the light.   15
And you, my father, there on the sad height,
Curse, bless, me now with your fierce tears, I pray.
Do not go gentle into that good night.
Rage, rage against the dying of the light.

Background note	Dylan Thomas's father was blind when he died.

EXPLORATIONS

Before reading

1. Imagine how you would feel if someone you care about was critically ill. Try to describe the thoughts that would go through your mind as you waited by their bedside.

2. What do you think the poet means by 'that good night'? Does it mean the same as 'the dying of the light', or do you feel this might be a reference to the father's blindness?

3. How, according to Thomas, should 'Old age' react 'at close of day'?

4. What do 'wise' men know in stanza two? Do they act according to their knowledge? Critics have interpreted 'forked no lightning' as meaning: 'were not inspired by the words'. Does this make sense to you?

5. How do 'Good men' react in the third stanza? Has 'the last wave' something to do with a last wave of the hand or the last wave in the sea?

6. What is the poem saying about how 'Wild men' lived their lives?

7. There is paradox in seeing with 'blinding sight' as the 'Grave men, near death' do. What do you think the poet is trying to suggest here? If you are unsure, leave the question and come back to it later. Did you notice the pun in 'Grave men'?

8. What is Thomas asking his father to do in the final stanza? Have you any idea of what he means by 'fierce tears'?

9. Read the poem aloud. What tone of voice should you adopt? What is the effect of the refrain in the final line of each stanza? How, for example, should 'Rage, rage' be read? Does the sound give you an idea of how the poet feels? Should the poem be read at a brisk or slow pace? Why?

10. Do you get a sense from the poem about how life should be lived according to the poet?

11. How does the poet feel about his father?

12. Why do you think the final stanza is four lines long when the other stanzas contain three?

13. Look at the images of light and darkness that run through the poem. What does light symbolise for the poet? What does darkness represent?

14. What emotions does the poet feel in the poem? What words or images suggest how he feels?

15. How do you imagine the poet's father? What kind of a person was he? How do you think he lived his life?

16. State briefly what the theme of this poem is. Can you sum up your understanding of the text in one or two sentences?

17. Do you find the poet's language unusual or difficult? Write about any two features of the writer's style.

18. Is the poet sincere in what he has to say about his father? Justify your answer.

Fourth reading

19. Does this poem build up to a climax? Can you see any structure in how the poem is developed?

20. Do you think the effort involved in understanding this poem was worthwhile? Do you think that critics who complained about the obscurity of Dylan

Thomas's poems were justified? Does any line or phrase from the poem stick in your mind? Can you relate to the poet's feelings?

21. 'No paraphrase will ever do justice to the verse of Dylan Thomas.' Would you agree with this statement? Consider how sound, sense and imagery combine to produce the overall impact.

22. 'Dylan Thomas is intense and passionate.' Comment on the poem's emotional atmosphere. How do you react to Thomas's portrayal of feelings? Are you moved by the poem?

23. What is the poet's attitude to death as displayed in the poem?

Edwin Morgan (1920–)

Morgan was born in Glasgow, was first published in 1952 and was still being published in 1996. Such a long career is marked by an ability and vision to write poetry inspired by a wide and varied list of subjects, from space travel to mythological goddesses. His prolific output includes libretti, plays, criticism and translations from Anglo-Saxon and Russian. His poems are as varied in form as they are in material, showing, for example, similarities to medieval Latin writing on the one hand and e. e. cummings on the other.

Strawberries

prescribed for exam in 2011

There were never strawberries
like the ones we had
that sultry afternoon
sitting on the step
of the open french window   5
facing each other
your knees held in mine
the blue plates in our laps
the strawberries glistening
in the hot sunlight   10
we dipped them in sugar
looking at each other
not hurrying the feast
for one to come
the empty plates   15
laid on the stone together
with the two forks crossed
and I bent towards you
sweet in that air
in my arms   20
abandoned like a child
from your eager mouth
the taste of strawberries
in my memory
lean back again let me love you   25

let the sun beat
on our forgetfulness
one hour of all
the heat intense
and summer lightening   30
on the Kilpatrick hills

let the storm wash the plates

EXPLORATIONS

First reading

1. The poet suggests that food connected with special moments has a special taste. Would you agree with him? Have you any special memories where the food seemed to taste especially good?

2. What impression do you get of the setting for this poem? Do you find it a surprising setting for a poem? Why?

3. What sort of a relationship do you think these two people have? Choose two phrases from the poem to support your view.

Second reading

4. What is the weather like as the couple eat the strawberries? Does it tell you anything about their feelings?

5. 'the empty plates
laid on the stone together
with the two forks crossed'

Why do you think the poet introduces this image into the poem at this point? Does it have any connection with the couple?

6. How does the poet use the weather to suggest the intensifying of their emotions? Do you think that this is a successful device or is it rather over-dramatic?

Third reading

7. 'not hurrying the feast
for one to come'

Eating is a sensual experience. Can the 'feast' of strawberries be seen as a preparation for another equally sensual 'feast'? What is your reaction to this connection of ideas?

8. Eating is also an important social activity. Can you think of occasions where sharing food has a special significance, perhaps even suggesting a change in the nature of a relationship? How would you feel if you had to share a table in a restaurant with a stranger, or if you were invited to a friend's home for a meal?

9. Why do you think the poet chose to write this poem without any punctuation? Was he trying to suggest something about the moment, or perhaps about the way that he remembers the moment?

10. This is a remembered moment. Do you think that this affects the way in which the poet views the scene? Can memories be trusted? Does it matter if they are unreliable?

Howard Nemerov (1920–1991)

Howard Nemerov was born in New York in 1920. After he graduated from Harvard in 1941, he served as a pilot in the Royal Canadian unit of the US Army Air Force. He flew throughout the Second World War and he became a first lieutenant. He married in 1944.

Following the war, Nemerov taught in a number of American universities while writing poetry, novels, short stories, essays and criticism. He was awarded numerous prizes for his poetry, including the prestigious Pulitzer Prize for Poetry in 1978 for *The Collected Poems of Howard Nemerov*.

Nemerov became the third Poet Laureate of the United States of America in 1988. He died in 1991.

Wolves in the Zoo

prescribed for exam in 2014

They look like big dogs badly drawn, drawn wrong.
A legend on their cage tells us there is
No evidence that any of their kind
Has ever attacked man, woman, or child.

Now it turns out there were no babies dropped   5
In sacrifice, delaying tactics, from
Siberian sleds; now it turns out, so late,
That Little Red Ridinghood and her Gran

Were the aggressors with the slavering fangs
And tell-tale tails; now it turns out at last   10
That grey wolf and timber wolf are near extinct,

Done out of being by the tales we tell
Told us by Nanny in the nursery;
Young sparks we were, to set such forest fires
As blazed from story into history   15
And put such bounty on their wolvish heads

As brought the few survivors to our terms,
Surrendered in happy Babylon among
The peacock dusting off the path of dust,
The tiger pacing in the stripéd shade.   20

EXPLORATIONS

First reading

1. (a) In the first line of the poem, Nemerov describes the wolves as 'big dogs badly drawn'. How do you picture the wolves from this description? (b) Do you find it a surprising image to use about the wolves? Why?

2. (a) What does the notice on the wolves' cage say? (b) Why do you think Nemerov decided to put this piece of information at the very beginning of his poem?

Second reading

3. (a) How is the wolf usually portrayed in the 'Little Red Riding Hood' story? (b) What does Nemerov have to say about this portrayal? (c) What other untrue story was told about wolves?

4. What effect did these untrue stories have on (a) the young children who heard them and (b) the world's wolf population?

5. 'As blazed from story into history'

   (a) Explain the difference between a 'story' and 'history'?
   (b) What is Nemerov suggesting happened to the untrue tales told about wolves?

Third reading

6. (a) What type of scene can you picture from the images in the final stanza of the poem?
   (b) Do you think that the wolves, the peacock and the tiger are really 'happy'? Why?

7. 'now it turns out, so late,

   That Little Red Ridinghood and her Gran

   Were the aggressors'

   'Done out of being by the tales we tell'

   'As brought the few survivors to our terms,

   Surrendered in happy Babylon'

   (a) What do these lines suggest about the way humans have treated the wolves? (b) Do you agree with this point of view? Why/why not?

8. The forming of people's attitudes and the consequences of those attitudes are ideas that occur in this poem. (a) Did thinking about this poem make you reconsider your attitude to wolves? (b) Might this poem encourage you to reconsider some of your other attitudes?

9. Explain the theme, or central message, of this poem in your own words. Use quotations from the poem to support your explanation.

10. Write a letter to the newspaper either in favour of or against the practice of keeping animals in zoos.

Richard Wilbur (1921–)

Richard Wilbur was born in New York and educated at Amherst College and Harvard University. He served in the American army during the Second World War and has been a teacher at Harvard and other universities. Among his collections of poetry are *The Beautiful Changes and Other Poems* (1947); *Ceremony and Other Poems* (1950); *Things of This World: Poems*, which won a Pulitzer Prize in 1956; and *New and Collected Poems* (1988). Wilbur believed that one of the main functions of poetry is to examine the inconsistencies and disharmony of modern life. He was made Poet Laureate of the United States in 1987.

The Writer

prescribed for exam in 2011

In her room at the prow of the house
Where light breaks, and the windows are tossed with linden,
My daughter is writing a story.

I pause in the stairwell, hearing
From her shut door a commotion of typewriter-keys   5
Like a chain hauled over a gunwale.

Young as she is, the stuff
Of her life is a great cargo, and some of it heavy:
I wish her a lucky passage.

But now it is she who pauses,   10
As if to reject my thought and its easy figure.
A stillness greatens, in which

The whole house seems to be thinking,
And then she is at it again with a bunched clamor
Of strokes, and again is silent.   15

I remember the dazed starling
Which was trapped in that very room, two years ago;
How we stole in, lifted a sash

And retreated, not to affright it;
And how for a helpless hour, through the crack of the door,   20
We watched the sleek, wild, dark

And iridescent creature
Batter against the brilliance, drop like a glove
To the hard floor, or the desk-top,

And wait then, humped and bloody,   25
For the wits to try it again; and how our spirits
Rose when, suddenly sure,

It lifted off from a chair-back,
Beating a smooth course for the right window
And clearing the sill of the world.   30

It is always a matter, my darling,
Of life or death, as I had forgotten. I wish
What I wished you before, but harder.

Notes

[1]	**prow:**	the pointed front of a ship
[2]	**linden:**	a lime tree
[5]	**commotion:**	a loud mixture of noises
[6]	**gunwale:**	the top edge of the side of a ship
[14]	**clamor:**	a loud noise
[18]	**sash:**	a window
[22]	**iridescent:**	shimmering colours

EXPLORATIONS

1. Imagine that you are in your bedroom and your Mum or Dad is in the next bedroom trying to put together a new set of self-assembly shelves. Write a short piece describing the different sounds that you hear and what you can picture happening to make these sounds. As a class, you might like to read some of the pieces aloud.

First reading

2. The poet's daughter and the starling are both struggling. Describe in your own words (a) how his daughter is struggling and (b) how the starling is struggling.

3. (a) The poet cannot see his daughter in lines 1–15, so what sense does he use to work out what she is doing? Choose *two lines* where you feel that the poet uses this sense to help you to imagine what is happening.

   (b) What sense does the poet use in his description of the starling in lines 16–30? Again, choose *two lines* where you feel that the poet uses this sense to help you to imagine what is happening.

Second reading

4. 'Young as she is, the stuff
   Of her life is a great cargo, and some of it heavy:'

   (a) Do you agree with the poet's view that no matter how old you are life can be complicated and difficult to cope with? (b) Can you suggest how his daughter's writing might be related to her trying to cope with her life? (c) How does he feel about his daughter struggling with her life and her writing? Refer to the poem to support your answer.

5. (a) Choose *one image* from the poet's description of the starling's struggle in lines 16–30 that shows how difficult it was for the bird. (b) How does the poet feel as he watches the starling struggle? (c) What do you think the poet learned about struggling from the sparrow's successful escape?

6. 'It is always a matter, my darling,
   Of life or death,'
   'I wish
   What I wished you before, but harder.'

   Examine these two quotations and explain how they show a change in the poet's attitude to his daughter's struggle in the course of the poem.

7. (a) In lines 1–15, the poet uses an unusual extended metaphor that compares his daughter's struggle with writing to her being on a ship setting off on a voyage. Pick out the lines in the poem that convey this idea. (b) Can you suggest ways in which writing could be seen as going on a voyage?

8. Wilbur has said that he was inspired to write this poem when he felt 'two ideas, two images come together'. Did you find that his linking of (a) the image of his daughter struggling to write with (b) the image of the trapped starling helped you to understand what he was saying in the poem, or did you find this link confusing? Refer to the poem in your answer.

9. Wilbur's writing has great elegance because of his confident and skilful use of literary devices. (a) Consider how his use of alliteration in 'Batter against the brilliance' helps to reinforce the meaning of this phrase. (b) Discuss how his use of the simile 'drop like a glove' conveys the way in which the exhausted starling fell.

10. Imagine that you are Wilbur's daughter and he has slipped this poem under your door. After you have read the poem, you decide to write a response to him. Write what you would say.

A Summer Morning

prescribed for exams in 2012 and 2013

Her young employers, having got in late
From seeing friends in town
And scraped the right front fender on the gate,
Will not, the cook expects, be coming down.

She makes a quiet breakfast for herself.   5
The coffee-pot is bright,
The jelly where it should be on the shelf.
She breaks an egg into the morning light,

Then, with the bread-knife lifted, stands and hears
The sweet efficient sounds   10
Of thrush and catbird, and the snip of shears
Where, in the terraced backward of the grounds,

A gardener works before the heat of day.
He straightens for a view
Of the big house ascending stony-gray   15
Out of his beds mosaic with the dew.

His young employers having got in late,
He and the cook alone
Receive the morning on their old estate,
Possessing what the owners can but own.   20

Notes

[7]   **jelly:** jam
[11]   **catbird:** a black and grey North American bird whose song often sounds like a cat mewing
[16]   **mosaic:** a picture or pattern that is made up of small coloured pieces of stone or glass

EXPLORATIONS

First reading

1. (a) Why do the cook and the gardener not expect their 'young employers' to be 'coming down' on this summer morning? (b) What does the line 'And scraped the right front fender on the gate' suggest to you about the condition that the 'young employers' were in when they arrived back late? (c) What does this incident tell you about the attitude of the 'young employers' to the things they own?

2. Lines 5–11 describe the scene inside the house where the cook is preparing her breakfast. (a) Based on your reading of these lines, how do you picture the kitchen that she is working in? (b) Do you think the cook looks after the kitchen well? What evidence can you find for your answer?

3. Lines 12–20 move the poem outside to the garden of the house. (a) Describe how you imagine the garden from the images that the poet uses. (b) The gardener takes a moment to look at the garden and the house and 'his beds mosaic with the dew'. What do his action and the use of 'his' suggest about the gardener's attitude to this garden?

First reading continued

4. Wilbur uses the senses of sight and hearing in the poem to help us to appreciate how special this summer morning on the 'estate' is. Choose *one image for each sense* and explain why you particularly like it.

Second reading

5. 'He and the cook alone
    Receive the morning on their old estate'

    (a) The word 'Receive' has a number of meanings, two of which are (i) to accept or take something that has been offered and (ii) to welcome and entertain a guest. Consider how each of these meanings can be applied in the lines above. (b) Do you think that these lines suggest that the cook and the gardener enjoy working on the 'estate' Why? (c) Is it significant that they think of it as '*their* estate'? Explain your answer.

6. 'Possessing what the owners can but own.'

   (a) Based on your reading of the poem, discuss how each of the people engages with (functions with, thinks and feels about) the 'estate'. (b) Do you think that how you engage with something is part of the difference between 'possessing' and 'owning'? Why? (c) Do you agree with the poet that there is a difference between possessing and owning? Use references from the poem to support your view.

7. (a) Both the cook and the gardener use the term 'young employers' rather than the individual names of their employers. What does this tell you about the kind of relationship that the cook and the gardener have with these people? (b) How do you think the cook and the gardener feel about the way that the 'young employers' treat the estate? Refer to the poem in your answer.

8. (a) Based on Wilbur's descriptions of the kitchen and the gardens, how would you describe the mood of this summer morning? (b) He uses a very regular rhyme scheme in each quatrain (group of four lines): line 1 rhymes with line 3; line 2 rhymes with line 4. This can be written as *a,b,a,b*. Do you find that this scheme adds to the overall mood that is created in the poem? In what ways does it do this?

9. We have seen what the cook and the gardener are doing while the 'young employers' are still asleep. Write a piece describing what you think will happen in the kitchen and the garden when the 'young employers' do eventually come down.

10. (a) Imagine that this estate is going to be sold. The auctioneer has asked 'the young employers', the cook and the gardener to write a short piece about the estate to be included in the information booklet. Do you think the three descriptions would be the same? Explain your answer. (b) Try writing a paragraph for each of them in the way that you think they would write about the estate.

Denise Levertov (1923–1997)

Denise Levertov was born in Essex in England. Her father had converted from Judaism to become an Anglican parson. She was educated completely at home and at five years old decided that she would become a writer. At the age of twelve she sent her poetry to T. S. Eliot, who responded very positively to her work. She published her first poem at seventeen and her first collection in 1946. During the Second World War she worked as a civilian nurse during the bombing of London.

In 1947 she married an American and soon after moved to the USA with him. By 1956 she had become an American citizen. Her poetry became much less formal and she was heavily influenced by poets such as William Carlos Williams. Her second American volume, *With Eyes at the Back of Our Heads* (1959), established her as one of the great American poets, and her British roots were by now a thing of the past. During the 1960s she became very involved in activism and feminism. She was strongly opposed to the Vietnam War. *The Sorrow Dance*, which expressed her feelings about the Vietnam War and the death of her sister, was a passionate, angry collection. In all she published more than twenty volumes of poetry. She died in December 1997.

What Were They Like?

prescribed for exams in 2011 and 2012

---

1. Did the people of Vietnam
      use lanterns of stone?
2. Did they hold ceremonies
      to reverence the opening of buds?
3. Were they inclined to laughter?   5
4. Did they use bone and ivory,
      jade and silver, for ornament?
5. Had they an epic poem?
6. Did they distinguish between speech and singing?

1. Sir, their light hearts turned to stone.   10
      It is not remembered whether in gardens
      stone lanterns illumined pleasant ways.
2. Perhaps they gathered once to delight in blossom,
      but after the children were killed
      there were no more buds.   15
3. Sir, laughter is bitter to the burned mouth.
4. A dream ago, perhaps. Ornament is for joy.
      All the bones were charred.
5. It is not remembered. Remember,
      most were peasants; their life   20
      was in rice and bamboo.
      When peaceful clouds were reflected in the paddies
      and the water buffalo stepped surely along terraces,
      maybe fathers told their sons old tales.
      When bombs smashed those mirrors   25
      there was time only to scream.
6. There is an echo yet
      of their speech which was like a song.
      It was reported their singing resembled
      the flight of moths in moonlight.   30
      Who can say? It is silent now.

EXPLORATIONS

Before reading

1. What do you know about the Vietnam War? Find out about it and discuss it.

First reading

Lines 1–9

2. Read the questions. What does the questioner want to find out?

3. What do these questions tell us about the questioner – for example: what preconceptions does s/he have about the Vietnamese; what is his/her profession – journalist, historian, archaeologist or what?

4. Read the questions aloud in the tone of voice you would expect the questioner to ask them. Discuss the tone and manner of the questioning.

5. What responses would you expect to each of these questions? Suggest sample answers.

Second reading

Lines 10–31

6. Are the answers as you expected? What do you find surprising or unexpected? Do you think the answers might have surprised the questioner? Why?

7. From the answers, what do we learn about the way of life of the Vietnamese?

8. What is the chief preoccupation of the person who replies? What preys on his/her mind and colours all the replies?

9. Do you think the tone of the answers differs from that of the questions? Explain your views on this and discuss them in your group or class.

Third reading

10. What is your favourite image or phrase in the poem?

11. Examine each of the metaphors individually: the light, the bud, laughter, decoration, heritage and culture. What is suggested by each metaphor? What do they contribute to the atmosphere of the poem?

Third reading continued

12. What impression is given of the attitude to life of Vietnamese people after the war? Where is this suggested?

13. Are there any signs of hope for the future in this poem?

Fourth reading

14. Were you moved by the poem? Discuss your reaction with your group or class.

Fourth reading continued

15. What do you think the poem is saying? Write two or three paragraphs on this.

16. Have you previously read a poem that took the format of a 'question and answer' sequence? What do you think of this format? Is it effective in this case? Explain your views.

Patricia Beer (1924–1999)

Patricia Beer was born in Exmouth, Devon, into a Plymouth Brethren family. Her father was a railway clerk and her mother a teacher; Beer wrote a vivid account of her stern upbringing in *Mrs Beer's House* (1968). Patricia won a scholarship to Exmouth Grammar School and achieved a first-class honours degree at Exeter University. She went on to St Hugh's College, Oxford, and lived in Italy teaching English during the period 1947–53. After a succession of temporary jobs Beer was appointed lecturer in English at Goldsmiths' College in London in 1962, where she remained for six years. In 1964 she married an architect, John Damien Parsons, with whom she refurbished a Tudor farmhouse in Up Ottery, Devon, where she lived for the rest of her life.

Patricia Beer left teaching to become a full-time writer in 1968.

In all, Beer published nine volumes of poetry, one novel and an academic study, *Reader I Married Him*, an analysis of the major nineteenth-century women novelists and their female characters. Patricia Beer made her poems out of the ordinary events of daily life with a wry humour and a sharp eye for detail.

The Voice

prescribed for exam in 2014

When God took my aunt's baby boy, a merciful neighbour
Gave her a parrot. She could not have afforded one
But now bought a new cage as brilliant as the bird,
And turned her back on the idea of other babies.

He looked unlikely. In her house his scarlet feathers   5
Stuck out like a jungle, though his blue ones blended
With the local pottery which carried messages
Like 'Du ee help yerself to crame, me handsome.'
He said nothing when he arrived, not a quotation
From pet-shop gossip or a sailor's oath, no sound   10
From someone's home: the telephone or car-door slamming,
And none from his: tom-tom, war-cry or wild beast roaring.

He came from silence but was ready to become noise.
My aunt taught him nursery rhymes morning after morning.
He learnt Miss Muffett, Jack and Jill, Little Jack Horner,   15
Including her jokes; she used to say turds and whey.

A genuine Devon accent is not easy. Actors
Cannot do it. He could though. In his court clothes
He sounded like a farmer, as her son might have.
He sounded like our family. He fitted in.   20

Years went by. We came and went. A day or two
Before he died, he got confused, and muddled up
His rhymes. Jack Horner ate his pail of water.
The spider said what a good boy he was. I wept.

He had never seemed puzzled by the bizarre events   25
He spoke of. But that last day he turned his head towards us
With the bewilderment of death upon him. Said
'Broke his crown' and 'Christmas pie'. And tumbled after.

My aunt died the next winter, widowed, childless, pitied
And patronised. I cannot summon up her voice at all.   30
She would not have expected it to be remembered
After so long. But I can still hear his.

EXPLORATIONS

First reading

1. What impression of the aunt do you get from the first stanza? How do you visualise her?

2. 'He looked unlikely.' What do you think the author means by this?

3. How do you imagine the aunt's home looked? Examine the detail in the two opening stanzas.

4. Why do you think the aunt taught the parrot nursery rhymes? Is there a connection with the loss of her baby son?

5. 'He fitted in.' How did the parrot fit in?

6. Why do you think the author 'wept'? How does she feel about the parrot?

7. What do you think the poet means by 'pitied | And patronised'? What does this tell us about how people perceived the aunt?

Second reading

8. Read the poem aloud. Jot down what you notice about its sounds and rhythms.

9. How do you react to the first sentence? Is it an effective opening?

10. Comment on the 'jungle' simile in the second stanza.

11. Do you get a sense of place from the references to Devon and the local pottery? Does this enrich the poem?

12. 'With the bewilderment of death upon him. Said |

    "Broke his crown" and "Christmas pie". And tumbled after.'

    Comment on these lines. Do you think the lines work well? Can you detect some humour in the clever phrasing?

13. What evidence is there in the poem that the parrot was regarded more as a family member than as a mere household pet?

14. How do you feel about the aunt's life? Can you suggest why we are not told her name?

Third reading

15. Briefly state what the theme of the poem is.
16. Would you agree that there is genuine warmth of feeling in this poem?
17. How do you react to the style in which the poem is written? Comment on any three features. You might consider the poet's conversational

language, her wry humour, her eye for detail and her use of imagery.

18. What is the mood of this poem? What choice of words and images suggest the mood? Look closely at the final stanza.
19. What have you learned about the character of the author from reading the poem?

Fourth reading

20. Write a paragraph giving your personal reaction to 'The Voice'. Would you recommend it?

Richard Murphy (1927–)

Richard Murphy was born in County Mayo in 1927 and now lives in South Africa. He has published numerous collections of poetry, which have won many awards in Ireland, Britain and the USA. His collected poems *In the Heart of the Country* was published by Gallery Press in 2000. He is a member of Aosdána.

Moonshine

prescribed for exams in 2011 and 2012

To think
I must be alone:
To love
We must be together.

To think I love you   5
When I'm alone
More than I think of you
When we're together.

I cannot think
Without loving   10
Or love
Without thinking.

Alone I love
To think of us together:
Together I think   15
I'd love to be alone.

EXPLORATIONS

Before reading

1. What sort of ideas, feelings and images do you usually find in a love poem?

First reading

2. What do you notice on first reading this?

First reading continued

3. What kind of person do you think the speaker is here?

4. The speaker is expressing a dilemma or conflict. Describe the dilemma in your own words.

Second reading

5. What do you find unusual about this love poem?

6. Which of the possible meanings of the title do you think best suits the poem, or could they both apply? Explain your opinions.

7. Do you think the poet is taking this love stuff seriously? Explain.

Maya Angelou (1928–)

Maya Angelou, originally Marguerite Johnson, was born on 4 April 1928 in St Louis, Missouri. Her older brother gave her the name 'Maya'. Her early life was unsettled and traumatic and for many years Maya had to struggle to overcome her childhood experiences.

Maya's parents divorced when she was three and Maya and her brother lived for five years with their grandmother in Arkansas, a state where racial segregation was practised.

When Maya was eight she and her brother went back to their mother. During this time, Maya was raped by her mother's boyfriend. Deeply traumatised, Maya withdrew into herself, speaking only to her brother. Once again, the children returned to Arkansas and through the loving support of her grandmother and her study of literature and music, Maya recovered full speech by the age of twelve.

Maya had a son at the age of sixteen and embarked on a series of jobs that ranged from being the first female streetcar conductor to dancing in musicals. In the late 1950s, Maya moved to New York to pursue her singing and acting career. This proved to be a turning point in her life and Maya Angelou has since developed into a playwright, a civil rights activist, a lecturer and a director, among other occupations. In 1993, she read one of her poems at the inauguration of President Bill Clinton and she has developed a close friendship with Oprah Winfrey.

Phenomenal Woman

prescribed for exam in 2012

Pretty women wonder where my secret lies.
I'm not cute or built to suit a fashion model's size
But when I start to tell them,
They think I'm telling lies.
I say,   5
It's in the reach of my arms
The span of my hips
The stride of my step,
The curl of my lips.
I'm a woman   10
Phenomenally.
Phenomenal woman,
That's me.

I walk into a room
Just as cool as you please,   15
And to a man,
The fellows stand or
Fall down on their knees.
Then they swarm around me,
A hive of honey bees.   20
I say,
It's the fire in my eyes,
And the flash of my teeth,
The swing in my waist,
And the joy in my feet.   25
I'm a woman
Phenomenally.
Phenomenal woman,
That's me.

Men themselves have wondered   30
What they see in me.
They try so much

But they can't touch
My inner mystery.
When I try to show them,   35
They say they still can't see.
I say,
It's in the arch of my back,
The sun of my smile,
The ride of my breasts,   40
The grace of my style.
I'm a woman

Phenomenally.
Phenomenal woman,
That's me.   45

Now you understand
Just why my head's not bowed.
I don't shout or jump about
Or have to talk real loud.
When you see me passing   50
It ought to make you proud.
I say,
It's in the click of my heels,
The bend of my hair,
The palm of my hand   55
The need of my care,
'Cause I'm a woman
Phenomenally.
Phenomenal woman,
That's me.   60

EXPLORATIONS

First reading

1. (a) Having read this poem for
    the first time, would you
    describe your overall reaction
    to it as a positive or a negative
    one? (b) Choose a particular
    extract from the poem that
    really triggers this response in
    you and try to explain why it
    affects you in this way.

Second reading

2. What effect does Angelou
    have on men when she goes
    into a room?

3. Why do you think that the
    'Pretty women' want to know
    her 'secret'?

4. How do (a) the 'Pretty women'
    and (b) the 'Men' react when
    Maya tries to reveal her secret
    to them?

5. 'The stride of my step,' 'The
    swing in my waist', 'The sun of
    my smile'.   Which of the
    following words would you use
    to describe the tone, or
    emotion, expressed in the
    quotations above: positive,
    confident, assured, happy?

Third reading

6. Angelou explains where her
    secret lies in lines 6–9, 22–25,
    37–45 and 53–56. Can you
    suggest a connection between
    these lines and her repetition
    of the phrase 'I'm a woman'?

7. 'When you see me passing | It
    ought to make you proud.'
    Bearing in mind the difficulties
    that Angelou has faced in her
    life, why do you think that she
    feels that we should be 'proud'
    when we see her 'passing'?

8. (a) From your reading of the
    poem, sum up, in your own
    words, the qualities that
    Angelou feels make her a
    'Phenomenal Woman'.
    (b) Do you agree with her that
    she is, indeed, a 'Phenomenal
    Woman'?

9. (a) What is the theme, or
    central message, of this poem?
    (b) In your opinion, could this
    theme apply to both males
    and females?

10. Write a short passage of
    prose, or a poem, entitled
    'Phenomenal Man' or
    'Phenomenal Person', outlining
    the characteristics and qualities
    that you find admirable.

Fleur Adcock (1934–)

Fleur Adcock was born in New Zealand
and lived there at various times, but
has spent much of her life in England.
Her volumes of poetry include *The Eye
of the Hurricane* (1964), *Tigers* (1967),
High Tide in the Garden (1971), *The
Inner Harbour* (1979), *The Incident
Book* (1986), and *Time Zones* (1991).
She is considered one of the foremost
feminist poets of the age, famous for
her 'anti-erotic' style of love poems.
'For Heidi with Blue Hair' is taken from
The Incident Book and is dedicated to
her god-daughter, Heidi Jackson.

For Heidi with Blue Hair

prescribed for Ordinary Level exams in 2011 and 2013

When you dyed your hair blue
(or, at least, ultramarine
for the clipped sides, with a crest
of jet-black spikes on top)
you were sent home from school   5

because, as the headmistress put it,
although dyed hair was not
specifically forbidden, yours
was, apart from anything else,
not done in the school colours.   10

Tears in the kitchen, telephone-calls
to school from your freedom-loving father:
'She's not a punk in her behaviour;
it's just a style.' (You wiped your eyes,
also not in a school colour.)   15

'She discussed it with me first –
we checked the rules.' 'And anyway, Dad,
it cost twenty-five dollars.
Tell them it won't wash out –
not even if I wanted to try.'   20

It would have been unfair to mention
your mother's death, but that
shimmered behind the arguments.
The school had nothing else against you;
the teachers twittered and gave in.   25

Next day your black friend had hers done
in grey, white and flaxen yellow –
the school colours precisely:
an act of solidarity, a witty
tease. The battle was already won.   30

EXPLORATIONS

First reading

1.   What details of the story stand
     out? What in particular do you
     notice on a first reading?

2.   Visualise the scene in the
     kitchen. What details do you
     notice? How do you hear the
     voices? Comment on the tones
     of voice, or say the words aloud
     as you imagine them.

3.   Read the second stanza aloud
     as you imagine the
     headmistress would say it. How
     would you describe the tone?
     What kind of person do you
     think she is? Explain.

First reading continued

4.   What kind of person do you
     think the father is?

Second reading

5.   Why do you think Heidi dyed
     her hair?

6.   Why did Heidi's black friend
     have hers done? Explore the
     last stanza for clues.

7. 'It would have been unfair to mention | your mother's death, but that | shimmered behind the arguments.' What do you imagine people were thinking? Write out the thoughts that the father, or the headmistress or the teachers, might have had. What might Heidi herself have thought? Comment on the word 'shimmer'.

8. What kind of school do you suppose it was? Comment on the school's attitude and outlook as revealed in the poem. Do you think it was strict, 'stuffy', 'posh', reasonable, or what? Read the entire poem again before committing yourself.

9. Do you think the poem accurately reflects the demand for conformity found in school life? Do you find it true? Explain.

Third reading

10. Would you consider the father's attitude usual or unusual for a parent? Explain.

11. What truths about the life of a teenager do you find in this poem?

12. Do you think the poem is humorous? Mention two ways in which this humour is created. Is this note of humour maintained all the way through?

13. Make notes on the main themes and issues you find dealt with in the poem.

Mary Oliver (1935–)

Mary Oliver was born in 1935 in a small town in the Ohio countryside. Her direction in life was established at an early age when, as she puts it, 'I quickly found for myself two . . . blessings – the natural world and the world of writing.' Oliver attended Ohio State University and Vassar College but left without a degree so that she could devote herself to her writing. She believes that she developed her unique poetic 'voice' during the years she spent working alone on her writing with no desire for publication because, as she explains, 'I had to make my own decisions, without any social response.' However, she did receive very positive feedback following the publication of her first poetry collection in 1963 and has gone on to win numerous prizes for her writing, including the prestigious Pulitzer Prize

for Poetry. Although she is one of the most popular poets in the USA, she is reluctant to have her photograph used on her books or to talk about her private life, preferring to keep the emphasis on her work. 'I believe it is invasive of the work when you know too much about the writer, and almost anything is too much.'

The Sun

prescribed for exams in 2012 and 2013

Have you ever seen
anything
in your life
more wonderful

than the way the sun,   5
every evening,
relaxed and easy,
floats towards the horizon

and into the clouds or the hills,
or the rumpled sea,   10
and is gone –
and how it slides again

out of the blackness,
every morning,
on the other side of the world,   15
like a red flower

streaming upwards on its heavenly oils,
say, on a morning in early summer,
at its perfect imperial distance –
and have you ever felt for anything   20

such wild love –
do you think there is anywhere, in any language,
a word billowing enough
for the pleasure

that fills you,   25
as the sun
reaches out,
as it warms you

as you stand there,
empty-handed –   30
or have you too
turned from this world –

or have you too
gone crazy
for power,   35
for things?

EXPLORATIONS

1. Which do you prefer, the sunrise or the sunset? Why? If you have seen one in reality try to recall how it looked and what you felt as you watched it. You might like to write a short piece describing your experience.

First reading

2. Oliver has created a wonderful 'word picture' of the sun. Choose *one image* from the poem that you particularly like and explain why it appeals to you.

3. (a) What is being described in lines 5–11? (b) Are there any particular words in these lines that clearly suggest to you that this is the end of the day?

4. 'like a red flower

   streaming upward on its heavenly oils,

   say, on a morning in summer,

   at its perfect imperial distance – '

   (a) Do you think that the poet's use of 'a red flower' as a metaphor for the rising sun is effective? Why? What aspects of the sunrise does it suggest to you?

   (b) How does the poet suggest in these lines that a sunrise has a spiritual/religious quality?

   (c) How can the sun be said to be 'imperial'?

Second reading

5. (a) Do you agree with the suggestion found in lines 1–4 and lines 20–21 that sunrises and sunsets touch us not only visually, but also emotionally? (b) Why do you think that these moments can inspire 'such wild love' and 'pleasure' in people?

6. How are the reactions of the people in the final stanza to the sunrise and sunset different from the reactions that you considered in question 5? (b) Do you agree with the view that the poet expresses in the final stanza? Explain your answer.

7. (a) What effect does the absence of punctuation in lines 1 – 4 have on the speed, or pace, at which these lines are read? (b) What emotions are being expressed in these lines? (c) Do you feel that the pace of reading and the emotions in these lines work well together? Why?

Second reading continued

8. Now examine lines 5–9.
    (a) What effect do the four commas used here have on the pace of reading? (b) What is happening in these lines? (c) Does the poet's matching of the pace of reading to the meaning help you to imagine the scene? Explain your answer.

Third reading

9. Oliver is known for her exquisite 'lyrical' poetry. (a) What features of the lyric form are evident in this poem? (b) Do you consider this to be a successful lyric poem? Refer to the poem to support your answers.

10. Mary Oliver once wrote of nature, 'How can we ever stop looking? How can we ever turn away?' Has this poem encouraged you to keep 'looking' at nature or are you happy to 'turn away'? Write a piece outlining your feelings about the world of nature.

Brendan Kennelly (1936–)

Born in Ballylongford, County Kerry in 1936, Brendan Kennelly was Professor of Modern Literature at Trinity College Dublin for more than thirty years until his retirement in 2005. He has published over thirty books of poetry, among them *My Dark Fathers* (1964), *Dream of a Black Fox* (1968), *Salvation the Stranger* (1972), *Cromwell* (1983), *The Book of Judas* (1991) and *Poetry Me Arse* (1995).

A prolific poet, he writes about everything: love, nature, history, Kerry, and being alive. And he communicates in very direct, colloquial, down-to-earth language.

A Glimpse of Starlings

prescribed for exams in 2011 and 2012

I expect him any minute now although
He's dead. I know he has been talking
All night to his own dead and now
In the first heart-breaking light of morning
He is struggling into his clothes,   5
Sipping a cup of tea, fingering a bit of bread,
Eating a small photograph with his eyes.
The questions bang and rattle in his head
Like doors and canisters the night of a storm.
He doesn't know why his days finished like this   10
Daylight is as hard to swallow as food
Love is a crumb all of him hungers for.
I can hear the drag of his feet on the concrete path
The close explosion of his smoker's cough
The slow turn of the Yale key in the lock   15
The door opening to let him in
To what looks like release from what feels like pain
And over his shoulder a glimpse of starlings
Suddenly lifted over field, road and river
Like a fist of black dust pitched in the wind.   20

EXPLORATIONS

First reading

1. 'I expect him any minute now although | He's dead.' Judging by this first line, what do you expect you might find in this poem? Discuss in pairs or groups.

Second reading

2. Write three sentences about what you think is happening in this poem. Discuss in pairs or groups.

3. Focus on the first twelve lines, where the poet imagines what his recently dead father is thinking and feeling, his 'thoughts inside the head'.
   (a) What does he imagine the father doing on that morning?
   (b) How would you describe how the father feels – is he happy, sad, or what is he feeling? (c) What images make you think that? Explain.
   (d) 'Eating a small photograph with his eyes'. Discuss in pairs or groups what you think this might mean. Do you think it is an effective expression?
   (e) 'The questions bang and rattle in his head like doors and canisters the night of a storm'. Do you think this simile/comparison works well? Explain your thinking.

4. Do you think that, after death, our spirits may be like the father's – confused, disorientated, bewildered, needing the familiar, needing love? Discuss this.

Third reading

5. Focus on the final eight lines. The image of the father is realised through remembered familiar sounds. What are they?

6. 'The door opening to let him in | To what looks like release from what feels like pain'. (a) In your own words, what might the father be thinking here?
   (b) What is the effect of the qualifying phrases 'What looks like' and 'what feels like'?

7. (a) In the final three lines the focus moves beyond the father to 'a glimpse of starlings'. What does the image suggest to you? Discuss in groups.
   (b) The image then develops into a simile/comparison: 'Like a fist of black dust pitched in the wind'. Is this out of place or might it be appropriate in the circumstances? Discuss this.

Fourth reading

8. Do you think the poet was 'close to' his father? Explain your thinking with reference to words and phrases and to the emotions/ tone of the poem.

9. The poem is written in the present tense. What is the effect of this?

10. What do you like about this poem? Discuss it in pairs or groups and then write up your opinions.

Night Drive

prescribed for exams in 2013 and 2014

I

The rain hammered as we drove
Along the road to Limerick
'Jesus what a night' Alan breathed
And – 'I wonder how he is, the last account
Was poor.'   **5**
I couldn't speak.

The windscreen fumed and blurred, the rain's spit
Lashing the glass. Once or twice
The wind's fist seemed to lift the car
And pitch it hard against the ditch.   **10**
Alan straightened out in time,
Silent. Glimpses of the Shannon –
A boiling madhouse roaring for its life
Or any life too near its gaping maw,
White shreds flaring in the waste   **15**
Of insane murderous black;
Trees bending in grotesque humility,
Branches scattered on the road, smashed
Beneath the wheels.
Then, ghastly under headlights,   **20**
Frogs bellied everywhere, driven
From the swampy fields and meadows,
Bewildered refugees, gorged with terror.
We killed them because we had to,
Their fatness crunched and flattened in the dark.   **25**
'How is he now?' Alan whispered
To himself. Behind us,
Carnage of broken frogs.

II

His head
Sweated on the pillow of the white hospital bed.   30
He spoke a little, said
Outrageously, 'I think I'll make it.'
Another time, he'd rail against the weather,
(Such a night would make him eloquent)
But now, quiet, he gathered his fierce will   35
To live.

III

Coming home
Alan saw the frogs.
'Look at them, they're everywhere,
Dozens of the bastards dead.'   40

Minutes later –
'I think he might pull through now.'
Alan, thoughtful at the wheel, was picking out
The homeroad in the flailing rain
Nighthedges closed on either side.   45
In the suffocating darkness
I heard the heavy breathing
Of my father's pain.

EXPLORATIONS

Before reading

1. Have you ever been travelling in a car in severe weather conditions? If so, describe the weather, as you remember it.

First reading

2. How would you describe the weather in Section I? What images, words or phrases convey this best?

3. Think about the description of the Shannon:

   'A boiling madhouse roaring for its life
   Or any life too near its gaping maw'
   and also the image of 'Trees bending in grotesque humility'.

   Working in pairs, explore all possible suggestions from these lines. Use a dictionary for any difficult words.

4. What do you notice about the frogs? (a) What words or images are most effective? (b) How do you feel on reading these lines? (c) How does the writer feel about them? Where is this suggested? (d) What do the frogs add to the atmosphere of the section?

Second reading

5. What do you thin is happening in this poem? Who is in the car?

6. (a) How would you describe the atmosphere in the car? What words or phrases convey this best? (b) What do you notice about the differences between the two men?

7. What do you notice about the sick man in the hospital bed?

   What similarities and differences do you notice between the journeys to and from the hospital? Do you think the sick man will pull through? Explain your thinking.

Third reading

8. What does this poem say to you about death, love, and families? These are the themes.

9. Consider the descriptive language of this poem. Discuss some examples that you think particularly good.

10. Suggest a number of ways by which the poet conveys the tense, worried atmosphere.

Marge Piercy (1936–)

Marge Piercy was born on 31 March 1936 in a Detroit shattered by the economic hardships caused by the American Depression. Her father Robert, like many men at the time, had struggled to find work until he finally got a job installing and repairing machinery. Piercy credits her mother and grandmother as major influences in her life, both in stimulating her imagination and love of reading and in encouraging her to develop a strong sense of her Jewish heritage. Piercy began to write at the age of fifteen. She has always written both poetry and fiction and frequently writes both at the same time. Often she finds herself developing themes from a novel she is working on in her poetry: an approach that she claims, with some humour, helps her to avoid the dreaded 'writer's block'. Piercy was very much a part of the feminist movement of the 1960s and still works to improve the position of women as well as that of society itself in her wider political activism. She lives, and works, with her

husband, the writer Ira Wood, and a number of her beloved cats in Cape Cod. For Piercy, poetry is essential to the human condition because, as she explains,' you have to know why, you have to know who you are, you have to know what you're doing and why you're doing it. You have to know what you believe in . . . That's mostly poetry.'

Will we Work Together?

prescribed for exams in 2013 and 2014

You wake in the early grey
morning in bed alone and curse
me, that I am only
sometimes there. But when

I am with you, I light   5
up the corners, I am bright
as a fireplace roaring
with love, every bone in my back
and my fingers is singing
like a tea kettle on the boil.   10
My heart wags me, a big dog
with a bigger tail. I am
a new coin printed with
your face. My body wears
sore before I can express   15
on yours the smallest part
of what moves me. Words
shred and splinter.
I want to make with you
some bold new thing   20
to stand in the marketplace,
the statue of a goddess
laughing, armed and wearing
flowers and feathers. Like sheep
of whose hair is made   25
blankets and coats, I want
to force from this fierce sturdy
rampant love some useful thing.

Notes

[20] **bold:** brave, daring, courageous
[23] **armed:** bearing weapons
[27] **sturdy:** strong, powerful
[28] **rampant:** occurring in an unrestrained way, growing wildly,
      out of control

EXPLORATIONS

First reading

1. (a) How does the poet imagine her lover reacting to her not being beside him when he wakes up? (b) Does she seem to be offended by the fact that he curses her? (c) Why do you think she feels this way about his cursing?

2. (a) How do you feel when you wake up to a 'grey' morning? (b) Can you suggest why Piercy decided to open this poem with the image of her lover waking in the 'grey' morning?

3. Much of the poem, lines 4–18, is given over to the poet reminding her lover of how it is when she is there. Choose *one image* from this section that you feel really suggests the strength of her feelings, and explain the reasons for your choice.

4. Examine how the poet creates a strong sense of the physicality of her feelings in lines 4–18 by: (a) references to parts of the body; and (b) references to the senses of sight and touch.

First reading continued

5. 'I am bright | as a fireplace' (a simile); 'like a kettle on the boil' (a simile); 'My heart wags me, a big dog | with a bigger tail' (a metaphor); 'I am | a new coin printed with | your face' (a metaphor).

   Take each of the similes and metaphors quoted above and, in your own words, explain what she is trying to tell her lover about her feelings by using that simile or metaphor.

Second reading

6. 'I want to make with you some bold new thing'.

   (a) What do these lines tell you about what the poet wants to happen with their love? (b) Are you surprised that she feels this way given what she has said in lines 4–18, or can you understand her feelings?

7. 'the statue of a goddess laughing, armed and wearing flowers and feathers.'

   In ancient times a statue of a goddess was treated with great respect by the crowds in the marketplace and it would often survive for centuries. So the poet wants their relationship to involve respect and to be long-term. (a) Can you suggest what characteristics the other elements in the goddess's appearance stand for? (b) Do you think that they are good characteristics to have in a relationship? Why?

8. 'I want
   to force from this fierce sturdy rampant love some useful thing.'

   (a) How do these lines suggest the energy of their love?

   (b) Can you explain, in your own words, what the poet wants to do with this energy? (c) Do you think that she has been brave to tell him all this? Why?

Third reading

9. Do you see this as a poem about love or passion or commitment, or perhaps all three? Use references from the poem to support your view.

10. Imagine that you want to persuade Marge Piercy to come to your school to talk about this poem. Write a letter to her explaining why you particularly like this poem and why you think it is relevant to you and your fellow pupils.

Roger McGough (1937–)

Roger McGough was born in Liverpool and studied modern languages at Hull University. Along with Adrian Henri and Brian Patten, he popularised poetry in the 1960s as part of the Mersey Beat poets based in Liverpool. Their poetry put heavy emphasis on live performance and was therefore funny and accessible. It dealt with real concerns for ordinary working-class people. His poetry has been used a lot

in schools and he continues to be as popular today as he was in the 60s. He is often asked to promote poetry for events such as National Poetry Day. These days his poetry has become more conventional and he uses it to promote social and human rights issues.

Bearhugs

prescribed for exam in 2012

Whenever my sons call round we hug each other.
Bearhugs. Both bigger than me and stronger
They lift me off my feet, crushing the life out of me.
They smell of oil paint and aftershave, of beer
Sometimes and tobacco, and of women   5
Whose memory they seem reluctant to wash away.

They haven't lived with me for years,
Since they were tiny, and so each visit
Is an assessment, a reassurance of love unspoken.

I look for some resemblance to my family.   10
Seize on an expression, a lifted eyebrow,
A tilt of the head, but cannot see myself.

Though like each other, they are not like me.
But I can see in them something of my father.
Uncles, home on leave during the war.   15

At three or four, I loved throse straightbacked men
Towering above me, smiling and confident.
The whole world before them. Or so it seemed.

I look at my boys, slouched in armchairs
They have outgrown. See Tom in army uniform   20
And Finn in air force blue. Time is up.

Bearhugs. They lift me off my feet
And fifty years fall away. One son
After another, crushing the life into me.

EXPLORATIONS

First reading

1. (a) How would you explain the word 'Bearhugs'? (b) Did this title make you want to read the poem? Why?

2. McGough recalls his sons coming to visit him. Choose one image that helps you to picture the scene and explain why you chose it.

3. Using the information in the poem, describe McGough's two sons.

Second reading

4. What does the first stanza tell you about the type of relationship that the poet has with his sons?

5. 'They haven't lived with me for years,
   Since they were tiny, and so each visit
   Is an assessment, a reassurance of love unspoken.'

   (a) Why are his sons' visits very special to McGough? (b) Do you think he might feel differently if he had lived with them when they were growing up? Why?

6. (a) Who do his two sons remind him of? (b) In McGough's view, what characteristics and qualities do his sons share with his father and uncles?

Second reading continued

7. (a) Compare the way that McGough, as a boy, felt about his father and uncles with the way that he, as an adult, feels about his sons. (b) Are there any similarities between his feelings?

Third reading

8. 'I look for some resemblance to my family.'

   (a) Can you suggest why the poet wants to see if his sons look like him or the rest of his family? (b) Might this desire have anything to do with the fact that he did not live with them during their childhood?

9. Although McGough does not directly describe himself in the poem, there are clues about his physical appearance and his personality. Try to find as many of these clues as possible and then use them to write a description of how you picture him.

10. Imagine that you are one of McGough's sons. Write a diary entry of one of your meetings with your Dad, including what happened and your feelings.

Michael Longley (1939–)

Michael Longley was born in Belfast on 27 July 1939, of English parents. His father fought in the trenches in the First World War and was gassed, wounded, decorated, and promoted to the rank of captain. In *Tuppenny Stung*, a short collection of autobiographical chapters published in 1994, Longley describes his family, primary and secondary education and the forces of his early cultural formation: Protestant schoolboys' fears of the dark savageries supposedly practised by Catholics; an English education system dismissive of Irish culture and history; and Protestant Belfast's fear and resentment of the Republic. His early education and local socialisation made him aware of conflicting classes and religions, and of the duality of Irish identity.

Later he was educated at the Royal Belfast Academical Institution and in 1958 he went to Trinity College, Dublin, where he studied classics and wrote poetry but felt very under-read in English literature until taken in hand by his friend and young fellow-poet Derek Mahon.

Longley worked for the Arts Council of Northern Ireland in the period 1970–91, when he took early retirement. His work for the arts was driven by a number of guiding principles, including nurturing indigenous talent and providing support for artists, not just the arts, allied to the need to transcend class barriers and bring the arts to the working class. He was a champion of cultural pluralism, fostering the artistic expression of both sides of the religious and political divide.

His collections include: *No Continuing City* (1969); *An Exploded View* (1973); *The Echo Gate* (1979); and *Gorse Fires* (1991), which is centred on Longley's adopted second home of Carrigskeewaun in County Mayo.

Michael Longley is a fellow of the Royal Society of Literature and a member of Aosdána. He is married to the critic and academic Edna Longley.

Badger

For Raymond Piper

prescribed for exam in 2013

I

Pushing the wedge of his body
Between cromlech and stone circle,
He excavates down mine shafts
And back into the depths of the hill.

His path straight and narrow   5
And not like the fox's zig-zags,
The arc of the hare who leaves
A silhouette on the sky line.

Night's silence around his shoulders,
His face lit by the moon, he   10
Manages the earth with his paws,
Returns underground to die.

II

An intestine taking in
patches of dog's-mercury,
brambles, the bluebell wood;   15
a heel revolving acorns;
a head with a price on it
brushing cuckoo-spit, goose-grass;
a name that parishes borrow.

III

For the digger, the earth-dog   20
It is a difficult delivery
Once the tongs take hold,
Vulnerable his pig's snout
That lifted cow-pats for beetles,
Hedgehogs for the soft meat,   25

His limbs dragging after them
So many stones turned over,
The trees they tilted.

[2] **cromlech:** a name formerly used for the remains of a portal tomb; here the poet uses it to mean the horizontal slab on top of the upright stones

[14] **dog's mercury:** a herbaceous woodland plant, usually regarded as toxic

[19] **a name that parishes borrow:** the poet refers to broc, the Irish for 'badger' (in fact the element Broc found in place-names – for example Domhnach Broc, anglicised Donnybrook – is the man's name Broc)

EXPLORATIONS

First reading

Section I

1. Think of section I as a picture or painting. What do you see? Consider the setting described, the background, the lighting, and the main subject.

2. What do you notice about the badger? How do you visualise the animal? Examine the connotations of descriptive words and phrases, such as 'the wedge of his body'; 'Night's silence around his shoulders'; 'he | Manages the earth'. How do the badgers' paths differ from those of other animals, and what might this suggest about the nature of the badger?

3. What is suggested here about the animal's relationship with the earth? Consider his association with cromlech and stone circle; how he 'manages' the earth; how he 'Returns underground to die.'

4. Do you think the badger has particular significance for the poet? Explain.

5. How would you describe the atmosphere of section I? What words or phrases help to create it?

Second reading

Section II

6. What do you notice about the badger's diet?

7. What other aspects of the badger's environmental function are referred to in section II?

8. 'a head with a price on it . . . a name that parishes borrow.'

   What do these lines suggest about human attitudes to the badger?

Third reading

Section III

9. What do you think is happening in section III?

10. Contrast the humans' treatment of the environment in section III with the badger's management of the earth in sections I and II.

11. Do you think the poet has some sympathy for the animal in this section? Which phrases or images might suggest this?

12. Explore the ironies in the first stanza of this section.

Fourth reading

13. What point is the poet making about humankind's interaction with the environment?

14. What other themes do you notice in the poem?

15. Would you agree that 'Longley displays the scientific assurance of a naturalist'?

16. 'Longley's view of the west of Ireland is a realistic rather than a romantic one.' On the evidence of the poem 'Badger' would you agree with this statement? Refer to the text to support your argument.

17. Summarise your thoughts and feelings on this poem.

Tess Gallagher (1943–)

Tess Gallagher was born in 1943 in Port Angeles, Washington, USA, the eldest of five children. Her father Leslie worked as a logger, a dockhand and on the small ranch owned by the family. Writing was very much a part of her life from an early age and she wrote both poetry and fiction. Indeed, her first published work was a short story. It was when she joined a creative writing class conducted by the eminent poet Theodore Roethke at the University of Washington that, as Gallagher put it, 'poetry did rather kidnap me'. Her first, award-winning, book of poetry was published in 1976 and reflected Gallagher's roots 'in that generation of women writers who stepped forth out of the feminist revolution'. In later years, Gallagher has returned to short story writing, encouraged by her late husband, the writer Raymond Carver; and in poetry, her exploration of what it is to be a woman has become an honest inquiry into the nature of being human. Since the late 1960s, in between writing, teaching and working on films, Gallagher has visited Ireland regularly and has embraced Irish culture: delighting in singing 'traditional Irish dirge'; counting many Northern poets as her friends and collecting stories from the Irish story-telling tradition.

The Hug

prescribed for exams in 2013 and 2014

A woman is reading a poem on the street
and another woman stops to listen. We stop too,
with our arms around each other. The poem
is being read and listened to out here
in the open. Behind us   5
no one is entering or leaving the houses.

Suddenly a hug comes over me and I'm
giving it to you, like a variable star shooting light
off to make itself comfortable, then
subsiding. I finish but keep on holding   10
you. A man walks up to us and we know he hasn't
come out of nowhere, but if he could, he
would have. He looks homeless because of how
he needs. 'Can I have one of those?' he asks you,
and I feel you nod. I'm surprised,   15
surprised you didn't tell him how
it is – that I'm yours, only
yours, etc., exclusive as a nose to
its face. Love – that's what we're talking about, love
that nabs you with 'for me   20
only' and holds on.

So I walk over to him and put my
arms around him and try to
hug him like I mean it. He's got an overcoat on
so thick I can't feel   25
him past it. I'm starting the hug
and thinking, 'How big a hug is this supposed to be?
How long shall I hold this hug?' Already
we could be eternal, his arms falling over my
shoulders, my hands not   30
meeting behind his back, he is so big!
I put my head into his chest and snuggle

in. I lean into him. I lean my blood and my wishes
into him. He stands for it. This is his
and he's starting to give it back so well I know he's   35
getting it. This hug. So truly, so tenderly,
we stop having arms and I don't know if
my lover has walked away or what, or
if the woman is still reading the poem, or the houses –
what about them? – the houses.   40

Clearly, a little permission is a dangerous thing.
But when you hug someone you want it
to be a masterpiece of connection, the way the button
on his coat will leave the imprint of
a planet in my cheek   45
when I walk away. When I try to find some place
to go back to.

EXPLORATIONS

First reading

1. For Gallagher, 'the image is still the important element' in her poetry. Choose *one image* from 'The Hug' that you find particularly striking and explain the reasons for your choice.

2. (a) Describe, in your own words, the events that lead up to the poet giving her partner a hug in line seven. (b) Can you suggest why these events made her feel like hugging?

3. (a) What is her partner's reaction when the man asks 'Can I have one of those?' (b) How does the poet feel about this reaction? (c) How would you feel if your partner said it was fine for you to hug a stranger?

4. (a) Why do you think she decides to 'walk over' and hug the stranger? (b) Which one of the following words best describes how she feels as she begins to hug the stranger: happy, shy, uncomfortable? Explain your answer. (b) Would you feel the same if you were in her position? Why?

Second reading

5. (a) 'Suddenly a hug comes over me and I'm
    giving it to you'
    'I finish but keep on holding you.'
    Based on these lines, would you say that this is a one-person or a two-person hug? What clues lead you to this conclusion?

    (b) 'I lean my blood and my wishes
    into him. He stands for it. This is his
    and he's starting to give it back'

From your reading of these lines, would you say that this is a one-person or a two-person hug? Explain your answer.

6. 'He's got an overcoat on
    so thick I can't feel
    him past it.'
    'This hug. So truly, so tenderly, we stop having arms'

    (a) How do these lines show that her hug with the stranger changes from a physical action to an emotional one? (b) Is there any sense of this change in the description of her first hug with her partner in lines 7–11? Support your answer by reference to the poem. (c) Which of the two hugs, do you think, is closest to being 'a masterpiece of connection'? Give reasons for your answer.

Third reading

7. 'He looks homeless because of how | he needs'. (a) Can you suggest why the poet makes this link between being 'homeless' and having 'needs'? (b) Is the stranger the only person who 'needs' in this poem? Give reasons for your answer.

8. 'When I try to find some place | to go back to.' (a) Do you think that the poet is referring to a 'real' physical place, or an emotional 'place' or both, in these lines? (b) What 'place' was the poet in, before she hugged the stranger? (c) How does her sense of this 'place' change as she hugs the stranger in lines 36–40? (d) Discuss whether the poet could also be seen as being 'homeless' at the end of the poem.

9. Gallagher has related how some 'hardcore poetry people' wanted her to take 'The Hug' out of her book of poems because, as she explains, 'In the United States, if you have any jollity in a poem, it can't be a poem with a capital P.' (a) Can you suggest what the differences might be between a poem with a capital P and a poem with a small p? (b)Where do you think the 'jollity', or fun, lies in this poem? (c) Do you think that a poem can be fun and still be a poem with a capital P?

10. Imagine that you have decided to read 'a poem on the street'. What poem, from those that you have studied on the Leaving Certificate course, would you choose to read? Explain the reasons for your choice.

Paul Durcan (1944–)

Among the more notable of Paul Durcan's many collections are *The Berlin Wall Café* (1985), *Daddy Daddy* (1990), *A Snail in My Prime* (1993), *Christmas Day* (1996) and *Greetings to Our Friends in Brazil* (1999). He focuses on contemporary Ireland, particularly the west, and also on themes of political violence, love and marriage, and religion. He is well known for his satires directed at Church and state and for his zany wit. But much of his most moving poetry springs from his own life experience, for example the breaking up of his marriage in *The Berlin Wall Café* and the love–hate relationship with his father in *Daddy, Daddy*. 'Going Home to Mayo, Winter, 1949' is taken from the collection *Sam's Cross* (1978).

Going Home to Mayo, Winter, 1949

prescribed for exams in 2011 and 2012

Leaving behind us the alien, foreign city of Dublin
My father drove through the night in an old Ford Anglia,
His five-year-old son in the seat beside him,
The rexine seat of red leatherette,
And a yellow moon peered in through the windscreen.   5
'Daddy, Daddy,' I cried, 'pass out the moon,'
But no matter how hard he drove he could not pass out the moon.
Each town we passed through was another milestone
And their names were magic passwords into eternity:
Kilcock, Kinnegad, Strokestown, Elphin,   10
Tarmonbarry, Tulsk, Ballaghaderreen, Ballavarry;
Now we were in Mayo and the next stop was Turlough,
The village of Turlough in the heartland of Mayo,
And my father's mother's house, all oil-lamps and women,
And my bedroom over the public bar below,   15
And in the morning cattle-cries and cock-crows:
Life's seemingly seamless garment gorgeously rent
By their screeches and bellowings. And in the evenings
I walked with my father in the high grass down by the river
Talking with him – an unheard-of thing in the city.   20

But home was not home and the moon could be no more outflanked
Than the daylight nightmare of Dublin City:
Back down along the canal we chugged into the city
And each lock-gate tolled our mutual doom;
And railings and palings and asphalt and traffic lights,   25
And blocks after blocks of so-called 'new' tenements –
Thousands of crosses of loneliness planted
In the narrowing grave of the life of the father;
In the wide, wide cemetery of the boy's childhood.

Note

[4]   **rexine:** the brand name of a type of artificial leather used in upholstery

EXPLORATIONS

First reading

1. In the first part of the poem, what does the child notice about the journey? What aspects give it a magical quality for him?

2. What does the young boy like, in particular, about the family home in Turlough? What do you notice about the atmosphere of the place and how it is created? Look at the sights and sounds.

3. In the first part of the poem what evidence is there that the child is unhappy in Dublin?

Second reading

4. What do you think he means by the phrases 'But home was not home' and 'the moon could be no more outflanked'?

5. What images are used to signify the city, and what atmosphere is created? Describe the city as you think the speaker sees it.

6. In the poem, how does life in the city contrast with life in the country?

Second reading continued

7. How do you think the poet feels about both the country and the city? What exactly leads you to say this?

Third reading

8. What do you discover about the relationship between father and son in this poem?

9. Do you think Durcan captures well the child's view of the world? Refer to specific images or phrases of dialogue to support your views.

10. How do you understand the final three lines of the poem?

Fourth reading

11. Briefly explain the main themes you find in the poem. What has it to say about the country versus the city; one's place of origin; holidays; dreams and reality; a child's view of the world?

12. On the evidence of this poem, would you consider Durcan to be an idealist, a nostalgic person, or what?

13. Do you find this to be a sad or a happy poem? Comment.

Liz Lochhead (1947–)

Liz Lochhead was born in Scotland, in a Lanarkshire mining village, on 26 December 1947. As a child, she spent much of her time drawing and painting. She attended Glasgow School of Art from 1965 to 1970 and then taught art until 1979, when she became a full-time writer.

Although her early writing was mainly poetry, in the 1980s Lochhead also began to write for the stage. Much of her poetry explores what it is to be Scottish and what it is to be a woman, often in a humorous way; while her work as a playwright, featuring a number of adaptations of ancient Greek plays, explores what it is to be human.

Liz Lochhead has won many prizes for her work and in 1998 was listed

among 'Scotland's Fifty Most Influential Women' in a Scottish Sunday newspaper. She now lives in Glasgow with her architect husband.

Kidspoem/Bairnsang

prescribed for exam in 2014

---

it wis January
and a gey dreich day
the first day Ah went to the school
so my Mum happed me up in ma

good navy-blue napp coat wi th rid tartan hood   5
birled a scarf aroon ma neck
pu'ed oan ma pixie an' my pawkies
it wis that bitter
said noo ye'll no starve
gie'd me a wee kiss and a kid-oan skelp oan the bum   10
and sent me aff across the playground
tae the place Ah'd learn to say
it was January
and a really dismal day
the first day I went to school   15
so my mother wrapped me up in my
best navy-blue top coat with the red tartan hood,
twirled a scarf around my neck,
pulled on my bobble-hat and mittens
it was so bitterly cold   20
said now you won't freeze to death
gave me a little kiss and a pretend slap on the bottom
and sent me off across the playground
to the place I'd learn to forget to say
it wis January   25
and a gey dreich day
the first day Ah went to the school
so my Mum happed me up in ma
good navy-blue napp coat wi th rid tartan hood,
birled a scarf aroon ma neck,   30
pu'ed oan ma pixie an' my pawkies
it wis that bitter.
Oh saying it was one thing
but when it came to writing it
in black and white   35
the way it had to be said
was as if you were posh, grown-up, male, English and dead.

EXPLORATIONS

First reading

1. Explain, in your own words, what is happening between the little girl and her mother in this poem.

2. What picture do you get of the little girl from the images that Lochhead uses to describe her?

Second reading

3. Pick out two lines from the poem that you think sound very Scottish and explain why they sound Scottish to you.

4. (a) Find the same two lines that you chose for Question 2 in the English-sounding version and explain why they sound English to you. (b) Which version do you prefer? Why?

5. From the clues in the poem can you guess where the little girl spoke with a Scottish accent and where she spoke with an English accent?

6. (a) Can you suggest which accent the little girl felt most comfortable with? Why do you think that she felt like this?

Third reading

7. 'but when it came to writing it
   in black and white
   the way it had to be said

   was as if you were posh, grown-up, male, English and dead.'

   What does the tone, or the emotion, of these lines tell you about the little girl's feelings when she was made to write in this way?

8. Do you feel that Lochhead is correct in her description of the way you are expected to write in school as 'posh, grown-up, male, English and dead'? Give reasons for your answer.

9. (a) Do you think that the lines 1–12 might put some readers off finishing this poem? Why? (b) Would you advise them to keep on reading? Why?

10. (a) Imagine that you have just come home from a shopping trip or from a match. Write out the description you would give of your experience to (i) a friend of your own age and (ii) an adult you know. (b) In which piece were you most 'yourself'? Why do you think this was?

Penelope Shuttle (1947–)

Penelope Shuttle was born in Middlesex, England in 1947. From an early age Shuttle was very aware of the natural world, feeling that she was 'part of a continuum with nature and weather' and, as a teenager, she read, and was excited by, a wide range of poetry. In 1969 she met the poet and teacher Peter Redgrove and, in spite of a sixteen-year age difference, the two were drawn together by their 'affinity as poets'. Their marriage was immensely successful both personally and creatively with Shuttle and Redgrove continuing to write poetry and prose as individuals and as a collaborative pair until Redgrove's death in 2003. Their move to Cornwall in 1970 was equally successful, and Shuttle continues to live there today because for her 'Cornwall is an artist itself . . . with its glittering light and its granite shadows'.

Shuttle received the first of her many awards for writing in 1974 and she continues to participate actively in all aspects of the world of poetry, ranging from judging poetry competitions to giving readings of her work.

Jungian Cows

prescribed for exams in 2011, 2012 and 2013

In Switzerland, the people call their cows
Venus, Eve, Salome, or Fraulein Alberta,
beautiful names
to yodel across the pasture at Bollingen.

If the woman is busy with child or book,   5
the farmer wears his wife's skirt
to milk the most sensitive cows.

When the electric milking-machine arrives,
the stalled cows rebel and sulk
for the woman's impatient skilful fingers   10
on their blowzy tough rosy udders,
will not give their milk;

so the man who works the machine
dons cotton skirt, all floral delicate flounces
to hide his denim overalls and big old muddy boots,   15
he fastens the cool soft folds carefully,
wraps his head in his sweetheart's sunday-best fringed scarf,
and walks smelling feminine and shy among the cows,

till the milk spurts, hot, slippery and steamy
into the churns,   20
Venus, Salome, Eve, and Fraulein Alberta,
lowing, half-asleep,
accepting the disguised man as an echo of the woman,
their breath smelling of green, of milk's sweet traditional climax.

Notes

Jungian: Carl Jung was a Swiss psychiatrist whose work in psychology is still influential today. His ideas have also influenced a number of poets, including Penelope Shuttle and her husband Peter Redgrove.

Cows: One of Jung's theories concerns the 'collective unconscious' (the feelings and thoughts about universal themes, or archetypes, that humans as a group inherit from earlier groups).

Jung identified several key archetypes that recur, e.g. the mother. One of the symbols used to represent the mother archetype is the cow. So, for example, the ancient Egyptian goddess Hathor was often shown as a cow to emphasise her 'motherly' qualities. The cow has also been used to symbolise qualities traditionally held to be feminine, e.g. concern for the community or group, being instinctive. Jung believed that men have some feminine elements within them.

[4]   **Bollingen:** a small village located on the north bank of Lake Zurich, Switzerland. Jung built a holiday home there and lived in it for several months each year.

[9]   **stalled:** to stop; to be put in a compartment in a cowshed

[11]   **blowzy:** rough-looking

[14]   **flounces:** a frill

EXPLORATIONS

First reading

1. Do you find this an amusing poem? Pick out the parts of the poem that amused you.

2. Using the clues in stanza 2, who, do you think, usually milks 'the most sensitive cows'? Can you suggest a reason why this is?

3. (a) What does stanza 3 tell you about how the cows reacted to the 'electric milking-machines'? (b) Are you surprised by their reaction? Why?

4. (a) What did 'the farmer' and 'the man who works the machine' do to persuade the cows to give the milk? (b) From your reading of the poem, would you say that the men were comfortable or uncomfortable about what they had to do?

5. (a) Do you think the cows were really fooled by what the men did? Refer to the poem to support your view. (b) Can you suggest why the cows decided to co-operate?

Second reading

6. (a) Divide a page into two columns. Put the heading 'Female' on one column and 'Male' on the other. Go through the poem and pick out all the words and phrases that are connected to 'Female' and write them in the female column and then do the same for 'Male' in the male column. (b) Using your lists, write a description, in your own words, of how being 'Female' is portrayed in the poem, and then do the same with 'Male'. (c) Do you agree with the two portrayals? Explain your answer.

7. (a) Who would you say holds the most power in this poem, the male figures or the female figures? Support your view with quotations from the poem. (b) Given the lists that you made for question 7, are you surprised by this distribution of power? Why?

8. 'till the milk spurts, hot, slippery and steamy'; 'their breath smelling of green, of milk's sweet traditional climax'.

   (a) How does the poet suggest in these lines that milk is a comforting and nourishing food that promotes life?

   'Venus, Eve, Salome and Fraulein Alberta,'

   'accepting the disguised man as an echo of the woman'

   (b) What do you think the poet is suggesting here about the connection between female figures and the production and collection of milk, the promoter of life?

Third reading

9. The poet uses the word 'traditional' in the final line of the poem. A tradition is a custom passed down through the generations. (a) What traditions can you find in this poem? (b) Do you think we should always keep to the traditional way of doing things? Why?

10. Tell the story of this situation from the point of view of either (a) 'the man who works the machine' or (b) one of 'the stalled cows'.

Zoo Morning

prescribed for exam in 2014

Elephants prepare to look solemn and move slowly
though all night they drank and danced, partied
and gambled, didn't act their age.

Night-scholar monkeys take off their glasses,
pack away their tomes and theses,   5
sighing as they get ready for yet another long day
of gibbering and gesticulating, shocking
and scandalising the punters.

Bears stop shouting their political slogans
and adopt their cute-but-not-really teddies' stance   10
in the concrete bear-pit.

Big cats hide their flower presses, embroidery-frames
and watercolours;
grumbling, they try a few practice roars.
Their job is to rend the air, to devour carcasses,   15
to sleep-lounge at their vicious carnivorous ease.

What a life.
But none of them would give up show-business.

The snakes who are always changing,
skin after skin,   20
open their aged eyes and hinged jaws in welcome.

Between paddock and enclosure
we drag our unfurred young.
Our speech is over-complex, deceitful.
Our day is not all it should be.   25
The kids howl, baffled.

All the animals are very good at being animals.
As usual, we are not up to being us.
Our human smells prison us.

In the insect house   30
the red-kneed spider dances on her eight light fantastics;
on her shelf of silence she waltzes and twirls;
joy in her hairy joints, her ruby-red eyes.

EXPLORATIONS

Before reading

1. Think back to a visit you made to the zoo or to nature programmes you watched on television. How would you describe each of the following animals to a young child? Elephants, monkeys, bears, big cats, snakes and spiders. Jot down words and phrases that capture how they move and behave.

2. On first reading this poem what do you notice?

3. Did you enjoy the descriptions of the dual life of elephants? Explain your reaction.

4. (a) What do the monkeys in their night life personas remind you of? (b) Do you think she describes the day life of the monkeys well? Explain.

5. (a) How does she imagine the hidden life of bears? (b) How does she feel about everyday bears? Do you think her description has caught an essential truth about the animals?

6. In pairs, explore: (a) The contrast between daytime and night-time lives of big cats. What do you notice? (b) What words or phrases best catch their frightening fierceness? (c) What patterns are emerging in this poem? (d) Can you suggest what the poet might be up to?

Second reading

7. (a) When you saw the snakes opening their hinged jaws did you feel welcomed? (b) Does this description fit in with the tone of the poem?

8. (a) 'Between paddock and enclosure . . .' Do you think this section describes accurately the experience of some family outings to the zoo? Develop your ideas. (b) 'our unfurred young.' What is the poet suggesting here, do you think? (c) 'our speech is complex, deceitful'. Discuss what this might mean and how it links to the rest of the poem.

9. Do you agree with what the poet is suggesting about human beings here?

10. Do you think the poet admires the spider? Explain your thinking. How does this stanza link with the previous one?

Third reading

11. The poet is turning the world as we see it on its head to make us view it afresh and really think about it. What does this poem make you think about? These are the themes.

12. Will your next visit to the zoo provoke new thoughts? Explain.

Noel Monahan (1948–)

Noel Monahan taught English at St Clare's College, Ballyjamesduff, County Cavan. He grew up on a farm near Granard, County Longford, and was educated at Maynooth College where he studied English, history and philosophy.

He has published four collections of poetry: *Opposite Walls* (1991); *Snowfire* (1995); *Curse of the Birds* (2000); and *Funeral Games* (2004), from which the poem 'All Day Long' is taken. His poetry has been translated into Italian, Romanian, French and Russian. He has won many awards for both poetry and drama.

All Day Long

prescribed for exams in 2011 and 2012

At school we see
Ink spilt on the floor.
Children get bored
Counting, conjugating verbs . . .
All day long.   5

You never know
When some disappear
You never know
Where to find them.

Teachers are patient,   10
See with their eyes.
Children, not easily tamed,
See with their hearts,

And are made to sit in rows,
In blue and navy uniforms.   15

How can you know
When some disappear?
How can you know
Where to find them?

Principals, Deputy Principals,   20
Constantly counting the children,
Mornings and afternoons
Names and numbers put on files.

One never knows
When they go missing   25
One never knows
Where to find them.

EXPLORATIONS

Before reading

1. Choose any school day this
    week. In your mind, re-run the
    main events from morning to
    evening. In the main, was the
    day enjoyable, boring, helpful,
    a waste of time, or what?
    Describe how you felt about
    the day.

First reading

2. Look at the details in the first
    stanza. (a) What do you notice
    about the state of the
    classroom and about the
    lesson being conducted? (b) Is
    this different from the
    classroom and the lessons you
    are used to nowadays?

First reading continued

3. Now read the rest of the poem again. (a) What do you notice about the teachers? (b) What are their preoccupations concerning the school? (c) Do you think the teachers are coping well with issues in the school? Discuss this in pairs or groups.

Second reading

4. In groups, discuss how relevant you think school is to your lives. (a) In what ways is it relevant and in what ways irrelevant? (b) What do you usually do when you find that some lessons are not relevant, not interesting or just too difficult?

Second reading continued

5. Where do the children in the poem disappear to? Using insight from your own experience, describe their state of mind.

Third reading

6. What do you think the poem is saying about schooling and education? Refer to the text to support your views.

7. How would you describe the poet's attitude to the teachers?

8. Do you think he understands students well?

9. Read the title aloud. Do you think it accurately conveys the main theme of this poem? Explain.

Kerry Hardie (1951–)

Kerry Hardie was born in Singapore in 1951, grew up in County Down, studied English at York University and now lives in County Kilkenny. She has won many prizes for her poetry. Among her collections are: *In Sickness* (1995); *A Furious Place* (1996); *Cry for the Hot Belly* (2000); *The Sky Didn't Fall* (2003), from which 'Daniel's Duck' is taken; and *The Silence Came Close* (2006).

Daniel's Duck

prescribed for exams in 2011, 2012, 2013 and 2014

I held out the shot mallard, she took it from me,
looped its neck-string over a drawer of the dresser.
The children were looking on, half-caught.
Then the kitchen life – warm, lit, glowing –
moved forward, taking in the dead bird,   5
and its coldness, its wildness, were leaching away.

The children were sitting to their dinners.
Us too – drinking tea, hardly noticing
the child's quiet slide from his chair,
his small absorbed body before the duck's body,   10
the duck changing – feral, live –
arrowing up out of black sloblands
with the gleam of a river
falling away below.

Then the duck – dead again – hanging from the drawer-   15
      knob,
the green head, brown neck running into the breast,
the intricate silvery-greyness of the back;
the wings, their white bars and blue flashes,
the feet, their snakey, orange scaliness, small claws, piteous   20
      webbing,
the yellow beak, blooded,
the whole like a weighted sack –
all that downward-dragginess of death.

He hovered, took a step forward, a step back,   25
something appeared in his face, some knowledge
of a place where he stood, the world stilled,
the lit streaks of sunrise running off red
into the high bowl of morning.

She watched him, moving to touch, his hand out: 30
What is it Daniel, do you like the duck?
He turned as though caught in the act,
saw the gentleness in her face and his body loosened.
I thought there was water on it –
he was finding the words, one by one,   35
holding them out, to see would they do us –
but there isn't.
He added this on, going small with relief
that his wing-drag of sounds was enough.

Notes

[1]   **mallard:** a type of wild duck
[6]   **leaching:** being drained away or sucked out
[11] **feral:** wild
[12] **sloblands:** muddy ground or land
[21] **piteous:** pitiful

EXPLORATIONS

First reading

1. Focus on the first two sections. (a) Describe in sequence what happens. (b) What do you notice about the kitchen, the reaction of the children and the reaction of the adults?

2. Focus on the description of the duck in the third section. Read it a number of times, then close your eyes and imagine it in detail. Now write a brief but detailed description of it.

3. What are your feelings on reading the description of the dead duck? Discuss them in groups.

4. Read the fourth section. Imagine you are Daniel. (a) What do you see? (b) What thoughts are going through your head? (c) What thoughts might be going through the mother's head?

5. This incident provokes a moment of insight or new understanding (an epiphany) for each of the participants, the writer, the mother and Daniel. Describe each of these, using evidence from the text to support your ideas.

6. What do you think are the main issues or themes this poem deals with? Develop your ideas on this.

7. Do you think the poet has a very good eye for observation? Support your ideas with evidence from the poem.

8. Imagine that you meet Daniel as an adult in later years and he remembers the incident. Write the dialogue as you think it might occur.

9. Write three paragraphs on what you liked about this poem and why.

10. How different from your own is the world of this poem?

11. Do you think the writer should have brought the duck into the kitchen?

Paul Muldoon (1951–)

Paul Muldoon was born in County Armagh and educated at Queen's University, Belfast. After leaving college he went to work as a producer for BBC Radio in Belfast. He also lived for a while in Dingle, County Kerry. Since then he has worked mainly as an academic; much of his teaching has been in the creative writing programme at Princeton University in the USA. Recently, he was appointed to the prestigious position of Professor of Poetry at the University of Oxford.

Muldoon is a brilliant technical poet. He is equally at ease writing sonnets and long poems, lyric and narrative poetry. Some of his poetry is written about the North, but often only incidentally. He uses puns and word associations in a very deliberate way. His collections include *Mules*, *New Weather*, *Why Brownlee Left*, *Quoof*, *Meeting the British*, *Madoc: A Mystery*, *The Annals of Chile* and, most recently, *Hay*. His *Selected Poems* (1968–94) is probably the best introduction to his work.

Anseo

prescribed for exams in 2011, 2012 and 2013

When the Master was calling the roll
At the primary school in Collegelands,
You were meant to call back Anseo
And raise your hand
As your name occurred.   5
Anseo, meaning here, here and now,
All present and correct,
Was the first word of Irish I spoke.
The last name on the ledger
Belonged to Joseph Mary Plunkett Ward   10
And was followed, as often as not,
By silence, knowing looks,
A nod and a wink, the Master's droll
'And where's our little Ward-of-court?'

I remember the first time he came back   15
The Master had sent him out
Along the hedges
To weigh up for himself and cut
A stick with which he would be beaten.
After a while, nothing was spoken;   20
He would arrive as a matter of course
With an ash-plant, a salley-rod.
Or, finally, the hazel-wand
He had whittled down to a whip-lash,
Its twist of red and yellow lacquers   25
Sanded and polished,

And altogether so delicately wrought
That he had engraved his initials on it.

I last met Joseph Mary Plunkett Ward
In a pub just over the Irish border.   30
He was living in the open,
In a secret camp
On the other side of the mountain.
He was fighting for Ireland,
Making things happen.   35
And he told me, Joe Ward,
Of how he had risen through the ranks
To Quartermaster, Commandant:
How every morning at parade
His volunteers would call back Anseo   40
And raise their hands
As their names occurred.

EXPLORATIONS

Before reading

1. What are your own memories of primary school, your teachers, friends and characters in your own class – especially the ones that got into a lot of trouble?

First reading

2. What does the word 'Anseo' mean? When was it used in school?

3. Describe the 'master'. What does his title say about him?

First reading continued

4. Why are Ward's forenames important?

5. What is Ward's life like at the end of the poem?

6. What do you imagine his soldiers' lives are like under his command?

Second reading

7. Why do you think Ward takes such care with the stick? Suggest reasons.

8. The narrator of the poem and the master use puns. Isolate each pun and explain what they are referring to.

11. How do the first and last verses mirror each other? What point do you think the poet is making here?

Third reading

9. The tone in the first verse is very unemotional. What effect does this have on your reading of the poem? Does the tone change later on? If so, how?

10. What contradictions are in the poem?

Fourth reading

12. 'What comes around goes around.' Do you think that this saying is relevant to the poem?

13. What is your own reaction to the life and experiences of Joseph Mary Plunkett Ward?

14. What do you think this poem is saying about life?

Julie O'Callaghan (1954–)

Julie O'Callaghan was born in Chicago in 1954 and moved to Ireland in 1974. Her poetry for children is particularly popular and appears in a number of children's anthologies. Her poetry for adults is highly regarded and in 2001 she won the Michael Hartnett Poetry Award.

In April 2003, Julie O'Callaghan was made a member of Aosdána in recognition of the contribution that she has made to the arts in Ireland. She lives in Kildare with her husband, Dennis O'Driscoll, who is also a writer.

Problems

prescribed for exam in 2013

Take weeds for example.
Like how they will overrun
your garden and your life
if you don't obliterate them.
But forget about weeds   5
– what about leaves?
Snails use them as handy
bridges to your flowers
and hordes of thuggish slugs
will invade – ever thought about *that*?   10
We won't even go into
how leaves block up the gutters.
I sure hope you aren't neglecting
any puddles of water in your bathtub
– discoloration will set in.   15
There is the wasp problem,
the storms problem, the grass
growing-between-the-bricks-in-the-driveway problem.
Then there's the remembering to
lock-all-the-windows problem.   20
Hey, knuckleheads!
I guess you just don't appreciate
how many problems there are.

Notes

[4]   **obliterate:** destroy completely
[9]   **thuggish:** behaving in violent and lawless ways
[21] **knuckleheads:** stupid people

EXPLORATIONS

First reading

1. (a) Count the number of problems mentioned in the 23 lines of this poem. Would you agree with the poet's decision to give this poem the title 'Problems'? Explain your answer. (b) Some of the problems are vividly described. Choose the two descriptions you like the most and explain why you like them.

2. A lot of the lines in this poem are short, made up of only four or five words. (a) What effect does this have on the pace, or speed, at which this poem is read? Experiment with reading it quickly and slowly and discuss which sounds better. (b) Does the pace that you agreed on suggest anything to you about the speaker's feelings?

Second reading

3. ' – ever thought about that?'
   'Hey, knuckleheads!'
   'I guess you just don't appreciate how many problems there are.'

   (a) How would you describe the speaker's tone of voice in these lines? (b) What does this tone reveal about the speaker's attitude to the way in which other people view the problems that she is worried about? (c) Do you think she is right to worry about these problems? Why?

4. ' – what about leaves?
   Snails use them as handy
   bridges to your flowers
   and hordes of thuggish slugs
   will invade . . .'

   (a) Describe in your own words the picture that you see when you read these lines. (b) How does the poet's use of rhyme in the phrase 'thuggish slugs' help to make the image of the slugs more memorable?

5. The speaker in the poem tends to exaggerate her problems. Do you think she does this because she is trying to be funny or because she is worried? Explain your answer.

6. In one sentence, sum up what you think the theme, or message, of this poem is.

7. Examine how the poet creates the impression that the speaker in this poem is in conversation with someone else. You might like to look at (a) the type of language used, (b) the structure of the phrases and (c) the use of questions.

8. A dramatic monologue is where a person speaks and through what is said reveals his/her character. From your readings of this poem, how would you describe the character of the speaker?

9. Imagine that you are a magazine 'Agony Aunt/Uncle' answering problems sent in to you by readers. You have received this poem in the post. Write your reply.

10. The writer of this poem, Julie O'Callaghan, has said ' I think it (poetry) should be a haven of quietness where you can hear yourself think.' What has this poem made you think about?

The Net

prescribed for exam in 2011 and 2014

I am the Lost Classmate
being hunted down the superhighways
and byways of infinite cyber-space.
How long can I evade the class committee
searching for my lost self?   5

I watch the list
of Found Classmates
grow by the month.
Corralled into a hotel ballroom
Festooned with 70s paraphernalia,   10

bombarded with atmospheric
hit tunes, the Captured Classmates
from Sullivan High School
will celebrate thirty years
of freedom from each other.   15

I peek at the message board:
my locker partner,
out in California, looks forward
to being reunited with
her old school chums.   20

Wearing a disguise, I calculate
the number of months left
for me to do what I do best,
what I've always done:
slip through the net.   25

Notes

[4]   **evade:** avoid
[9]   **Corralled:** to be put into an enclosure, often used in
      connection with cattle or other animals
[10] **paraphernalia:** various objects
[11] **bombarded:** to attack with objects or to question a person
      constantly

EXPLORATIONS

Before reading

1. (a) The title of this poem is 'The Net'. How many different types of net can you think of? You might like to collect pictures to show the types of 'net' that you have suggested. (b) Do the different types of net have anything in common?

First reading

2. (a) What type of net is described in the first stanza of the poem? (b) Pick out the words that lead

First reading continued

you to this conclusion. (c) From your reading of lines 1–8, can you explain what is being organised using this net?

3. (a) Why do you think the poet describes herself as 'the Lost Classmate' in line one? (b) Can you explain why she refers to the person that she was when she was at school as 'my lost self'?(b) Do you agree with the poet's view that as a person goes though life he/she can have different 'selves'? Give reasons for your answer.

First reading continued

4. (a) In your own words, describe how the poet imagines the scene in the 'hotel ballroom' in lines 9–12. (b) Do the images she uses suggest that she considers it a pleasant or an unpleasant experience?

Second reading continued

Sullivan High School to make her react in the way that she does to the reunion?

8. Given the poet's reaction to the class reunion, are you surprised that she keeps checking the reunion website? Why?

Second reading

5. Using the clues in the first and last stanzas, do you get the impression that the poet does or does not want to be found by the 'class committee'?

6. (a) List all the different words that you would use to describe someone who is your 'friend'. (b) Do the words 'locker partner' in line 17 suggest to you that this person was a 'friend' of the poet's? Explain your answer.

7. From your reading of the poem, what do you think happened during the poet's time at

Third reading

9. 'slip through the net'. (a) How is the net that appears in the final line of the poem different from the net that was described in the first stanza? Explain your answer. (b) As far as the poet is concerned, what are the two nets trying to do to her?

10. Imagine that you are the poet when she was in her teens attending Sullivan High School. Write her diary entry in which she describes her experiences during a day at school.

Carol Ann Duffy (1955–)

Carol Ann Duffy was born in Glasgow of Irish parents but grew up in Staffordshire, England. She attended university in Liverpool, where she studied philosophy. Her poetry very often gives voice to the powerless or the mad. She is very adept at putting herself in somebody else's head and then writing from their perspective, be they psychopaths, maids or tabloid editors. Her poetry has a wry humour and a lot of people who would not regularly read poetry are comfortable with her style.

She has won many awards for her

collections, which include *Standing Female Nude* (1985), *Selling Manhattan* (1987), *The Other Country* (1990), *Mean Time* (1993) and *The World's Wife* (1998). This last collection featured a series of poems written from the perspective of the forgotten female: Mrs Midas, Queen Kong, Mrs Lazarus and others.

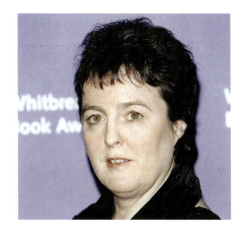

Valentine

prescribed for exams in 2011 and 2014

Not a red rose or a satin heart.
I give you an onion.
It is a moon wrapped in brown paper.
It promises light
like the careful undressing of love.   5
Here.
It will blind you with tears
like a lover.
It will make your reflection
a wobbling photo of grief.   10
I am trying to be truthful.
Not a cute card or a kissogram.
I give you an onion.
Its fierce kiss will stay on your lips,
possessive and faithful   15
as we are,
for as long as we are.
Take it.
Its platinum loops shrink to a wedding-ring,
if you like.   20
Lethal.
Its scent will cling to your fingers,
cling to your knife.

EXPLORATIONS

Before reading

1. What do you associate with Valentine's Day?

First reading

2. What is your first reaction on reading this poem? Discuss the various reactions.
3. The onion is given four times. With what is it associated each time?
4. Is there anything at all romantic about this poem?

Second reading

5. How long will the taste of onion stay on the lover's lips? How long will the couple last?
6. What type of relationship do the couple have? Have they been in love for long?
7. How does the onion promise light?

Third reading

8. How would you feel if you were given an onion for Valentine's Day?
9. The poet uses very short lines regularly in the poem. What effect do these short lines have?
10. Describe each metaphor that the speaker uses to describe the onion.

Fourth reading

11. Read 'My mistress's eyes . . .' by William Shakespeare and compare it with this poem.
12. This poem manages to be 'cold and passionate'. How?
13. Do you think that this is a good love poem? What makes it good or bad?
14. 'Love is particular to individuals and can't be represented by Love Hearts and Teddy Bears.' Does the poet agree? Do you?

Peter Sirr (1960–)

Born in County Waterford in 1960, Peter Sirr went on to attend Trinity College, Dublin before spending some years in the Netherlands and Italy. During this time, his poetic talent gained early recognition when he was awarded the Patrick Kavanagh Award in 1982, and the publication of his first collection of poetry, *Marginal Zones*, in 1984 excited considerable interest. On his return to Dublin, he became the first Director of the Irish Writers' Centre, holding this post until 2003 when, as he puts it, he 'opted for the fruitful wilderness of freelance-dom'. Subsequently, while working as a freelance writer and translator, he also acted as the editor of *Poetry Ireland Review* for a number of editions, relishing the 'poetic adventure' of hunting for poems that 'cause the hair on the back of the neck to stand up'. For Sirr, a poem is the result of a finely balanced interaction between emotion and words, as he explains: 'The poem which makes a successful emotional appeal must have a core of ice, must be built on formal attentiveness to language, line break, diction, syntax, technique.' Peter Sirr lives in Dublin with his wife, the poet and teacher Enda Wyley, and their daughter.

Madly Singing in the City

after Po Chü-i

prescribed for exams in 2013 and 2014

And often, when I have finished a new poem,
I climb to the dark roof garden
and lean on a rail over an ocean of streets.
What news I have for the sleeping citizens
and these restless ones, still shouting their tune   5
in the small hours. Fumes rise from the chip-shop
and I am back at the counter, waiting my turn.
Cod, haddock, plaice, whiting.
The long queue moves closer;
men in white coats paint fish with batter,   10
chips leap in the drying tray.
There's a table reserved for salt and vinegar
where the hot package is unswaddled,
salted, drenched, wrapped again
and borne out into the darkness.   15
In darkness I lean out, the new words ready,
the spires attentive. St. Werburgh's, St. Patrick's, Nicholas
Of Myra. Nearby the Myra Glass Company
from where we carried the glass table-top.
In a second I will sing, it will be as if   20
a god has leaned with me, having strolled over
from either of the two cathedrals, or from the green
and godly domes of Iveagh Buildings.
Ever since I was banished from the mountains
I have lived here in the roar of the streets.   25
Each year more of it enters me, I am grown
populous and tangled. The thousand ties of life
I thought I had escaped have multiplied.
I stand in the dark roof garden, my lungs swelling
with the new poem, my eyes filled with buildings   30
and people. I let them fill, then,
without saying a word, I go back down.

Po Chü-i: a poet who lived in China from AD772 to 846. He worked as a government official but, because of his determination to speak out against those in power and to highlight social problems, he was banished on a number of occasions. His poetry is characterised by simplicity and clarity and flashes of sharp humour.

[13] **unswaddled:** unwrapped. Babies were once swaddled: cloth was wrapped closely around the baby's arms, body and legs to make a type of cocoon.

[17] **St. Werburgh's:** a church in Dublin. The original was built in 1178 and was later rebuilt in 1715.

[17] **St. Patrick's:** St Patrick's Cathedral, Dublin, Ireland's largest church, which dates from the thirteenth century. Said to have been founded beside a well used by St Patrick for baptisms in AD450.

[17] **Nicholas of Myra:** the Church of St Nicholas of Myra, Dublin, built in the seventeenth century. For a time it acted as a Pro-Cathedral.

[22] **two cathedrals:** St Patrick's and Christchurch Cathedrals

[23] **Iveagh Buildings:** buildings commissioned by the Earl of Iveagh to replace the slums that surrounded St Patrick's Cathedral in Edwardian Dublin

[27] **populous:** densely inhabited, full of people

EXPLORATIONS

Before reading

1. Think back to a time when you were working really hard at something that took lot of effort but when you finished you were really pleased with the result. It could be when you had a summer job, or doing your homework, or fixing something, or a sports training session, or finishing an exam, etc. (a) Describe what you were doing. (b) How did you feel as you were working on the task? Did you want to give up at any stage? If you did, what stopped you giving up? (c) How did you feel when it was finished and you knew that you had done really well? Did you tell anyone about how good you felt? Did you do anything to celebrate? You might like to tell your story to the class and then to write a short piece describing your experience.

2. (a) Why does the poet feel like celebrating? (b) How does he want to celebrate successfully completing his task? (c) Are there any similarities between his feelings and the feelings that you remembered in Question 1?

3. In your own words, describe how you picture the scene that the poet looks down on in lines 1–6.

4. (a) Do you find it easy to imagine the chip shop based on the poet's description in lines 7–15? Why? (b) Are you surprised to find a chip shop appearing in a poem? Can you suggest why the poet decided to include it in his description of Dublin? (c) How do you feel about the idea of a poet going into a chip shop?

5. (a) From your reading of the poem, can you work out how long the poet has been living in Dublin? Support your answer by reference to the poem. (b) Would you say that he has settled in well there? Why?

6. 'What news I have for the sleeping citizens
and these restless ones, still shouting their tune' (lines 4–5)
'In darkness I lean out, the new words ready' (line 16)
'In a second I will sing, it will be as if
a god has leaned with me' (lines 20–21).

   The lines above show how the poet is on the verge of 'singing' his poem out over the city on a number of occasions. However, each time he is distracted by something. For each of the quotations above, examine the poem to find out what it is that distracts him from singing.

7. 'I stand in the dark roof garden, my lungs swelling
with the new poem, my eyes filled with buildings
and people. I let them fill, then, without saying a word, I go back down.'

   (a) Given that the title of this poem is 'Madly Singing in the City', are you surprised that the poet goes 'back down' without making a sound? Why? (b) Can 'Singing' be an internal as well as an external experience? (c) 'Singing' can mean celebrating something in verse. What do you think the poet celebrates in verse in this poem?

(d) What does his use of the word 'Madly' suggest about his feelings? You may find it helpful to look up 'Madly' in the dictionary.

8. Sirr uses everyday conversational language in this poem, but he arranges it in such a way that we really see and feel what he is writing about. (a) Examine how his use of the word 'ocean' in line 3 helps you to 'see' the view as he stands in the roof garden. (b) Why do you think Sirr uses the word 'unswaddled' to describe unwrapping the chips in line 13? What is he trying to tell us about how the chips were wrapped? (c) How do the commas and the rhythm of the words in line 14 suggest the feeling of people working quickly to keep the chips warm? (d) Choose another line where you think Sirr uses a word or phrase that really helps you to see or feel what he is writing about, and explain why you chose it.

9. In this poem, Sirr celebrates his space in the world, the centre of Dublin city, where he mixes with people and buildings, eats, makes memories, forms relationships and writes poetry: in short, the space where he lives. Write a paragraph or a poem entitled 'My Space' celebrating the space in the world where you live.

10. Peter Sirr has written, 'Poets can often seem to be working a narrow little seam of private experience. They don't seem to get out much.' Write a presentation, to be given to your class, entitled ' My views on what makes a good poet'. Use references or examples from your work on the Leaving Certificate Poetry course to illustrate your talk.

Simon Armitage (1963–)

Simon Armitage was born in Huddersfield and studied geography at Portsmouth Polytechnic. He is a very prolific poet, having published seven books since 1989: *Zoom!* (1989); *Kid* (1992); *Book of Matches* (1993); *The Dead Sea Poems* (1995); *Cloudcuckooland* (1996); a book about Iceland, *Moon Country* (1996); and a prose book about life in Northern England, *All Points North* (1998). Most recently he edited a major anthology of British and Irish poetry.

He is a very popular poet and is the youngest writer in many anthologies. A lot of his poems have been influenced by his work as a probation officer. He provides good social observations into the thinking of people, especially young people, who are marginalised. Some of his poetry is said to have been influenced by the work of Paul Muldoon.

It Ain't What You Do, It's What It Does To You

prescribed for exam in 2011

I have not bummed across America
with only a dollar to spare, one pair
of busted Levi's and a bowie knife.
I have lived with thieves in Manchester.

I have not padded through the Taj Mahal,   5
barefoot, listening to the space between
each footfall picking up and putting down
its print against the marble floor. But I
skimmed flat stones across Black Moss on a day
so still I could hear each set of ripples   10
as they crossed. I felt each stone's inertia
spend itself against the water; then sink.

I have not toyed with a parachute cord
while perched on the lip of a light-aircraft;
but I held the wobbly head of a boy   15
at the day centre, and stroked his fat hands.
And I guess that the tightness in the throat
and the tiny cascading sensation
somewhere inside us are both part of that
sense of something else. That feeling, I mean.   20

EXPLORATIONS

Before reading

1. What usually comes after the line 'It ain't what you do'? Would it have the same effect?

First reading

2. There are three things that the poet has not done and three things that he has. Compare them. Which are the more attractive to you?

3. What emotion does he get from living with thieves? How would this compare with the feeling he would get if he was hiking across America?

4. How does he justify comparing a lake in Manchester to one of the 'seven wonders of the world'?

5. What would helping a boy at the day care centre make him feel?

6. How would the boy feel?

Second reading

7. Have you ever had the sensation that the poet has in the final verse? When? Describe it.

Third reading

8. How does the poet use repetition in the poem?

Fourth reading

9. Is the last sentence in the poem completely necessary?

10. What type of guy do you think the poet is?

Enda Wyley (1966–)

Born in Dublin in 1966, Enda Wyley's literary career began at the age of nine, when, boosted by her parents' encouragement, she entered a poetry competition and won first prize. At the time, she was living in Glenageary, County Dublin and attending school in Dalkey. Indeed, Wyley looks back on her schooldays as 'the place where poems for me truly began'. A creative primary teacher helped to awaken Wyley to the wonders of the imagination. Some years later, it was in the school hall that the thirteen-year-old Wyley met the poet Brendan Kennelly, resulting in the two corresponding regularly about her poetry. Such support strengthened Wyley's determination to write and she 'soon owned several notebooks, filled with scribbles, quotes, half-lines – all the stuff of poetry being made'. Although she has published three anthologies to date, it is this fascination with the making of poetry that drives Wyley, as she explains: 'it isn't the publishing of poetry, but the making of it that is most important.' As a primary school teacher she enthusiastically encourages her own pupils to set off on 'the adventure of writing', just as she was once encouraged. Enda Wyley lives with her husband, the poet Peter Sirr, and their daughter in Dublin.

Poems for Breakfast

prescribed for exam in 2014

Another morning shaking us.
The young potted willow
is creased with thirst,
the cat is its purring roots.
Under our chipped window   5
the frail orange flowers grow.
Now the garden gate clicks.
Now footsteps on the path.
Letters fall like weather reports.
Our dog barks, his collar clinks,   10
he scrambles, and we follow,
stumble over Catullus, *MacUser*,
Ancient Greek for Beginners,
cold half-finished mugs of tea,
last week's clothes at the bed's edge.   15
Then the old stairs begin to creak.

And there are the poems for breakfast –
favourites left out on the long glass table.
We take turns to place them there
bent open with the pepper pot,   20
marmalade jar, a sugar bowl –
the weight of kitchen things.
Secret gifts to wake up with,
rhythms to last the whole day long,
surprises that net the cat, the dog,   25
these days that we wake together in –
our door forever opening.

Notes

[12]   **Catullus:** a Roman poet who lived in the first century BC
[12]   **MacUser:** a computer magazine

EXPLORATIONS

Before reading

1. Describe what you see and hear when you first wake up on a school-day morning. How do you feel about getting up to go to school? Is there anything that makes you feel a bit happier about having to do this?

First reading

2. (a) Line 1 tells us that this poem happens in the 'morning'. What events in the first section of the poem reinforce the idea that it is 'morning'? (b) Do any of these events happen when you are getting up in the morning?

3. 'Another morning'. (a) What does this phrase suggest to you about the mood of the couple as they start to get up? (b) Are there any images or sounds in the first section that you think reinforce this mood? Explain your choice.

4. (a) Does the state of the room help to improve the poet's mood? Refer to the poem to support your view. (b) How would you feel waking up in such a room?

Second reading

5. (a) What is unusual about the breakfast table in the second section of the poem? (b) How would you feel if you came down one morning to find the breakfast table set like this? Why?

6. (a) Can you explain how the 'Secret gifts' got onto the table? (b) How do these 'gifts' affect the mood of the couple as they face 'Another morning'? (c) Do you think you might change the reaction you described in Question 5 if you knew that someone you really cared for had taken the time and effort to leave these 'Secret gifts' just for you? Why?

Third reading

7. 'rhythms to last the whole day long,
   surprises that net the cat,
   the dog,
   these days that we wake together in –
   our door forever opening.'

   (a) How do these lines show a change in the poet's attitude towards her surroundings and the day? (b) In what ways could reading the poems create 'rhythms to last the whole day' in the poet and her partner?

(c) Consider what the image of the 'door forever opening' suggests to you. Could it refer to the type of relationship that they share? Does it tell you how their attitude to life is affected by sharing this relationship? Have you another suggestion?

8. Wyley creates a very vivid image of the couple waking up in the morning, not only by using 'pictures' that we can see, but also by including sounds in her description. (a) How do the sounds in the first section of the poem help to make this scene real for you? (b) Can you suggest why sound does not feature as much in the second section?

9. Wyley values clarity in her writing and often edits her work ruthlessly to cut out words or phrases that she feels interfere with the clarity of the piece. Clarity can be defined as clearness, simplicity and intelligibility. Would you agree that each of these characteristics is present in this poem? Refer to the poem to support your view.

10. Using the title 'Secret Gift', write a short story or a poem about the effects that a simple act of loving kindness can produce.

David Wheatley (1970–)

Born in Dublin in 1970, David Wheatley was educated at the Royal Irish Academy of Music and Trinity College Dublin. He now teaches English literature at the University of Hull. Among his published collections of poetry are *Thirst* (1997), *Misery Hill* (2000) and *Mocker* (2006).

Chronicle

prescribed for exams in 2013 and 2014

My grandfather is chugging along the back roads
between Kilcoole and Newtown in his van,
the first wood-panelled Morris Minor in Wicklow.
Evening is draped lazily over the mountains;
one hapless midnight, mistaking the garage door   5
for open, he drove right through it, waking my father.

The old man never did get to farm like his father,
preferring to trundle his taxi along the back roads.
Visiting, I stand in his workshop door
and try to engage him in small talk, always in vain,   10
then climb the uncarpeted stairs to look at the mountains
hulking over soggy, up-and-down Wicklow.

Cattle, accents and muck: I don't have a clue,
I need everything explained to me by my father.
Clannish great-uncles somewhere nearer the mountains   15
are vaguer still, farming their few poor roods,
encountered at Christmas with wives who serve me oven-
      baked bread and come to wave us off at the door.

My grandfather pacing the garden, benignly dour,
a whiskey or a woodbine stuck in his claw,   20
a compost of newsprint in the back of his van.
You're mad to go live in Bray, he told my father,
somewhere he'd visit on rare and timorous raids,
too close to 'town' to be properly *Cill Mhantáin*.

All this coming back to me in the mountains   25
early one morning, crossing the windy corridor
to the Glen of Imaal, where schoolchildren read
acrostics to me of 'wet and wonderful Wicklow',
and driving on down to Hacketstown with my father
we find grandfather's grandfather under an even   30

gravestone gone to his Church of Ireland heaven,
and his grandfather too, my father maintains,
all turned, long since turned to graveyard fodder
just over the county line from their dear old Wicklow,
the dirt tracks, twisting lanes and third-class roads   35
they would have hauled themselves round while they endured,

before my father and I ever followed the roads
or my mountainy cousins first picked up a loy
or my grandfather's van ever hit that garage door.

EXPLORATIONS

Before reading

1. Explore your own genealogy. Try to trace your family tree, the record of your father's and your mother's family going back a few generations. Where did they live and what did they do for a living? Do you visit aunts and uncles and meet with cousins?

2. What is your attitude to these older generations? Do you feel proud of them, interested in their lives, sorry for them, couldn't care less, or what do you feel? Jot down your thoughts or discuss in groups.

First reading

3. What do you notice: (a) about the setting; (b) about the people in this poem?

4. Can you see why the title is appropriate?

5. Do you find the poet's family interesting? Explain your views.

Second reading

6. Focus in particular on stanzas 1 and 4. Would you agree that the grandfather is a 'larger than life' figure? What is the evidence for this?

7. The pace of life is slow. What words, phrases and images suggest this throughout the poem?

8. (a) This poem draws heavily on the geography of County Wicklow. Would you agree? Explore the poem in detail for evidence. (b) All the people mentioned have a particular love of County Wicklow. Write about this, referring to details from the poem to back up your views.

Third reading

9. Write two paragraphs on the main issue or theme dealt with in this poem.

10. Images of roads and of journeys taken or not taken form recurring patterns here. How do these tie in with the meaning?

11. How does the poet feel about his family and relations? Discuss this in pairs or groups and then write up your conclusions using references to the poem as evidence.

12. Do you think this poem says something important about families and native place or 'áit dúchais'? Discuss this and write up the conclusions.

Unseen Poetry: Approaching the Question

An Approach to a Poem

Like any other work of art, such as a painting, sculpture, film or building, a poem needs many viewings or readings before we come to appreciate it fully. All the usual techniques we employ when viewing any new or unusual object can be of use here: first noticing the particularly striking or unusual features; then focusing in on a small area of it; drawing back and trying to see the whole structure; circling around it; finding words to describe it to ourselves; asking ourselves what we like about it; and so on. And so by circling the object and zooming in and out to examine interesting features, gradually we pick up more and more of the detail until the entire object makes sense for us. Many readings are the key to understanding.

Here are some questions you might ask yourself as you read and reread:

What do I notice on a first reading?

List any and every thing I notice on first reading the poem. This gives me the confidence to say something about it, even though I don't yet understand the full picture.

What do I see?

- Where is it set? What scene or scenes are featured?

- What pictures strike me as interesting? Focus on a setting or an image. What are my thoughts on it?
- Follow the images through the poem. Is there a sequence or a pattern? Have the images anything in common?
- Do the images or settings suggest anything about the themes or issues the poem might be dealing with?
- What atmosphere or mood is suggested by the visual aspects? Which words or images are most powerful in creating this atmosphere?

What is the poem doing, and how is it structured?

(1) Does it tell a story?

- Is there a narrative structure to this poem? If so, what is happening? What is the sequence of events? Am I clear about the story line?
- What is my reaction to this story?
- Is there a main idea behind the narrative? What is the poet's central concern?
- What do I notice about the shape of the poem?
- If a narrative poem, is it in the genre of a ballad, epic, allegory, etc.?
- Is it serious, humorous, satirical, or what?

(2) Is it a descriptive piece, re-creating a scene?

- Is its primary purpose to re-create the atmosphere of an event or the mood of a moment?
- Is it mainly decorative? Or has it a point to make, or a moral to transmit?
- How does the poet want me to feel? What mood is created in this poem? What words or phrases help to create this mood?
- If a lyric poem, is it in the form of a sonnet, ode, villanelle, sestina, or what?
- What is the poet's central concern (theme)?
- Leaving technical terms aside, how would I describe what the poem sets out to do?

The speaker

- Who is the speaker in the poem? What kind of person do I imagine him or her to be? What state of mind is the speaker in? What words or phrases reveal most about the attitude and state of mind of the speaker? Consider the tone of the poem and how it is created.
- What point of view is being put across in the poem? Am I in sympathy with it or not?
- Who is the speaker addressing in the poem?
- What do I notice about the poet's style?
- Does the poet rely heavily on images? If so, what do I notice about them?
- Does the poet use the musical sounds of words to create effects: alliteration, assonance, onomatopoeia, etc.? Does he or she use rhyme? What is the effect? What do the sounds of words contribute to the atmosphere of the poem?
- What do I notice about the type of words (diction) most frequently used – are they ordinary, everyday, learned and scholarly, technical, or what?
- Does the poet use regular metre (rhythm or regular beat in the lines) or do the lines sound more like ordinary conversation or a piece of prose writing? What is the overall effect? Explore the rhythm of the language.
- Are any of these features particularly noticeable or effective? What do I like?

What is my reaction to it?

- Can I identify with the experience in this poem? Has there been any similar experience in my life?
- What are my feelings on reading this poem, and what words, phrases, images or ideas spark off these reactions in me?
- How do I react to it? Do I find it amusing, interesting, exciting, frightening, revolting, thought-provoking, or what?
- What seems to me most important about the piece?
- At a critical level, do I think it is a well-made poem? What in particular do I think is effective?

Some basic questions

A final line-by-line or stanza-by-stanza exploration should bring the poem into clearer focus and facilitate answers to the basic questions:

1. What is the poem about (theme)?

2. Is it an interesting treatment of this theme?
3. What is important about the poem?
4. How is the poem structured (form and genre: narrative or lyric, ballad, ode, sonnet, etc.)?
5. What are the poet's feelings and attitudes (tone)?
6. How would one describe the atmosphere or mood of the poem, and how is it created?
7. What features of poetic style are noticeable or effective?
8. What are my reactions to the poem?

Comparing a newly read poem with a prescribed poem

Which ideas are similar? Which are different?
Which poem made the greater impact on you, and why?

What insights did you get from each poem?
What is the attitude of the poet in each case? Are there similarities or differences in tone?
How does each poet differ in use of language, imagery, etc.?
Comment on the form and genre in each case.

Practice

To practise answering similar questions on unseen poems, use any of the poems in this anthology which are not on your prescribed course.

Past Examination Questions
(Higher Level)

William Shakespeare

'Choosing Shakespeare's sonnets.'
Imagine your task is to make a small collection of sonnets by William Shakespeare from those that are on your course. Write an introduction to the poems that you would choose to include.

(Higher Level 2002)

Emily Dickinson

What impact did the poetry of Emily Dickinson make on you as a reader? Your answer should deal with the following:
- *Your overall sense of the personality of the poet*
- *The poet's use of language/imagery*

Refer to the poems by Emily Dickinson that you have studied.

(Higher Level 2005)

Elizabeth Bishop

'Introducing Elizabeth Bishop.'
Write out the text of a short presentation you would make to your friends or class group under the above title. Support your point of view by reference to or quotation from the poetry of Elizabeth Bishop that you have studied.

(Higher Level 2001)

'The poetry of Elizabeth Bishop appeals to the modern reader for many reasons.'
Write an essay in which you outline the reasons why poems by Elizabeth Bishop have this appeal.

(Higher Level 2002)

'Reading the poetry of Elizabeth Bishop.'
Write out the text of a talk that you would give to your class in response to the above title. Your talk should include the following:
- *Your reactions to her themes or subject matter.*
- *What you personally find interesting in her style of writing.*

Refer to the poems by Elizabeth Bishop that you have studied.

(Higher Level 2006)

Gerard Manley Hopkins

'There are many reasons why the poetry of Gerard Manley Hopkins appeals to his readers.'
In response to the above statement, write an essay on the poetry of Hopkins. Your essay should focus clearly on the reasons why the poetry is appealing and should refer to the poetry on your course.

(Higher Level 2004)

W. B. Yeats

Write an article for a school magazine introducing the poetry of W. B. Yeats to Leaving Certificate students. Tell them what he wrote about and explain what you liked in his writing, suggesting some poems that you think they would enjoy reading. Support your points by reference to the poetry by W. B. Yeats that you have studied.

(Higher Level 2005)

Robert Frost

'We enjoy poetry for its ideas and for its language.'
Using the above statement as your title, write an essay on the poetry of Robert Frost. Support your points by reference to the poetry by Robert Frost on your course.

(Higher Level 2003)

'Robert Frost – a poet of sadness?'
Write an introduction to the poetry of Robert Frost using the above title. Your introduction should address his themes and the impact of his poetry on you as a reader. Support your points with reference to the poems you have studied.

(Higher Level 2007)

Patrick Kavanagh

Imagine you were asked to select one or more of Patrick Kavanagh's poems from your course for inclusion in a short anthology entitled 'The Essential Kavanagh'. Give reasons for your choice, quoting from or referring to the poem or poems you have chosen.

(Higher Level 2004)

Philip Larkin

Write an essay in which you outline your reasons for liking and/or not liking the poetry of Philip Larkin. Support your points by reference to the poetry of Larkin that you have studied.

(Higher Level 2001)

'Writing about unhappiness is the source of my popularity.' (Philip Larkin) In the light of Larkin's own assessment of his popularity, write an essay outlining your reasons for liking/not liking his poetry. Support your points with the aid of suitable reference to the poems you have studied.

(Higher Level 2008)

Adrienne Rich

'The desire to be heard – that is the impulse behind writing poems, for me.' (Adrienne Rich) Does the poetry of Adrienne Rich speak to you? Write your personal response, referring to the poems of Adrienne Rich that do/do not speak to you.

(Higher Level 2008)

Sylvia Plath

If you were asked to give a public reading of a small selection of Sylvia Plath's poems, which ones would you choose to read? Give reasons for your choices supporting them by reference to the poems on your course.

(Higher Level 2003)

'I like (or do not like) to read the poetry of Sylvia Plath.' Respond to this statement, referring to the poetry by Sylvia Plath on your course.

(Higher Level 2004)

'The poetry of Sylvia Plath is intense, deeply personal, and quite disturbing.' Do you agree with this assessment of her poetry? Write a response, supporting your points with the aid of suitable reference to the poems you have studied.

(Higher Level 2007)

Seamus Heaney

Dear Seamus Heaney . . . Write a letter to Seamus Heaney telling him how you responded to some of his poems on your course. Support the points you make by detailed reference to the poems you choose to write about.

(Higher Level 2003)

Derek Mahon

'Speaking of Derek Mahon . . .'
Write out the text of a public talk you might give on the poetry of Derek Mahon. Your talk should make reference to the poetry on your course.

(Higher Level 2004)

'Derek Mahon explores people and places in his own distinctive style.'
Write your response to this statement supporting your points with the aid of suitable reference to the poems you have studied.

(Higher Level 2008)

Eavan Boland

Write a personal response to the poetry of Eavan Boland.
Support the points you make by reference to the poetry of Boland that you have studied.

(Higher Level 2002)

'The appeal of Eavan Boland's poetry.'
Using the above title, write an essay outlining what you consider to be the appeal of Boland's poetry. Support your points by reference to the poetry of Eavan Boland on your course.

(Higher Level 2005)

Past Examination Questions
(Ordinary Level)

William Wordsworth

It is a Beauteous Evening, Calm and Free

1. (a) What words suggest the presence of God in the first eight lines of this sonnet? (10)
   (b) 'The poem gives us a sense of a beautiful calm evening.'
   Do you agree? Explain your answer. (10)
   (c) How does Wordsworth feel about the child in the poem? Refer to the poem in your answer. (10)
2. Answer **ONE** of the following: [Each part carries 20 marks]
   (i) From your reading of this poem, what things are important to Wordsworth? Support your response with reference to the poem.

OR

(ii) You have been asked to suggest a poem for a collection called 'Peaceful Moments'. Say why you would choose this poem.

OR

(iii) This poem was written around 200 years ago. Do you think it is still worth reading? Explain why or why not.

(Ordinary Level 2004)

W. B. Yeats

An Irish Airman Foresees His Death

1. (a) What, in your view, is the attitude of the airman to the war in which he is fighting? (10)
   (b) Write out the line or phrase from the poem that best shows his attitude. Give a reason for your choice. (10)
   (c) Write a short paragraph in which you outline your feelings towards the airman. Support your view by quotation from the poem. (10)

2. Answer **ONE** of the following: [Each part carries 20 marks]
   (i) 'I balanced all, brought all to mind'
   What are the kinds of things the airman is referring to in this line from the poem?

OR

   (ii) Imagine the airman has to give a short speech to his fellow pilots as they prepare for battle. Write out the text of the speech he might give.

OR

   (iii) Suggest a different title for the above poem. Give reasons for your answer, supporting them by quotation from the poem.

(Ordinary Level 2002)

Robert Frost

Out, Out–

1. (a) Which words and phrases in the first twelve lines (ending at '. . . *when saved from work*') help to give you a clear picture of the place where the poem is set?
   Explain your choice. (10)
   (b) Describe the boy's reaction when he realised that his hand had been badly damaged by the saw. (10)
   (c) Do you think the poet shows sympathy for the boy?
   Explain your answer. (10)

2. Answer **ONE** of the following: [Each part carries 20 marks]
   (i) Write the diary entry of the boy's sister, in which she records her experiences and feelings on the day the accident happened.

OR

(ii) People have said that this is a very dramatic poem. Do you agree? Explain your answer.

OR

(iii) Which of the following statements best describes your response to the poem?
- *I found the poem cruel because . . .*
- *I found the poem dramatic because . . .*
- *I found the poem sad because . . .*

Give reasons for your answer.

(Ordinary Level 2007)

Patrick Kavanagh

Shancoduff

1. (a) How does the poet show that he likes Shancoduff, his home place? Support your answer by reference to the poem. (10)

   (b) Where in the poem does he show that life in Shancoduff can be harsh? Support your answer by reference to the poem. (10)

   (c) On balance, do you think that Shancoduff would be a likeable or a harsh place to live in? Give a reason for your answer. (10)

2. Answer **ONE** of the following: [Each part carries 20 marks]

   (i) Imagine Patrick Kavanagh puts his farm up for sale. Write the advertisement that might appear in the local newspaper. Base your advertisement on the poem.

OR

   (ii) 'They are my Alps and I have climbed the Matterhorn . . .' Why, in your opinion, does Kavanagh refer to the Alps and the Matterhorn in this poem?

OR

   (iii) What do you think is the cattle-drovers' view of Kavanagh's way of life? Refer to the poem in your answer.

(Ordinary Level 2005)

W. H. Auden

Funeral Blues

1. (a) How did this poem make you feel? (10)

   (b) Do you think that the poet really loves the one who has died? Explain your answer. (10)

   (c) Do you like the way the poet expresses sadness at the death of his friend? Give a reason. (10)

2. Answer **ONE** of the following: [Each part carries 20 marks]
- (i) Imagine that the poet wanted to choose a line or two from the poem to be written on his lover's tombstone. Which line or lines would you advise him to choose? Write the lines and give reasons for your choice.

OR

- (ii) Imagine you wanted to perform this poem to music with a group of musical friends. How would you perform it so that people would remember the experience?

OR

- (iii) What things did you learn about the poet W. H. Auden from reading the poem? Refer to the poem in your answer.

(Ordinary Level 2003)

Howard Nemerov

Wolves in the Zoo

1. (a) What, in your opinion, is the poet's attitude to wolves? Give a reason for your answer, based on the poem. (10)
   (b) Why do you think the poet talks about '*Little Red Ridinghood and her Gran*'? Explain your answer. (10)
   (c) Choose two lines from the poem that especially appeal to you. Explain your choice. (10)
2. Answer **ONE** of the following: [Each part carries 20 marks]
   - (i) 'This poem tells us a lot about the attitude of human beings to wild animals.'
     Would you agree with this statement? Give reasons for your answer based on the poem.

OR

   - (ii) A company is publishing a book of nature poetry for young adults called *Our Animals – Our Friends*. You have been invited to choose a poem for publication. Explain why you would or would not choose *Wolves in the Zoo* for inclusion.

OR

   - (iii) You are a wolf in the cage in the zoo. Describe your thoughts and feelings. You may use the material in the poem to support your response.

(Ordinary Level 2007)

Philip Larkin

The Explosion

1. (a) What impression of the miners do you get from reading the opening four stanzas of the above poem? Support your view by reference to the text.

(10)

(b) Stanza five ('At noon, there came a tremor . . .') describes the moment of the explosion. What effect does the poet achieve by describing the event in the manner in which he does? Give a reason in support of your view. (10)

2. Why, in your opinion, does Larkin end the poem with the image of the 'eggs unbroken'? Support your answer by reference to the poem. (10)

3. Answer **ONE** of the following: [Each part carries 20 marks]
   (i) Compare *The Explosion* with any other poem by Philip Larkin that you have studied as part of your course.

OR

   (ii) What, in your opinion, can we learn about Philip Larkin himself, the things he values or considers important from reading this poem? Support your view by brief reference to the poem.

OR

   (iii) Imagine that the wife of one of the men killed in the explosion were to write an article describing the event for her local newspaper. Write out a paragraph that you think she might include in her article.

(Ordinary Level 2002)

Denise Levertov

What Were They Like?

1. (a) What impression does the poet give us of the people of Vietnam? Refer to the poem in your answer. (10)
   (b) From the 6 answers given in the second part of the poem, choose an answer that for you creates the clearest picture of the horrors of war. Explain your choice. (10)
   (c) Did you like this poem? Give a reason for your answer. (10)

2. Answer **ONE** of the following: [Each part carries 20 marks]
   (i) The shape of this poem is unusual – a set of questions followed by a set of answers. Do you think it is a good way to write the poem? Explain your answer.

OR

   (ii) Imagine you were asked to make an anti-war video in which this poem is spoken. Describe the music and images you would use as a background to the reading of the poem.

OR

   (iii) Do you think the title of the poem, *What Were They Like?*, is a good one? Explain your view.

(Ordinary Level 2005)

Patricia Beer

The Voice

1. (a) What picture of the poet's aunt emerges from this poem? Refer to the poem in your answer. (10)

 (b) In your opinion, what part did the parrot play in the aunt's life? Explain your answer by referring to the words and events in the poem. (10)

 (c) Which of the following statements best describes your response to the poem? Give a reason for your answer.
 - *I found the poem amusing*
 - *I found the poem sad*
 - *I found the poem both amusing and sad* (10)

2. Answer **ONE** of the following: [Each part carries 20 marks]

 (i) Imagine that the poet was asked to make a speech at the 'funeral' of the parrot. Write out the speech that you imagine she might deliver.

 OR

 (ii) *'Nature's creatures should not be kept in cages for our amusement.'* Write a short piece outlining your views on this topic. You should refer to the poem to support the points you make.

 OR

 (iii) Imagine you were asked to make a short film or video using **one moment or event** from this poem. Describe the moment or event you would choose and explain the kind of film or video you would make.

 (Ordinary Level 2006)

Maya Angelou

Phenomenal Woman

1. (a) From your reading of Stanza 1 (lines 1–14) what, according to the poet, is her secret for women? (10)

 (b) *'Men themselves have wondered*
 What they see in me.'
 What answer does the poet give to the men in Stanza 3 (lines 31–46)? (10)

 (c) Having studied the poem, do you think the poet is a '*Phenomenal woman*'? Explain your answer. (10)

2. Answer **ONE** of the following: [Each part carries 20 marks]

 (i) Did you enjoy reading this poem? Write a piece where you give your views in response to this question.

 OR

(ii) This poem is about self-confidence. Choose two examples from the poem which you feel reveal this quality of self-confidence in a special way. Give reasons for your answer.

OR

(iii) If you were to write a poem entitled 'Phenomenal Man', what qualities would you give that man? (In writing your answer, you may, if you wish, present the male qualities as the female ones are presented in the last 9 lines of the poem,
'I say,
It's in the . . .
That's me.')

(Ordinary Level 2008)

Adrienne Rich

Aunt Jennifer's Tigers

1. (a) Why in your opinion does the poet's aunt choose the theme of tigers for her screen? Give a reason for your answer, based on your understanding of the poem.   (10)

   (b) *The massive weight of Uncle's wedding band*
   Sits heavily upon Aunt Jennifer's hand.
   What impression do you get of Aunt Jennifer's marriage from these lines? Explain your answer.   (10)

   (c) Choose one of the following phrases which in your opinion best reveals the poet's attitude towards her aunt:
   - *she admires her*
   - *she pities her*

   Explain your choice.   (10)

2. Answer **ONE** of the following: [Each part carries 20 marks]

   (i) This poem is full of movement and colour. Choose some words and phrases of both movement and colour which especially appeal to you. Explain your choices.

   OR

   (ii) 'Adrienne Rich's poems are very gloomy.' Write a piece in which you agree **or** disagree with this statement. Your response should include some reference to **one** or **both** of the other Rich poems on your course – *'Storm Warnings'* and *'Power'*.

   OR

   (iii) In this poem, the poet speaks **for** her Aunt Jennifer. Write a piece in which Aunt Jennifer tells her **own** story. You may use the material in the poem to support your response.

(Ordinary Level 2008)

Sylvia Plath

The Arrival of the Bee Box

1. (a) What impression of the poet, Sylvia Plath, do you get from reading this poem? (10)

   (b) What words or phrases from the poem especially help to create that impression for you? (10)

2. The following list of phrases suggests some of the poet's attitudes to the bee box:

   - *She is fascinated by it*
   - *She is annoyed by it*
   - *She feels she has great power over it*

Choose the phrase from the above list that is closest to your own reading of the poem. Explain your choice, supporting your view by reference to the words of the poem. (10)

3. Answer **ONE** of the following: [Each part carries 20 marks]

   (i) Imagine you were asked to select music to accompany a public reading of this poem. Describe the kind of music you would choose and explain your choice clearly.

OR

   (ii) 'The box is only temporary.'
        What do you understand the last line of the poem to mean?

OR

   (iii) Write a paragraph in which you outline the similarities **and/or** differences between *The Arrival of the Bee Box* and the other poem on your course by Sylvia Plath, *Child*.

(Ordinary Level 2003)

Fleur Adcock

For Heidi with Blue Hair

1. (a) What impression of Heidi do you get from the above poem? (5)

   (b) Where does the language used by the poet especially create that impression for you? (10)

2. (a) From the following list, choose the phrase that is closest to your own reading of the poem:

   - *a funny and clever poem*
   - *an important poem about people's rights*
   - *a sad poem.*

Explain your choice, supporting your view by reference to the words of the poem. (10)

(b) 'The battle was already won.' What do you understand the last line of the poem to mean? (5)

3. Answer **ONE** of the following, (i) or (ii) or (iii). [Each part carries 20 marks.]
   (i) 'It would have been unfair to mention
   your mother's death, but that
   shimmered behind the arguments.'
   How do these lines from the fifth stanza affect your attitude to Heidi and what she had done? Give reasons for your answer.

   OR

   (ii) Does Heidi remind you of anyone you know in real life? Write a short paragraph that shows how that person is most like Heidi. [N.B. You should not give the persons's real name.]

   OR

   (iii) What impression of Heidi's father emerges from the poem? Support your answer by reference to the text.

   (Ordinary Level 2001)

Seamus Heaney

A Constable Calls

1. (a) What overall impression of the constable do you get from the above poem? (5)
   (b) Where in the language of the poem is that impression most fully created? (10)
   (c) What signs are there in the poem that the constable's visit causes tension in the house? (15)
2. Answer **ONE** of the following, (i) or (ii) or (iii). [Each part carries 20 marks]
   (i) 'His boot pushed off
   And the bicycle ticked, ticked, ticked.'
   What effect does Seamus Heaney create by using this image as an ending to the poem?

   OR

   (ii) Imagine you are the constable. Write the report you would make about your visit to the house once you had returned to the barracks.

   OR

   (iii) How does the young boy in the poem feel about the constable? Support your answer by reference to the poem.

Derek Mahon

After The Titanic

1. (a) What effect did the sinking of the *Titanic* have on Bruce Ismay, the speaker in this poem? (10)

   (b) Do you sympathise with him after reading this poem? Give a reason. (10)

   (c) What details in the poem make you sympathise with him, or not sympathise with him? (10)

2. Answer **ONE** of the following: [Each part carries 20 marks]

   (i) 'This poem gives you a vivid picture of the disaster.' Would you agree? Support your answer with reference to the poem.

   OR

   (ii) 'Letter from a ghost.' Imagine you are one of the people who drowned on the *Titanic*. Write a letter to Bruce Ismay telling him about your memories of that night. Use details from the poem in your letter.

   OR

   (iii) In this poem Mahon speaks *as if he is* Bruce Ismay. How well do you think he gets into Bruce Ismay's mind? Give reasons for your answer.

   (Ordinary Level 2004)

Derek Mahon

Antarctica

1. (a) A friend asks you to tell him/her what this poem is about. Write what you would say. (10)

   (b) Choose some words and phrases which you think create the sense of the terrible climate experienced by the explorers. Explain your choices. (10)

   (c) *'I am just going outside and may be some time.'* How does the poet show that Oates (the speaker of the first line of the poem) is moving further and further away from his companions in the tent? Explain your answer. (10)

2. Answer **ONE** of the following: [Each part carries 20 marks]

   (i) Imagine that you are one of Oates's companions. Write what you would say to him in order to persuade him not to leave the tent.

   OR

   (ii) You are Edward Oates. Write the diary entry you would like to leave behind to explain your conduct in walking out into the snow to die.

   OR

(iii) 'The final four lines are the finest lines in the poem.'
Do you agree with this statement? Explain your answer.

(Ordinary Level 2008)

Eavan Boland

This Moment

1. (a) Why in your opinion does the poet call the poem, *This Moment*?   (10)
   (b) Write out two images from the poem that best help you to picture the neighbourhood at dusk. Give a reason for your choice in each case. (10)
   (c) Taken as a whole, does this poem give you a comforting or a threatening feeling about the neighbourhood? Explain your answer. (10)
2. Answer **ONE** of the following, (i) or (ii) or (iii). [Each part carries 20 marks]
   (i) Imagine you were asked to make a short film based on the poem, *This Moment*. Describe the sort of atmosphere you would try to create and say how you would use music, sound effects and images to create it.

   OR

   (ii) *Stars rise.*
   Moths flutter.
   Apples sweeten in the dark.
   Do you think these lines provide a good ending to the poem? Give reasons for your opinion.

   OR

   (iii) Write a short letter to Eavan Boland in which you tell her what her poems on your course mean to you.

(Ordinary Level 2001)

Paul Durcan

Going Home to Mayo, Winter 1949

1. (a) What is the poet's attitude to Dublin city in this poem? Explain your answer.   (10)
   (b) His attitude to Mayo is very different. How is this shown in the poem?
                                                                            (10)
   (c) What do we learn about the relationship between father and son from the poem? Explain your answer.   (10)
2. Answer **ONE** of the following: [Each part carries 20 marks]
   (i) Using one of these as an opening, write about the overall mood of the poem:
     • *I think this is a happy poem because . . .*
     • *I think this is a sad poem because . . .*

   OR

(ii) Imagine that the poet keeps a diary. Write his diary entry at the end of his first day at his father's mother's house.

OR

(iii) Pick out a couple of your favourite lines or images from the poem and explain why you like them.

(Ordinary Level 2008)

Carol Ann Duffy

Valentine

1. (a) 'I am trying to be truthful.'

    In your opinion, what is the speaker of the poem trying to tell her lover about her feelings? 10)

   (b) Write down one line or phrase from the poem that tells you most about the kind of relationship the lovers have. Say why you think it is an important line. (10)

   (c) How do you imagine a lover would feel if he or she received this poem on St Valentine's Day? Explain your answer. (10)

2. Answer **ONE** of the following: [Each part carries 20 marks]

   (i) In what way is this poem different from the normal poems or rhymes that lovers send to each other on Valentine's Day?

OR

   (ii) In your opinion, what reply might the lover write to this Valentine? You may, if you wish, write your reply in verse.

OR

   (iii) 'Lethal.

     Its scent will cling to your anger,

     cling to your knife.'

     Do you think that this is a good ending to the poem? Explain your view.

(Ordinary Level 2003)

Simon Armitage

It Ain't What You Do, It's What It Does to You

1. (a) What kind of life does the poet say he has not lived? (10)

   (b) What do the things he has done tell you about him? Refer to the poem in your response. (10)

   (c) Do you think he creates a feeling of stillness in the following lines?

     'But I

     skimmed flat stones across Black Moss on a day

     so still I could hear each set of ripples

     as they crossed. I felt each stone's inertia

spend itself against the water; then sink.'
Give a reason for your answer. (10)

2. Answer **ONE** of the following: [Each part carries 20 marks]

   (i) Armitage thinks that titles are very important. Do you think he has chosen a good title for this poem? Refer to the poem in your response.

   OR

   (ii) Someone asks you to suggest a poem to be included in a collection for young people. You recommend this one. Explain why.

   OR

   (iii) 'That feeling, I mean.'
   What kind of feeling do you think Armitage is describing in the last stanza? Do you think he describes it well? Explain your view.

   (Ordinary Level 2004)

Acknowledgements

The author and publisher are grateful to the following for permission to reproduce copyright material:

The poems by W.B. Yeats are reproduced by kind permission of A P Watt on behalf of Gráinne Yeats; 'The Tuft of Flowers', 'Mending Wall', 'After Apple-Picking', 'The Road Not Taken', 'Birches', "Out-Out-", 'Spring Pools', 'Acquainted with the Night', 'Design' and 'Provide, Provide' from *The Poetry of Robert* athem.

84, 1939,
y, copyright
by Robert
esley Frost
anagh are
edited by
04), by kind
Estate of the
ugh the
y; 'An
ddings',
ees', 'The
produced by
ber Ltd; 'The
The Bight',
ova Scotia',

'The Prodigal', 'Questions of Travel' and 'Sestina' from *The Complete Poems 1927-1979* by Elizabeth Bishop. Copyright © 1979, 1983 by Alice Helen Methfessel. Reprinted by permission of Farrar, Straus and Giroux, LLC.; Poems by Thomas Kinsella are reproduced by kind permission of Carcanet Press Limited; 'The Uncle Speaks in the Drawing Room', 'Our Whole Life' from *Collected Early Poems 1950-1970* by Adrienne Rich. Copyright © 1993 by Adrienne Rich. Copyright © 1967, 1963, 1962, 1961, 1960, 1959, 1958, 1957, 1956, 1955, 1954, 1953, 1952, 1951 by Adrienne Rich. Copyright © 1984, 1975, 1971, 1969, 1966 by W.W. Norton & Company, Inc. Used by permission of the author and W.W. Norton & Company, Inc. 'Aunt Jennifer's Tigers', 'Storm Warnings', 'Living in Sin', 'The Roofwalker', 'Trying to Talk with a Man', 'Diving into the Wreck', 'From a Survivor' and 'Power' from The Fact of Doorframe: *Selected Poems 1950-2001* by Adrienne Rich. Copyright © 2002 by Adrienne Rich. Copyright © 2001, 1999, 1995, 1991, 1989, 1986, 1984, 1981, 1967, 1963, 1962, 1961, 1960, 1959, 1958, 1987, 1956, 1955, 1954, 1953, 1952, 1951 by Adrienne Rich. Copyright © 1978, 1975, 1973, 1971, 1969, 1966 by W.W. Norton &